Meyer London

Meyer London

*A Biography of the Socialist
New York Congressman,
1871–1926*

GORDON J. GOLDBERG

McFarland & Company, Inc., Publishers
Jefferson, North Carolina, and London

LIBRARY OF CONGRESS CATALOGUING-IN-PUBLICATION DATA

Goldberg, Gordon J., 1933–
    Meyer London : a biography of the socialist New York congressman, 1871–1926 / Gordon J. Goldberg.
    p.   cm.
    Includes bibliographical references and index.

    ISBN 978-0-7864-7216-1
    softcover : acid free paper ∞

    1. London, Meyer, 1871–1926. 2. Legislators—United States—Biography. 3. Jewish legislators—United States—Biography. 4. United States. Congress. House—Biography. 5. Jews, Russian—United States—Biography. 6. Socialists—United States—Biography. 7. Socialism—United States—History—20th century. 8. Lower East Side (New York, N.Y.)—Politics and government. 9. New York (N.Y.)—Politics and government—1898–1951. 10. United States—Politics and government—1901–1953. I. Title.
    E748.L84G65 2013
    328.73'092—dc23   2012047467
    [B]

BRITISH LIBRARY CATALOGUING DATA ARE AVAILABLE

© 2013 Gordon J. Goldberg. All rights reserved

No part of this book may be reproduced or transmitted in any form or by any means, electronic or mechanical, including photocopying or recording, or by any information storage and retrieval system, without permission in writing from the publisher.

Front cover image: Meyer London (Harris & Ewing Collection, Library of Congress)

Manufactured in the United States of America

McFarland & Company, Inc., Publishers
   Box 611, Jefferson, North Carolina 28640
   www.mcfarlandpub.com

Table of Contents

Acknowledgments vi
Introduction 1

1. The Early Years: 1871–1901   5
2. London and the Labor Movement   16
3. Prelude to Victory: The Elections of 1910 and 1912   41
4. Victory in 1914   64
5. Preparing for Congress: Issues of War and Peace   78
6. The Sixty-Fourth Congress: The Specter of War   97
7. The Sixty-Fourth Congress: In Pursuit of Constructive Reform   121
8. The Sixty-Fifth Congress: War Declared   153
9. The Sixty-Fifth Congress: Champion of Civil Liberties   174
10. The Elections of 1918 and 1920   203
11. The Sixty-Seventh Congress: Opposition to Postwar Conservatism   239
12. Meyer London: The Final Years   266

Epilogue: Failure of a Dream   275
Chapter Notes   277
Bibliography   309
Index   315

Acknowledgments

This book began as my dissertation, and I was fortunate to have the late Dr. Joseph A. Dowling of the Department of History at Lehigh University direct my work. I would also like to thank the late Dr. Lawrence Leder and Dr. William Shade, both members of my dissertation committee, for their many useful comments and suggestions. I would like to express my gratitude to my colleague Dr. Mike Gabriel of Kutztown University who has helped me in so many different ways. Finally, my great appreciation goes to my late colleague Professor Moshe Kennet and my late father-in-law Morris Yaker for their invaluable help in translating Yiddish materials. The American Jewish Historical Society gave me a research grant and published my article on London's contribution to the fight for social security, unemployment benefits and universal health care.

During the course of my research I benefited from the guidance of librarians and archivists at the old Tamiment Institute Library, the YIVO Institute, the New York Public Library, the Library of Congress, the Kutztown University Library and the Lehigh University Library. I also corresponded with librarians at Duke University, Cornell University, and the Milwaukee Historical Society. Dorothy Swanson of the old Tamiment Institute gave invaluable assistance and made its collections available to me. Erica Gottfried of the Tamiment Library/New York University has been very helpful.

Also a special thanks to the extended London family, particularly Keith (family archivist) and Lauren Grober and Rosalyn Baxandall for their interest and help. Thank you Kara, Mickey and Tom.

My family has supported and encouraged me throughout this endeavor. I owe a deep debt of gratitude to my late parents Harry and Esther and my brother Leonard. Unfortunately, they are no longer here to enjoy this moment. My children, David and Debra, have listened patiently when I expressed frustration. Finally, I would like to dedicate this book to the love of my life, Rose Lee. Her interest has helped sustain me and her advice and editorial assistance immeasurably improved the manuscript.

Introduction

This book is an updated revision of my doctoral dissertation, *Meyer London: A Political Biography*, completed at Lehigh University. I decided to revisit the subject for several reasons. We are rapidly approaching the one hundredth anniversary of World War I which began in Europe in 1914 and ended in 1918. Elected to Congress in 1914, London served for the duration of the war. As the only Socialist, London sought to present the Socialist Party's position on the war and America's intervention in April 1917, while dealing with the reality of serving as a minority of one. London urged strict neutrality, opposed Wilson's preparedness program, and voted against war with Germany and Austria-Hungary. However, he broke with the party and supported the American war effort. His opposition to American intervention and his support for the war demonstrated great courage as he faced criticism from both pro-war and anti-war elements. During the conflict, London emerged as one of the principal champions of civil liberties. He fought against the adoption of the Espionage Act, and vigorously protested in the House against suppression of Socialist publications and the arrest and imprisonment of Socialist leaders such as Eugene Debs. He also took a leading role in the amnesty movement.

Another reason for this book is that London, a Russian Jewish immigrant from New York's Lower East Side, became an important spokesman for the urban immigrant worker. He fought for old age pensions, workmen's compensation, and a national health care system. He won unanimous approval in the House Labor Committee for his National Social Insurance Resolution which the House narrowly rejected during the Sixty-Fourth Congress. A disappointed London nevertheless persisted, and helped educate his colleagues as to the need for what we now refer to as the "safety net": Social Security, Medicare, Medicaid and the Affordable Health Care Act. London also opposed the effort to restrict immigration, an issue of great importance to the American Jewish community and other so-called "New Immigrants."

This biography also seeks to highlight London's involvement in the Socialist and trade union movements. As counsel and adviser to the Workmen's Circle, the International Ladies' Garment Workers' Union, the International Fur Workers' Union, transport workers, jewelers and other trade unions, London guided them in their formative years and thereafter. Grateful for his efforts, these organizations made possible his election to Congress in 1914, 1916 and 1922.

Finally, the only published biography, *Meyer London: An East Side Epic*, commissioned by the Meyer London Memorial Committee, appeared in 1930, four years after his death. Written by Harry Rogoff, a Socialist journalist, it dealt primarily with London's congressional career and is eulogistic in tone. As I rewrote my dissertation, I conducted additional research in order to utilize more recent scholarship in the area of American Jewish studies and American labor history. As a result, I gained new insights about London's place within the Jewish community on the Lower East Side, his role and contributions to the union movement and his efforts in Congress on behalf of the urban immigrant.

Meyer London's life spanned the period from 1871 until his death in 1926. Born in the Russian-Polish province of Suwalki, in the Pale of Settlement, he moved with his mother and younger siblings to New York in 1891 to join his father. Unlike many Russian Jewish intellectuals, London entered the public arena as a lawyer and politician. His law practice, by choice, never became lucrative, as he found fulfillment in the trade union and Socialist movements. He dedicated his life to the struggle for social and economic justice.

As a member of the Socialist Party, London advocated peaceful and evolutionary methods and the ballot box, rather than violence and revolution to end industrial capitalism and to usher in the cooperative commonwealth. Well-versed in Socialist theory, London refused to take a rigid doctrinal position on contemporary problems, but sought to adapt Socialist principles to the American scene. As a Socialist, his goal was to end industrial capitalism not to reform it.

Defeated by the corrupt Tammany machine in 1910 and 1912, as the Socialist candidate in New York's Ninth and Twelfth congressional districts respectively, London, with strong support from largely Jewish and Socialist-led unions, achieved victory in 1914, the first Russian Jew and the first Socialist from the East Coast. He was reelected in 1916 and 1920, but lost in 1918 when the Democrats and Republicans fused on the platform of "100 percent Americanism." In 1922, a last-minute gerrymander of the Twelfth Congressional District arranged by Republicans and Democrats in the New York Legislature deprived London of his Jewish working-class support and made further election impossible.

During three terms in Congress, London proved that he was no ordinary politician. As a Russian Jew, London offered a different perspective in the House. He emerged as a leading spokesman for the labor movement and the urban immigrant. From his vantage point on the House Labor Committee, he waged a vigorous fight for unemployment insurance as well as disability, old age and health insurance. Although ultimately unsuccessful in his own time, he helped educate Congress on these vital issues.

London also advocated abolition of injunctions in labor disputes and prohibition of child labor. He blamed capitalism for the plight of the working class. Economic democracy, he maintained, would occur when the workers owned the principal means of production. London also fought against all attempts to restrict immigration, and defended the urban immigrant community from its detractors.

In regard to foreign policy issues, London proved independent minded. When war began in Europe in 1914, London urged strict neutrality and later opposed the Wilson administration's preparedness program. He opposed war with Germany and Austria-Hungary. Like later critics of American intervention in Vietnam and Iraq, London's loyalty was impugned by the press, by leaders in the German Jewish community, by former president Theodore Roosevelt and by his House colleagues.

However, after America entered the war, he refused to follow the Socialist Party's opposition. At first, London abstained from voting on military measures. His belief, however, that German militarism constituted a worldwide threat led him to support the American war effort. As a result, left-wing Socialists denounced him and demanded his expulsion from the party. On the other hand, conservative congressmen continued to criticize his anti-war votes and his initial refusal to support military measures. London remained steadfast in his beliefs and won the grudging respect of his colleagues in the House.

Another example of his independent thinking involved his response to events in Russia. London welcomed the overthrow of the Czar in March 1917, reflecting the views of his Russian Jewish constituents and the Socialist Party. Ambivalent about the Bolsheviks, he would eventually reject the repressive Lenin-Trotsky regime and the separate peace with Germany. Nevertheless, he argued against Allied-American military intervention in Russia and called for diplomatic recognition. Once again London's conservative colleagues attacked him, as did left-wing Socialists who supported the Bolsheviks.

London steadfastly opposed all threats to American civil liberties. He supported quasi–Socialist measures vital to the war effort, viewing them as an important step toward the cooperative commonwealth, and advocated American participation in an international league.

Defeated in 1918, London returned to Congress in 1921 faced with the conservative, pro-business Harding administration. London opposed Republican tax policies and increased tariff duties. He urged amnesty for political prisoners and a reduction of military spending, and he continued his efforts against immigration restriction and on behalf of the labor movement. In foreign affairs, he presented the Socialist plan for an international league and called for American recognition of Russia. London left Congress in March 1923, and, until his sudden death in 1926, devoted himself to his law practice and to opposing communism within the labor movement.

During his short life, Meyer London was first and foremost an American. He loved his adopted country and favored assimilation. Secondly, he was a Socialist who sought to end industrial capitalism and replace it with a more just and humane society—a cooperative commonwealth. Thirdly, he was a Russian who did not forget his native land or his fellow Russians in their time of need. Finally, London was a Jew. Although he did not practice Judaism and was not a Zionist or cultural nationalist, he was proud of his Jewish heritage. He fought immigration restriction and anti–Semitism wherever it reared its ugly head. Perhaps above all, Meyer London's contemporaries regarded him as a *mensch*—a caring, decent human being.

In my research, I have utilized the London Papers which are located at the Tamiment Library and Robert F. Wagner Labor Archives, now part of the Bobst Library at New York University. Unfortunately, after completing his work on London, Harry Rogoff destroyed most of the papers. Despite the handicap this created for a later biographer, a great amount of material, particularly on London's political career, exists in a variety of other sources. The *Daily Forward*, the leading Yiddish Socialist daily; the *New York Call*, an important English Socialist daily; the labor press as well as other Socialist and non–Socialist publications have proved indispensable in piecing together London's political campaigns. The *Minute Books of the Socialist Party of Local New York*, also available at Tamiment, shed much light on Socialist campaign activities and London's relationship with New York Socialists. The *Congressional Record* and various publications furnish an excellent account of London's work in Congress and insights on how a minority of one, in this instance a Socialist, functioned and can make a difference.

London, unfortunately, did not keep a journal nor did he write an autobiography. However, he did write articles that discussed his activities in Congress on a variety of domestic and international issues. These proved very helpful. Much sought after by the mainstream press, London agreed to interviews with journalists writing for papers such as the *New York Times*. An examination of the bibliography will present a fuller picture of the extent of my research. It should be noted, however, that the American Socialist Party Papers at Duke University, a major collection, had nothing to offer on London.

1
The Early Years: 1871–1901

> The American workingman awoke! To assist them in grasping the truths of Socialism, I joined the Social Democracy.—*Meyer London, Social Democrat, February 18, 1898, 1.*

The partitioning of Poland in the eighteenth century brought a majority of its Jews under Russian rule and resulted in their confinement in the Pale of Settlement.¹ Throughout the nineteenth century, except for a brief interval in the 1860s, the czarist government promulgated restrictive measures which severely tested traditional Jewish middle-class roles and reduced Russia's Jews to poverty. Coercion eventually led to violence with the "spontaneous" outbreaks of 1881, the massacres of Kishinev in 1903 and the pogroms that followed.²

Against this background of growing tsarist suppression, Meyer London was born on December 21, 1871, in the town of Kalvariya, Lithuania, then part of Russia, near the Polish border. His mother, Rebecca Berson, came from a family of rabbis. His father, Ephraim, a Talmudic scholar, wrote articles for Hebrew magazines in which he expressed radical political and religious views. Like many intellectuals in Russia at this time, he had no trade or profession and no regular income.³

Seeking to escape the poverty of his native town, Ephraim London joined the multitude of Jews continuously on the move within the Pale and took his family southward to the Ukraine. There he established himself as a grain merchant at Zenkov in the province of Poltava. His fortunes did not improve. Unable to provide for his family, Ephraim and his second son Louis, a boy of thirteen, emigrated to America in 1888.⁴ "This movement from village to town to city, the migration from one section of the Pale to another, and the exodus overseas were all part of the mass flight from poverty."⁵

The oldest son, Meyer, remained in Russia to continue his training for an intellectual career. At the "cheder" he studied Hebrew, the Bible and the Talmud.⁶ Meyer also attended the gymnasium where he began his secular education. His early education, he recalled some years later, had not been "a very practical preparation for the struggle among hard realities. But our people knew only their books and what they held." He supported himself by tutoring younger boys.⁷

While at the gymnasium, Meyer associated with a group of students imbued with radicalism. They "talked a lot about the revolution and had not the slightest idea what a revolution actually meant." His father heard about Meyer's flirtation with radical ideas and warned his son not to commit to revolutionary causes. He urged Meyer to "study, think, observe and wait," until he knew more about world conditions.⁸

In 1886, however, an era of liberalism, during which Jews were readily admitted to the gymnasia and universities, ended. Authorities placed a 10 percent quota on Jewish admissions to gymnasia, real schools and universities.⁹ Angered by this course of action, and despite his father's warnings, London became involved in anti–Czarist activities.¹⁰

In 1891 the family decided to join Ephraim and Louis in New York. Meyer interrupted his studies to accompany them.¹¹ His decision to emigrate at this time may have resulted from the police attention he attracted because of his revolutionary sympathies. He fled Russia, disguised as a peasant, in order to escape exile to Siberia for his revolutionary activities.¹²

In the meantime, Ephraim London had set up a small printing shop on Suffolk Street in the heart of New York's crowded Lower East Side. Here the family reunited in the fall of 1891. Ephraim's economic position had barely improved. A hand press was his most important possession which he used to print Yiddish, Russian and English materials. Ephraim's political views had become more extreme; he had joined the anarchists. For a short time, Ephraim published a radical Yiddish weekly, the *Morgenstern*.

Contributors represented diverse elements of the radical movement, but it printed news almost exclusively from anarchist organizations. Like much of the radical literature of the day, it was theoretical and unrelated to the contemporary scene.¹³

After arriving in New York, Meyer worked in his father's print shop. Business was poor, and he found it necessary to seek employment elsewhere. He entered the cigar maker's trade which required no special skill. It could be learned easily in three or four weeks. He also began to tutor again. Meyer later obtained a position as an assistant librarian with the Educational Alliance, located in the heart of the Lower East Side. It required only four hours a day of his time. This made it possible for him to continue his education at the Alliance which had been established by the New York German Jewish community to speed the Americanization of their Eastern European brethren.

Meyer worked hard to learn English, and read everything he could find that dealt with English and American history and politics. He studied great orators such as Burke, Pitt and Webster in order to teach himself to become a public speaker. In 1896, the same year he became a citizen, Meyer entered the New York University law school. He continued to work part time at the Alliance library while attending evening classes. Two years later, he was admitted to the New York bar.[14]

The exact origin of London's involvement with socialism remains unclear. At the time that he emigrated to America, Marxism did not have a large following among Jewish students and workingmen in Russia. London had participated in the anti–Czarist movement in his native land, and had no doubt been exposed to radical social ideas. It appears, however, that London's belief in socialism, as in the case of other Russian Jewish immigrants, developed on New York's Lower East Side.

By the time Meyer London arrived in America, thousands of Russian Jews had fled Russia to escape the repressive actions that followed the assassination of Czar Alexander II as well as deteriorating economic conditions. A large number had settled on the Lower East Side among mostly non–Jewish Germans who had left their native land following the unsuccessful revolution in 1848. Many of these Germans were Social Democrats linked directly to Karl Marx both intellectually and politically. Here, they organized their German brethren into socialist trade unions and established a flourishing German-language press. In 1877, they created the first successful Socialist party in the United States—the Socialist Labor Party.

Welcomed by these German Socialists, a number of Russian Jewish intellectuals, including Morris Hillquit, Abraham Cahan, Benyomen Faygnboym, Louis Miller and Mickhail Zametkin, were introduced to socialism. Russian Jewish intellectuals attended lectures in "Little Germany," read German newspapers, and interacted with Johan Most, a former Social Democrat who became America's preeminent anarchist, and Sergius Schewitsch, editor of the German Socialist daily the *New Yorker Volkszeitung*.

Russian Jewish intellectuals were attracted to Social Democratic thinking by its inclusiveness and its promise of a more just society to be achieved through trade union activity and political action rather than revolution. In order to organize Yiddish-speaking workers, many learned Yiddish. Energized by the Great Upheaval of 1886, they helped create a Jewish labor movement (the United Hebrew Trades), Yiddish-speaking sections of the SLP and a flourishing Socialist press by 1900.[15]

Meyer London entered this vibrant Russian community where he met many radicals, primarily anarchists, who gathered in his father's shop. He listened with great interest to their discussions. In addition, he attended numerous lectures and Socialist meetings where he no doubt listened to Abraham Cahan, Louis Miller and Morris Hillquit.

Among the more popular gathering places for young people were the Friday-evening debates on contemporary problems at the Educational Alliance. Meyer spoke in hesitant English; Yiddish was banned at the Alliance until 1899. On numerous occasions he defended radical ideas. The logical presentation of his views compensated for his lack of style. He acquired a reputation as an outstanding debater.[16]

In 1894, London joined the Socialist Labor Party (SLP), and two years later, he ran for the New York Assembly in the Sixteenth Assembly District.[17] The SLP had come under the control of Daniel De Leon in the early 1890s.[18] De Leon's primary political goal was to gain control of the trade unions through the tactic of "boring from within." The SLP concentrated its efforts on turning the American Federation of Labor (AFL) and the Knights of Labor to Socialist principles. In both instances the Socialist Laborites were rebuffed. Undeterred, De Leon, in December 1895, created a new revolutionary union, the Socialist Trade and Labor Alliance, to rival the AFL.[19]

De Leon's efforts to create the Socialist Trade and Labor Alliance wrecked the illusion of unity within the Socialist Labor Party. Trade unionists in New York City, especially from the Jewish unions, showed no sympathy for the new organization. They refused to abandon the policy of "boring from within" and still believed that the SLP could convert the AFL to socialism through continuous agitation and education while protecting the economic interests of its members.[20]

Two Jewish Socialist newspapers in New York, the *Abendblatt* and *Arbeiter-Zeitung*, attacked De Leon's policies. The editorial staffs of these papers, which included Abraham Cahan, Morris Winchevsky and Louis E. Miller, opposed De Leon's trade union tactics, his authoritarian control of the SLP and his refusal to acknowledge his Jewish background. De Leon attempted, but with no success, to crush this opposition at the Socialist Labor Party Convention in 1896.

Subsequently, these disaffected journalists abandoned hope of reforming the SLP. At a meeting on January 30, 1897, socialists and union leaders who were also opposed to De Leon joined with them to establish a new press association and decided to publish a Yiddish paper, the *Daily Forward* (*Forverts*), with Abraham Cahan as editor.[21] In the meantime, several dissident Jewish sections of the SLP led by Meyer London, Isaac Hourwich and Joseph Barondess, also left the SLP. In late June of 1897, they organized Local Number 1 of the newly created Social Democracy of America.[22]

This socialist party was created at a convention in mid-June of 1897 in Chicago through the efforts of Eugene V. Debs, president of the American Railway Union, and Victor L. Berger, Milwaukee Socialist and newspaper editor. The convention adopted a platform calling for the creation of a cooperative commonwealth, public ownership of all monopolies, mines and systems of transportation, a public works program for the unemployed, creation of a postal savings bank, and adoption of the initiative, referendum, recall and proportional representation. Its most controversial and unique provision called for unemployment relief by colonizing a western state with the ultimate objective of gaining political control of the state.[23]

Like many East Side socialists who left the Socialist Labor Party, London had apprehensions about certain aspects of the new party. The Social Democracy contained a conglomeration of elements: church reformers, Christian Socialists, silver leaguers, economic clubs, single taxers and anarchists, all of whom London believed had no solid foundation in Socialist thought. London also rejected the colonization scheme in favor of a political-action-only policy.[24]

Despite these doubts, the Social Democracy attracted him because he

> saw labor wallowing in the mire of simple trade-unionism.... I saw the toiler worshiping the gods his own hands have made, fighting all battles but his own, and I despaired. I watched with envy the triumphant march of Socialism abroad, while here all was chaos and stagnation. The Social Democracy came as a delightful surprise. In unequivocal words it declared relentless war on capitalism. At the helm of the organization stood battle-scarred veterans of the laborer's cause. It was not theoretical speculation, but the bitter and expensive school of experience that gave birth to American Socialism. The shortcomings of simple trade-unionism were now clearly seen by the noblest labor organization — the American Railway Union. The American workingman awoke! To assist them in grasping the truths of Socialism, I joined the Social Democracy.[25]

Faced with revolt on New York's East Side, the National Executive Committee of the Socialist Labor Party appealed to and won the support of the national party membership. Controversy continued, however, and finally, on July 4, the Executive Committee of the SLP for Greater New York expelled the already-resigned Jewish journalists and the members of the four Jewish assembly districts that supported them.[26]

These Jewish radicals, including Meyer London, then joined the Social Democracy of America. It held a convention between July 31 and August 2, attended by fifty-eight delegates who claimed to represent approximately 1,200 members of the Socialist Labor Party and 10,000 trade unionists. London; Isaac Hourwich, a lawyer and economist; and Joseph Barondess, a popular labor leader, appeared on August 1 before the convention as representatives of Local Branch Number 1 of the Social Democracy to explain the objectives of the new organization and to convince the delegates to join Debs' movement.

In an hour-long speech, London emphasized the American origin and character of the Social Democracy. He deplored the failure of the SLP to respond to the appeal of the Social Democracy. In the name of international socialism, he urged the delegates to join the new party. After a lengthy debate, the delegates voted 40 to 10 to approve affiliation with the new organization.

At a mass meeting that evening, London introduced a resolution stating, "We, Jewish-speaking Socialists of ... New York, ... herewith declare ourselves in accord with the principles of the Social Democracy of America, as well as declare that we greet with joy this new movement of liberation, and pledge our energies to the support of this new party which will lead the laboring class over the broad road of scientific socialism, to the final goal of humanity — to the emancipation of the laboring class from the yoke of capitalism and the replacement of the competitive system by the co-operative commonwealth." The delegates adopted the resolution with "a rousing yea."[27]

The Social Democracy of America did not last out the year. From its inception factionalism plagued the party. The political actionists, led by Victor Berger, devoted their efforts to winning elections and accepted most Marxist principles, including the class struggle. Their main support came from Milwaukee, Haverhill, Massachusetts, and New York's Lower East Side, where London, Isaac Hourwich and Abraham Cahan, noted journalist and editor of the *Forward*, had obtained support for the Social Democracy from the two hundred members of the Forward Association. The *Forward* emerged as the champion of socialism on the East Side, attracting unattached Socialists and disillusioned Socialist Laborites to the political action wing of the Social Democracy.[28] A second faction supported the utopian scheme of colonization but had little knowledge of, or in many instances rejected, Marxist theory, including class struggle. Most of the colonizers came from old Populist strongholds in Chicago and the Western cornbelt and mining areas.[29]

The colonization-political action controversy came to a head at the party's second convention in June 1898. Berger's Milwaukee followers and the *Forward* Socialists, with whom London was allied, argued for rejection of colonization as a utopian scheme and adoption of political action and Socialist propaganda.[30] When the issue came to a vote, the colonizers had a majority of 52 to 37.

The political action group immediately withdrew from the convention and organized a new Social Democratic Party led by Victor Berger and Eugene Debs.[31] The party platform rejected colonization and declared itself "a class-conscious, revolutionary, social organization." It emphasized independent political action and trade unionism as the principal means to liberate the working class.[32]

During the following year, Social Democratic political success in Massachusetts encouraged Meyer London and some less doctrinaire party members to consider the feasibility of fusion with non–Social Democrats during elections.³³ Although the National Executive Board disapproved of such coalitions, the Social Democratic New York branches challenged the board's policy.³⁴

Among Social Democrats, London was a leading proponent of cooperation with the Independent Labor Party, organized by trade unionists after the Brooklyn Trolley Strike of 1899.³⁵ At a meeting of the Social Democrats of Greater New York held on August 28, he introduced a motion to join the Independent Labor Party in the coming municipal election. After a "spirited" debate, the motion carried with but four dissenting votes.³⁶

Cooperation proved short-lived. Trade union leaders refused to accept the socialist-oriented party program. Some Social Democrats contended that nothing could be gained by cooperating with a non-socialist party even under a socialistic platform. The controversy erupted at an Independent Labor Party Conference held on September 21 when party officials, despite objections from Social Democrats, seated several supporters of William Jennings Bryan. The Social Democratic delegates immediately withdrew from the conference.

At a meeting of the branches of the New York Social Democrats on September 23, the members, by the narrow margin of two votes, defeated a resolution calling for withdrawal from the Independent Labor Party. London was among those Social Democrats who voted to continue. He believed that they could make the Independent Labor Party a Socialist organization. On September 28, however, the Social Democrats reversed their position and voted 50 to 32, with London in opposition, for withdrawal. Social Democrats would neither cooperate with the Independent Labor Party nor accept its nominees.³⁷

The Social Democratic Party's National Executive Board had observed these events with keen interest, and the behavior of the New York Socialists greatly disturbed it. About the same time the New Yorkers severed relations with the Independent Labor Party conference, the board "condemned all deviations from straight Socialist politics,"³⁸ and ordered them to recall their delegates from the Independent Labor Party conference and to withdraw immediately from the party or face suspension.³⁹ London opposed the board's position and defended the proponents of cooperation at the Social Democratic National Convention in 1900.⁴⁰

In the meantime, another split occurred within the Socialist Labor Party. As in 1897, dissatisfaction with the policy of dual unionism and discontent with the leadership of Daniel De Leon precipitated the revolt. Led by Morris Hillquit, this anti–De Leon faction of the SLP known as the "Kangaroos" held a convention at Rochester, New York, on January 29, 1900. The delegates repudiated the Socialist Trade and Labor Alliance and recommended that all party members join the organization of the trades to which they belonged.

The convention chose its presidential ticket for the coming election and then approved a resolution calling for unification with the Social Democrats. It authorized a committee to attend the Social Democratic National Convention, scheduled to begin on March 6 in Indianapolis, to work out details of the union.[41]

The unity proposal of the Social Laborite insurgents met with hostility from some Social Democrats. Among those adamantly opposed were the Jewish Social Democrats of New York with whom Meyer London closely associated. They had not forgotten that two years earlier, the same Social Laborites who now espoused merger, supported De Leon in his quarrel with the *Forward*.[42]

The most persistent opposition came from the Social Democratic leaders in Wisconsin and Illinois. Victor Berger and his associates inalterably opposed any change in the party's name, its philosophy or its tactics.[43] More important, Berger feared that they might lose control of the party to the Social Laborites.[44] It soon became apparent that those opposed to merger were in the minority and would have to fight a rearguard action at the party's national convention. London attended the Social Democratic National Convention held at Indianapolis in March 1900 as a delegate. The convention elected London to the platform committee along with Victor Berger and Eugene Debs.[45]

Prior to considering the unity question, London vigorously defended the New York branches that had supported the Independent Labor Party. He stated that the New York comrades believed that their efforts would have benefited the Socialist movement. The New Yorkers, London declared, deserved praise rather than being "discountenanced" and threatened with suspension by the National Committee.

Isadore Phillips, a fellow New Yorker, took strong exception to London's position. The Independent Labor Party, Phillips countered, was unworthy of Socialist support. Furthermore, the Social Democratic Party branches had achieved the "acme of puerility" when they joined a group that seated delegates who supported William Jennings Bryan. Despite London's pleas, the convention voted almost unanimously to uphold the action of the National Committee.[46]

With completion of debate on the platform, the delegates turned to the important unity question. Both Morris Hillquit and Job Harriman, who represented the Socialist Labor Party committee on unity, urged union. They pointed out that the two parties fundamentally agreed and that personalities, not issues, kept them apart. Hillquit expressed a willingness to accept the name Social Democratic if it would further Socialist success. The former members of the SLP were then seated as delegates.[47]

On the motion of Debs, the convention appointed a committee of fourteen, including London, to study the unity problem.[48] Subsequently, the committee presented majority and minority reports to the convention. Both recommended that the convention appoint a committee to negotiate a treaty of union. The majority report insisted, however, that under no circumstances should the party name be altered. The minority report merely recommended that the name Social Democratic Party be retained.[49]

During the debate on the convention floor, London and several other delegates supported the majority report. London agreed with Berger's view that acceptance of the minority report would be equivalent to surrender to the former Socialist Laborites, and would destroy the work that many had done in building the party. The delegates, after hearing Hillquit's statement against the majority position, adopted the minority report and proceeded to select a unity committee.[50]

The final business, nomination of candidates for the presidency and vice presidency of the United States, caused further confusion among the delegates. Debs refused the nomination primarily for health reasons. James F. Carey and William Mailly nominated the Socialist Labor faction candidates Job Harriman and Max Hayes. London pointed out that Harriman and Hayes were unacceptable as non-party members. A delegate reminded London that his support for the Independent Labor Party in New York had aided Republicans and Democrats.

Amidst mounting confusion, Berger, Heath and Stedman supported London, and only a hurried motion to adjourn ended the turmoil. The matter was finally resolved when Debs reconsidered and agreed to become the party's presidential candidate. The next day the convention nominated Debs and Harriman by acclamation and adjourned. Most of the delegates left Indianapolis convinced of the imminence of a unified Socialist party.[51]

The unity committees of the Social Democratic Party and the Social Laborites met in New York on March 25, 1900, to work out final details. Disagreement flared anew, and during the following months little progress occurred.[52] London had little tolerance for the constant quibbling which plagued the American socialist movement throughout its existence. He had no desire to fight his comrades. The working class, he believed, could not afford to expose its weaknesses to its capitalist enemies.

During these trying times, London and Max Pine, an important East Side Labor leader, helped retain the support of six East Side and Brooklyn branches for the Social Democratic Party National Executive Board. The *Daily Forward*, with which London was closely allied, also "strongly supported" the National Board.[53] Although top-level Socialist leaders reluctantly cooperated during the campaign, the fact that the Debs-Harriman ticket polled 94,700 votes clearly proved the desirability of unity.

By 1901, a large majority of socialists in the two parties, buoyed by the campaign and the election, had become convinced of the need for union. The Chicago board, swept along by growing demands for unity, called a convention to once more consider the issue. A short time later, the membership of both parties approved a convention which met on July 29, 1901, in Indianapolis to found the Socialist Party of America.[54]

A spirit of compromise prevailed at Indianapolis. The convention never seriously discussed the question of Socialist unity since it took the matter for granted. The platform, however, did bring acrimonious debate and developed new factional lines. The divisive issue involved the fundamental problem of immediate political and economic demands. One faction, known as the "impossibilists," opposed the inclusion of immediate demands. They claimed that workers could not obtain quick relief under capitalism and that immediate demands would only divert the working class and delay the coming of socialism. The other faction, dubbed "opportunists" by their opponents, also desired the cooperative commonwealth, but believed they could obtain it through evolutionary methods. Immediate demands enabled Socialists to reach and to educate workers; they alleviated the hardships of the working class under capitalism.

The issue crossed party lines. Hillquit and other former Social Laborites supported Berger and the Chicago faction. The convention voted 5,358 to 1,315 to include immediate demands in the platform. The delegates unanimously passed a resolution on trade unions that favored complete cooperation with all bodies representing organized labor. After reaching accord on the platform, the convention drafted a constitution, adopted the name Socialist Party of America, formed an executive committee and established party headquarters in St. Louis.[55] Socialist unity had become reality.

Meyer London did not attend the Indianapolis convention. Nevertheless, his career indicates that he embraced much of the meeting's accomplishments. As a member of Congress, he advocated bills which sought to improve the social and economic position of the working class. London, unlike many socialists, was too practical a politician to isolate himself from the mainstream of American life by taking a rigid doctrinal position. He rejected the revolutionary course of the "impossibilists" for a more moderate, evolutionary approach which would pave the way for the cooperative commonwealth. This brought him into conflict with the left wing of the Socialist Party, but did not deter him from his position.

London's close association with the labor unions was also indicative of his agreement with the Indianapolis platform. He consistently advocated close ties between the unions and the Socialist movement. As a result, the left wing attacked him repeatedly for collaborating with the "reactionary" American Federation of Labor.

1. The Early Years

In the years immediately following his arrival in the United States, London became actively involved in the Socialist movement. Among the first to break with De Leon's Socialist Labor Party, he subsequently played an important role in founding the Social Democratic Party on New York's Lower East Side. He played a lesser role in establishing the Socialist Party of America. During the years between 1891 and 1901, his interests, however, went beyond socialism. Like many of the young Russian Jewish intellectuals who came to the United States, London became intimately involved with the emerging Jewish trade union movement on the Lower East Side. After beginning his law practice, these ties deepened, and London became an important legal adviser to Jewish unions and other working-class organizations, many with Socialist sympathies.

2

London and the Labor Movement

> Meyer London was "the oracle, the prophet, the pillar of fire which lights the way for the 75,000 cloakmakers." —*New York Call*, August 8, 1910, 2

The Jewish labor movement emerged on New York's Lower East Side in the 1880s from the utopian ideals that stirred the former Russian students who lived and worked in the squalid tenements and sweatshops. The early Jewish unions lacked solid organization and financial resources, and disappeared almost as quickly as they appeared.[1] Meyer London later recalled that in the early days of the garment unions, "we had unions ... they existed on paper. We had agitators who were irritators only. We had a movement that moved backwards. We talked about a social revolution and had a seventy-hour week. We talked about reorganizing the whole world in a day, and down under our very noses people slaved in the sweat shops."[2] Despite recurrent failure, the Jewish labor movement succeeded as educator and inspirer. The unions broke through the harsh conditions and brought hope to the tenement and sweatshop.

As legal adviser to the Jewish unions in these difficult formative years, London helped place them on a solid foundation. He made lasting contributions to the International Ladies' Garment Workers' Union, the International Fur Workers' Union and other unions.

After London began his law practice in 1898, he became deeply involved in the Jewish labor movement. His first case involved a strike, and thereafter, he specialized in labor litigation. He acted as legal adviser to unions on the East Side, negotiated contracts and fought injunctions.[3] This involved much hard work with little prospect of financial success. London developed a substantial practice but frequently refused fees from impoverished unions or individuals, choosing to work pro bono.[4]

Thus, prior to and for some time during the garment workers strike, London received no payment for his services. The union leadership decided to give him $2,000. Abraham Rosenberg presented the check, but London refused to accept it. He told Rosenberg to give it to the striking workers. The latter informed him that the union would not permit him to work for nothing. If London refused the payment, they would not retain him. London accepted the check. This is merely one example of London's selflessness. To Meyer and his wife Anna, a dentist, whom he married in 1898, "life was worthwhile only if one used it for a useful purpose — primarily to help those who needed help" whether it was an individual, union or the Socialist Party.[5]

The International Ladies' Garment Workers' Union (ILGWU) was founded on June 3, 1900, in New York by representatives of six cloak, suit and skirt makers' organizations. In the first ten years of the ILGWU's existence, the union had to overcome many challenges in order to become an effective organization. Leaders lacked organizational experience, and internal conflict and dissension plagued various locals. The large influx of immigrant labor from Eastern Europe was unfamiliar with and antagonistic to trade unionism. In addition, there was the seasonal nature of the industry.[6] By 1904, the ILGWU included sixty-six locals with approximately nine thousand members. Nevertheless, in 1905 it seemed on the verge of collapse due to increased pressure from employers and internal difficulties.[7]

In this most critical period, London not only served the union in a legal capacity, but as an inspirational leader. He readily gave advice, guidance and financial assistance. When the income of the International dwindled to practically nothing during the financial crisis of 1907–1908, only London and Abraham Rosenberg, who became union president during the crisis, voiced words of hope. In addition, London gave the New York Joint Board twenty-five dollars to pay its rent.[8] Though the future looked bleak, encouraging signs appeared.

In 1907, the New York reefer makers went out on strike.[9] These workers were among the least skilled in the ladies' garment industry, and the shops in which they labored had the worst conditions in the trade.[10] Since reefer making required little skill, it attracted the newly arrived Russian immigrants who willingly worked for the lowest wages in the cloak industry.

On March 22, 1907, after the employers had responded to union demands with a lockout, some 1,200 workers went out on strike. The ILGWU's New York Joint Board led by London, Rosenberg, and Benjamin Schlesinger, manager of the Cloak Makers' Union, brought to bear labor's fullest resources.[11]

After seven weeks the Reefer Manufacturers' Association agreed to terms with the union. The strike settlement established the closed shop, reduced the workweek from fifty-nine to fifty-five hours, freed the workers from paying for needles, straps, and shuttles, specified that the employers would provide sewing machines, and abolished inside sub-contracting among the pressers.[12] The victory, although a limited one, encouraged the active members of the ILGWU.

The optimism created by the success of the reefer makers was dampened by the depression which gripped the country late in 1907. One-third of organized labor in New York was unemployed; the unorganized were affected even more severely.[13] The ILGWU survived these dark days. With the end of the depression in the middle of 1909, a turning point in garment trade unionism occurred in both the men's and women's branches of the industry.[14]

Restlessness grew within the shirtwaist industry during the summer and fall of 1909. Major grievances included low wages, long hours, inside subcontracting, excessive charges for needles and electricity, and fines for lateness and spoiled work. In New York, Ladies' Waist Makers Union, Local 25 of the ILGWU declared a strike against the Triangle Waist Company on September 27, 1909.[15] At Cooper Union, on the evening of November 22, London; Samuel Gompers; Abraham Cahan; Benjamin Feigenbaum, a leading Jewish Socialist and writer; and Mary Dreier, president of the New York Women's Trade Union League, addressed a waistmakers' meeting called to consider a general strike.[16] Stirred by impassioned pleas from Clara Lemlich, a teenage activist, the local approved the strike. The ILGWU later endorsed this decision.[17] The strike, which became known as the "Uprising of the Twenty-Thousand," lasted until February 15, 1910. Some twenty thousand waist makers, mostly young women between sixteen and twenty-five, left their shops.

Police and private guards clashed with the workers manning picket lines. London joined several attorneys recruited to defend the arrested pickets.[18] As violence increased against the pickets, public sympathy grew. The Women's Trade Union League, the Central Federated Union, and the United Hebrew Trades provided financial aid and direction. On December 20, the strike spread to Philadelphia, but no settlement on an overall basis was reached in either city. A conference between the union and the employers produced a tentative compromise agreement. The agreement did not, however, provide for union recognition or a union shop, and on December 27, the strikers overwhelmingly rejected the proposed settlement. The union, thereupon, negotiated individually with various employers and settled with some 360 firms. The strike raised hope among workers in other branches of the industry and bolstered the confidence of ILGWU leaders. The membership of Local 25 increased from one hundred to over ten thousand by 1911. Moreover, the shirtwaist workers had demonstrated the effectiveness of a general strike.[19]

The successful shirtwaist strike encouraged ILGWU leaders to launch a major drive to organize cloak and suit shops. They subsequently called a general strike of the cloak and suit workers. Their grievances were similar to those of the shirtwaist makers: long hours, low wages, inside subcontracting, homework, unreasonable charges and fines, irregularity of pay, poor sanitary conditions, and insecurity of employment.

Unlike the shirtwaist strike, however, the ILGWU had carefully planned the cloak strike. As early as July 1908, the New York Joint Board of the Cloak and Suit Makers' Union began a campaign among the cloak makers for a general strike. The following month Meyer London, Max Pine, and H.B. Weinstein, a noted labor organizer engaged by the Joint Board, spoke at a meeting, sponsored by the board and the United Hebrew Trades. They made the first appeal to the cloak makers for a general strike.

However, progress proved slow. Not until the success of the shirtwaist makers' strike did the movement gain momentum. By June 1910, more than ten thousand workers had joined various locals of the Joint Board in anticipation of the strike. In the same month, the tenth convention of the ILGWU met in Boston and approved a resolution authorizing a general strike when deemed advisable. Preparations continued under the direction of the General Executive Board of the International and the Joint Board of New York. The American Federation of Labor, in response to a request for help, assigned John B. Lennon, treasurer of the Federation, to advise the strikers.[20]

Some doubt, however, still existed about the feasibility of a general strike. At a conference called by the *Daily Forward* in early June, London expressed confidence in the cloakworkers.[21] A mass meeting held on June 30 in Madison Square Garden dispelled lingering doubts. An overflow crowd responded enthusiastically to speeches by London, Abraham Cahan, John Mitchell and Samuel Gompers. In his brief remarks, London declared that the walkout of seventy-five thousand would resound all over the world. He pledged to assist the workers in their fight for the eight-hour day, but bluntly warned that if they did not stick to the union, they would return to work on an eighteen-hour basis and take bundles home.[22]

On July 2 and 3, the cloak makers voted on a general strike. The results, announced on July 4, showed 18,771 in favor with only 615 in opposition.[23] The strike was set for July 7 at 2:00 P.M., but the workers were not informed until that very morning when they received copies of the *New Post*, the publication of the Joint Board. At the appointed hour, some sixty thousand cloak makers, union and non-union, left their shops. By the end of the week, the reefer makers, raincoat workers and Brownsville cloak makers had joined the walkout, and upwards of seventy-five thousand participated in the strike.[24]

During the nine-week strike, London, as union counsel, led negotiations, attended all conferences, represented the union in court, spoke to union members in order to boost morale and raised needed funds. He worked eighteen-hour days. From time to time, he never returned home, spending his time at union headquarters. He told a *New York Call* writer that his practice was "going to the dogs"; he had not been in his office for weeks. But who, London exclaimed, could worry about clients when this "great war" was taking place![25] Apparently, London was so consumed that he failed to worry about the needs of his wife Anna and his young daughter Isabel. Although Anna remained very supportive and proud of her husband's achievements, Isabel, writing many years later, described her mother's "discomfort, loneliness, physical and financial insecurity."[26]

Shortly after the strike began, London drafted a statement on behalf of the Strike Committee. The committee, it stated, refused to apologize for the general strike. If anything, the committee owed the exploited workers an apology for not having aroused them earlier. The cloak industry, the statement continued, served as an excellent example of an industry in which "survival of the fittest" now meant "survival of the meanest." The employer who most exploited his workers had the best chance for success. The cloak manufacturers had ruined the trade developed by industrious workers and had corrupted their morale by encouraging "treachery, slavishness and espionage." "This general strike," London declared, "is greater than any union. It is an irresistible movement of the people. It is a protest against conditions that no longer can be tolerated. We ask for humane treatment; we demand the right to live; we refuse to be annihilated." London concluded with an appeal to the American people for help.[27]

In a letter dated July 5, 1910, the Settlement Committee sent a proposed agreement to each manufacturer containing the union demands. It included recognition of the ILGWU, a closed shop (hiring of only union members), the forty-eight-hour week, with a half holiday on Saturday, ten paid legal holidays, abolition of subcontracting and homework, adjustment of the wage scale, provision by the employers of electrically driven sewing machines and other accessories without charge, the right of representation of the union in the shop by a delegate, weekly payments in cash, arbitration of disputes without work stoppages, abolition of overtime during slow periods.[28]

A number of smaller manufacturers, the "moths of Division Street," who could not afford a protracted conflict, quickly settled with the union. Another sixty settled within the first five days, and after three weeks, 350 had signed agreements. However, the larger manufacturers, who resented interference in their business by either government or labor, organized the Cloak, Suit and Manufacturers' Protective Association shortly after the strike began. Each member signed a pledge to address shop grievances, improve sanitary conditions, and to refrain from signing an agreement with any organization, union or otherwise, which would mean relinquishing control and management of his business.

Although the latter provision seemed to preclude union recognition, the Association members were not the "diehards" of the industry. They did not object to resolving the real grievances of the workers, for they saw an opportunity to strike a blow at the smaller unscrupulous manufacturers who, through their exploitative practices, prevented rationalized organization of the garment industry and an end to industrial anarchy.[29]

The day after the strike began, Michael J. Regan, the industrial mediator of the New York State Board of Mediation and Arbitration, sent a letter to the union Settlement Committee and the Manufacturers' Association requesting each to appoint a conference committee. The Executive Committee of the Association on July 11 decided, however, not to enter into negotiations unless the union waived its demands for recognition, the closed shop, and a signed contract from the Association.[30] London, who had worked closely with the Settlement Committee, characterized the demands of the manufacturers as preposterous. If, he maintained, the manufacturers believed the union's demand for recognition unjust, they should prove it, and then convince union leaders in a face-to-face meeting.[31]

Meanwhile, new efforts had begun to end the strike. On July 21, the very day that preliminary negotiations had broken off, Meyer Bloomfield, a Boston lawyer and social worker, acting on behalf of A. Lincoln Filene, held discussions with both sides in an effort to restart negotiations. Filene, a leading Boston department store owner and civic figure, had taken an immediate interest in the cloak strike. A prominent member of the Boston branch of the National Civic Federation, he was deeply interested in industrial peace with justice for both employer and worker. Moreover, both Filene and Bloomfield had previous experience with Jewish labor and the ladies' garment industry.

As a result of Bloomfield's talks with representatives of the union and the Association, both sides agreed on July 22 to invite Louis D. Brandeis to New York to establish a fair basis for negotiations. Contacted by Filene, Brandeis consented. He arrived on July 23 with a proposed agreement which omitted either a closed or open shop.[32]

Brandeis conferred with the Strike Committee on July 23 and 24. He persuaded a majority of the committee to waive the closed shop demand and to draft a statement of grievances. Having conceded to the Association's conditions for negotiations, the manufacturers agreed to a conference with union officials on July 28. At this juncture, a split almost occurred within the union. Abraham Rosenberg, president of the ILGWU, and those members of the Strike Committee who disagreed with the decision to waive the closed shop demand, threatened to boycott the conference upon learning that John Dyche, secretary-treasurer of the ILGWU, had modified a vital union demand calling for non-discrimination against the strikers. Instead of insisting on this point, Dyche had agreed to discuss it at the conference. At this critical juncture Samuel Gompers intervened and worked out a truce between the conservative and radical factions of the Strike Committee.[33]

On July 27, London and Julius Henry Cohen, attorney for the Manufacturers' Association, asked Brandeis to serve as chairman of the conference. Brandeis agreed.[34] London, enthusiastic about the conference with the employers, denied a statement by the manufacturers that Brandeis opposed the closed shop, and attributed it to misinformation on their part. Brandeis, London noted, had championed the cause of labor when he defended the ten-hour day for women.

London hoped that the conference would not only resolve the workers' present grievances, but would make it possible to settle future grievances through an arbitration court composed of an equal number of representatives from each side. In view of the employers' complaint that the union sought to ruin their business, London hoped they would welcome such a court.[35] London realized his objective in the final agreement, the Protocol of Peace, which provided that future disputes be settled by a Committee of Grievances and by a Board of Arbitration.

Representatives of the union and employers met from July 28 to July 30. Each side was represented by ten men in addition to their attorneys—London and Julius Henry Cohen.[36] Both London and Cohen showed a conciliatory spirit in their opening remarks. London informed the manufacturers, "We do not come to control your business; we do not come to control your trade. I personally would have liked to see a state of affairs where mankind should control everything in co-operative effort, but I realize in the year 1910 and in the cloak trade it is hardly possible of realization, and I have advised my clients, and they have agreed with me in that view."[37]

In order to facilitate a quick settlement, Brandeis, with the assistance of London and Cohen, arranged the conference agenda so the least disputed matters came first. Implementation of the agreement, which might cause difficulty, would be discussed only after the settlement of all problems in the dispute. At the conclusion of the first session, Brandeis, encouraged by the tone of the discussions, expressed confidence. In a joint statement, London and Cohen agreed that "considerable progress" had occurred.[38]

The proceedings continued to move smoothly, and the conferees reached an understanding on specific grievances presented by the cloak workers. When the vital question arose pertaining to a method for enforcing the agreement, negotiations deadlocked. Union members viewed the closed shop as the only way to establish a self-enforcing agreement. If the union gave up the closed shop, it could not promise to create or maintain standards for non-union members. To employers, on the other hand, the closed shop meant losing control of their factories.

John Lennon attempted to introduce the closed shop, but Brandeis held that it violated the pre-conference agreement. Moreover, he rejected London's suggestion that the closed shop be considered if no other remedy emerged. However, Brandeis permitted discussion of a union shop agreement after dismissing Cohen's argument that it also violated the agreement not to discuss the closed shop.

Faced with an impasse, Brandeis introduced a compromise plan, the preferential union shop, whereby employers gave preference to union men who were "equally competent" to non-union men. While the manufacturers agreed to accept the Brandeis plan, the union representatives rejected it.[39] London objected to the term "equally competent" and asked for the omission of the word "equally." He maintained that "if you will attempt to draw fine distinctions in any paper you will submit to our people, the more refined the distinction is the less they will understand it, and think they will be deceived."[40]

The question, London contended, could be settled if the manufacturers consented to employ union men as long as competent union men were available. The union realized, however, that the manufacturers had the right to employ non-union help when it was impossible to obtain competent union men.[41] In the final analysis, Brandeis' proposal proved too new and too untested for the union representatives. They found it difficult to believe that an employer would prefer a union man to a non-union man.[42]

In order to avoid a complete breakdown of negotiations, Brandeis suggested that the conference adjourn and that Cohen and London meet with him on August 1 to devise a plan acceptable to both sides as the basis for further bargaining.[43] On that day, Brandeis received a tentative written proposal from Cohen which contained articles dealing with the grievances discussed at the conference. It also provided for the establishment of Joint Boards of Arbitration and Sanitary Control. On the vital issue of union control, the manufacturers agreed to cooperate with and strengthen the union, accept the preferential union shop, and express their sympathy for the union. Brandeis made several modifications in the preferential union shop clause and sent the proposal, with Cohen's approval, to London.

After studying the proposed contract, London reiterated the union's position on the closed shop. He disclaimed, once more, any union desire to control or regulate the business of the manufacturers, and emphasized that the union was open to every person no matter how poor.[44]

On August 3, the union rejected the manufacturers' proposal and negotiations ended. In an explanatory letter to Cohen, London wrote, "Our people fear that the establishment of what you designate as an experiment ... will enable unscrupulous manufacturers to discriminate against the union man, so that his factory will become ... a closed shop against the union man."[45]

London asked Cohen to advise his clients to reach an understanding with the union on wages and hours and to agree to employ competent union men. London stated he would not hesitate to recommend Cohen's proposal thus modified as the basis for settlement of the strike. Cohen rejected London's letter and termed it a "distinct violation" of the union's pledge not to discuss the closed shop.[46]

Shortly after the rupture in negotiations, Cohen applied for a permanent court order to restrain the strikers from picketing and the newspapers from encouraging the strikers.[47] On August 6, at a hearing before Judge Irving Lehman of the Supreme Court of New York County, London argued against the injunction. Judge Lehman granted a temporary, limited injunction restraining the union from coercing any cloak maker to leave work through force, threat, fraud or intimidation. He also ordered the union to show cause why the injunction should not be made more sweeping and permanent.[48]

Despite Lehman's ruling, London expressed optimism that the manufacturers would not obtain their objective. "I feel confident that the rights of men will not be subordinated to the rights of property and that the manufacturers will fail in their efforts to have a general strike declared a conspiracy."[49] Strike leaders shared this view.

The injunction hearing took place on August 12 before Justice Goff of the New York Supreme Court. Cohen sought a sweeping injunction. He referred to the strike as an illegal combination in restraint of trade and a conspiracy. London opposed the action. In his statement, London maintained that the Supreme Court was not superior to the will of the people. "We are determined," he said, "to exercise all the rights given to us by our laws and by the Constitution. No court can deprive us of our rights."[50] There was no need for a court order to restrain "force, fraud and intimidation" as requested by the manufacturers. Such acts have long been prohibited, he declared, and furthermore, the police could handle the situation.

As to Cohen's contention that the general strike was a conspiracy, London stated, "His claim is that we want a monopoly of union labor, and labor being a commodity, a monopoly of union labor is unlawful. Strange reasoning indeed! As soon as all workingmen join the union you will become a monopoly, and will violate the law. In other words, we may have unions, but they must be weak; we may have strikes, but not successful ones."[51]

London noted that the New York Court of Appeals had upheld, in a series of cases, contracts between a union and employer providing for exclusive employment of union members. "If a contract for a closed or union shop is valid when made with one manufacturer, ... does the contract lose its lawful character when made with the 110 manufacturers who constitute the Manufacturers?" Cohen, he continued, had failed to understand that a union was not organized to keep non-union workers jobless. To the contrary, the union wanted non-unionists to join, and gave them every chance to do so. London denied that Cohen spoke for the non-union workers or the poor people. "It is not the people that he is representing here, but the manufacturers, the sweaters, and the exploiters. They talk of patriotism and Americanism, yet these same lovers of liberty ... are bleeding their victims for a wage of $3 a week." London declared that public policy dictated that intelligently led and well-organized unions should organize the workers, educate them and guide them. "The trade union is not only a necessity. It is a blessing." In conclusion, he asked that the manufacturers' suit be dismissed, for they had neither incurred property damage nor could they prove such damages.

The union won a temporary victory when Justice Goff reserved decision on Cohen's application until the following week.[52] London expressed confidence that the manufacturers would not secure the injunction. Their claims were "ridiculous and contradictory."[53]

As the strike wore on, workers and the employers alike experienced increasing economic hardship. The strikers and their families suffered from hunger and could not pay their rent. Strike benefits were small and irregular as the union lacked adequate financial resources for a protracted struggle.[54]

In commenting on the strike, London said, "You know it takes my breath away when I think about it. Think of the grandeur of this struggle. Think of it, 75,000 men leaving their shops and standing up for their demands. When I think into how many homes this strike ... penetrates, how many children are anxiously asking whether papa has won out against the bosses, how many wives, in spite of the fact that the grocer and butcher have a long and heavy bill to show them, send their husbands to the meeting halls with the words, 'Fight to win' on their lips—when I think of this, I sometimes cannot sleep for hours."[55]

Though negotiations remained deadlocked, Filene, Bloomfield and Dr. Henry W. Moskowitz, a social worker and later adviser to Governor Alfred E. Smith, continued their peacemaking efforts. They enlisted the assistance of the wealthy New York financier Jacob H. Schiff, and Louis Marshall, a prominent constitutional lawyer and a leader of American Jewry, who arranged a meeting with London and Cohen.

At this conference held on August 25, Marshall persuaded London and Cohen to accept a revision of the latter's earlier proposal. The agreement included a preferential union shop clause and a statement that the union did not seek a closed shop but a union shop.[56] After a heated debate, the Strike Committee, split on the preferential strike clause, decided to submit the proposal to the workers without recommendations. On August 27, the strikers "overwhelmingly" rejected the proposed settlement. They were determined to continue their fight for the closed shop and the eight-hour day.

On the very day that the strikers rejected the new proposal, the union incurred a severe blow. Justice Goff granted a sweeping injunction which prohibited the strikers from picketing or interfering with the operation of the cloak factories. Goff held the strike to be a common law, civil conspiracy since its goal was to win the closed shop and not to improve the workers' position.[57]

United by Goff's ruling, the Strike Committee declared that the union would challenge the ruling. They would appeal, London commented, regardless of the strike's outcome. The decision seriously threatened the labor movement, and if sustained would have far-reaching consequences. "Because of its influence in other labor troubles, if not on account of its present effect, we should have to fight the injunction with every weapon in our command." London challenged the basis of Justice Goff's decision. He noted that the circumstances in the case cited by Goff as precedent were dissimilar to those in the present cloak strike. Goff's precedent involved one union fighting another union; this case involved employer and employee.[58]

At an election rally on behalf of London's candidacy for Congress in the Ninth Congressional District, he bitterly denounced Judge Goff and the injunction. He reminded the audience of more than two thousand that Goff owed his election to workers' votes though he had not run on a ticket supported by a working-class organization. "His campaign was not made upon the issue of the world for the producers of wealth; therefore he stands opposed to your interests." London declared that the workers would continue to fight for their rights. They would take the appeal to the United States Supreme Court "to find if these judges will declare the general strike to be a conspiracy. If they do, then we will know that these judges are the greatest conspirators in the land." The workers, London concluded, would win this fight and establish their rights.[59]

Meanwhile, Filene and Moskowitz intensified their efforts to get union officials to accept the proposed settlement previously rejected by the union on August 27. The General Executive Board of the ILGWU, as a result of the injunction and the efforts of Filene and Moskowitz, reevaluated its position and dropped its demand for a closed shop.[60]

On September 1, London made public the union's new position in a letter to Acting Mayor Mitchell. In view of Judge Goff's decision, London wrote, the union had adopted a resolution requesting employers "to maintain a union shop, and to employ none but members of the union as long as union members can be obtained to do the work required by the employer." The union had thus agreed to a settlement based on the proposal rejected on August 27. He also sent a copy of the resolution to the Association.[61]

On the same day, Filene finally persuaded both sides to resume negotiations. London and Cohen met with Louis Marshall, and by the afternoon of September 2, they reached an agreement on a basic settlement. The Manufacturers' Association accepted the proposal, and at six o'clock that evening, some two hundred shop chairmen ratified the agreement, thus ending the nine-week general strike.[62] The "Protocol of Peace," as the landmark agreement became known, provided significant gains for the workers.[63] The cloak makers obtained a fifty-hour week, double pay for overtime, satisfaction of wage demands (making arbitration on this matter unnecessary), abolition of inside subcontracting and charges for power. A rewritten preferential union clause eliminated the objectionable terms "non-union men" and "equal ability." The employer would now choose between one union man and another, and could employ non-union help only when union labor was unavailable.

Equally important, the Protocol established mechanisms to oversee the industry's labor relations. It included provisions to set up a Joint Board of Sanitary Control to maintain shop standards, a Board of Grievances to deal with minor disputes, and as the highest authority, a three-man Board of Arbitration. Though either side could withdraw from the agreement at will, no termination date existed. The Protocol was intended as a permanent peace treaty for the garment industry.[64] As such, it represented a major breakthrough in industrial relations.

An elated London, who along with Brandeis, Marshall and Cohen must be given much credit for this achievement, expressed delight with the settlement. "I am physically exhausted, otherwise I would dance for joy. It is a victory. It is an honorable settlement. I am particularly happy that the settlement has not pounded the bosses into submission, but that we converted the bosses to the view that trade unionism has come to stay."[65] London had achieved the goal shared with Brandeis, Filene and others: to bring order out of chaos and to establish a basis for industrial peace in the garment industry.

The days following the end of the strike gave Meyer London little respite. Before a majority of the workers could return to their shops, price schedules for piecework had to be established. London participated in numerous meetings between committees of employers and the union. Workers anxious to return to their jobs grew impatient. Rumors spread that the strike had not ended and that another general strike or numerous smaller strikes would be called. London reassured the workers that the rumors had no foundation. Preparing price lists for such an "army of workers" took time, he pointed out, but "in the course of the next few days every cloak maker will be at work. We are adjusting prices as fast as possible."[66]

London also expressed satisfaction with the attitude of the manufacturers who seemed more inclined than ever to favor the union. He attributed this to the manufacturers' acceptance of the need for organization in the cloak industry as well as other industries. Employers found it much easier to deal with organized labor than with individual workers. London voiced confidence that the cloak strike would be a matter of history in a few days.[67]

As counsel for the ILGWU, implementation of the Protocol continued to require much of London's time and effort. At first little difficulty occurred. With the arrival of the slack season in November 1910, it became apparent that the Committee of Grievances could not handle the growing number of complaints brought to its attention. Improvements in the grievance machinery were necessary, but such efforts proved fruitless.

Dissatisfaction with the Protocol grew among the workers and the manufactures. Finally, on January 17, 1911, Julius Cohen filed a formal complaint with the Board of Arbitration. London responded for the union. He noted that the complaint was vague, and requested a specific statement before replying in detail. He later attended a meeting called in order to get the manufacturers to withdraw charges; they refused to do so. At the request of Henry Moskowitz, London prepared a list of countercharges for consideration by the Arbitration Board. Moskowitz hoped that with the presentation of charges and countercharges both parties could be persuaded to settle their differences through conciliation rather than the Board of Arbitration.[68]

London attempted to delay the formal presentation of his countercharges hopeful that the Association would withdraw its complaint. On January 26, he wrote Moskowitz a detailed account of the union's grievances. The manufacturers, London charged, had not adhered to the Protocol's wage scales and had dismissed workers for demanding union scale. Moreover, some Association members had threatened to reduce their labor force in order to compel their employees to accept less than scale. London also claimed that employers sent work to shops in other cities over which the ILGWU had no control. Additional charges included discrimination against active union men; failure to install electric machines, to improve sanitary conditions, to cooperate with the Grievance Committee; and, finally, failing to pay weekly workers for legal holidays by discharging them before the holiday and rehiring them.

Nevertheless, London reiterated his confidence in the Protocol. No one had expected, he stated, that all abuses would be remedied in four months. London once more urged the manufacturers to withdraw their complaint. If the manufacturers failed to do so, the union would file its charges, and "there will be charges and countercharges galore, to the great delight of those who believe that the cloak industry should be governed by the divine principle of 'Dog eat Dog.'"[69]

Further efforts to reach a compromise failed. London received instructions to present formal charges to the Board of Arbitration against the Association for failing to abide by the "letter and spirit" of the Protocol. On February 23, the union presented both its response to the Association's charges and its own countercharges. The latter were similar to those included in London's letter to Moskowitz except the charges of discrimination were strengthened, and the union charged the Association with obstructing its efforts to acquire evidence of non-compliance with the Protocol. Brandeis was thus forced to call the Board of Arbitration on March 4, 1911.[70]

This first meeting of the board lasted three days. Brandeis acted as chairman. Morris Hillquit represented the unions and Hamilton Holt the manufacturers. London presented the union's position. He accused the manufacturers of acting in bad faith. "As soon as they believed that a strike no longer threatens them, they have no use for an association." Moreover, he noted, "almost every member of their Executive Committee violates the agreement." It became clear, as the hearing proceeded, that most of the difficulty stemmed from faulty operation of the Committee of Grievances. Brandeis requested Holt and Hillquit to prepare a plan to strengthen the committee. This resulted in the adoption of more clearly defined procedures for investigating grievances and for enforcing committee decisions. Thereafter, both sides accepted rulings of the Board of Arbitration, and for a time, the Protocol functioned smoothly.[71]

Other branches of the New York garment industry adopted agreements similar to the Protocol.[72] In September 1911, the Ladies' Tailors and Dress Makers' Union, Local 38 of the ILGWU, conducted a general strike involving some three thousand workers. As counsel for Local 38, London helped extend "protocolism" to the ladies' tailoring trade. London and Julius Cohen, the latter representing the manufacturers, implored Brandeis to accept chairmanship of the ladies tailors' Board of Arbitration. They assured him that the board would meet infrequently as they had agreed privately not to go before the board except on "really important and vital issues." Brandeis agreed, but London's and Cohen's optimism proved misplaced.[73]

Within Local 38, those opposed to surrendering the right to strike gained control. Dissatisfaction with the Arbitration Board's failure to take prompt action to resolve issues lingering from the general strike led to a number of shop strikes. London, Cohen and Brandeis, in order to facilitate decisions of the Board of Arbitration, accepted Henry Moskowitz's suggestion for an industry economic study.

Although harassed while gathering information by officials of the local who sympathized with the strike proponents, London submitted a detailed report on overtime payments in unionized industries and a selected statement of wage and employment conditions within the ladies tailors' industry. Cohen persuaded members of the Merchants' Society of the Ladies Tailors and Dress Makers of New York to allow accountants to examine the books of sixteen manufacturers. The accountants prepared a statement which they forwarded to Brandeis.[74]

The Board of Arbitration heard additional evidence and considered briefs from mid–December 1911 to mid–February 1912. Cohen sought to introduce other controversial issues, but London insisted that the board consider only those questions left unsettled by the general strike. Upon resolution of these questions, London agreed that the board should inquire into other differences.[75]

On February 27, 1912, the board rendered its decision. It upheld London's contention as to questions referred to it by the peacemakers of the general strike. On the vital question of overtime pay and payment on legal holidays, it ruled that overtime pay be one and three-fifths of regular wages, with the employers determining the number of men to work overtime, and that the workers receive payment on two of the five holidays and double pay for work done on any holidays.[76]

The board's decision satisfied neither the strike proponents of Local 38 nor the Manufacturers' Society. The former vowed to continue their obstructive tactics. They also refused to recognize the manufacturers' right to determine the number of workers for overtime. On the other hand, the employers agreed to comply with the decision, but insisted that the overtime pay not be made retroactive to September 19, the date of the Protocol. London disagreed with the employers and insisted that the Protocol explicitly made the board's decision retroactive. As for the manufacturers' plea that some would go bankrupt, London replied that if some went bankrupt because of this just decision, then "they deserved to go to the ground."[77]

As conditions within the cloak industry stabilized toward the end of 1911, improvement of working conditions ended, and antagonism toward the Protocol persisted. Workers blamed the Protocol for their problems. They claimed that it prevented them from legally striking. In addition, the radicals among the workers considered the Protocol "class collaborationist" and harmful to the class struggle and the liberation of the working class. On the other hand, the employers felt that they had made too many concessions and had received too little in return, for shop stoppages and strikes continued to harass them.[78]

Personality clashes among union leaders, quarrels between the conservative leadership of the ILGWU and the more radical officers of the New York Joint Board, and friction between the union and the Manufacturers' Association increased during the fall of 1912.[79] These were merely forerunners of events which subjected the Protocol to a severe trial during the following year.

The first clash occurred in January 1913 when a dispute in the shops of Goldfield and Lachman led to a breakdown of the Grievance Board machinery. At a meeting of the Board of Grievances on January 27, Julius Cohen stated that the Association would not deal with the Joint Board since the Protocol had been negotiated with the International rather than the local unions or the Joint Board. The manufacturers realized that the conservative officers of the International were more willing to cooperate with them. Furthermore, they hoped to take advantage of the dispute between the Joint Board and the International as to which had the authority to speak for the local union.[80]

Dr. Isaac A. Hourwich, newly appointed chief clerk of the Joint Board, insisted that the Protocol had been signed with the Joint Board and not the International. Hourwich denied the authority of the International to interfere in the internal affairs of the local unions.[81] Hourwich viewed himself as a champion of the rank and file and industrial democracy. "If you desire to deal with the shadow instead of the body it is your privilege," he warned, "but you must be aware that they cannot deliver the goods."[82]

London prevented John Dyche, secretary treasurer of the International, angered by Hourwich's references to the union, from precipitating an open fight between the International and the Joint Board. London, feared the consequences of a rift within union ranks He believed that despite the existence of differences within the union, it had to maintain a united front against the Association. Since Cohen raised the question of union jurisdiction, London held it imperative that the International back Hourwich's position. He persuaded Dyche to sign a letter written by Hourwich to the Association in which the International agreed that the manufacturers must deal with the Joint Board.[83]

Although the Association still rejected this view, the Board of Arbitration in early February upheld Hourwich's arguments. The board ruled, however, that the International, as "guarantor" of the Protocol, had to make certain that the Joint Board fulfilled its obligations. Since both sides had agreed to accept the findings of the Board of Arbitration, the crisis was surmounted.[84]

The rift between the International and the Joint Board, however, widened with the passage of time, and the Protocol remained under continuous attack. Dr. Hourwich led the onslaught. Flushed with the success of his first confrontation with the International and the Association, Hourwich drafted a comprehensive plan to modify the Protocol. "He became the center around which the bitterly contested issues of the garment industry swirled — arbitration versus conciliation; 'protocolism' versus class war; radicalism of the New York locals versus conservatism of the International."[85]

Hourwich seized upon a minor dispute that occurred on April 14, 1913, to push his demand for reform. When the Board of Grievances failed to settle the dispute, it referred the matter to the Board of Arbitration. London prepared the union's complaint against the Manufacturers' Association. Like Henry Moskowitz, acting secretary for the Board of Arbitration, he hoped to resolve the dispute without going before the board.

As time passed without action, Hourwich became convinced that binding arbitration had to replace mediation. He met with Brandeis in Washington on May 9 and demanded a more effective arbitration system. Brandeis maintained that mediation and conciliation were preferable to arbitration. Failing to convert Hourwich to his views, Brandeis suggested that the Joint Board prepare amendments for improving the Protocol. These would then be considered by a joint conference of union and Association representatives. Hourwich agreed and obtained the approval of the Joint Board.[86]

On May 17, Hourwich sent Brandeis a fifteen-point proposal and requested an immediate conference. The most important item was point 15. It enlarged the Board of Arbitration to make it more accessible to the concerned parties. Four days later London sent a similar letter to the Association. Hopes for immediate action vanished when Moskowitz informed Hourwich that a conference could not convene before the end of June.

A disappointed Hourwich, in a letter to Brandeis, referred ominously to the "memorable summer" of 1910 and stated that he could not predict the results if the Association maintained its unyielding attitude. Brandeis, disturbed by Hourwich's "threats," appealed to London and Moskowitz to reason with him. London expressed surprise that Hourwich would make such a "threat" without consultation. He promised Moskowitz that he would deal with Hourwich.[87]

During the month of June, anti–Protocol agitation intensified. The *New Post*, in close alliance with Hourwich, kept up a constant barrage against the Protocol. Internal pressures grew within the Joint Board. A majority feared for the very existence of the Protocol. Hourwich opposed efforts by the Joint Board to supervise the editorial policy of the paper. He offered his resignation in protest. The Joint Board, fearful that Hourwich's resignation would cause an internal upheaval, refused to accept it and sought compromise. Within the union, however, the split widened between Hourwich supporters and foes. Hourwich's tactics and his insistence upon arbitration in place of conciliation were largely responsible for the internal conflict.[88]

Henry Moskowitz hoped that London would assume the role of mediator within the union. Moskowitz believed that London, while "straddling" the arbitration question, had enough sense as a good trade unionist to appreciate the impracticality of arbitration. According to Moskowitz, London was too

2. London and the Labor Movement 33

Isaac M. Hourwich Law Office. From left to right, secretary, clerk, wife Anna Rosenson London, unknown man, Meyer London and Hourwich, circa 1910. Photographic Collection, Tamiment Library, New York University.

much an idol of the garment workers to risk alienating their affections. Nevertheless, his strategic position within the union gave rise to Moskowitz's expectation that at the proper time London would come to the rescue.

This hope died when friction developed between London and Hourwich. The two men had been close associates for many years, and at first held similar opinions regarding the value of the Protocol. Hourwich, however, aroused London's ire when he began to arrogate the union counsel's duties. He also wrote irritating letters to London. As a result, their friendship gradually deteriorated. Although London had come to doubt Hourwich's approach to resolve grievance deadlocks, he did not openly express these doubts. Thus, the rift between them was imperceptible at first.[89]

The joint conference finally met on July 8 and remained in session until July 30, 1913. Due to close cooperation between London and Julius Cohen, the conference got off to a good start. During the following week discussions deadlocked, but private negotiations between London, Cohen, and Hourwich produced an agreement on a modified version of the all-important fifteenth point. They agreed to enlarge the Board of Arbitration by providing two alternates for each member. This would enable the board to function without the regular arbitrators. The conferees accepted this amendment but could not reach an agreement on other vital issues such as wages and sub-manufacturing. They referred the question of Protocol reform to the Board of Arbitration.[90]

The Board of Arbitration met from August 3 to August 6 to consider the questions referred to it by the conferees. Brandeis objected to the proposed addition of six men to the board and received the support of his fellow arbitrators. On the wage matter, the board called for an investigation of garment industry wages, since no reliable statistics existed.

Hourwich refused to accept the board's decision, and denounced Brandeis' "paternalism" and "dictatorial attitude."[91] London accepted the decision and convinced the Joint Board to do the same. Moreover, London successfully persuaded Hourwich to cooperate with the wage investigation and with Cohen and himself in formulating an acceptable program to improve the grievance machinery. Nevertheless, Hourwich attempted to introduce some reforms unilaterally.

As a result, animosity toward Hourwich intensified within both the union and the Manufacturers' Association. London finally broke with him toward the end of September and joined the Joint Board's anti-Hourwich faction. London feared that Hourwich would drive the workers into a general strike which he believed would be disastrous for the union movement in the cloak industry.[92]

Due to the activities of Hourwich, the Manufacturers' Association requested another meeting of the Board of Arbitration. At the board sessions on October 3 and 4, Julius Cohen asked that Hourwich be censured for articles in the *New Post* which, he charged, inspired hostility to the Association and the Protocol. The board upheld the Association. It censured both the *New Post* and Hourwich, stating that the latter's views constituted an act of "insurrection and rebellion" against the Protocol.[93]

The Board of Arbitration met again on October 12 and 13 to consider wage increases and the question of reforming the grievance machinery of the Protocol. It granted limited wage adjustments where adequate data existed. Although the board made no change in the Board of Grievances, it did agree to further study the matter.[94]

These decisions represented reversals for Hourwich and his more radical supporters. On the other hand, they strengthened the more moderate position of the International officers and those on the Joint Board who sought reconciliation between the two.

Through London's peacemaking efforts, the split was slowly healed. At a meeting of the Joint Board on October 18, London introduced a conciliatory resolution in order to clarify the relationship between the Joint Board and the International. Although opposed by Hourwich, a majority of the delegates supported it. The resolution called for continuous cooperation between the Joint Board and the International, expressed disapproval of any action that could cause personal conflict between the two organizations, endorsed a free press but warned the official publications of both parties to refrain from personal attacks upon each other and to treat respectfully the employers with whom they had friendly relations. It also provided that the Joint Board should elect three of the five members of the Grievance Board and the International the remaining two, so that there would be friendly and united action in dealings with the Manufacturers' Association. The International accepted the conciliatory resolution of the Joint Board and notified the Association that it would assume responsibility for enforcing the board's October decisions.[95] London's efforts had apparently resolved the differences between the Joint Board and the ILGWU.

However, in early November, London's peacemaking initiative unraveled. Abraham Rosenberg, president of the ILGWU, in a letter to the Joint Board castigated Hourwich's conduct. Stung by Rosenberg's attack, Hourwich who had considered resigning as chief clerk changed his mind and sought reappointment. Furthermore, he insisted upon several conditions, including recognition as the union's only lawyer in its dealings with the Association — a rebuff of London.

On November 24, the Joint Board voted not to reappoint Hourwich, and also refused to hold a referendum on the question. The Joint Board, however, under pressure from Hourwich supporters, reversed itself and agreed to a referendum in mid–December. The members would vote on five conditions Hourwich had imposed for his continuance as chief clerk. But this still did not satisfy a vindictive Hourwich who insisted on a referendum on one question: the removal of Meyer London and his appointment as the lone counsel for the union.[96] The referendum resulted in an "overwhelming" vote in favor of Hourwich who gained recognition as the principal lawyer for the union in dealing with the Association on matters involving the Protocol.[97]

On December 16, a deeply hurt London resigned as counsel for the Joint Board. The vote, he explained, had limited his authority and amounted to a vote of no confidence by the cloakworkers.[98] London's true feelings surfaced at the Twelfth Convention of the ILGWU in Cleveland in June of 1914. In brief remarks to the delegates he commented that "he had not for one minute thought of deserting the cloak makers, but when the ship was on fire, having on board a captain (Hourwich) who was blind and sailors who were drunk, I thought it a sensible thing to step aside so that I could come at the proper time and lend a helping hand."[99]

The Manufacturers' Association refused to accept the referendum and called upon the International to remove Hourwich. The manufacturers refused to take part in any discussions under the Protocol until this condition was met. At the next meeting of the Board of Arbitration on January 18, 1914, the board took up the Hourwich problem. It ruled that the manufacturers did not have the right to compel Hourwich to withdraw. If, however, he chose to resign voluntarily, out of loyalty to the union and the Protocol, "a continuance of the protocol in our opinion would be assured, and a dangerous and anomalous crisis ... would be averted."[100] Although the board acknowledged that each side had the right to terminate the Protocol at a moment's notice, it suggested an eight-day truce. Both sides accepted the proposed cooling-off period.[101]

On the following day, Hourwich offered his resignation to the Joint Board. The so-called "Hourwich affair" ended on January 22, when the board accepted his resignation.[102] The struggle ended in a victory for London, Brandeis, Cohen, and others who believed that disputes in the garment industry could be settled through the procedures established in the Protocol.

The success of the garment workers and the corresponding growth of the ILGWU in 1909–1910 were marred by the tragic Triangle Shirtwaist Factory fire on March 25, 1911. One hundred forty-six workers, mostly young Jewish and Italian women, perished. A week after the fire, an angry London addressed a large protest rally at Cooper Union. He attributed the fire to a system of "greed." In a sarcastic vein, London predicted that an investigation would occur. It would "result in a law [bill] being referred to a committee that will report in 1913. And by 1915 a law will be passed — and after that our grafting officials will not enforce it."

London's prediction proved wrong. Responding to intense public pressure, the Democratic Tammany-controlled state legislature, led by Robert Wagner and Al Smith, created the Factory Inspection Commission. It subsequently proposed fifteen bills to the legislature dealing with fire hazards, factory inspection, sanitation, and employment of women and children. Eight passed with bipartisan support.[103]

During the years following the cloak makers' strike, London also played an important role in creating the furriers' union. Earlier efforts had ended in failure. Encouraged by the successful strikes elsewhere in the garment industry, eighty fur operators met in the fall of 1909 and laid the groundwork for reorganization of the union. Membership grew at a disappointing rate until the spring of 1911 when the United Hebrew Trades extended financial and organizational support. By the spring of 1912, some three thousand fur workers had joined the union.[104]

Isadore Cohen, union organizer and later president of the International Fur Workers' Union, recalled that London first came to the union to address a mass meeting several days after the disastrous Triangle Waist Company fire. "London came, spoke and remained with us. That evening he took our infant organization to his heart, and bestowed upon it all the passionate affection of which he was capable. There was no spoken or tacit arrangement regarding the services or compensation. We just adopted him as our father and he assumed his fatherly duties and responsibilities with cheerful eagerness."[105]

By the spring of 1912, union officials, encouraged by the surge in membership and three thousand dollars in the union treasury, began preparations for a general strike. They set up a General Strike Committee and drafted demands for union recognition, a nine-hour day and a fifty-four-hour week, paid legal holidays, abolition of homework and subcontracting, and improved sanitary conditions. On June 14 and 15, the union members voted overwhelmingly for a general strike. Union leaders designated June 20 as the date for the proposed walkout and selected Meyer London as their legal adviser.

On June 19, the Associated Fur Manufacturers and the Mutual Protective Fur Manufacturers rejected the union's demands. The following day approximately seven thousand fur workers, from four hundred shops, responded to the strike call. With virtually the entire trade at a standstill, union leaders predicted an early victory. London shared that view. He predicted that since the fur industry demanded skilled labor the manufacturers would find it impossible to utilize professional scabs.[106]

Despite this early optimism, it soon became apparent that the fur workers faced a long and difficult struggle. The fur manufacturers rejected union demands for recognition and the closed shop. The two manufacturers' associations, representing some three hundred employers, agreed not to enter into any contract, agreement, or secret understanding that would conflict with the principle of the open shop.[107] The fur manufacturers' position resembled that taken previously by the cloak employers.

Soon after the strike began, London held secret conferences with the employers. The manufacturers informed him that they would not deal with the union. They would treat London not as a union representative, but as a private individual. London reminded them that other "big capitalists" dealt with unions, and he could not understand why the fur manufacturers refused to do the same.[108] The employers, on the other hand, saw no need to negotiate. They believed that the workers, as during past strikes, would return to their shops after a few weeks.[109] As a result, initial efforts to settle the strike failed.

The manufacturers underestimated fur workers' determination. The strike wore on for twelve weeks as the fur workers continued their demand for union recognition. During these weeks, London once again devoted himself, to the exclusion of other professional and personal commitments, to the furriers' cause. "He was there to inspire his men with his oratory; he was there to comfort and guide the strike leaders; he was there to plead with the bankers for loans and with fellow labor organizations for help. He was there ... to negotiate the peace terms with the employers."[110]

A breakthrough occurred toward the end of August when the manufacturers agreed to negotiations. A secret meeting took place between representatives and lawyers of the union and the manufacturers on the evening of August 20. After seven hours, the employers acceded to nearly all the union demands, including union recognition. The agreement also provided for a half-day holiday on Saturday for the first eight months of the year. It did not include the closed shop.[111]

On August 22, the striking fur workers assembled at two meetings to hear reports by London on the proposed settlement. The crowds greeted London with prolonged cheers and applause. The strikers shouted, "We want a half holiday on Saturdays throughout the year." London commended the furriers for holding out for ten weeks in order to obtain their demands. He urged them to listen carefully and to study the proposed settlement upon which they would later vote. London then discussed the agreement point by point. He paid particular attention to the controversial provision for a half-day holiday on Saturdays and indicated that they would probably get more than that. The proposal also included ten paid legal holidays, abolition of subcontracting, readjustment of wage rates twice a year, a joint board of sanitary control, a joint arbitration board to settle all grievances that might arise, and a committee of ten to settle all matters unresolved by the strike. The proposal embraced the principles of the Protocol of Peace.

In conclusion, London urged the strikers to vote intelligently on the proposals. He received prolonged cheers when he admonished them to stick by the union until victorious. Samuel Gompers, who followed London to the rostrum, also advised the workers to weigh carefully the proposed settlement. If dissatisfied, they should continue to strike until the employers yielded to their demands.[112]

The strikers did not get the opportunity to vote on the proposed settlement. On the following day, the manufacturers' associations denied that they had agreed to a tentative settlement subject to ratification by both sides. In response, the strikers made it clear that they would not return to their jobs until the employers gave them a half holiday on Saturdays the whole year round.[113] The day after the meeting London predicted that the workers would vote overwhelmingly against the proposals. He based his opinion on the reaction of the workers at the meeting when he mentioned the half holiday on Saturdays.

During the next two weeks negotiations continued. When asked about the strike situation, London commented that he felt more confident in this fight than in the victorious strike of the cloak makers in 1910. The employers might hold out a few more days, he declared, but eventually they would have to grant the strikers' demands.

On September 8, the twelve-week general strike ended. With the exception of the closed shop and the abolition of contracting, the fur workers had won many important gains, including their demand for the Saturday half holiday. London expressed pleasure with the settlement. "It was a splendid fight," he said, "and ... well worthwhile. The conditions have been so improved that I believe the workers will never permit the old conditions to be reinstalled."[114] As news of the settlement spread during the early morning hours of September 8, thousands of joyous strikers surged through the streets. They marched to London's house at 274 East Broadway, and "he was dragged from his bed and ... carried to the window" from where he addressed the cheering crowd. For almost an hour after London had retired, the crowd remained in front of his residence.

Encouraged by its success, the union, in 1913, joined with local fur unions in other cities to form the International Fur Workers' Union and affiliated with the American Federation of Labor.[115] Although London's later congressional activities prevented him from taking an active part in union affairs, he continued to serve the union in a legal capacity through the remaining years of his life.

In the years following the successful strikes of the garment workers and the furriers, London staunchly supported conciliation and arbitration, as established in the Protocols of Peace, as the best means for resolving industrial disputes.[116] Great changes had occurred in industry, politics, and legislation, but most trade union methods, London maintained, were passé. With the exception of the railroad and mining industries, the strike had become "entirely futile" as a weapon. The use of violence by employers and workers, London insisted, was never in date. "Both sides have been violent, but violence has never been lastingly effective or even temporarily wise for either side."

Political activity and educational propaganda, London believed, were the best means to advance the cause of the labor movement. "I would have every union transform itself into an educational center, even though that changed extensively ... the leadership. Leaders must grow as the world grows, in labor or elsewhere." Furthermore, the worker had to recognize his duty as a citizen, an obligation in which he had "failed lamentably." Though labor talked loudly about the brotherhood of man, it failed to stand together. "This is a failure not only to grasp the right idea of the individual's duty to society, but is a failure to grasp the right idea of the worker's duty to his fellow workers."

London believed that the final objective of the socialists was an industrial democracy where "everyone participating in the State's burdens shall also participate in its benefits." He considered capital and labor mere words. His interest lay neither in capital nor labor, but in the welfare of all human beings.

If workers educated themselves, there was nothing that they could not achieve in America. "They have the votes. All that is needed is powerful concerted action."[117] London maintained that an educated, enlightened working class could realize its objectives through political action. The vehicle for translating goals into realities was the Socialist Party.

Although London saw some of his contemporaries attain wealth and prominence as corporate lawyers and businessmen, he fervently believed that there was no higher honor than to represent the labor movement. Nothing, he said, gave him more pleasure than the building up of the "mighty" Cloakmakers' Union.[118]

During this troubled period London had worked with leaders of the established American Jewish community such as Louis Brandeis, Jacob Schiff, Louis Marshall, Julius Cohen and Henry Moskowitz among others. Despite his Socialist beliefs, he won their respect for his intellect, his reasonableness, and his steadfastness in the pursuit of economic justice for the workers he represented.

His selfless devotion to the labor movement did not go unnoticed. Labor leaders, including Samuel Gompers, with whom he developed a lasting working relationship, deeply appreciated London's tireless efforts on behalf of working men and women. Union members embraced London and gave him their wholehearted political support. They were largely responsible for making London the first Socialist congressman from the East.

3

Prelude to Victory: The Elections of 1910 and 1912

> Thinking men would vote for the man who has given himself to the workers for the last twenty years, and who cried out for the Jewish victims of the Russian pogroms.—*Daily Forward, November 3, 1910, 10.*

In 1910, the Local New York branch of the Socialist Party nominated Meyer London for Congress in the Ninth Congressional District. The popular labor lawyer had run unsuccessfully for the New York Legislature in several earlier campaigns. This was his first bid for a national office. The party's decision to select London rather than Morris Hillquit indicated that it recognized the need to support candidates closely identified with the Jewish immigrants. London's dedicated service to the trade unions, his support for the Russian revolutionary movement and his advocacy of free immigration had won the affection and respect of the people. With this campaign, London emerged as a major political figure on the Lower East Side.

The Lower East Side of New York, the scene of Meyer London's political career, is situated at the southern tip of Manhattan Island. Bounded roughly by the East River and the Bowery to the east and west and by Fourteenth Street and Market Street from north to south, it had become an "immigrant Jewish cosmopolis" by the first decade of the twentieth century.[1] Predominately German and Irish prior to 1870, the Lower East Side took on an immigrant Jewish complexion, for almost all European Jews arriving after 1870 found their way initially to this district. By 1914 one-sixth of New York's population resided south of Fourteenth Street upon one eighty-second of the city's real estate. The number of Jews in New York was estimated at 80,000 in 1870, but increased to approximately 1,400,000 by 1915, representing 28 percent of the city's total population. Seventy-five percent of the Jews of New York lived on the Lower East Side in 1892, as compared to 50 percent in 1903, and 23 percent in 1916.[2]

Unfamiliar with English and with insufficient means, Jewish immigrants

Map of New York's Lower East Side circa 1910. Reprinted by the permission of the publisher from *The Promised City: New York's Jews, 1870–1914*, Revised Edition, by Moses Rischin, p. 77, Cambridge, MA: Harvard University Press, Copyright 1962, 1977 by the president and Fellows of Harvard College. Copyright renewed 1990 by Moses Rischin.

found little reason to move elsewhere. Most lacked training to find employment in a trade or skilled industry. However, production of consumer goods such as clothing, cigars and household wares required little skill, and immigrants could readily compete.[3]

Low wages, long hours and irregular employment were reflected in the living conditions of the people. Tenements lay crammed together with business and industry. Crowded and unsanitary conditions characterized the three- and four-room flats of the six- to seven-story walk-up dumbbell tenements, so called because of their shape. Only one room in each apartment received direct light and air, and the four apartments on each floor had common water closets. Since few families could afford the monthly rent of ten to twenty dollars, they took in boarders to help meet expenses. This added to congested conditions. In 1906, thirty-seven of the fifty-one blocks in New York with over three thousand inhabitants each were on the Lower East Side.[4]

Fire posed a constant danger to tenement dwellers. Flimsy fire escapes and narrow stairways, cluttered with junk, made passage almost impossible. Thirty-eight percent of the deaths in Manhattan fires between 1902 and 1909 occurred on the Lower East Side. However wretched conditions were during the winter months, they became unbearable during the humid summer heat. Crowded quarters and sweatshop employment did not lessen ambitions. "Optimism and hope engulfed every aspect of immigrant life. For a people who had risen superior to the oppressions of medieval proscriptions, the New York slums acted as a new found challenge."[5]

Optimism and hope alone, however, could not free Lower East Side Jews from the sweatshop and ghetto-life existence. Some managed to become employers. Others entered the professions, while many fled New York for neighboring towns and cities. The great majority sought leaders to show them the way.

The young Russian Jewish intellectuals, such as Meyer London, who came to the Lower East Side with the first wave of Eastern European immigrants in the early 1880s and thereafter, took up the struggle. Energies previously devoted to the Jewish emancipation struggle and the fight against czarist oppression now fought the dire conditions confronting Jewish immigrants on New York's Lower East Side. They sought social justice and industrial democracy through political and labor agitation.

Meyer London found himself equally at home within the Jewish labor movement and the Socialist Party which became the principal vehicles for reform. Like many of his fellow Socialists, London was a perennial candidate for public office on the Socialist ticket. From the point of view of immediate results these campaigns proved fruitless. Undismayed by slow progress and occasional setbacks, London and other Socialists ran for office primarily because election campaigns provided an excellent vehicle to educate their listeners.[6]

Newly arrived Eastern European Jews viewed government with suspicion, and lacked knowledge of its forms and functions. Not tied to the Republicans or the Democrats by interest, habit or sentiment, "they wandered in a haze of impotence from Tammany to reform to revolution."[7] This presented Socialist candidates with a threefold task: to educate immigrants about their responsibilities as Americans, to preach the Socialist doctrine, and to expose the connection between Tammany politicians and crime and vice on the Lower East Side.

London began his work for the Socialists in 1894. As a member of Daniel De Leon's Socialist Labor Party, he delivered the Socialist message from soapboxes on Lower East Side street corners at a time when the people knew little about Socialist principles. Unlike many of his fellow Russian Jewish intellectuals, London preferred English to Yiddish, which he used sparingly. The young Socialist spoke in halting English as an American to Americans. "He never ranted, never clowned, though these methods of speech-making were then popular on the East Side, and were considered infallible. London spoke on the assumption that he was addressing men and women of his own mental caliber. He shared his thoughts and emotions with his audience."[8]

Meyer's first bid for political office occurred in 1896, when he received the Socialist Labor Party's nomination for the New York Assembly in the Sixteenth Assembly District, located in the Ninth Congressional District where Daniel De Leon was the party's nominee for Congress.[9] London received 1,114 votes, a considerable margin behind the two old-party candidates.[10]

After the election, London broke with the Socialist Labor Party and helped form the Social Democracy in New York.[11] Under the new party's banner, he again ran for Assembly in 1898, this time in the Fourth Assembly District. During the campaign the Social Democracy and Socialist Labor candidates frequently forgot the major parties and concentrated their fire on each other.[12] The *Daily Forward* implored the voters to cast their ballots for London, Louis Miller and Joseph Barondess who had helped the workers in their greatest battles and greatest victories over capital. "Do not," the *Forward* stated, in a slap at the doctrinaire SLP, "be taken in by those who tell you to 'vote for a principle' without paying attention to personalities. Vote for the Social Democratic Party, the only honest party that has a good chance to have its candidates elected."[13]

Not only did London run well behind the Democratic and Republican candidates, but he trailed the Social Labor candidate by better than two to one.[14] Nevertheless, the *Social Democratic Herald*, the official publication of the Social Democratic Party, termed it an "excellent beginning." Renewed effort would bring better results next time.[15] In 1899, London again ran unsuccessfully as the Social Democratic candidate in the Fourth Assembly District.[16] He received only 272 votes, less than one percent of the total vote

During the years immediately following this election, the Socialist Party of America was created.[17] By 1904 its membership had grown to over twenty thousand, and the party nominated Eugene Debs as its presidential candidate. London made his final effort for the New York Assembly in the Fourth District in the same year. He called upon the citizens of the district to abandon "the soul-crushing traditions of the past ... to embrace a new political faith if convinced of its soundness ... and to pledge to us your cooperation and aid and there shall be heard in the legislative hall in Albany the voice of the true champions of the people, the voice of militant Socialists."[18] Despite a vigorous campaign, London suffered defeat once more.[19]

In the period between 1904 and 1909, London devoted much of his time to the labor movement and to assisting Russian Jewish revolutionaries and the victims of Russian pogroms.[20] The massacres and brutality that shook the Jewish Pale of Settlement in Russia stirred New York. Yiddish newspapers published front-page reports of the Russian struggle for freedom and the violence against fellow Jews. The Russian-Jewish community on the East Side quickly rallied to support their oppressed brethren. They created aid societies to raise funds for pogrom victims and the revolution.[21]

Events in Russia posed a dilemma for London. Although in sympathy with the Bundist movement,[22] London rejected its nationalistic program. Like many Jewish Socialist leaders, he believed that Jewish nationalism should be subordinated to making socialism a success. Cosmopolitan in outlook, London and many of his fellow Jewish Socialists hoped to merge with their radical American comrades. Although London valued the Jewish cultural tradition, he hoped it would become a part of American culture. London thus belonged to the "assimilative" school of Socialists.[23] Some years later he wrote, "The Jew in America looks upon America as the land of promise. To him it is his homeland. Here he is free to pursue his spiritual ideals without hindrance. I do not believe in a divided allegiance. I do not believe that America can permit itself to be divided along the lines of nationality, race or religion. No matter what a man's religion or former nationality, or racial origin may be, unless he is willing to be a part of the American people, he is a stranger."[24]

Stirred, however, by the dramatic developments in Russia, the East Side Socialists put aside their cosmopolitanism and actively battled for the Jews as Jews.[25] With his usual enthusiasm, London devoted himself to the revolutionary cause. Although wholeheartedly American, he could not remain indifferent to his native land or his fellow Jews. "Whether we are nationalists or not, whether we believe in assimilation or not, whether we are religious or not, I deem it a duty of the Jew everywhere to remain a Jew as long as in any corner of the world the Jew is being discriminated against. To this extent I am a Jewish nationalist."[26] London addressed numerous meetings and soon gained recognition as the most effective speaker for his fellow Russian Jews.

Seeking financial assistance, the Bund sent envoys to the large New York Russian community. In 1903, the first Bund representatives, Arcady Kremer and Michael Berg, arrived in New York.[27] London spoke at the first rally called to greet them. Greatly impressed with his "revolutionary intuition," they chose London to plead their cause in the United States. When Gregory Maxim, the leader of the rebellion in the Baltic provinces, reached New York in the spring of 1906, London agreed to assist Maxim in fund-raising efforts. London closed his law office and traveled with Maxim around the country speaking on behalf of the Bund.

"Practical men" considered London a fool for neglecting his legal career in order to work for the Bund without remuneration. His wife Anna, speaking about the hardships of their early married life, noted that Meyer's law practice had begun to do reasonably well and their fortunes had improved, but then he closed his office and the family became dependent on the income from her dental practice. Meyer's daughter, some years later, stated that the lack of money never affected her because everyone else lacked money. "Our traditions did not include money as a problem to be discussed.... My mother ... did the managing and protected me from real want, even though she lived for long periods on bread and coffee."[28]

London resumed his political career in 1909 when he accepted the Socialist nomination for judge of the Supreme Court of New York County. Although defeated, he received over seven thousand votes, a very credible showing.[29]

In May of the following year, due to Morris Hillquit's poor showing in the 1908 congressional campaign in the Ninth Congressional District, the New York local of the Socialist Party bypassed Hillquit and nominated London as its candidate in the Ninth. East Side workers greeted London's nomination with great enthusiasm. The *New York Call* referred to him as "one of the wittiest, sarcastic and ... effective campaigners of the East Side." It expressed optimism about London's chances and stated that the coming campaign would be one of the most vigorous conducted by the Socialist Party in New York.[30]

Located in the heart of the Lower East Side, the Ninth Congressional District of New York was the most densely populated Russian-Jewish area and the center of a vigorous radical movement. In 1904 Joseph Barondess, the district's Socialist Party candidate, polled 21 percent of the total vote. Two years later, Morris Hillquit increased the Socialist share to 26 percent.[31] However, in 1908 his vote declined to 21 percent.[32] This severe setback for the Socialist movement on the Lower East Side led to some soul-searching among local Socialist leaders.

Socialist commentators, writing in the *Daily Forward*, the *New York Call*, and the *Zukunft*, attributed Hillquit's poor showing to several factors. All, however, ignored significant ethnic issues in the Ninth District, issues which figured decisively in his defeat.³³ Hillquit, although a Russian-Jewish immigrant, declared early in the campaign that he recognized no special interests on the Lower East Side.³⁴ Hillquit expressed the Socialist Party position which responded least, of all the parties on the Lower East Side, to purely ethnic interests.

While Hillquit's interests and ambitions transcended the parochialism of East Side politics, his opponents continued to campaign on this level, and Hillquit left himself open to charges of indifference to the Jewish community. The *Tageblatt*, which generally supported the Democratic Party, pointed to Hillquit's ambivalence on the immigration question and labeled him a restrictionist and a foe of the immigrant worker. In fact, Hillquit, seeking to placate the AFL, sought to identify Socialist Party restrictionist sentiment with cheap Asian labor. But East Side Jews would accept nothing less than unrestricted immigration.³⁵

The immigration issue and Hillquit's seeming indifference to local matters became overriding issues in the final weeks of the 1908 campaign. Democratic congressman Henry M. Goldfogle, a German Jew born in the United States, had opposed immigration restriction. Goldfogle's weakness lay in his connection with Tammany and his voting record on economic and social issues vital to the Lower East Side. Despite Socialist efforts to brand him as Tammany's tool, Goldfogle decisively defeated Hillquit. However, Hillquit ran well ahead of Eugene Debs, the Socialist Party's presidential candidate. Ballot splitting in the Ninth Congressional District gave Hillquit 21.23 percent of the vote as compared to Debs' 13.56 percent. Hillquit had attracted non–Socialist support, but "appeared in too controversial and equivocal a light to command the broad support of the population of the Jewish community."³⁶

The decision to nominate Meyer London for Congress in 1910 indicated that the Local New York branch of the Socialist Party had "grudgingly" recognized "that socialism operating in the ghetto must acknowledge the legitimacy of ethnic loyalties of its inhabitants."³⁷ Unlike Hillquit, London had remained firmly tied to the Lower East Side, and he willingly responded to its citizens' needs. Although many older labor and Socialist leaders had expected London to leave the Lower East Side, he did not.³⁸ As previously discussed, he served as legal counsel to various trade unions and to the Workmen's Circle.³⁹ He gave himself wholeheartedly to the Russian revolutionary movement.

Furthermore, London opposed immigration restriction. At the Socialist Party convention in 1910, London, a delegate of the Jewish Agitation Bureau, argued against the exclusion of all Asian immigrants.[40] However, he supported Hillquit's compromise resolution which denied exclusion on the basis of race or nationality.[41] Immigration restriction, London pointed out, was contrary to the position taken by the Stuttgart Congress of the Second International of 1907.[42] "I feel that we ought to take all the resolutions," a frustrated London declared, "and send them back to a Resolution Committee of intelligent men, and then we can get an intelligent resolution."[43]

London charged that exclusion violated a fundamental Socialist principle which prohibited racial discrimination. "When you say we will exclude people because they are Japanese ... Chinese ... and Hindoos [sic], you violate ... one of the elementary principles of international Socialism, and you will have declared the bankruptcy of Socialism."[44] Rejection of the Stuttgart Resolution position meant that the American Socialist Party was breaking with the international Socialist movement. "I speak in behalf of all oppressed races, and I say by adopting a resolution pointing to particular races they will point the finger of scorn at you and will say that the Socialists of America have put upon the great mass of Japanese and Chinese the stamp of inferiority.... You want to turn America back; you claim to be progressive; you are taking a step backward. Do not be such little politicians in Heaven's name."[45] The convention adopted the Hillquit resolution by a narrow margin, 55 to 50.[46] Although subsequent conventions attempted to change this policy, the Hillquit resolution remained the party's official stance on immigration.

The 1910 Socialist campaign on the East Side began during the great Cloakmakers' Strike. Max Pine, secretary of the United Hebrew Trades, and Abraham Cahan spoke at a rally on July 29 called to ratify London and other Socialist candidates. Pine emphasized one of the principal themes of London's campaign, his close association with and his unceasing efforts on behalf of the worker. London, Pine pointed out, had grown up with the laboring people of the East Side. He had defended them, had suffered with them, and now devoted all his time and energy to the striking cloak makers. Cahan reminded the audience that although the struggle for immediate amelioration of conditions was proper, socialism aimed to end capitalism. This election, he stated, afforded the workers the opportunity to deal the system an initial blow by sending London to Congress.[47]

London's campaign officially began on the evening of September 26 when he opened campaign headquarters at the M & L Jarbulowsky Building, 165 East Broadway. He was thirty-nine years old, of average build, attractive in appearance and of confident bearing. A skilled speaker, London urged the audience of approximately one thousand to begin work to send a working-class representative to Congress. A Socialist congressman would represent the cause of labor, rather than engage in petty fights over district leadership and dispensing graft.[48]

In an interview with the *New York Call*, London stated that the outlook for a large Socialist vote appeared good for several reasons. Republicans and Democrats, he explained, represented capitalist interests. London pointed out both parties had nominated Judge Vann for the Court of Appeals. Vann had opposed organized labor every time he ruled in a labor case. The gubernatorial candidacy of Charles Edward Russell on the Socialist ticket offered another reason for an increased socialist vote. "Russell made the people talk radicalism in years past. His presence at the head of the Socialist Party ticket in this campaign will make people talk Socialism now." Furthermore, the success of the Milwaukee Socialists would inspire the New York socialists. Finally, greater unity existed on the East Side than ever before as evidenced by the active role of the Labor Zionists and the Social Revolutionaries in the campaign. "All of these things together," London concluded, "ought to make the campaign this year a record breaker."[49]

The New York branch of the Socialist Party shared London's optimism. According to Socialist analysis, the Ninth District contained the factors necessary for success: capitalist repression, numerous militant Socialists, and a constituency of impoverished workers. George S. Gelder, the Socialist campaign manager, stated that the Socialists would make a special effort to reach every voter in the Ninth.[50] The National Executive Committee also recognized the chances for a breakthrough. At a meeting held in New York on October 16, London's district was among four congressional districts chosen to receive financial assistance. It received the largest appropriation, two hundred fifty dollars.[51]

The East Side labor movement provided invaluable assistance to London's campaign. Among those unions which supported his candidacy were the United Hebrew Trades, Cutters' Union Local 10, the Brotherhood of Painters and Paperhangers, and the International Ladies' Garment Workers' Union. The cloak makers, grateful for London's leadership during their recent successful strike, campaigned vigorously on his behalf. Abraham Rosenberg, president of the ILGWU, reminded workers that London had put aside his law practice for nine weeks in order to fight their battles in conferences and the courts. "Upon you, cloakmakers in particular," Rosenberg declared, "devolves the duty of voting for Meyer London.... Send one of your own class, the Socialist candidate, Meyer London, to Congress and the working people of the United States will extend to you deep, heartful thanks."[52]

Eight large cloak shops in New York started a Meyer London Campaign Fund. They also established a committee to raise funds throughout the city.[53]

In addition, during the third week of the campaign, the cloak makers organized a Cloakmakers' Meyer London League in order to coordinate their activities on London's behalf.[54] Throughout the campaign the garment workers distributed literature, campaign buttons, conducted meetings, and raised funds to secure London's election.

London's campaign received further impetus from the labor movement when Samuel Gompers warmly endorsed his candidacy on September 10. London's devotion to labor, Gompers declared, had rarely been equaled by any man and never exceeded by any attorney engaged to protect workers' interests. "His knowledge, his energy, his devotion and his integrity should win for him the undying devotion of every union man living within the 9th Congressional district."[55]

Prominent Socialist leaders such as Charles Edward Russell, Gustave Strebel, Dr. Karl Liebknecht and Morris Hillquit also urged London's election. Russell and Strebel, Socialist candidates for governor and lieutenant governor respectively, campaigned actively on London's behalf.[56] On October 11, Dr. Karl Liebknecht, leader of the German Social Democrats lecturing in the United States, pointed out the role of Russian Jews in championing socialism and stated that American Jews would be no less faithful to international socialism. This faith would elect London to Congress.[57]

On November 5, three days before the election, Morris Hillquit belatedly endorsed London. In a letter to the voters of the Ninth Congressional District, printed in the *New York Call*, Hillquit referred to his previous campaigns in the district as "among the most pleasant recollections of his life." This time, however, he appealed to the citizens of the Ninth District on behalf of "my friend and comrade, Meyer London." No one, he asserted, could better lead the Socialist fight against human misery, injustice, and oppression in the Jewish quarter of the Lower East Side. With London in Congress, American workers would have an eloquent spokesman in Washington. The situation in the Ninth District, he concluded, had never before been so favorable. Voters should not waste the opportunity.[58] A number of Socialist organizations on the Lower East Side ratified London's candidacy and worked on his behalf. The Workmen's Circle, the Socialist Jewish benevolent society which London served as legal counsel from 1905 until his death, established the Meyer London Workmen's Circle Campaign League and opened a headquarters at 163 East Broadway. Like the Cloakmakers' League, it sponsored rallies, solicited funds, distributed literature, and conducted canvasses.[59]

The Poale Zion, the first organization of Socialist Zionists begun in the United States in 1903, endorsed London on September 22.[60] Dr. Chalm Zhitlowsky, at one time prominently connected with the Socialist Revolutionary party in Russia, declared that London was the man best fit to represent the

East Side in Congress. He knew the needs of the people and would steadfastly defend the rights of the workers. London accepted Poale Zionist support but indicated that he would not run on a Zionist platform, and he "believed" that they did not expect him to modify his views. He would run, London asserted, as a Socialist, on a Socialist platform, without modification or restriction.[61]

London recognized that in order to win he needed to woo non–Socialist progressive voters. In 1908, the *Forward* had characterized Hillquit as the representative of the working class and not of the larger Jewish quarter.[62] During the 1910 campaign, the *Forward*, reflecting London's new strategy, described London as the representative of the "thinking people" of the large colony of Jewish workers, peddlers, and small businessmen.[63] Thus, London, if elected, would serve as the spokesman for the entire Jewish community and not merely the working class.

Within the Socialist Party a more militant element considered such an appeal contrary to Socialist principles, and wanted to emphasize the anticapitalist aspects of socialism. They remembered Hillquit's first campaign in 1904, when his supporters were accused of appealing to the "good men," the non–Socialist reform element in the Ninth District. These charges agitated the local Socialist movement for some time thereafter, and the "sour taste" left by them had not completely disappeared by 1910.[64]

No doubt London realized some would oppose a campaign conducted on this basis, but London, like Victor Berger and other pragmatic right-wing socialists, wanted to win elections. London characterized the Socialist campaign in the Ninth District as "thoroughgoing." It would bring results, because it reached out to all voters. Never before had trade unions allied so closely to the Socialist movement. London unabashedly admitted that his campaign aimed at professional classes and businessmen disgusted with the old political machines. "These men have voted for Jerome, they voted for Hearst, they voted for Gaynor. Now the feeling is general among them that the time has come to break away from the old political machines."[65]

Among non–Socialist elements in London's campaign were the East Side Peddlers' Association and the Meyer London Professional League.[66] The latter, about 120 of the "most prominent" professional men in the district, issued a circular letter calling upon the intelligent voters of the Lower East Side to assert themselves and to elect London. The letter described Goldfogle as a typical professional politician and an obedient servant of Tammany. He did not represent the interests of the district, and had lost the people's trust. The Republican, John W. Block, was an unknown whose record did not justify his nomination. To the contrary, London, who lived on the East Side for nearly twenty years, had devoted his life to helping the downtrodden.[67]

In yet another appeal, the Professional League urged the election of a representative who would fight the trusts and monopolies. Every "fair-minded" man should give the Socialists an opportunity in Congress. With the support of the independent voter, London's election was a certainty.[68]

As the campaign unfolded, London aimed some of his sharpest barbs at the Democratic and Republican parties. The former, he declared, had nothing to offer while the latter suffered from internal dissension, and had no solutions for the important problems of the day. The people were abandoning the Republican Party; it had become a synonym for trust rule. On the other hand, the Socialist movement, although it lacked representation in Congress, significantly influenced Republican and Democratic policies as evidenced by the popularity of Theodore Roosevelt and Robert La Follette who posed as radicals. London accused the old party candidates, and in particular Roosevelt, of raising "all sorts foreign and impersonal cries in order to detract from the real issues of the campaign.... It is noise, noise and nothing else that we hear during the campaign. Each of the old party candidates tries to outdo the others in dodging the real vital questions."[69]

London and other Socialist candidates considered economic justice the paramount issues in the campaign. At a meeting of the cloak makers, London stated, "In this land of great wealth where it is possible for a president to enter office practically a poor man and come out independently wealthy for life; in this land where the Supreme Court judges stoop to do the bidding of their masters the great capitalists of the country; in this land where the vast majority are the slaves of their economic masters, here the Socialist party pitches its camp and hurls its defiance to the master class." Charles Edward Russell, at the same rally, declared that only economic justice should appeal to workers. "That is the issue upon which the Socialist Party makes this campaign, has made every campaign in the past and will make every campaign in the future."[70]

Henry M. Goldfogle, the Democratic incumbent, also came under withering attack. William Karlin, London's running mate in the important Eighth Assembly District, called Goldfogle Tammany's "errand boy." He attacked the "shameful" stand of Goldfogle and Tammany against organized labor. Workers had not chosen their own representative. They had allowed Tammany to send its man to Congress. Only by electing London would the voice of labor be heard in Congress.[71] The *Daily Forward* described Goldfogle as a typical cigar-smoking, Tammany official who made promises that he never fulfilled. In the past, the *Forward* charged, Goldfogle had taken advantage of the people's ignorance. He had ignored the issues in favor of hand shaking and cigar giving. The Socialist campaign challenged these old techniques. Voters now discussed issues and expressed interest in socialism. Goldfogle could not compete in such a campaign, the *Forward* declared.[72]

3. Prelude to Victory

Both the *Forward* and the *New York Call* criticized Goldfogle's record in Congress. They accused him of failing to speak out on behalf of labor and of either voting against or dodging legislation vital to the working man. The *Forward* noted that Goldfogle had said little during ten years in Congress. To extract his record from the *Congressional Record* was as hard as "digging a ton of coal." Goldfogle, the *Forward* further charged, had defended the trusts against regulation. To the contrary, London and the socialists believed that the government should help the poor against the rich "thieves."[73]

The Socialist Party dominated the campaign on the Lower East Side. Although the Republican Party nominated candidates, it gradually receded into the background, leaving the battle to Tammany and the Socialists. In 1910, the Republicans nominated John W. Block, who also ran on the Independent League ticket.[74] His campaign received slight attention. For that matter, Goldfogle did not conduct a very vigorous campaign, apparently relying upon Tammany's henchmen on Election Day.[75] However, the *New York Call* pointed out that the East Side Tammany papers which supported Goldfogle remained silent because there was little to say in his defense. Even the staunchest friends of Tammany, the *Call* declared, found it impossible to defend a congressman who joined with the "corruptest of Republican congressmen" to support Speaker Joseph Cannon. They adopted the much safer course of saying very little about Goldfogle's record in Congress.[76]

Two conservative Yiddish dailies that supported Goldfogle, the *Tageblatt* and the *Jewish Daily News*, appealed to the orthodox Jewish vote by questioning London's religious beliefs. Throughout the campaign they referred to him as a non-orthodox Jew. In addition, they attacked his labor record and asserted that businessmen could best defend their interests by electing their friend Henry Goldfogle.[77] These efforts, both the *Forward* and *Call* reported, had created pessimism among Goldfogle supporters. Unlike previous campaigns, conservative Democrats and Republicans questioned Goldfogle's chances due to London's strong appeal among the voters of the Ninth District.[78]

This pessimism within the Goldfogle campaign encouraged Socialist optimism and spurred London supporters to even greater efforts. As Election Day approached, numerous meetings took place under the auspices of the Socialist Party Campaign Committee, the Cloakmakers' League, the Workmen's Circle Campaign League and other organizations active in London's behalf.[79] Meetings and parades, however, represented only one aspect of the campaign. The *Call* reported, three days before the election, that the Campaign Committee, with the assistance of union workers, had distributed more than two hundred thousand pieces of literature. In fact, every voter received literature at least three times.[80]

In addition, the Cloakmakers' League distributed thousands of Meyer

London campaign buttons in the Ninth District.[81] The Canvass Committee of the Socialist Party Campaign Committee, assisted by hundreds of volunteer workers, conducted a doorbell-ringing, stair-climbing, block-by-block canvass to obtain votes for London. "Hundreds" of voters could not be found at the addresses from which they had registered. The *Call* accused Tammany of colonizing the district with floaters and repeaters. George Gelder, Socialist Campaign Committee manager, called it the crude work of "election crooks." Two-thirds of the untraceable voters, he charged, were Tammany Hall floaters and repeaters. The Campaign Committee retained lawyers to find and prosecute such persons before the election. A meeting of all union secretaries, secretaries of the various branches of the Workmen's Circle and election district captains considered the best methods for exposing and prosecuting Tammany floaters and repeaters. London and Gelder urged poll watchers to prevent the use of floaters and repeaters and to ensure a fair count.[82]

On November 5, the *Call* charged that the Republican and Democratic machines, faced with the prospect of a London victory, had "joined hands" to ensure his defeat. It reported that Republican ward captains had received orders, to turn over their votes to the Tammany candidate, Henry Goldfogle.[83] Three days later the *Call* stated that it had "definitely" learned that the Republicans had decided to scratch Block in at least two Assembly Districts containing about six hundred Republican voters.

Despite this alleged Republican — Tammany agreement, the Socialist Campaign Committee, encouraged by a *Daily Forward* canvass showing London in the lead, remained confident about a Socialist victory in the Ninth.[84] Fear existed, however, that Tammany might steal the election unless sufficient Socialist watchers manned the polls. In the final days before the election, repeated pleas were made for volunteers to work both within and outside the polls. A large number of outside watchers were needed to prevent Tammany "thugs" from frightening away Socialist voters as in the past.[85]

As the election approached, the *Daily Forward* intensified its efforts on London's behalf. The *Forward* printed the names and addresses of all registered voters in the Ninth. It urged union members and others to find the name of a union brother or friend and to make sure that he voted for London.[86] London, the *Forward* stated, knew the people of the Lower East Side and what they needed. Although he would not accomplish wonders if elected to Congress, it would be good to have at least one friend there. He would represent the workers and guard against harmful laws. The Jewish workers and businessmen of the Lower East Side needed one person in Congress to defend them. The Russian, Polish and Romanian Jews needed a voice against Russian despotism on behalf of Jewish "freedom fighters."[87] For years, the *Forward* pointed out, the most corrupt officials of the Democratic Party had ruled the

3. Prelude to Victory 55

East Side. Every two years the voters had sent Goldfogle to Congress, but this year the Jewish citizens would revolt. The average Jewish voter, the *Forward* declared is not a Tammany slave. Thoughtful voters in the Ninth District would vote for Meyer London, the man who dedicated himself to the workers for the last twenty years and who "cried out" for the Jewish victims of Russian pogroms.[88]

On November 8, Election Day, London and Charles Edward Russell visited every polling place in the district. Enthusiastic crowds cheered and applauded wherever they appeared. The *New York Call*, in its Election Day edition, predicted a London victory.[89] However, the final count revealed that London trailed Goldfogle by 1,284 votes. London had received 3,322 votes, Goldfogle 4,606 and Block 1,850.[90]

In his election post-mortem, London attributed Goldfogle's victory to a Democrat and Republican fusion behind Goldfogle. However, the fact that the Republican Block received 1,850 votes belies London's charge that the two older parties had fused. Anticipating criticism, London also noted that he had run better than two to one ahead of Charles Edward Russell, he regretted that so much ballot splitting had occurred, but he felt flattered by the large personal vote. Looking forward to his next campaign for Congress, London called for enfranchisement of East Side workers and more effective political organization in the district. "The businessmen, the manufacturers, and all the elements whom I, as a Socialist have been fighting all my life, have the vote. The only salvation lies in enfranchising the workingman who lives on the East Side." London also noted that the "conservative elements," despite their victory, threatened to change the boundaries of the Ninth Congressional District in order to make a Socialist victory impossible.[91]

In the final analysis, London's defeat resulted from a number of factors: many Jews did not become citizens and could not vote, the failure of London's campaign to effectively coordinate various groups who supported his candidacy, and an inability to prevent election irregularities and secure an honest count. Orthodox Jewish hostility toward London, support for Goldfogle from businessmen opposed to London because of his labor record and Tammany's intimidation of voters also contributed to London's defeat. Tammany workers pressured peddlers and small businessmen in the district to support Goldfogle. They threatened peddlers with loss of their licenses and businessmen with rigid enforcement of the Sunday closing laws. Furthermore, the police indicated that they would no longer tolerate obstruction of the sidewalks with boxes and merchandise.[92]

Although London's 33.09 percent of the vote was 11.86 percent better than Hillquit's 1908 showing, not everyone expressed satisfaction with the results. In an article in the *New York Call* shortly after the election, Louis B.

Boudin, a prominent left-wing Socialist, questioned the tactics of the London campaign. Boudin pointed to the large split vote for London. Milwaukee had only a 5 percent difference between the gubernatorial candidate and the congressional candidate. On the other hand, in the Ninth Congressional District, London's percentage was twice that of Charles Edward Russell.

According to Boudin's analysis, campaign tactics accounted for the difference between Milwaukee and New York. Milwaukee Socialists had utilized Socialist principles to address workers' needs. In London's district, however, Socialists addressed themselves to the progressive element. In addition, an appeal had been made on ethnic grounds. Socialists had appealed to Russian Jews to vote for London, because he was a Jew. Boudin asserted that such an appeal represented "a positive menace" to the Socialist movement. Socialism had taken a step backwards.[93]

During the following weeks, a series of articles appeared in the *Call* in response to Boudin's article. London did not respond to Boudin, but Max H. Danish, a member of the Ninth Congressional Campaign for the three previous elections, sought to refute Boudin's charges. He noted that similar criticisms about un–Socialistic methods were made repeatedly after every election on the East Side. Danish denied that London's campaign had neglected Russell. He challenged Boudin to produce evidence that the committee had neither spoken in the name of the party nor stood squarely upon and on behalf of Socialist principles. Danish admitted that London had been nominated because of his "tremendous popularity with the workers of the East Side, his magnetic personality and his unswerving earnestness and devotion to the cause of labor." Only by selecting such candidates could the Socialists hope to elect congressmen and assemblymen on the East Side. As to Boudin's charge that the campaign had appealed to "racial prejudices," Danish replied that "we have not made any stronger use of it, notwithstanding the temptations which came from the enemy, than has been made in the columns of the *Call* whenever speaking about Comrade London's candidacy."[94]

Despite Boudin's view that an appeal to ethnic sentiment violated Socialist practice, the candidacy of Meyer London in 1910 indicated that Local New York recognized the existence of special interests on the Lower East Side. London had immersed himself in the important movements in the Jewish community. Moreover, although not a devout Jew, London was proud of his Jewish heritage and was willing to fight for Jewish causes. Thus, the local party organization considered him an ideal candidate and highly electable. In this respect, London's campaign differed little from Victor Berger's successful 1910 congressional campaign which was "adroitly designed" to woo non–Socialist votes.[95]

Though London had suffered defeat in his first congressional campaign, he and other Socialists could take heart at party successes elsewhere. Victor Berger became the first Socialist elected to Congress. The party also elected nineteen members to various state legislatures, carried five counties, and won municipal elections in Milwaukee and eleven other cities. Moreover, for the first time in six years, the Socialist vote, which had remained relatively stable, increased by 50 percent. This impressive showing underscored the need for continued agitation and efficient organization. It boosted morale and held out the prospect that better times lay ahead.

Encouraged by gains throughout the country, London and his fellow New York Socialists looked forward to the municipal election of 1911 and the congressional campaign in 1912. London's defeat had underscored the need to build a political organization capable of challenging the Tammany machine. Moreover, it had revealed the possibilities of a campaign designed to woo non-socialist voters.

In 1911 London once again took to the political hustings, this time as one of three Socialist candidates for the New York Supreme Court in the First Judicial District. London received 18,178 votes which placed him well behind the three successful Democratic candidates who each polled over 200,000 votes.[96] The New York Socialists failed to capture any municipal offices, but elected a member to the New York Legislature.[97] Elsewhere in the country, the party made impressive gains. When the full results were in, Socialists rejoiced at the election of some one thousand comrades to office in 337 towns and cities. In addition, party membership rose from 58,011 in 1910 to the all-time high of 125,826 in May 1912.[98]

In New York, where the 1912 campaign began late in June, Socialists were highly optimistic about party prospects.[99] However, London's fears that the Democratic-controlled legislature would change the boundaries of the Ninth Congressional District became reality.[100] The Ninth now became the Twelfth District. London was nominated by Local New York as its congressional candidate in the new district. Despite this change, London believed he would win. He pointed out that for the first time in many years there would be a four-cornered race. In the past Republicans and Democrats had united to defeat the Socialist candidate, but the current campaign differed. The candidacy of Henry Moskowitz on the Progressive ticket lessened the possibility of a last-minute deal between the old parties. With a Progressive candidate in the field, and the expectation of an increased Socialist vote over 1910, London saw a Socialist victory as a distinct possibility.[101]

Once more London received the enthusiastic support of organized labor. The Cloakmakers' Union endorsed the entire Socialist ticket, but concentrated its efforts on London's behalf. The union organized the Cloakmakers' Meyer London Campaign League and rented stores throughout the Twelfth District in order to hold meetings and to reach East Side citizens.[102] They levied a voluntary assessment of twenty-five cents upon each union member in an attempt to raise more than five thousand dollars for London's campaign.[103]

The *Ladies' Garment Worker*, the official publication of the International Ladies' Garment Workers' Union, referred to London as the ideal candidate not only of the Socialist Party but of the workers. "Meyer London is the man par excellence who through thick and thin has for many years stood with the people, with the working class as against the oppressors." The *Ladies' Garment Worker* reminded its readers that Gompers had advised the workers to vote for London two years earlier.[104] Since 1910 he had gained even greater esteem among the workers. Every enfranchised workman should, therefore, vote for Meyer London.[105] The Furriers' Union, grateful for London's successful leadership during its recent strike, also campaigned vigorously on his behalf. Along with the cloak makers, they contributed heavily to London's campaign fund, and shared in the tedious work of the campaign.[106]

As in 1910, London had the support of non–Socialist groups on the East Side; among them were the Meyer London Professional League, the Businessmen's League, the Citizen Peddlers' Association, the East Side Citizen's League, the Independent Voters' League and the Women's Meyer London League. These organizations sponsored meetings, raised funds, distributed literature and sought to attract non-socialist votes.[107]

The City Executive Committee of Local New York became more directly involved in London's campaign. Due to the large split vote for him in 1910, Local New York was criticized for its conduct of the campaign.[108] In response, the East Side Campaign Committee promised that campaign manager Nathan Weiser would submit reports of meetings, and would inform Julius Gerber, the executive secretary of Local New York, as to the dates of large rallies.[109]

On October 26, however, nine days before the election, the Central Committee of Local New York took charge of the campaigns in the Eleventh, Twelfth, and Thirteenth congressional districts, all located on the East Side. State party secretary U. Solomon, Louis Lichstein, Alexander Gilbert, and F. Sumner Boyd were elected to the East Side Campaign Committee, with Julius Gerber serving as an *ex officio* member. The *New York Call* reported that the Central Committee took this step to better coordinate the various elements active in the campaign.[110] It also indicated dissatisfaction with the conduct of the campaign on the East Side.

Despite these organizational problems, London, buoyed by the results of his previous congressional effort and the optimistic outlook for the present campaign, waged a vigorous fight for election. Crisscrossing the district, London tirelessly hammered away on the issues at countless indoor and outdoor meetings. Conscious of the criticism leveled at tactics that had produced the large split vote in 1910, London made it clear that the workers should not support him alone, but should vote for the Socialist Party and its principles.

London told more than five hundred cloak makers gathered at Apollo Hall on October 15, "I do not come to you as Meyer London, as the attorney of your union, but I come as a representative of the working class—the Socialist party. Don't vote for me as an individual. I don't want it. Don't elect me because I am London for it is not right that you should do so. Eliminate my personality entirely from this campaign, because this is not a fight for individuals. It is above that. It is a fight for principles." If elected, London promised, he would represent in Congress the same idea that Victor Berger had represented: the elimination of poverty wherever it exists.[111]

Although the candidacy of Progressive Henry Moskowitz ensured a four-cornered race, London, like Eugene Debs, feared that Progressives would attract Socialist votes.[112] During the campaign London questioned the sincerity of Progressives and the possibility of reforming capitalism. He charged that many politicians, including Theodore Roosevelt, had become Progressives only a few months before the election. He admitted that "thousands" of sincere men and women believed in the Progressive Party. "It is, however, impossible to separate the disappointed politicians of the old parties who had flocked into the ranks of the Progressives from the sincere believers in social justice." The salvation of the country, London insisted, lay in voting for the Socialist Party which sought to emancipate the working class from political and industrial oppression.[113]

London also criticized the Progressive platform. Despite its promises, London told a capacity audience at the University Settlement House on October 14, the Progressives failed to offer satisfactory solutions for two pressing problems confronting the workers—rent and unemployment. Rent took one-fourth of the workers' income. With private ownership of land, landlords would quickly take advantage of any increase in wages to raise rent and eat up their gains. "Private ownership of land," London declared "is as absurd as private ownership of the air."

As for unemployment, the Progressives, London asserted, had little to offer. "We say, let us take care of ourselves when we are strong through our economic and political organizations. We workers don't want to be like Vanderbilt's dogs, fed three good meals a day and taken out once in a while in an automobile. That's what the Progressives want." The Progressives would do everything for the worker as long as he remained a worker. The time for halfway measures had passed. The Socialists demanded nothing less than the emancipation of the working class.[114]

As in 1910, the Socialist candidate aimed his sharpest barbs at the incumbent Tammany congressman Goldfogle. London and his supporters attacked Goldfogle's lackluster record in Congress and his association with Tammany. Goldfogle, they charged, had consistently ignored legislation vital to the workers. Like other capitalist candidates, he voted for capitalist interests.[115]

Furthermore, the corrupt Tammany machine was despised throughout the country, and should not represent the district. "Nothing," London pointed out, "is heard from them until a month before the election when they come to the district and indulge in mud-slinging about their opponents, hand out compliments to the citizens, and beg for votes. Nowhere has it been written that Timothy D. Sullivan should be the representative of 300,000 Jews."[116]

As the campaign closed, a number of leading Socialists and labor leaders came into the Twelfth District to speak on London's behalf. The highlight was Eugene V. Debs' appearance at a large rally in Rutgers Square on October 21. More than ten thousand cheering people greeted the popular Socialist Party presidential candidate. Debs, who followed London to the rostrum, recalled their first meeting seventeen years earlier. "It is not necessary to tell you that he is a pioneer on the East Side. London has been absolutely true to you from the start. And if you are as true to him as he is to you, Meyer London will be the next Congressman from this district." Debs noted that the wage earners of the district have never had a representative in Congress. What, he asked the crowd, has Goldfogle ever done for you? "He has never lifted his hand to improve your condition, or to raise your wages.... He never raised his voice in labor's behalf. He has no interest in you; he does not associate with you. But ... if Meyer London is elected ... you, for the first time, will be represented by a truly working class representative."[117]

In addition, party workers and volunteers from the unions were busy with last-minute preparations. Canvassers visited voters to present the Socialist views, to invite them to party meetings, to distribute literature, and to uncover Tammany floaters and repeaters.[118] The East Side Campaign Committee appealed for an additional one hundred canvassers to assist in exposing some 1,500 floaters and repeaters reported to be in the Twelfth District. The committee also called for one hundred watchers to prevent corruption and vote stealing.[119]

The *New York Call* and the *Daily Forward* strongly supported London's campaign. The *Call* extensively covered Socialist activities on the East Side. It reminded the workers that Goldfogle only thought of them around election time. As in the 1910 campaign, the *Forward* listed in its pages the names and addresses of the district's registered voters and urged its readers to find the name of a union brother, a relative or a friend and to see that he voted for London.[120] The *Forward* warned the citizenry that they would throw away their votes if they supported the three capitalist parties. A vote for London, however, would strengthen socialism and help break Tammany's hold over the Jewish quarter.[121]

As the campaign drew to a close, the *New York Call* reported that the Socialist campaign in the Twelfth District had grown to such proportions that "Tammany is shuddering with fear that its 'grafting claw' will be severed." Furthermore, Tammany, faced with certain defeat, was "concocting schemes" to keep London out of office. A secret conference of Democratic and Republican leaders, the *Call* charged, on October 27, included Goldfogle; Samuel B. Koenig, chairman of the Republican County Committee; Judge Leonard A. Smitkin; and several other East Side politicians. The conference lasted for over two hours behind closed doors. The *Call* reported that they had agreed that Alexander Wolf, the Republican candidate, would be "sacrificed on the altar of capitalist politics" in order to save Goldfogle. Similar tactics had been used in 1910.[122] Although the Socialists had conducted their best-organized campaign to date, Goldfogle defeated London by 956 votes. London received 3,646 votes, 324 more than he had obtained in 1910. But his percentage had declined from 33.09 to 31.22.[123]

The failure of London's campaign organization to prevent voting irregularities and to get Socialist votes counted proved once again a major factor in his defeat. Tammany "goons" intimidated voters and expelled Socialist watchers from the polls. In addition, Tammany inspectors and watchers delayed the count in order to ascertain how the vote was going. In many election districts, the count began only after Socialists had called the police. Moreover, Socialist watchers observed poll clerks not counting Socialist ballots and split votes for London.

Perhaps equally significant, Socialists underestimated Henry Moskowitz's strength. He attracted Progressive support that might otherwise have gone to London. Moskowitz no doubt benefited from the popularity of former president Theodore Roosevelt, the Progressive Party presidential candidate, and Oscar S. Straus, the Progressive candidate for governor and former member of the Roosevelt cabinet.[124]

London complained that Tammany had stolen the election, a charge repeated by the Socialist press. Tammany had once again used strong-arm tactics at the polls, had used repeaters and floaters and had intimidated Socialist poll watchers who were undermanned. London indicated that he would seek a recount insisting that an honest vote would give him a majority.

On the following day, November 6, London informed the *Call* that the Socialist Party Campaign Committee would consider a recount in the Twelfth District. If necessary, they would take the matter to the highest court. London stated, "The result of this election has made a foundation for Socialism so that it will have to be reckoned as a highly important factor in determining

... future elections." Despite the outcome, he expressed satisfaction with Socialist progress in New York.[125]

On November 6, London appeared before the Executive Committee of Local New York to review the election results. After considerable discussion, the committee decided to secure a recount in the Twelfth Congressional District and to prosecute the election and police officials responsible for illegal handling of the vote.[126] London secured a restraining order pending the recount. The recount subsequently confirmed Goldfogle's reelection.[127]

Undiscouraged by this setback, London once again entered the political arena in 1913. He sought the party's mayoralty nomination, which subsequently went to Charles Edward Russell.[128] Instead, London received the nomination for district attorney of New York County. His opponent, District Attorney Charles S. Whitman, had the support of both the Democrats and the Republicans.[129] London's primary reason for running was to keep his name before the public, looking ahead to the 1914 congressional election. Due to his involvement with the trade unions, London's campaign did not formally get under way until October 24.[130] Although London limited his campaign to approximately two weeks, he polled 13,136 votes as compared to 229,169 for Whitman. In Manhattan, however, London ran ahead of Charles Edward Russell who received 11,859 votes.[131]

While unsuccessful in electoral contests in the years prior to 1914, New York City Socialists built a strong socialist-labor coalition. The Socialist Party had a detailed plan for an improved society and had gained the support of workers and others who sought the same objective. Furthermore, the Socialist Party filled a void created by Tammany's failure to provide for certain underprivileged groups in the city. Impoverished immigrant workers, largely from Eastern Europe, who sought a better future, flocked to the Socialist banner. Unfortunately, organized labor did not present a solid front in the important elections of these years. The older, conservative craft unions tended to support the Democratic machine; whereas, the newer, immigrant unions, particularly those in the needle trade industries, leaned toward the Socialists. These unions became "the financial backbone and the chief organizational props of the Socialist Party."[132]

London, who played a prominent role in the organizational strikes of the International Ladies' Garment Workers, the International Fur Workers' Union and other East Side unions, received working-class support. With each campaign his vote and popularity increased. Pragmatic and gradualist in approach, London stressed the need for reform and an intelligent disciplined working class to prepare for the cooperative commonwealth. He sought the support of Socialists, non–Socialists, trade unionists, immigrant and non-immigrant and other citizens.

3. Prelude to Victory

While unsuccessful prior to 1914, London and his fellow New York Socialists had obtained invaluable political experience. Most important, they had learned the need for better organization and coordination of their campaign activities in order to defeat Tammany. With this in mind, and with the bitter experience of London's defeat in 1912 to spur them on, they began preparations for the next congressional campaign.

4
Victory in 1914

> What I expect to do is to take to Washington the message of the people, to give expression there to the philosophy of Socialism. I want to show them what the east side of New York is and what the east side Jew is.—*Meyer London,* New York Times, *November 9, 1914, 1.*

For Meyer London, 1914 was a year marked with both disappointment and crowning success. In January, the "Hourwich affair" ended when the Joint Board of Cloakmakers accepted the resignation of Dr. Hourwich.[1] London and those who believed in the arbitration procedures established in the Protocol had emerged victorious in this bitter and protracted struggle. But after the International Ladies' Garment Workers' Union Convention in June, the new leadership of the International appointed Morris Hillquit as its counsel, retaining London in merely an advisory capacity.[2] Hurt by this turn of affairs, London had little time for remorse.[3] He planned to attend the International Socialist Congress in Europe in late August.

In addition, he had to prepare for the coming congressional elections. London and his fellow Socialists were determined to prevent Tammany from stealing the election, as many Socialists claimed it had done in 1912. Efficient organization and the experience of two congressional campaigns finally brought victory to the "East Side's beloved labor tribune."[4] He became the first Socialist congressman from the East and the first New York City Socialist elected to any office.

The Hourwich affair had caused dissension within the ILGWU which surfaced at the Twelfth Annual convention of the union convened in Cleveland on June 1, 1914. The Hourwich affair was fully discussed and resolved.[5] The delegates criticized Rosenberg, Dyche and the General Executive Board for failing to exercise the utmost tact in the dispute, but approved a resolution endorsing the action of the Executive Board "for having succeeded in restraining and preventing the Cloak and Skirt Makers' Union from entering into an unnecessary, unwarranted and useless fight with the ... Association."[6] Although renominated for office, both Rosenberg and Dyche declined.[7] The convention then unanimously selected Benjamin Schlesinger and Morris Sigman, president and secretary treasurer respectively, and on June 13, London installed the newly elected officers.[8]

Shortly thereafter, the new officers appointed Morris Hillquit as counsel for the International.[9] Neither Schlesinger nor the General Executive Board offered any reasons for the decision to replace London. His close association with Rosenberg and Dyche during the struggle between Hourwich and the Joint Board probably aroused some antagonism among Hourwich supporters. Thus, the new officers may have placated the dissatisfied elements by appointing Hillquit.

The General Executive Board of the International, however, on July 1, adopted a motion to engage London "to act in an advisory capacity only," for the remuneration of fifty dollars a month. The board also agreed to pay London $125 for services rendered at the Cleveland convention and to send Vice Presidents Metz, Kleinman and Lefkovits to represent the union at a farewell banquet honoring London who had been elected a delegate to the Socialist International Congress.[10] Hence, the decision to replace London did not repudiate the man who had served the International so well. Moreover, the union, as in London's previous campaigns, endorsed his candidacy in 1914, worked vigorously on his behalf and took credit for his election.

The 1914 Socialist campaign began in New York when the party's state convention convened in Rochester with some two hundred delegates on hand.[11] After adopting a state platform which emphasized issues with popular appeal rather than the basic tenets of socialism,[12] the delegates nominated a full slate of candidates for statewide offices, headed by Charles Edward Russell for United States senator and Gustave Strebel for governor.

London, a delegate to the convention, approved both the party ticket and platform. The nomination of Russell and Strebel, he stated, fulfilled the dream of the great Socialist teacher Ferdinand Lassalle. "He always said that the emancipation of the working class would come when the intellectuals and proletarians united in overthrowing capitalism." As for the platform, London said that it presented "the sound clear expression of the political side of the class struggle. He was particularly pleased with the women's suffrage provision. "The enfranchisement of one half of the human race will mark a milestone in the progress of the State of New York and will make the movement for the emancipation of women irresistible."[13] London agreed with the opinion expressed by Morris Hillquit, state party secretary U. Solomon and other delegates that the party had excellent prospects in the coming election.[14]

On July 12, the nominating convention of Local New York met to select Socialist congressional candidates and also to choose delegates to the 1915 New York State Constitutional Convention. London was once again the party's nominee for Congress in the Twelfth Congressional District. In addition, the convention nominated London, Morris Hillquit, and Abe Cahan as delegates to the State Constitutional Convention from the Eleventh District. Julius Gerber, executive secretary of Local New York, declared that an active fight would be waged in the Twelfth Congressional District and expressed optimism for Socialist chances.[15]

London's campaign began in early October after he returned from Europe. The Workmen's Circle and the ILGWU had chosen London to represent them at the International Socialist Congress in Vienna late in August.[16] Due to the beginning of World War I, the Congress was advanced to the first week of the month. London planned to accompany the American Socialist delegation which consisted of Victor Berger, Charles Edward Russell, Morris Hillquit, Emil Seidel, George R. Lunn and Oscar Ameringer. Shortly before they left, the delegates received information that the Congress would meet in Paris rather than Vienna. They met at Hillquit's home in New York to decide whether they should proceed to a congress that might never open. The majority believed it their duty to undertake the journey. Thus, London and his fellow delegates left New York on July 31. Ninety miles at sea they received a cable from the National office that the Congress had been canceled. London, alone, decided to proceed.[17]

Prior to and after London's departure, the Executive Committee of Local New York mapped out a vigorous campaign including a concerted effort in London's district. The Socialists believed that Tammany had stolen the 1912 election from London due to irregularities at the polls and insufficient organization. At a meeting held on July 10, the Executive Committee of Local New York established a Committee of Five to manage the campaign in conjunction with a committee elected by the various branches in the congressional district. The campaign manager and the treasurer of the Twelfth Congressional Campaign Committee would then be chosen by the campaign committee subject to the approval of the Executive Committee.[18] On September 26, the campaign committee reported that it had selected Louis Schaffer campaign manager and that everything was going well.[19]

In a statement to the *Call*, Schaffer announced completion of arrangements for the campaign which would open officially on October 2 with a rally at Forward Hall. He predicted the sending of Socialist legislators to both Washington and Albany, for the people of the East Side had never been so disgusted with the old parties. Unions had pledged support and would elect committees to cooperate with the party organization. In addition, thirty-two Workmen's Circle branches planned to establish a committee for each of the Twelfth's election districts. Shafer pointed out that an early division of work among the various election districts would procure an honest count of Socialist votes. In previous elections this had been left until the last minute, leaving no Socialist watchers to prevent old-party watchers from stealing Socialist votes. A finance committee consisting of officials of Jewish labor, Socialist and fraternal organizations was also created.[20]

The campaign in the Twelfth Congressional District opened as planned on October 2. An overflow crowd of three thousand heard London, who appeared publicly for the first time since his return from Europe, urge all workers "to get into the fray and help." London declared that he had been elected, but counted out two years ago. He was confident of going to Washington this year provided organized labor and the Socialists did their duty. Max Pine appealed to the members of "London-made unions" to engage in mass picket duty to prevent "old party gangsters" from stealing London's election by counting him out and by "browbeating" Socialist voters.[21]

As in his previous congressional campaigns, London received the wholehearted support of organized labor. The largest unions in the garment industry—the cloak makers, the furriers, the ladies' waist makers and the men's tailors—organized campaign committees and collected money in the shops for London's campaign. The unionists also established their campaign headquarters at 175 East Broadway. Although the unions worked primarily among union members, they cooperated with the Socialist campaign managers.[22]

The ILGWU, in particular, waged a vigorous fight for London's election. The union organized the Ladies' Garment Workers' Union Socialist Campaign Committee, and the New York Joint Board appointed Vice President Saul Metz as the manager of the committee. In addition, the union rented a number of stores as meeting places and centers for the distribution of campaign material.[23] The committee formally opened its campaign on October 16 with three large hall meetings in different parts of the Twelfth District.[24]

In his third campaign for Congress against the incumbent Henry M. Goldfogle, London once again aggressively courted non-socialist voters.[25] His campaign strategy subordinated the basic demands of the socialist movement to vote-getting issues. London did not ignore socialist propaganda, but made it secondary to repudiating the corrupt Tammany machine and its control of New York City. Throughout the campaign, he told audiences that so long as Tammany "henchmen" represented the East Side in Congress, the stigma of Tammany was on them and their district and that the East Side could not expect the respect of the American people.[26]

London and the socialist press reviled Goldfogle's connection with Tammany, his voting record in Congress, and his indifference to the interests of the Jewish quarter. In a speech before 1,200 pants makers on October 29, London declared that every time the people of the East Side needed a spokesman on the floor of Congress, Goldfogle was absent.[27] The *New York Call*, the *Daily Forward* and the *Zukunft*, a Yiddish monthly, appealed to their readers to rid themselves of the "Tammany Jew" and to elect London, the friend of labor and the immigrant.[28]

The non-socialist press also chastised Goldfogle. The *New York Evening Journal* declared him typical of the worst kind of "bossism." The Hearst paper called upon the voters of the Twelfth Congressional District to support London "who is a thousand times better a man, to put it mildly." The *Evening Journal* stated that it would be an excellent thing to have several intelligent radicals in Congress telling unpleasant truths to the conservatives.[29]

During the campaign the immigrant question emerged as a hot-button issue. Goldfogle and his supporters, in an effort to discredit London, charged that the Socialist Party had opposed unrestricted immigration at its convention in 1910. The *Tageblatt*, which supported Goldfogle, declared that London, as a loyal Socialist, would oppose Jewish emigration to the United States from the war-torn countries.[30] Goldfogle's supporters played upon Jewish fears of restricted immigration. They maintained that any restriction would adversely affect Jewish immigration.

London immediately responded to this charge. In a letter dated October 28, printed in both the *Call* and *Forward*, London unequivocally denied that he favored immigration restriction and the literacy test, and branded the stories circulated by Tammany as lies. He pointed out that in 1910 he had appeared before the House Committee on Immigration to oppose the literacy test and other "oppressive and humiliating" restrictions. The Democrats, he charged, had introduced all the anti-immigration bills in Congress. "I have been a member of the Socialist Party since its inception, but I assure you that I would not hesitate to fight my own party if it should betray its high ideals, and imitate the other parties attempt to close the doors of America to victims of oppression."[31]

The *Daily Forward*, the General Executive Committee of the Workmen's Circle and the Action Committee of the Jewish Federation defended London's position. They pointed out that London had consistently supported free immigration and declared that the *Tageblatt*, lacking other issues, had manufactured the charge.[32]

Fully aware that Tammany would go to any length to achieve Goldfogle's reelection, the East Side Campaign Committee made plans to safeguard the Socialist vote on Election Day. Louis Schaffer appeared before the Executive Committee of Local New York on October 12 to request assistance in preventing repeaters and floaters from voting in the Twelfth District. The Executive Committee instructed Julius Gerber, the local's executive secretary, to call a conference of London, Morris Hillquit and Henry L. Slobodin, chairman of the County Committee, to consider the matter.[33]

On October 17, the *Call* reported that the East Side Campaign Committee planned to have four watchers in each of the thirty-five election districts in the Twelfth.[34] Schaffer also sought and obtained assurance from the Honest Ballot Association and the district attorney's office that they would help the Socialists secure a clean election.[35]

In addition, the East Side Campaign Committee circulated a petition in the Twelfth District requesting Mayor Mitchell to instruct the police commissioner to protect the Socialists from dishonest politicians. In a letter to the mayor, Schaffer called upon Mitchell to meet with London, Hillquit and Russell in order to receive the petition and to discuss police protection at the polls. Mitchell, however, directed Schaffer to meet with Police Commissioner Woods. Subsequently, at a meeting between London, Russell and Woods, the latter assured them that "the police will not be allowed to overlook abuses should they occur."[36]

The presence of Tammany floaters and repeaters in the Twelfth also caused great concern. Alexander Kahan, the chairman of the Socialist Legal Bureau, produced evidence of Tammany's efforts to colonize the district. Assistant District Attorney Morningstar, who supervised the Election Bureau, informed Kahan that detectives would investigate the evidence submitted to him and that every illegal voter would be arrested.[37] The anti-Tammany *New York Tribune* also reported that Tammany had colonized on a "gigantic scale" throughout the city, mostly on the Lower East Side. As a result, District Attorney Whitman's office called upon the Volunteer Watcher's League, with a membership of eight thousand college men, to help guard the polling places.[38]

The *New York Call* and the *Daily Forward* urged vigilance at the polls to prevent London from once more being counted out. The *Call* noted two ways to elect London. "One is to cast sufficient votes to do so. The other, and most important, is to have them correctly tabulated."[39] The *Forward* pointed out that special precautions had been taken to see that the votes were correctly tabulated. Moreover, this year the Jewish quarter was determined to fight for the votes.[40]

The final week of the campaign was hectic, with meetings every night and many of the leading Socialists in the city coming into the district on London's behalf. Charles Edward Russell urged the voters of the Twelfth District to throw off Tammany's yoke by voting for London. "In intellect, as in character, he towers far above the kind of man we ordinarily send to Congress. The entire country would have reason to rejoice that such a man was to be in the National Legislature."[41] On November 2, the day before the election, Russell accompanied London in a caravan of twelve red automobiles on a "whirlwind" tour of the East Side. At a rally later that evening, Russell implored the citizens of the Twelfth to "vote for London and freedom." He reminded the audience that Goldfogle had been elected by fraud and intimidation in 1912. "Protest tomorrow against the tyranny that enabled Goldfogle to go to Washington."[42]

Enthralled Socialist workers intensified their activities. The East Side Campaign Committee conducted a house-to-house canvass in the Twelfth District. The results indicated that a large majority intended to vote for London.[43] The canvassers distributed thousands of copies of the *Call*, the *Forward* and other Socialist literature. In addition, they emphasized the need to elect Socialist candidates who would propose ways to obtain measures beneficial to East Side workers.[44] Once again the *Daily Forward* printed the names and addresses of the district's registered voters. It urged the residents of the Twelfth to find the names of relatives and friends and to encourage them to vote for London and all the Socialist candidates.[45]

On the evening of November 2, the East Side Campaign Committee completed its preparations for election day. Over two hundred watchers gathered at Forward Hall to receive instructions about their rights as watchers, their responsibilities at the polling places, and how to deal with problems at the polling places. The Garment Workers' Campaign Committee revealed that, for the first time, mass picketing would take place at each of the thirty-five polling places in the Twelfth District. The committee thus hoped to discourage Tammany efforts to intimidate voters and to protect Socialist watchers from "thuggery."[46]

On Election Day morning, the *Forward* expressed confidence in a London victory, but warned its readers that a "desperate" Tammany would use a variety of methods to avoid defeat. It instructed voters to vote early in order to avoid Tammany officials who might try to show them how to vote, to wait until the clerk placed their ballot in the box, to be unafraid, and if harassed to report to a Socialist watcher or to Socialist campaign headquarters. The Jewish quarter, the *Forward* declared, was determined to free itself from Tammany and to send one of its "own children" to Congress.[47]

The voters of the district took advantage of ideal weather to go to the polls in record numbers.[48] With the exception of a few disturbances, none of them serious, the election proceeded without disorder. Mass picketing at the polls helped maintain order, as twelve to forty union members remained in front of each poll until closing time. During the afternoon, the *Tageblatt* attempted some last minute "dirty work." Goldfogle's chief spokesman, in an attempt to win progressive support, published a statement that Dr. Henry Moskowitz, London's Progressive Party opponent in 1912, had spoken out against London. Moskowitz, who supported London's candidacy, repudiated the story by working for London. Moskowitz and Charles Edward Russell spent the day on the East Side visiting polling places and giving information and assistance to harried watchers.[49]

4. Victory in 1914

As the day wore on, excitement mounted on the East Side. Although the polls did not close until five o'clock, people began to gather in Rutgers Square, facing the Forward Building, where election returns would be flashed upon a large screen on the front of the building by means of a stereopticon. With each passing hour the crowd grew, until it overflowed Rutgers Square and filled nearby Seward Park and the adjoining streets. The *Call* estimated that by the time the polls closed some fifteen thousand people stood tightly packed in the square.[50] The *Forward* placed the crowd at fifty thousand and reported that it continued to grow throughout the evening.

Due to a new ballot, the congressional count did not begin until the gubernatorial and senatorial votes were completed. Thus, anxiety increased as time passed and rumors circulated that Tammany was delaying the count. Finally, at nine o'clock the first congressional returns from the Twelfth District appeared on the screen to the accompaniment of loud cheers.[51] As each election district completed its count, Socialist watchers transmitted the results to party headquarters at 151 Clinton Street, where they were tallied and made public.[52] Although the results were inconclusive, enthusiastic London supporters began to celebrate his victory as early as eleven o'clock.

During the night, the Yiddish conservative newspapers, the *Tageblatt* and the *Jewish Daily News*, issued extras announcing Goldfogle's reelection. The crowd refused to accept these unsubstantiated claims, and the *Forward* and *Call* printed numerous extra editions showing London in the lead.[53] A 2:30 A.M. bulletin gave London 4,340 votes to Goldfogle's 3,382, with eight districts still unreported.[54] Although Charles Edward Russell made a public statement claiming London's election, London refused to make any such declaration, and Socialist watchers maintained their vigil at the polls. As late as four o'clock, no word had been heard from the "Goldfogle precincts." At 4:20 A.M. London agreed to address a cheering throng of two thousand people gathered in Socialist headquarters. Reports already in showed him far ahead, but London refused to be caught off guard by Tammany. He told the crowd that they were not there for speeches and cheers. "We are here to man the count. It's only a little after 4 o'clock with enough time left for Tammany to do a lot of dirty work. My speech is that we don't want noise, but more watchers."[55]

Twelve hours after the polls closed, some ten thousand weary but excited persons remained outside the Forward Building. Abraham Cahan and other Socialists spoke to them from the second-story window.[56] At 5 A.M., Socialist watchers still manned the polls. Russell and Moskowitz continued to make their rounds, going from polling place to polling place, urging their comrades to keep on the job. Not until eight o'clock in the morning did London accept congratulations. He had steadfastly insisted that there would be plenty of time for "good tidings" after the completion of the count.[57]

According to the *New York Sun*, London left Socialist headquarters in the "early hours of the morning" and went to a restaurant on Division Street near Canal. There, friends told him of his victory. Several enthusiastic East Siders lifted London to their shoulders and marched him through the streets to his home at 372 East Broadway. Three different processions of jubilant East Siders, each headed by a band, also paraded to London's house. Marchers carried straw brooms to symbolize that Tammany's rule had been swept out.[58]

Morning papers such as the *New York World*, the *New York Press*, the *New York Sun* and the *New York American* mistakenly reported a Goldfogle victory.[59] In tabulating the election returns, these papers overlooked the Socialist vote and concluded that Goldfogle was victorious due to his large plurality over the Republican candidate Benjamin Borowsky.[60] Although the *Forward* reported London's election, confusion and anxiety existed among the people of the East Side.[61] Finally, the afternoon papers[62] proclaimed London's victory, and the morning papers carried the correct results the next day.[63] The final count showed that London defeated Goldfogle by a plurality of 1,022 votes. He received 5,969 votes or 47.98 percent of the vote as compared to Goldfogle's 4,947 votes or 37.98 percent.

Borowsky, the Republican, ran far behind with 1,133 votes or 8.67 percent of the vote. London carried the Second, Sixth and Eighth assembly districts. Although he lost the Fourth Assembly District, Goldfogle's plurality had been reduced from 1,098 votes in 1912 to only 174.[64] It would also appear that London received virtually all of the Progressive votes that had gone to Henry Moskowitz during the four-cornered race two years earlier. Though Goldfogle gained 355 votes, his percentage fell from 39.42 to 37.98, a loss of 1.44 percent. Borowsky added 294 votes, an increase of 1.49 percent. On the other hand, London gained 2,323 votes, and his percentage went from 31.22 to 47.98, an increase of 16.78 percent.

Moskowitz's support for London and dissatisfaction among Progressives with Tammany rule had played an important role in London's success. Discontent with existing economic conditions and the Socialist Party's excellent organization were also important factors. In the final analysis, however, London's victory was a tribute to the man who had championed the cause of the workers and who had defended the interests of the Jewish quarter. London was the only member of his party elected to office in New York City, and as in his previous congressional campaigns, he ran well ahead of the Socialist ticket.[65]

Commenting upon his victory in post-election interviews, London refused to stress the personal element in the campaign. He asserted that his victory represented the first effective blow delivered against Tammany Hall. The Socialists had succeeded where the reformers of all parties had failed. "I think," he said, "that the victory is especially significant for that reason, as well as for the reason that it is a victory for pure government over the tactics employed by Tammany Hall. I am convinced that we Socialists will yet be able to smash Tammany Hall utterly. This is only the beginning." Two factors had produced success: the increased intelligence of the Jewish worker and the general rebellion against Tammany politics. "I am proud that the first actual defeat Tammany has met upon its own grounds has been at the hands of the Socialists."[66]

In an interview with the *Call*, London asserted that his victory marked the beginning of a nationwide fight against capitalism. He would not remain alone in Congress very long. Through the ballot box the people would sweep the Socialist Party into control of the government. Once in power the Socialists would take the industries from capitalists and give them to the people. London told the *Call* that the "false" immigration issue had helped the Socialists on the East Side. He also praised the Socialist poll workers who had embraced their jobs with great vigor. Unlike 1912, Tammany could not steal the election because Socialist workers remained on guard.[67]

Socialist leaders were elated with London's victory. Charles Edward Russell declared, "It was a great day that saw London elected to Congress and the power of Tammany Hall on the East Side broken for the first time." Russell attributed London's success to "irresistible" Socialist principles, to London's "high" character, to a vigorous and ably directed campaign, and to a clean election made possible by Police Commissioner Woods and the Honest Ballot Association.[68] Morris Hillquit, in his analysis, asserted that no single issue was responsible for London's victory. Socialist sentiment had increased every year, "and this year a more intelligent mode of voting and a more honest count were assured by the introduction of the new ballot." Hillquit asserted that London's election made the Socialist Party a real political factor. It would encourage "thousands" of Socialist votes in the next election. On the national level, Walter Lanferseik, executive secretary of the Socialist Party, expressed gratification with London's election and Socialist successes elsewhere.[69]

London also received congratulatory letters from Cyrus Sulzberger and Louis D. Brandeis, two pillars of the Jewish establishment. The latter expressed delight at London's election. "It shows," Brandeis said, "the appreciation of your work by our people, and through it will come a wider appreciation of what you have done and are doing."[70]

The elated Socialist press looked forward to further gains. The *New York Call* attributed London's election to efficient organization and hard work. His victory represented an "important stride forward" for the socialist movement in New York.[71] The *Daily Forward* called the election of London the "first crack" in Tammany's stronghold. The Jewish quarter had finally divorced itself from Tammany which represented in Congress the interests of the capitalists and not the masses. The Jewish labor movement, the *Forward* asserted, had become a power in national politics.[72] The *Ladies' Garment Worker* referred to London's election as a victory for socialism and the workers. The workers had elected London for they knew him "intimately" and had confidence that he would vigorously promote labor's cause in the House of Representatives. "Congressman-Elect Meyer London is so versatile in his sympathies that he is rightly regarded as the fit representative of all sections of the people. He had the support of the businessman, the small dealer, the intellectual as well as of the worker and the trade unionist."[73]

The election of the first Socialist congressman from New York evoked great interest among the non–Socialist New York papers. London had accomplished what liberal and reform elements had failed to do for many years: He had defeated the Tammany tiger in its own lair. The *New York Post*, the *New York Tribune*, and the *New York World* congratulated him. The *Tribune* and the *Post* attributed London's victory to progressive support. London, the *Tribune* commented, had shown the people that he was no ordinary politician. He had stirred the district as rivals and reformers had not done in thirty years.

His triumph showed the "breakdown" of Tammany's domain on the Lower East Side and that the Progressives had lost their strength as the party of protest.[74] In a different vein, the *New York Times* lectured London on good behavior in Congress. It cautioned him not to let his newly won fame "agitate him." The *Times*, "in all friendliness," admonished London to follow Victor Berger's example and speak with sanity and moderation.[75]

In a number of interviews published in both the Socialist and non–Socialist press, London discussed his plans for Congress. The American people, he emphasized, would see a new type of Jew in Congress. Until now they had known only the representative of the Jewish businessmen and financiers. He would show them the representative of the Jewish laboring masses. At present London did not see any special Jewish problems, but if they existed he would give them his full attention. "I shall guard the interests of the Jewish masses," he promised, "and defend them when and where it will be necessary."[76] Noting his limitations as the lone Socialist congressman, London stated that he expected to be more the "propagator of an idea" than a legislator. He did not expect to bring about, single-handedly, great Socialist reforms. It was his responsibility to awaken Congress and the American people to the existence of serious social problems. Most Americans, London asserted, were not aware of these problems and did not realize the importance of social legislation. "I shall use the floor of the House as a forum from which I shall talk to the American people concerning the desires and aspirations of the Socialist party—the party which is here to emancipate the toilers from the bonds of wage slavery."⁷⁷ London acknowledged that although many believed the Socialists too radical, it was necessary to have some radicals in Congress if good was to be accomplished. "I am sure I am not saying too much when I say we shall do good to the country as a whole by being in Congress and by furnishing a new note in its discourses."⁷⁸

More specifically, London declared that he would propose "drastic measures" for trust regulation. The doctrine of individualism had permitted capitalists to gain control of the country's industries while the people who depended on these industries were placed at the "mercy of the exploiters." When an industry became a monopoly, London stated, it should be seized by the people and managed democratically. He would, therefore, urge government ownership of monopolies.⁷⁹

London declared that as a representative of the working class he would fight for the "most radical" labor legislation. He would advocate unemployment insurance, a minimum wage, a child labor law, a shorter working day and the overall improvement of working conditions. Government regulation of prices and the cost of living would be future objectives. London also stated that he would fight every effort in Congress to limit immigration. He took exception to the view of conservative labor leaders, such as Sam Gompers, that the influx of immigrants was harmful to local workers and unions.⁸⁰

When asked about the European conflict, London replied that talk would not stop it. He expressed doubt as to whether the United States could stop the war. If it was to be stopped, he said, war must be declared on war. As a first step, London proposed that Congress enact legislation to prohibit food exports and other materials vital to the belligerents' war efforts.

Nations that were starving could not fight, he maintained. Every shipload of supplies sent to the warring nations prolonged the war. In this way the United States could strike a "decisive blow" at England and Germany since both nations depended upon food imports. The military caste had caused the war in order to justify their existence. Militarism required food. "If we feed those nations [the belligerents] now, we will help them fight. If we starve them, we will make them quit. The people will revolt against a militarism that means starvation. And that will end the war." London also proposed making it illegal for American citizens to extend loans to belligerent governments. "Such an act should be counted treason — treason to the world."

Some radical measures, he explained, were needed to implement his proposals. The government should seize large food supplies and make them available to the people at low prices. If the warring nations, London concluded, could take control of industries "in order to kill more efficiently, we can surely take them over in order to keep folks alive."⁸¹ During these interviews, London also promised the people of the East Side that he would fulfill his campaign pledge to report periodically to them on his work and the work of Congress.[82]

On Sunday afternoon, November 8, fifteen thousand people gathered in Madison Square Garden to celebrate London's victory. Gold-lettered red banners representing more than a hundred Socialist organizations decorated the walls of the Garden. A brass band stirred the "noisy and enthusiastic" crowd. Each speaker who preceded London received cheers and applause, but when London appeared on the platform with his smiling wife and young daughter, the crowd cheered for almost fifteen minutes.

London told the audience not to expect him to accomplish wonders in Congress. "What I expect to do is to take to Washington the message of the people, to give expression there to the philosophy of Socialism. I want to show them what the east side of New York is and what the east side Jew is." London expressed confidence that he would get "fair play" in Congress. "I will have my say, but I shall not abuse the right." He warned the audience not to be misled by his success. Continued effort and organization were imperative to win further victories. Victory would be achieved not by violence, "but by the greatest of all forces, the force of human intellect."[83] People must be educated and made to think. "Ours is but a small beginning. We shall not rest until every power of capitalism has been destroyed and the workers emancipated from wage slavery."[84] Socialist notables Morris Hillquit, Abraham Cahan, Algernon Lee, James Larkin, Jacob Panken, William Karlin, Benjamin Feigenbaum and Morris Winchevsky also spoke. They characterized London's victory as a repudiation of Tammany and expressed optimism about future Socialist success.[85]

The *New York World*, which had criticized London in an editorial on November 8,[86] expressed pleasure that London had no illusions about his role in Congress. "Mr. London," the *World* wrote, "seems to have a keener appreciation of the dignity of Congress and a better understanding of an individual's relations thereto than many native Americans. He looks for fair play and he will not be disappointed. A member who intends to be heard but who respects his privilege is not likely to address an empty House or an inattentive country." London would probably make one important discovery in Washington, the *World* continued. He had fought Tammany as a Socialist, but he would learn quickly "that he is nothing more than an American Democrat in earnest."[87]

Thus, in 1914, the New York Socialists succeeded in electing the first Socialist to any office in New York City. London's victory represented a major defeat for the Tammany machine, and held out hope for further gains. The Local New York branch of the Socialist Party with invaluable support from the unions had developed a campaign organization capable of meeting Tammany on its own grounds. London had also demonstrated his ability to win non–Socialist votes. Many reform-minded citizens had turned to London out of disgust with Tammany. London's victory represented an endorsement of his fight for clean government and his efforts on behalf of the working man and the immigrant community.

London had no illusions about the challenges that awaited him. As a minority of one, he realized the difficulty in procuring needed legislation. However, he planned to propose bills beneficial to the working class, and would fight against capitalism and all efforts to restrict immigration. "If other Congressmen," London declared, "refuse to pass bills intended to help humanity, then they shall suffer in the end."[88]

5

Preparing for Congress: Issues of War and Peace

> I feel that every day the war continues means an ever growing danger of the infection of militarism. Every day the war continues the militarists gain strength. We should fight the propaganda of the jingo with the counter propaganda for international peace.—*Meyer London, New York Call, November 29, 1915, 1–2.*

The Sixty-Fourth Congress would not convene until December 6, 1915. During the thirteen month interlude following the election, London devoted much of his time to the peace movement, anti-preparedness agitation, the unemployment problem and women's suffrage. He supported the Socialist Party's proposal for an embargo by neutrals against the belligerent nations as a means for ending the war. As preparedness agitation intensified, London endorsed a general strike to prevent American involvement. In addition, he made plans to introduce a resolution in the House urging President Wilson to invite neutral nations to a peace conference. Although the European conflict increasingly diverted his attention from domestic matters, London prepared legislation to remedy the unemployment problem and worked on behalf of the Susan B. Anthony Amendment. He also studied various issues likely to arise in Congress and developed a "modest" program of action.

The outbreak of war in Europe during the summer of 1914 stunned American Socialists. The National Executive Committee of the Socialist Party, on August 12, 1914, expressed the party's opposition "to this and all other wars, waged upon any pretext whatsoever." It blamed the "ruling classes" of Europe for the conflict and pledged to assist the European Socialist parties "in any measures they might think it necessary to advance the cause of peace."[1] In December the party's "antiwar manifesto" set forth a Socialist analysis of the war. Its immediate causes were "thoughts of revenge ... imperialism and commercial rivalries..., secret intrigue, lack of democracy, vast systems of military and naval equipment..., jingo press ... and the ... capitalist system."

A large majority of the party membership approved this position in a referendum in September 1915.² London shared the view of his fellow Socialists. The war, he asserted, was not an accident. "There exists among the great masses of the people a notion that the present war is an accident, that somebody became crazy, particularly that a certain ruler with a long military moustache became crazy and that all is to be blamed upon the crowned individual. That is absurd." The primary cause of the war, London went on, was the clash of national economic interests.

London recognized that other factors contributed to the conflict. Prejudice and race hatred, he pointed out, could be utilized by "fools" at any time for any "vile" purpose. The German military caste believed that any one not in uniform was inferior. In Russia, with three-fourths of the population illiterate, the masses believed that the czar ruled by divine right. Furthermore, the presence of large armies and navies aggravated the economic struggle. "When two men get into a fight, if they have no revolvers they would not fight with revolvers, but if they have revolvers and ammunition and large stores of explosives at the very moment when their interests collide they will use the means they have at their disposal for destroying each other."³

London and his fellow Socialists could not explain why the strong socialist parties of Germany and France had not prevented the war.⁴ Delegates attending congresses of the Second International had voiced opposition to war. Yet, when it came, they rallied with a few notable exceptions to the defense of their respective homelands.⁵ The spectacle of Socialists killing Socialists, plus the collapse of the internationalism which proclaimed that the workers had no national allegiance, shocked American Socialists.

London noted with sadness that internationalism had failed to assert itself and that no serious attempt had been made to practice it. The leaders of the Second International had failed to support a general strike in order to prevent European war.⁶ Nonetheless, Socialists had no reason to apologize. In all the parliaments of Europe, they had protested against war until the last moment.⁷ The Socialists could not stop the war because they lacked numbers. "They had done their best, and they spoke honestly and not as patriots."⁸ Socialists, however, had been "easily" convinced that their respective countries faced invasion, and this fear replaced international cooperation with concern for protecting one's country against attack. Despite their efforts, the Socialists were swept off their feet and along with the rest of their fellow countrymen, "drawn into the maelstrom of confusion." Socialists, London said, could console themselves that the world had expected the Socialists "to overcome national prejudice and hatred, to defeat the secret plans of cabinets [and] to overpower the gigantic physical forces at the disposal of the rulers of the world."⁹ But no one, he commented, expected religion to do anything.¹⁰

In addition, clergymen had failed to confront the crisis in Europe. The "ministers of the Gospel" in Germany never uttered a word against militarism in that country. However, unlike the German clergymen, prominent German Socialist leaders went to jail for opposing militarism. Religion, London stated, had supported slavery in the South before the Civil War, and "it has been on the side of many another evil that had the endorsement of the governing forces of the community. Socialism is against religion when it is found in league with such forces."[11]

With characteristic vigor, London fought for peace and opposed preparedness, which he feared would draw the United States into the conflict. London wholeheartedly supported the Socialist Party's policy of neutrality. He believed that the party should maintain absolute neutrality so that its position would be respected and accepted as one of complete and unquestioned fairness in all matters.

This did not mean that Socialists should remain indifferent. Socialists of the neutral countries had to take a "militant stand" for peace. If they did not, London said, there would be little hope of rehabilitating the International in the near future. Moreover, a resort to arms would mean that the "gospel of force" had replaced every other gospel, human or divine. London proposed that the Socialist Party send representatives to Europe, preferably to the Hague. These representatives would act as peace ambassadors for the American Socialist Party, reporting the progress of events and seeking opportunities to work for peace.[12]

The Socialist Party, meanwhile, had embarked upon a peace program which included proposals for mediation by the United States, an international Socialist conference, and an embargo.[13] On September 19, 1914, Walter Lanferseik, national executive secretary of the party, sent telegrams to the Socialist parties of ten European nations requesting them to urge their respective governments to accept mediation by the United States. A week later the National Executive Committee called for an international Socialist conference in Washington to consider ways and means to end hostilities.

Socialist leaders in the belligerent nations rejected the proposal, but those in neutral European nations showed interest. They finally agreed to hold the conference in Copenhagen on January 15. American Socialists lost their enthusiasm when Socialists in the belligerent nations refused to send representatives. Therefore, rather than six delegates, only Morris Hillquit represented the American party. Hillquit, however, after being informed by the head of the International Bureau that European Socialists considered mediation futile, did not attend the conference. Shortly thereafter, the National Executive Committee, disillusioned with the Second International as a peace agency, refused to pay its dues to the International. The Socialist Party of America thus ended its affiliation with the Second International.[14]

Although London shared the disappointment of his American comrades, he still hoped to save the International. A few days after the National Executive Committee acted, London appealed for rehabilitation of the International as one of the foundations of socialism. "I believe it is our business to make the attempt to rehabilitate the International. I think that there is a great enough emergency to call for action and to justify action on the part of the National Executive Committee."[15]

In addition to the proposals for mediation and an international Socialist conference, the National Executive Committee initiated a campaign for an embargo against the belligerent nations. The party adopted a slogan, "Starve the war and feed America."[16] London endorsed the embargo, and called for an end not only to the shipment of food and supplies, but financial assistance as well. Clearly affirming his belief in neutrality, London argued that it was equally wrong to send food to Germany as it was to send ammunition to England. The neutral nations, London wrote, had not remained neutral, but had sent food and ammunition to the belligerents; the United States had been the "greatest sinner."[17] London intended to make the embargo a priority in Congress. "It will be contrary to all ideas of business. It will mean famine for food speculators. But it will knock militarism on the head. And it will mean full stomachs for millions of Americans who will otherwise go hungry."[18]

The Socialist campaign for an embargo received support from non–Socialist peace societies as well. London, who accepted a directorship in the New York Peace Society, favored Socialist cooperation with every "genuine" peace movement. Most Socialists, however, held the peace societies in low regard.[19] The agitation of Socialist and non–Socialist embargo proponents caused Congress and the Wilson administration to briefly consider the plan. Ultimately the belief that an embargo was not neutral prevailed, and the embargo movement virtually ended by October 1915.[20] London continued to support the embargo, but as the demand for preparedness increased, he also advocated a more radical response — a general strike.

Preparedness agitation began in October 1914 with a small but articulate group led by Theodore Roosevelt. Motivated by fear and distrust of Germany, Roosevelt believed that the United States should enter the war on the side of the Allies. Aware that public opinion strongly supported neutrality, the interventionists masked their objectives with patriotic exhortations to enlarge the American military. Initially, the interventionists made little headway. Most Americans did not consider the war a threat to the United States and, therefore, saw no reason to enlarge the army and navy. President Wilson's decision, in January 1915, to reduce the military budgets prompted preparedness spokesmen to increase the tempo and scope of their activities and propaganda. With the sinking of the *Lusitania* on May 7, preparedness agitation reached flood proportions. It became a virtual crusade as sentiment grew "that the United States had a vital interest in the conduct of the belligerents and the outcome of the war."[21]

As the preparedness campaign increased in intensity, Socialist and non-Socialist peace organizations launched an anti-preparedness movement. On April 15, London addressed a peace meeting of three thousand at Cooper Union sponsored by the Central Federated Union of Greater New York. He sarcastically remarked that those supporting preparedness "see an aeroplane in a bird, a submarine in a fish. The police department of New York ... could take care of all the trouble likely to arise on the Canadian border, as could ... a dozen cowboys on the Texan line."

He appealed to the workers to help end this war and all wars. The Socialists and the labor movements of the world had to make the continuance of the war impossible. The demand for peace would be effective only if it came simultaneously from the belligerents. American and neutral labor movements had to coordinate the efforts of the European working class. London stated that it would not be enough to send a delegation to Europe "to help pick up the torn threads of internationalism." American workers should refuse to participate in this destructive work. They should refuse to send either food or ammunition to belligerents. London went beyond the embargo and called upon the workers to paralyze "every industry that in any way helps to prolong the war. We do not care whom it shall strike and how much harm it will inflict upon ourselves, for the story of labor, is the story of martyrdom."[22] Thus, London joined a small group of American Socialists who publicly supported a general strike to end the conflict and to prevent American involvement.

At the conclusion of the meeting, London denied interventionists' charges that it had been pro-German. The meeting was "strictly neutral," and he had no information that it sought to promote German interests. As with the embargo, critics of the general strike charged that it was pro-German since the Allies received most of the American arms, munitions and food. London declared that he would have avoided participation in any meeting favoring either the Germans or the Allies. Moreover, during his address he had carefully avoided partiality. "I do not think," London said, "that there was any intention to aid the cause either of Germany or the Allies. Our only purpose was to protest against the war."[23]

The *New York Call* applauded the resolution adopted at the meeting as a start toward ending the conflict. The *Call* implored all Socialists to cooperate with organized labor to the fullest possible extent. "The general strike may be an untried and doubtful weapon, but when organized labor decides that is the only one available it devolves upon us to attempt to utilize it with all the power and skill we possess."[24]

The syndicalist origins of the general strike, however, made it unacceptable to those who dominated the Socialist Party, and the party never accepted it as part of its anti-war program.[25] The fact that London, a right-wing Socialist, adopted an anti-syndicalist measure illustrated his dedication to peace and his flexibility of thought.

The sinking of the *Lusitania* on May 7, 1915, represented a turning point in the preparedness movement.[26] Despite increased preparedness propaganda, the Socialist Party remained steadfastly opposed to war. London called the *Lusitania* sinking "the most awful crime in the annals of the war."[27] Nevertheless, he insisted that war could still be avoided. Germany, he told the *New York Call*, was not anxious for war with the United States. More important, the American people strongly desired peace. "The great mass of the people are calm and pacific. Ask the man in the street what he thinks about the war and he'll tell you it's terrible. He may have a preference as to one side or another, but he will not go to war for any of them." Once again London appealed to the labor movement. He urged labor to organize a committee and to invite delegates from all peace organizations to cooperate with it in making an effective protest in Washington against entering any offensive war.[28]

The resignation of William Jennings Bryan as secretary of state, on June 8, did not alter London's view regarding the possibility of war. In another interview with the *Call*, he challenged as unfounded Bryan's fears that war would result from Wilson's second note to Germany. Nevertheless, if Bryan had sincerely believed that the note would precipitate war, "it was honest for him to resign from the cabinet and state his reasons." London then rejected force as an instrument of diplomacy. Stress should be placed upon democracy in international affairs. The United States, which had contributed political democracy and religious freedom to civilization, could "easily afford to lead the world in extending democracy to international relations. Its standard need not be that of the militarist madhouse in Europe." Nations who disregard all standards of right and wrong cannot offend the United States. The United States, London concluded, as a democratic nation, should oppose war, since war undermined democracy.[29]

During the height of the preparedness campaign, London spoke at several important peace meetings. At a Women's Peace Party gathering on June 15 he responded to the National Security League, which had held a rally the previous evening in support of preparedness.[30] London warned that the League's ultimate goal was American intervention on behalf of the Allies. The *New York Times* reported that he aimed his sharpest barbs, however, at the metropolitan dailies. If these papers, he asserted, printed "headlines urging that national honor demands that we fight somebody for something, we will fight." How,

London asked, could we stop the people from being swept off their feet? Once again he emphasized the necessity of extending democracy to international affairs. Since European civilization and the social democratic movement had broken down, the United States must pursue the task. London also charged that certain labor leaders (no doubt he meant Sam Gompers) were not fulfilling their obligations during the present crisis. They should unequivocally oppose the war, he declared.[31]

Four days later London appeared at Carnegie Hall with William Jennings Bryan, Joseph D. Cannon, a representative of the Western Federation of Miners, and Congressman Frank Buchanan of Illinois to address a peace rally sponsored by the Central Federated Union. Both Bryan and London stressed the senselessness of the European war. London pointed out that the history of Europe was the "struggle for commercial supremacy, for new spheres of influence, [and] the striving to subjugate smaller nations." European nations, he continued, worshipped but one God, and that was the God of commercialism, London praised both the German Social Democracy and unions. The leaders of the workers in Germany had been "ridiculed, scorned and imprisoned" in their fight against the war. Europe now paid the price. This must not happen in the United States. Once more London rejected the idea that there was any danger of war. If a real danger existed, mass meetings would be insufficient. He repeated his demand for an embargo, as munitions makers would not voluntarily end their shipments. "They sell arms through the week and go to Church on Sunday."[32]

On the evening of June 21, London, Morris Hillquit and other Socialists addressed the first anti-war meeting held in New York under Socialist Party auspices. The large crowd cheered London and Hillquit who called for peace and an end to the arms traffic. London attacked the preparedness movement. He warned that a military buildup would lead to war. It had happened in Europe, and it could happen here. Only the Socialist Party of America could stop the "wave of war." London further warned that manufacturers would accuse those who supported peace of serving the Kaiser. But, he said, "I have as much love for the Kaiser as for Rockefeller."

Turning to naval armaments, London criticized proposals that the United States build a fleet large enough to defeat England, Germany and other nations. In order to have a fleet equal to that of several nations combined, the United States would "have to turn every canoe and scow into a warship." London stated that he would rather risk having the war go poorly for this country during the first months of a conflict than have American ideals and institutions destroyed by creating militarism.

Those who favored preparedness, he charged, promoted fear in this country of some possible enemy. "We should make it impossible for any jingo to repeat the crime of Europe. This is the one safe spot in the world for human beings. This is the nation of nations. This is the only spot where the oppressed found refuge. This is where they came from militarism, and we don't want the hatreds of Europe brought over to us." Every "liberty loving" man in this country must say, "We shall not be guilty of the crime of shedding human blood. We shall not fight mad men or a lunatic asylum."[33]

On July 1, London responded to a manifesto issued by the German Socialists urging the German government to begin peace negotiations. He proposed that the American Socialist Party organize an international Socialist conference to bring together the interested parties. London regarded the manifesto as a hopeful sign, but doubted that the German government would "consider with equanimity" the Socialist proposal for evacuating territory conquered by German and Austrian forces. Nevertheless, London believed that the German Socialists, by opposing the annexation of territory, had opened the way for the British, French and Russian Socialists to make similar demands upon their governments.

Although the German Socialists had issued the manifesto at a time when Germany held a military advantage, it would be unwise, London commented, if Socialists in other belligerent nations waited until they gained a similar position; they would only add to the bloodshed. He called upon his fellow Socialists to accept the German Socialists offer in a "fraternal spirit," and to rehabilitate the international movement. Moreover, American Socialists, as citizens of a great neutral power, should take the lead in urging Socialists in the belligerent countries to accept their German comrades' proposals. Socialists in all parts of the world, London asserted, should participate in the peace settlement. They could not afford to leave the settlement to the usual channels.[34]

The National Executive Committee also greeted the peace activities of the German Socialists with enthusiasm, but failed to act on London's proposal.[35] Instead, the committee designated July 18 as a day for Socialist peace demonstrations throughout the country.[36]

In the following months, London continued his efforts for both peace and against the preparedness movement.[37] During the fall election campaign of 1915, London declared that at no other time in American history was it so important to elect Socialist representatives. Those financially interested in large military expenditures had "terrorized" millions of Americans to believe that the country faced unknown dangers. Moreover, political leaders had indicated they intended to make preparedness the main issue in the next Congress and the 1916 presidential campaign.

The preparedness campaign, London asserted, not only threatened the "democratic and historical traditions" of the United States, but obscured the real issues which confronted the country and delayed, for generations, the solution of those problems. During the last decade the social conscience of the American people had been awakened as never before. The demand for large military expenditures jeopardized socialist pressure for labor legislation which had attracted the attention of state legislatures and the Congress.[38]

Shortly after this article appeared in the *New York Call*, Wilson formally declared for preparedness in a speech on November 4, 1915. Wilson urged preparation, not for war, but for defense. As expected, preparedness organizations applauded the president while anti-preparedness forces bitterly criticized him and made ready for the oncoming struggle.[39] In a speech to the Socialist Press Club on November 16, London questioned Wilson's program. The United States, he asserted, did not face a "serious danger" of invasion. European nations would never invade this country. "This jingoism has given me a bad headache for a long time. The whole world is mad, and now friends meet and gasp in whispers, 'What if someone should attack us?'"[40]

Several weeks later London conceded that under existing conditions the United States should "keep itself in a position to meet unjust attacks by foreign countries." London declared, however, that he would not support any measures that would cause other nations to fear that the United States was preparing to attack them.[41]

London elaborated upon the preparedness movement in an article which appeared in the December 1915 *Zukunft*. He wrote that the most important question the Sixty-Fourth Congress would consider was preparedness. In the last year, he noted, the United States had become more militaristic than in the preceding forty. Moreover, as war continued and more nations became involved, the United States would find it increasingly difficult to maintain its neutrality. Despite the hundreds of miles of ocean which separated the United States from the conflict, it had drifted toward militarism.

He charged that munitions makers had plotted to strengthen militarism. Moreover, Allied war orders had created a munitions industry in this country. London noted that the investment of millions of dollars meant that those involved would take any steps to protect their money and to continue the industry after the war. They had already won the press to their side, and had launched a propaganda campaign for militarism throughout the country. Munitions interests had also tied themselves to various political clubs and infiltrated peace organizations. In addition, theaters, moving pictures and comic pages all spread the doctrine of militarism.

Other elements had also helped create the militaristic mood in the country. American capitalists sought investment in profitable areas. They wanted the United States to pursue a vigorous colonial policy. Such a policy, London stated, would necessitate a change in this country's military posture, leading to colonial wars in contradiction to the policy advocated by the Democratic Party in 1900. Moreover, some argued that the United States was no longer isolated and should abandon Washington's policy of no entangling alliances. They insisted that the United States must become a great military power so that it could have a voice in international affairs. Some, London went on, advocated preparedness to protect the Monroe Doctrine since recent events had shown that doctrines alone meant little when a nation lacked power. Finally, militarists also stirred up fears over Alaska and the Panama Canal. They painted the situation in ever-darkening colors, and their influence had grown stronger.

London then discussed the opponents of preparedness. He divided the "pacifists" into two groups: The first, a small and unimportant group, maintained that the United States should not spend money for military expansion. These "Christian oriented" people believed that the United States should show that a nation could get along without an army or armaments. Nations would learn from our example as they had learned from the American Constitution. William Jennings Bryan exemplified this line of thinking.

The second and most important group of "pacifists," according to London, realized that the United States could not remain helpless while the rest of the world armed. Under such circumstances this country could not depend on other nations' good intentions. These "pacifists" warned that preparedness agitation should not lead the United States to militarism, If this occurred, America's neighbors would also begin to arm, militarism would accelerate and a world catastrophe would take place.

However, these "pacifists," London wrote, recognized the inadequacy of a negative program, and believed in an approach that would neither allow a nation to become defenseless, nor prevent it from becoming "drunk" with militarism. He proposed a plan that limited arms to defensive weapons; called for Congress to create a committee of experts to determine defensive and offensive weapons and how large a military establishment a secure nation needed; another committee appointed by Congress to investigate the relationship between the munitions industry and preparedness proponents; advocated government control of the munitions industry; and, most important, called for immediate action by the United States to end the war.

The president must take the initiative. He should call for a conference of neutral trading nations to determine a time and place to start peace negotiations. These nations, London stated, had already developed a plan for a lasting peace, based upon self-determination for all nations, freedom of the seas, and a court of international arbitration with power to enforce its decisions through a boycott. London declared that, as a Socialist, he could cooperate with these "wonderful pacifists" with a clear conscience. Moreover, as a Jew representing a Jewish district, he planned to point out the plight of Jews in the war-torn countries when discussing self-determination.

Wilson's preparedness program, London noted, attempted to deflate the preparedness forces while reassuring those who feared militarism. He had taken the middle way, but that way, London cautioned, could easily lead to extremes. Pacifists would be a minority in Congress, with a difficult job that could be made easier if people knew the reasons behind military agitation and its inherent dangers. The Socialist Party, London suggested, should therefore assume this job for it would benefit both the nation and the party.[42]

In an article written about the same time for the *American Socialist*, the official publication of the Socialist Party, London clearly embraced the views of the second group of pacifists. The foes of preparedness, he wrote, should not be satisfied with a negative program, but should demand an investigation of the sources of preparedness and the nationalization of the munitions industries. Furthermore, the United States should use "every influence as the greatest neutral nation ... to urge a settlement upon a permanent and durable basis." Once again London invoked the names of Karl Liebknecht and Keir Hardie, founder of the British Labor Party. How, he asked, could the American Socialist movement vindicate itself before history, if it failed to follow their example in promoting international peace?[43]

Meanwhile, on November 29, London informed the *New York Call* that, as the representative of the American Socialist movement, he would introduce a resolution in the House urging the president to convene a conference of neutral nations to work for a peace based upon the following principles: evacuation of invaded territory, liberation of oppressed nationalities, plebiscites by the people of Alsace-Lorraine, Poland and Finland to ascertain their allegiance or independence, removal of political and civil disabilities imposed on the Jewish people, freedom of the seas, gradual disarmament, and the establishment of an international court of arbitration, with the commercial boycott as a sanction.

As a Socialist, London felt an obligation to present a plan for world peace. He acknowledged that it was not original, but the plan represented the consensus of those who had given considerable thought to the question. "I feel that every day the war continues means an ever growing danger of the infection of militarism. Every day the war continues the militarists gain strength. We should fight the propaganda of the jingo with counter propaganda for international peace." London's peace proposal rejected the need for an organized military force. Such a force, he asserted, posed a "constant menace" to peace. "Unless the war is to be followed by substitution of other means than military force to enforce the decisions of the court of arbitration, we will have gained nothing and the world will revert to the doctrine of superior force."[44]

London's plan, one of the earliest Socialist attempts to define a just peace, bore a striking similarity to the international socialist peace aims and to the Fourteen Points of President Wilson.

On December 18, 1915, the National Executive Committee of the Socialist Party endorsed London's resolution. The committee also decided to circulate petitions, to send releases to Socialist newspapers, and to call upon socialist parties of other nations to approve similar proposals.[45] London's recommendations were later included in the 1916 Socialist Party platform.

One of London's proposals, as noted, called for the political and civil emancipation of Jews in the belligerent nations. Like many of his fellow American Jews, he was deeply concerned about the plight of Jews in these countries. Agitation had already begun within the American Jewish community on their behalf. On April 18, 1915, London addressed the National Women's Committee for Jewish Rights in the Belligerent Countries, the first of a series to promote equal rights for Jews, particularly in Russia. More than two hundred delegates, representing 177 Jewish labor organizations with more than three hundred thousand members attended. London expressed hope that the American people would assist persecuted Jews throughout the world. He told the audience that he expected the European Socialist parties to adopt the demands of Jewish congresses.[46]

In early September, London spoke about the plight of Russian Jews to more than three hundred delegates representing Jewish organizations from various parts of the country. The conferees sought to launch a movement for the emancipation of Russian Jews and to draft a plan urging the United States government to support equal rights for the Jews at the peace conference.[47]

In addition to these efforts to end discrimination, London served as chairman of the Jewish Relief Committee of America, established by the New York Socialist Party, a position he assumed in August 1915. This organization later affiliated with the American Jewish Joint Distribution Committee of Funds for Jewish War Sufferers and raised eight hundred thousand for overseas relief by July 1917.[48]

While London dealt with questions of peace and preparedness, he also remained active in labor affairs. Unions continued to consult him and to request his assistance. In January of 1915, he intervened on behalf of striking workers at the Williams and Clark Fertilizer Plant in Chrome, New Jersey, after deputies fired at strikers, killing one and wounding fifteen.[49] On yet another occasion, the Executive Committee of the United Hebrew Trades appealed to London to assist in the defense of Solomon Metz, president of the union, and seven officers of the International Ladies' Garment Workers' Union and the Joint Board of Cloakmakers who had been indicted for murder. Morris Hillquit, Abraham Levy and Jacob Panken were retained earlier by various East Side unions.[50] While London called for union solidarity and urged the workers not to rest until their "incarcerated brethren" were freed, he did not take an active part in the trial.[51]

Of particular concern to London was the persistent problem of employment. In the years following the depression of 1907, the American economy had experienced a series of upswings and recessions. An upswing took place in 1912, but a relapse which occurred the following year became a depression in 1914. Wages barely kept up with the rising cost of living, and unemployment mounted. Although statistics are inadequate for these years, unemployment in manufacturing, transportation, the building trades and mining was estimated at 16.4 percent in 1914, and 15.5 percent in 1915.[52]

On December 28, 1914, London spoke before the American Association for Labor Legislation in Philadelphia.[53] The Socialist congressman-elect discussed the causes of unemployment and proposed remedial measures. Unemployment, he told the delegates, was inevitable under the current system of production, a system characterized by industrial disorder from which the worker severely suffered. Society did not owe every man a living, he continued, but it owed him the opportunity to make a living. The failure of the American people to grasp the magnitude of the problem accounted for the inadequacy of the measures adopted to relieve the "evil."[54]

As the first step, London proposed a national system of labor exchanges to gather and systematize information. He then called for the adoption of a national compulsory unemployment insurance law. "We have learned," he said, "that there is an obligation upon the community to protect the worker against loss by involuntary idleness, which is not an accident, but a feature of our industrial system." Until the enactment of such a law, however, immediate relief was needed. He urged the Wilson administration to assist municipalities and states in their effort to assist the unemployed by implementing the conservation plank in the Democratic platform.[55]

Several weeks later the *New York Call* reported that the Socialist Party planned a state and national campaign for measures to alleviate unemployment. London would present bills in Congress incorporating a system of free national, state and municipal employment agencies, federal public work projects, federal loans to cities and states, and unemployment insurance.[56]

On January 21, the Socialist Party announced that as part of its unemployment campaign it would sponsor an unemployment day on February 12, in conjunction with the United Hebrew Trades and other unions.[57] Meetings would take place throughout the country. London would be the principal speaker at a mass rally in Union Square. The *New York Call* urged its readers to send resolutions containing the Socialist unemployment program to their congressman in order to force the government to supply jobs for the six million unemployed in the country. Their support would help London to win approval for the Socialist program in Congress.[58]

In an interview the day before the rally, London stated that a principal cause of unemployment was the lack of a social conscience in the country. "This lack of a social conscience is pitiable. Here we have all the features of a great national calamity and the country sits idly by." While some five hundred thousand men were jobless in New York City, authorities had failed to act on their behalf. London scored the cynicism of the people and officials. He suggested that the city build schools and extend loans to the unemployed. In addition, it should urge employers to divide work among more people. This would prevent extreme hardship and force all people to share the crisis. "But what is the use?" London asked. "You can't patch up a system based upon the individualistic philosophy of 'dog-eat-dog'!" The only way to solve the unemployment problem was "for the government to compete in all lines, until it has taken over all the industries of the nation. By producing for service and not profit, the government can pay good wages and institute the eight hour day." However, this "final solution" for unemployment lay in the future. Immediate relief was needed. He would, therefore, concentrate in Congress on the passage of a national unemployment insurance act.[59]

On February 12, some 3,500 people gathered in Union Square to participate in the Socialist demonstration against unemployment. For three hours the crowd listened as Socialist speakers criticized Mayor Mitchell and other city authorities for "meeting a breakdown in industry with nothing better than a deluge of old clothes." London lashed out once again at public apathy. He blamed the working people for the unemployment problem. "If the working class concentrated, it could compel action on the question.... It could compel employers to distribute work more equally and [it] could force municipalities to undertake as much public work as possible." London urged his listeners to write their representatives in Congress, the state legislature and the city administration demanding employment. "Surely all together must be able to do something. But nobody cares. They look upon the crisis as a temporary evil..., and therefore believe that no action is necessary."[60]

At this point, several people in the crowd interrupted London. What, they shouted, did he propose to do about the social revolution?[61] He replied that he planned to present the Socialist viewpoint in Congress. "I am elected for only two years and that is too short a time to bring about the Social Revolution, so I am going to leave the job until later. I am going to do hardly anything to bring it about. You see I have to be reelected in 1916 and I have to retain some votes in my district." When asked if he would vote with the Democrats and Republicans, London answered that he would if they offered good proposals.

London then proceeded to lecture his questioners on their responsibilities. "But if you really want to know what I would like to do it would be to make you fellows forget the sporting pages and the prize fights and buy books about your own problems and read, and read, and read. You see, I can't in Congress bring about the change you want. New habits of thinking will have to bring that change about." Only after the workers educated themselves and demanded change, London concluded, would Congress respond to their concerns.[62]

London's candid remarks at the Union Square meeting attracted the interest of the *New York Times* which printed an interview with him on February 21. In order to clarify any misunderstanding, London told the *Times* reporter that he had not attacked the Socialist Party or anyone else. He had pointed out how much the people could accomplish quickly if they determined to do so. They had the votes, but they needed concerted action to make themselves "all powerful."

Once again London decried the ignorance that existed on the unemployment question. No one even knew how many people were jobless. As to the causes of unemployment, he stated that the war had aggravated the present crisis. London reiterated, however, that unemployment was endemic to capitalism. Such distress was not new; it occurred approximately every ten years. "Overproduction and a glutted market, the result of a lack of intelligent adjustment between production and consumption, is an old story with us." Socialism, London went on, maintained that the worker did not receive a fair share of what he produced. As a result, his purchasing power declined and a glut followed because the people could not afford to buy goods. Hard times revealed the inefficiency of the system. Workers did not understand the causes of unemployment. They had a duty, therefore, as did society in general, to become better informed.

Labor and its leaders, London asserted, ignored difficulties until they became serious and affected them as individuals. London refused, however, to hold labor leaders responsible for this situation since they could not "be much better than the mass, nor the mass much better than the leaders." Hope for the future depended upon new educational opportunities. London once again suggested that workers could improve their intelligence by reading relevant topics. In addition, they should become familiar with existing laws and proposed legislation affecting workers.

London criticized labor leaders for using trade union tactics rooted in the past, even though important changes had taken place in politics, industry and legislation. Thus, the strike had become "entirely futile" in all monopolistic industries except railroads and mines. London called for other forms of action, including political activity and educational propaganda, to supplement the strike. He dismissed violence as never being in date. Although he acknowledged that both employers and workers had resorted to violence, London remarked that "violence had never been lastingly effective or either temporarily wise for either." Unions would never succeed entirely, he declared, until union leaders and the rank and file understood the laws governing modern industry. He suggested that every union become an educational center even though this produced extensive changes in union leadership. "Leaders must grow as the world grows, in labor or elsewhere."

Socialists, London stated, rejected the belief that reform would come from the "industrial magnates." He noted that some "noble souls" among them sought to improve conditions, but "generally speaking, people do not possess money, but are possessed by money. Men who have reached the ladder's top have to fight to stay there; few of them feel able to afford to stop and indulge in scruples."

When asked whether capital could oppress the worker if the worker showed the same ambition that made the employer a success, London replied that the worker must never think of himself as being alone. Unlike the capitalist who depended upon "intensification of his individualism," the rise of the worker rested upon the growth of "collective conscience." In the last fifteen years, he stated, thoughtful people had become aware of social problems. The nation had begun to realize that the community had an obligation to assist its weaker members. The ultimate objective of socialism, London declared, was a democratic society where everyone who participated in the state's burdens shared in its benefits. "Capital and labor! A mere phrase. I am not interested in capital and labor, but in human beings and their welfare."[63]

In the months following his election, London also participated actively in the women's suffrage campaign. After 1908, the Socialist Party took an active interest in the suffrage issue. Socialists campaigned for its adoption in those states which prohibited women's suffrage, and Socialist legislators introduced suffrage resolutions in states where the party had elected representatives.[64]

In New York the Socialists prepared a major effort to secure passage of a suffrage amendment which would appear on the ballot in the 1915 election. On February 28, 1915, designated by the Socialist Party as Women's Day, London and several other Socialists spoke to a large crowd on the "Women Question." London told the audience that debate on the issue tired him. "I don't care to speak about it and that's God's truth. The case in favor of women's suffrage is too elementary, too simple. It is an insult to any audience to offer to argue it out. It was a shame that there should be any question about the subject in this day." He expressed exasperation with those men who told women, "I can vote, but you can't because you are a woman." The Socialist

Uncle Sam greets the newly elected Congressman Meyer London. Translation: "Pleased to meet you" (top); "A truly new type of Jew — I like you." Cover of the *Groisser Kundes* (Big Stick), November 13, 1914.

Party, London declared, sought freedom for women to develop; suffrage was but one step in that movement. In the final analysis, he concluded, the main issue was how to prepare men and women to use the vote intelligently so they could cause peaceful change in the existing form of government.[65]

Shortly thereafter, London announced that he would carry on a "whirlwind" campaign for suffrage in New York State under the auspices of the Women's Committee of the Socialist Party. He would urge voters to cast an "overwhelming" vote for the women's suffrage amendment.[66] On June 7, at the National Women's Trade Union League Convention, he declared that the trade union movement and the suffrage movement were "inseparably united." Serving either cause, he said, was the highest kind of work for women of the working class.[67]

Several weeks later London spoke to five thousand people in Seward Park and declared that he expected the Twelfth Congressional District to give a larger vote for suffrage on Election Day than any other district in the country.

An overwhelming endorsement of suffrage at the polls by the Jewish community, he said, would show the whole country that no other district excelled its intelligence. Naturalized citizens, he went on, should be the last persons to oppose granting suffrage to American women. They owed it to those who had fought for political freedom in the past. "None need the vote more than the women of the East Side. When she gets it, down will go those tenement houses, and in their place will be reared comfortable ... homes fit for human beings to live in. The children will be taken out of the workshops, mills, mines, and factories, and women will no longer be forced to work in industry."

The right to vote, he asserted, was too important to be restricted to one part of the community. There should be no restriction of sex or property to the right to cast a ballot. Women had shown by their activities in the labor movement that they could work together for the common good. They would also organize on the political field to their benefit and that of their families. Suffrage, he concluded, would help create a better world politically, economically and socially.[68]

London favored federal rather than state action on the suffrage question. At a suffrage rally on August 16, he pledged to work for the Susan B. Anthony Amendment regardless of who introduced it in Congress. Once again he expressed his displeasure with the "antis." As an intelligent human being and a member of the community, a woman had the right to share in the lawmaking process. London pointed out that the question of equal rights was basically a federal rather than a state matter.[69]

He later elaborated this in the *New York Call*. The political emancipation of women, he wrote, was the next step in the progress of democracy. He reaffirmed his support for the Susan B. Anthony Amendment, but criticized those "well-meaning supporters" of suffrage who sought their objective by new and burdensome remedies.

While London urged continued agitation in the states, he warned against diverting the entire strength of the movement to the states. "The theory that the United States ... is an aggregation of states is no longer true. We are an industrial unit, we are a political unit and a national unit. There is no question, no difficulty, no evil which can confront a State without affecting the interests of the entire country. After all, the geographical and artificial separation into States cannot be permitted to stand in the way of the nation's progress."[70]

During the 1915 Socialist election campaign, in which London took an active role, he continued to fight vigorously for women's suffrage.[71] On October 17 and October 22, London and Eugene Debs shared the platform at rallies, and both urged passage of the New York suffrage amendment. London ridiculed anti-suffragists "who think as their ancestors did, or not at all." Women would be justified, he exclaimed, if they refused to obey any laws until they received recognition as human beings. He predicted, however, that women would win the ballot without any "strong revolutions."[72]

Despite London's efforts and Socialist Party support, the New York suffrage amendment went down to defeat by some two hundred thousand votes.[73] On November 3, the day after the election, London announced that he would reintroduce the Susan B. Anthony Amendment in Congress.[74] He feared, however, that it would not come up for a vote in the Sixty-Fourth Congress. The growth of interest in preparedness and the Wilson administration's lack of interest in the suffrage question indicated that the amendment would more than likely be buried somewhere in committee.[75]

The thirteen-month interval between his election and the meeting of the Sixty-Fourth Congress was hectic for Meyer London. He had continued his activities on behalf of the workers, and had championed the cause of women's suffrage. Believing, as did most Socialists, that selfish, commercial, imperialistic rivalries in Europe had brought the war, London maintained that it was the duty of the United States to avoid a war that would divert attention from needed domestic reform. Moreover, he insisted that the United States, as the leading non-belligerent, should do everything possible to end hostilities. Thus, when London took his seat in Congress on December 6, he continued his fight for peace and allied himself with the opponents of President Wilson's preparedness program. Despite the fact that the preparedness issue consumed most of his energy, London persistently pressed for social reform. Although opposed by conservatives on both sides of the aisle because of his "radical" beliefs, his colleagues in Congress generally respected him as the spokesman for the Socialist movement in the United States.

6

The Sixty-Fourth Congress: The Specter of War

> We must defend against attack. No sacrifice can be too great for that. We must not permit ourselves to be aggressors. We must oppose any policy that may lead to war.—*Meyer London,* Congressional Record, *64th Congress, 1st Session, 5,021.*

The Sixty-Fourth Congress convened in Washington on December 6, 1915, at a time when the Wilson administration and the country focused on the European conflict. Wilson had launched his preparedness drive, and would urge the new Congress to act upon his preparedness proposals. As the sole Socialist member of Congress, London voiced his party's opposition to the war, warned against the danger of preparedness, and proposed a Socialist plan to end the war. He also strongly opposed American intervention in Mexico. Although his voice proved a cry in the wilderness, London persisted in his fight against the war mania. He considered it his duty as an American and as a Socialist to sound the alarm.

London arrived in Washington a few days before his forty-fourth birthday. Buoyed by his election victory, he immediately concerned himself with the important issue of committee assignments.[1] Before leaving New York, he warned congressional leaders that unless he received seats on the Labor and Immigration committees, he would block "pet" private bills by refusing to give unanimous consent to such measures. The *New York Call* reported that Republican minority leader James R. Mann, who determined committee assignments for the Republicans, Progressives and other minority members, insisted that London receive only one committee assignment. London argued that he deserved two since Eugene Debs had received nearly one million votes in the 1912 presidential election. Democratic leaders indicated to the *Call* that they would resolve the matter.[2]

Determined to win at least two committee posts, London asked Democratic members of the House Ways and Means Committee for their assistance in obtaining seats on the Labor and Immigration committees. He pointed out that he had devoted most of his public life to the interests of labor and the immigrant, and that his constituents considered the immigration issue of vital importance. If assigned to the Labor and Immigration committees, he could continue in Congress the work that concerned him most. "In all fairness," London said, "I should not be denied that opportunity."

London subsequently met with various members of the Democratic leadership and informed them that he was not pleading, but stating his position with a full awareness of his rights and his opportunity to defend them. Several Democrats, including the majority leader, Claude Kitchin, agreed to help him. They recognized the justness of his demands and acknowledged that to allow Republican minority leader Mann to determine committee assignments for him constituted reasonable ground for complaint. Kitchin promised to do everything possible to get the Democratic caucus to protect London's independence.[3]

London achieved partial success. Due to an apparent compromise between the Democratic and Republican House leadership, the House rules were amended for London's benefit. The Ways and Means Committee and the Labor Committee were each increased by one member. The Republicans obtained an additional seat on the former, and London received an assignment to the latter.[4] He did not, however, attain a seat on the Immigration Committee.[5] Instead, he received seats on the Committee on Mines and Mining and the Committee on Expenditures.[6] Nevertheless, London won recognition as the representative of a minority separate and distinct from the Republican and Progressive parties. He also received assurances of friendship and cooperation from all sides in matters not affecting party policy. "Democrats, Republicans and Progressives," the *Call* commented, "have shown more than the ordinary courtesies to the new member."[7] Thus, from the beginning of his service in Congress, London established a cordial working relationship with the Democratic leadership.

Like Victor Berger, who preceded him in Congress, London faced responsibilities more demanding than other freshmen congressmen. London not only represented the people of the Twelfth Congressional District, but the nearly one million voters who had cast their ballots for Eugene Debs in 1912. Socialists everywhere believed that, as their sole representative in Congress, London should heed their desires. They flooded his mail with demands that he speak on a variety of subjects.[8] Fortunately, London had two able secretaries, Laurence Todd, a veteran Washington newspaperman, and Charles Solomon, a former *Call* writer, who handled much of the detail that might otherwise have overwhelmed him.[9] The *New York Call* pleaded with its readers to leave London free to work. "Do not burden him with casual questions and with a thousand requests for this and that. The whole working class needs him free to be constantly on the job, alert and keen."[10] London also received numerous invitations to speak at meetings, but seldom accepted them. He explained that he had too much to do in Washington even when Congress was not in session. Furthermore, his job was in Washington. Those on the other side, he warned, might wipe his out successes during his absence.[11] London seldom missed a session of Congress.

The Sixty-Fourth Congress opened at noon on December 6, and as his first legislative action, London introduced a Socialist proposal urging the president to summon a conference of neutral nations to offer mediation to the belligerents.[12] Matters proceeded routinely with the Democratic majority electing Champ Clark as Speaker of the House. London voted "present" rather than favoring either candidate.[13]

On the following day, President Wilson appeared before a joint session of Congress to deliver his Annual Message. Wilson emphasized preparedness, a new shipping bill, and patriotism. The American people, the president said, yearned for liberty and peace. They considered a just war as one which gave a people the right to defend themselves against aggression. If a defensive war should occur, it would require "disciplined might." The War Department, therefore, had developed plans to strengthen the army. Wilson described them in detail, and stated that they were "absolutely imperative now." The president then presented the Navy Department's five-year program to give the country a navy "fitted to our needs and worthy of our traditions."

Wilson called upon Congress to pass a shipping bill providing for a merchant marine that would help the country attain true economic and political independence. The United States also had to prove the sincerity of its professions about democracy; hence the need for legislation to expand self-government in the Philippines and Puerto Rico. In addition, new taxes were necessary to provide for enlarging the military. The president then denounced citizens of foreign birth who had "poured poison into the very arteries of our national life." Wilson requested legislation to preserve the honor and self-respect of the country. "Such creatures of passion, disloyalty, and anarchy must be crushed out."[14]

London, although captivated by the "beautiful language" of the message, found much to criticize. His first impression, he told the *New York Call*, was that Wilson's preparedness plan "was calculated to keep the mind of the country on remote and improbable difficulties, so as to divert it from questions calling for immediate answer." As for the hyphenate question, London stated that Socialists had no sympathy for those who utilized opportunities they enjoyed in this country to promote the interests of other governments. "But we would put under the same ban those who in the name of patriotism and in the name of Americanism, claim that the interests of the great masses of

Americans are identical with the interests of their exploiters." American Socialists, London declared, had a duty to repudiate the "monstrous doctrine" of ethnic distrust implicit in Wilson's message.[15]

London further elaborated on the president's address in the *American Socialist*. The Wilson administration, he charged, had joined the Republicans in betraying the country to militarism. The main theme of the address had been preparedness. But all the efforts to arm the country could not "compensate the United States for that loss of strength and that deep wound which will be caused by the attempt to divide the people into 'loyal' and 'disloyal.'"

London also criticized Wilson's failure to suggest remedies for the industrial evils revealed by the United States Commission on Industrial Relations. "The industrial program of the Democrats," he wrote, "seems to be exhausted, just as the labor issue had been met and all labor problems solved." London found it astounding that the president had not mentioned the important work performed by the Commission. This indicated the lack of thinking by the Democrats on the needs of an industrial nation. The president's proposal, London noted, to extend self-government to the Filipinos was characteristic. "The solemn statement is made that it is our duty to keep our promises to the helpless and to those dependent upon us. After this announcement we discover that no hope of emancipation is held out to the Filipino."

Nor for that matter had Wilson offered any new ideas on taxation. Those who had accumulated fortunes, a source of danger and corruption, were not threatened by taxes. The president had ignored the income tax. It appeared that the Democrats had run out of new ideas. The party expected "to thrive on intensifying national prejudices and ... in keeping the people directed toward distant and imaginary enemies ... so that they would ignore their real enemies, the captains of industry."[16]

From the beginning of the congressional session Wilson's preparedness program encountered difficulty. In the House of Representatives some fifty congressmen, including London, opposed expansion of the military. The core of this group consisted of approximately thirty Democrats from rural districts in the South and West, led by Claude Kitchin, the House majority leader. They knew, moreover, that a number of midwestern Republicans and usually loyal Democrats would support them when preparedness measures came to a vote.

Additional opposition came from congressmen who disliked the Continental Army scheme proposed by Secretary of War Lindley M. Garrison. Garrison's plan called for enlarging the Regular Army. He also proposed that the National Guard no longer serve as the ready reserve. A new reserve consisting of four hundred thousand men named the Continental Army would replace the Guard as the first line of defense. In addition to opposition to the Continental Army, a powerful National Guard lobby urged the House Military Affairs Committee to reject Garrison's plan and to rely for defense upon a strengthened National Guard. John Hay, chairman of the committee, although favoring the Guard, had agreed to support Garrison's plan out of loyalty to the administration.

Garrison failed to win support for the Continental Army scheme when he testified before the committee in early January 1916. Hay subsequently informed Wilson on January 11 that he could no longer support the Continental Army plan and that only three members of the Military Affairs Committee favored it. Hay proposed, instead, federalization of the National Guard. Despite administration efforts, the committee members refused to alter their position, and during the next month an impasse existed much to the delight of the anti-preparedness forces.[17]

Meanwhile, the House considered extending the emergency war taxes of 1914, due to expire on December 31, 1915. A sharp drop in import duties due to the disruption of international trade had necessitated these taxes. The administration, confronted with a deficit of from sixty to one hundred million dollars, had prodded Congress to impose a variety of internal taxes to raise an additional one hundred million dollars.[18] In his Annual Message on December 7, 1915, Wilson sought an additional three hundred million dollars to pay for his preparedness program.

During the debate on the emergency war taxes, London delivered his maiden speech in the House. The *New York Evening World* reported that on December 16, during "a fierce debate over the war tax bill, in which only party leaders and veterans participated, Meyer London suddenly stood in the well of the House and raising his hand bashfully to the Speaker, like a boy in school," asked for unanimous consent to address the House. London, the report went on, received ten minutes.

Speaking softly with a "distinct foreign accent," London asked the House to forgive his lack of modesty in seeking to address it on such a vital issue during his first two weeks in Congress.[19] He then announced, to the applause of the Democrats, that he intended to vote for the extension of the emergency war tax bill despite several "oppressive" provisions which imposed unnecessary burdens on the American people. London explained that he would support the measure because it was an emergency act in the fullest sense of the word.

London questioned the sincerity of Republican opposition. The Republicans had not offered a viable alternative. "It was perfectly sickening to listen to those worn-out repetitions of tariff, tariff, tariff.... They said nothing instructive, nothing definitive, nothing that would lead us to better things." The entire tax system, London proclaimed, needed revision. Not only was it unscientific; it was outmoded. Democrats and Republicans failed to realize that new times required new methods. As for himself, London stated that he favored an income tax, an inheritance tax and taxes upon land held for speculative purposes.[20] The House later approved the resolution extending the war revenue taxes for an additional year by a vote of 205 to 189, with London voting for the measure. At the conclusion of his comments, a number of congressmen surrounded London and "showered him with congratulations."[21]

A few days later Congress recessed for the holiday season, and London returned to New York. He told the *New York Call* that he hated to leave Washington, for much work remained to combat the militarists.[22] He would use the recess to fulfill his campaign pledge to review his activities in Congress with his Twelfth District constituents. He urged congressmen near their district to follow his example. By reporting on current business, they could either gain constituent support or enable them to "thrash out" differences.[23]

On the evening of December 22, London spoke to nearly one thousand persons. He warned the audience not to expect too much of him because complex congressional committee rules prevented a congressman from accomplishing very much. President Wilson, he went on, had impressed him as a "big man" behind whom many Democrats tried to hide their own smallness. Wilson, however, had played into the hands of those individuals who profited from preparedness. He was "frightened by a mere shadow flung across the ocean by the nightmare of war that is being enacted on the other side." Although London "theoretically" favored preparedness, he opposed the present agitation which was "largely foolish, artificial, and to a great extent political and entirely unjustifiable."[24]

London then discussed his peace resolution which he believed in accord with international socialism. London also touched upon the hyphenate question. He urged all naturalized citizens to abandon the hyphen and to merge themselves "heart and soul" with the American people.

After his remarks, the audience thanked him profusely. London protested that he did not deserve thanks for doing his duty. "I am a Socialist," he said. "If the doctrine of Socialism means anything, it means that an officeholder is the servant of the people. I am the servant of the East Side, and as such I owe to them a regular report."[25]

On the following evening, London addressed another meeting. He discussed domestic issues including social insurance, immigration, labor bills, suffrage, prohibition, and government ownership of public utilities.[26] Pleased by the response to his reports, London announced similar meetings on the last Saturday and Sunday of every month.[27] In a short time, he said, "people from surrounding districts will ask why their representatives don't report to them. When they discover why, they may replace them with individuals who will report."[28]

On January 4, 1916, London returned to his duties in the nation's capital, and on January 18, he delivered his first major speech in the House on the most important issue of the day, the international crisis. For almost forty-five minutes London received the close attention of House members as he presented a Socialist analysis of the war,[29] criticized preparedness and called for adoption of his peace resolution. His fellow congressmen frequently interrupted him with applause and peppered him with questions at the conclusion of his remarks. London pointed out that although everyone talked about preparedness, nobody questioned its purpose. It appeared, he stated, that because modern wars involved allied nations, the United States should prepare against the possibility of fighting a combination of nations. This country might, therefore, need a navy large enough to fight the combined navies of the world and the largest army in American history.

He then examined those elements who favored preparedness. The most important group was munitions manufacturers who profited from the sale of their "death-dealing instruments." A second group was American imperialists who wanted an army and navy "large enough to coerce Europe ... and the rest of the world into yielding to American capital new spheres of influence, new colonies, and new empires." London called the third group "the old women of both parties" who were "scared out of their wits," and who sincerely believed that someone was going to attack the United States.

Lastly was the political element, the Republican Party. The Republicans, he explained, knew that a larger army and navy would require additional taxes, and believed they would benefit politically from a tax increase passed by the Democrats. London pointed out the need to fight "the insanity of preparedness with the sane, rational, insistent demand for international peace." He had introduced his peace resolution for that reason. The principles contained in the resolution, he continued, resulted not from his imagination, but from serious study. Ten European peace groups had worked out a series of principles for a durable peace, and all of these groups favored a majority of the principles embodied in his resolution. International Socialist congresses had also adopted similar principles. His resolution, he declared, presented a consistent, logical, intelligent plan for addressing the peace issue.

Every member of Congress, he asserted, should study his proposal. They could do nothing nobler than to help end the war. Those who believed that congressional discussion of foreign policy was improper, London stated, were mistaken. He called for an end to the narrow view of patriotism which held "My country right or wrong." The American people should adopt a nobler and higher doctrine: "My country must always be right."

During the question-and-answer period that followed, several congressmen asked London for the position of the American Socialist Party if the United States was attacked. He responded that although the international Socialist movement opposed war, it recognized the right of a nation to defend itself. In the eventuality of attack, every Socialist would consider it his obligation to "rush to the defense of America." They also asked whether London thought the country could do without an army and navy. He replied that the less the United States relied on its military forces the better off it would be. But, he added, as long as other countries maintained military establishments, the United States needed some physical power.

London thus joined a number of prominent Socialist leaders, including Victor Berger, Morris Hillquit and Charles Edward Russell, who had ignored the official party resolution adopted in September 1915.[30] His views resembled those of Hillquit who had taken the position that the United States would be justified in strengthening its military establishment if there was any possibility of becoming involved in the war. But Hillquit denied that such a danger existed. Charles Edward Russell also supported preparedness, and was the first well-known Socialist to make a public demand for war against Germany. London was not prepared to go that far.[31]

In commenting on Russell's position, London said that he had seen Russell in Washington and "we agreed to disagree on the matter of preparedness." While he disagreed with Russell's position, London defended his right to express it. The Socialist movement understands that it must allow a great deal of latitude on such a question as preparedness due to world conditions. The war has caused so many problems that an individual must have an opinion on them. "Such problems cannot be reduced to a matter of dogma."[32] London, no doubt, had in mind his own views which were at odds with Socialist Party policy.

Victor Berger's *Milwaukee Leader* pointed out the contradiction between London's position on defensive war and that of the Socialist Party. "Unfortunately," the *Leader* commented, "if the policy to which the Socialist party has been committed should be pursued by the federal government all that Mr. London could do, all that any American citizen could do would be to sacrifice his life." Party instructions bound London to vote against preparedness. Unless, he ignored the party, he could not support any defense measure. The *Leader* questioned the necessity for this contradiction. Why, it asked, should any American Socialist be placed in London's position? The American Socialist did not differ from his German, French, or English comrades. "If necessity should arise, he would fight to defend his home and children." American Socialists had allowed "sentimentalists," who refused to face the facts, to commit them to a negative and unrealistic program. The party should "formulate a constructive policy and cease voicing a futile and insincere protest against the most natural of all instincts—the instinct of self-preservation."[33]

Not all American Socialists willingly accepted the concept of defensive war. The anti–*Forward* wing of the Jewish radical movement, consisting of the Jewish Socialist Federation, the Jewish Socialist Labor Federation and those in the anarchist movement, steadfastly opposed all capitalist wars, offensive and defensive.[34] Letters criticizing London's position appeared in the *New York Call* and the *American Socialist*. One writer denied London's right to commit every Socialist in the United States to fight for his country if attacked. Since the party had made no official statement as to a Socialist's duty in such an event, London had no right to speak for his fellow Socialists.[35]

The Kings County (Brooklyn) Socialist Local also objected to London's stance. Albert Pauly, the local's executive secretary, wrote London in March 1916 that it had resolved that "the working class had no country to defend," and that London's comments in Congress were considered "unsocialistic." He informed London that the local had refused to distribute his speech and requested him to attend a meeting to discuss his views.[36]

Despite criticism, London refused to modify his position. In a report to his constituents on January 30, he declared that he would never favor nonresistance. He refused, however, to support "any policy which might lead to a war for vengeance."[37] During the armed ship controversy, London pointed out that he had introduced a resolution urging Congress to declare "that, except when repelling an enemy invasion of the territory of the United States, there can be no justification for a resort to arms."[38]

London also struck back at his critics. At a meeting on March 26, he sharply criticized Socialists who wanted peace at any price. Socialists, he told the audience, opposed war as a matter of principle. "Our duty is to oppose all influences ... that will embroil us in combat. However, once in the war, the situation changes. No man is fool enough not to resist when his country is invaded. A revolutionist does not necessarily have to be a fool."[39]

Two days later, London told the House that he disagreed with Socialists who maintained that the working class was oppressed, and therefore, the worker had no home to defend. "Once again, he differentiated between a defensive war and a war of aggression. "We must defend against attack. No sacrifice can be too great for that. We must not permit ourselves to be aggressors. We must sternly oppose any policy that may lead to war."[40]

In the meantime, London continued his efforts on behalf of the peace resolution he had introduced in the House on December 6 and which Senator Henry Lane, a Democrat from Oregon, had subsequently introduced in the Senate on December 13. London, enthused by Lane's action, declared, "I am beginning to feel that I shall neither be alone or lonesome."[41] London's resolution, which was substantially in accord with the program adopted by the Socialist Party's National Executive Committee in May 1915, had been received favorably by Socialists and non-Socialists.[42] The *New York Call* urged Socialists to write their congressmen and senators in support of the resolution. London, the Socialist daily stated, "had done his job well, and it was now up to the rest of us to do ours."[43]

Berger's *Milwaukee Leader* questioned whether wars could be ended by resolutions. Nevertheless, London's plan had one important feature. It recognized that the question of war and peace interested all nations and not merely the belligerents. "It is based on the thought that peace, if it is to be more than a truce, must be determined by an international gathering of sufficient power to remove some of the causes of war." The adoption of London's resolution, the *Leader* concluded, might set in motion forces that would end the war or make peace more desirable.[44]

Louis B. Boudin, a leading left-wing Socialist and emerging London critic, wrote in the *New Review* that the Socialist Party of America was "to be congratulated on its good luck in having in Meyer London a representative who truly represented the sentiment of the great majority of its membership with respect to Peace, and who will do justice to its character of a true Peace Party." The introduction of London's peace resolution in Congress was very important, Boudin stated. "But even if it should not have the immediate result intended to be achieved thereby, ... it will nevertheless have done an immense service to the cause of Peace, by largely offsetting the great damage done that cause by President Wilson's preparedness message, and by serving as a clarion call to Socialist parliamentarians of some of the warring countries of how far they have wandered from the path of true Socialist internationalism."

Boudin noted, however, that London had erred in outlining the peace terms. This would detract from the peace resolution's value "as a crystallizer and unifier of Socialist sentiment in this country as well as abroad." Boudin recognized the difficulty in drafting peace terms that would satisfy all Socialists. Nevertheless, he said, a list of peace terms based upon the following rules would reduce friction to a minimum. First, include only those demands upon which most Socialists could agree in peace time. Second, eliminate those issues not directly related to the war. Finally, avoid including slogans of the belligerents or their supporters. London, Boudin asserted, had not followed these rules. Hence, his peace terms were "far from satisfactory."[45]

London's resolution received favorable comment abroad. An American newspaper correspondent in England, summarizing British press comment, stated that "quite unprecedented deference, not to say complaisance, characterizes the British reception of Mr. London's joint resolution." The British

6. The 64th Congress: The Specter of War 107

reaction was all the more striking, he went on, when compared with the statements made about Henry Ford's peace expedition. The *London Star* had called London's peace terms "within the range of practical politics." The *Manchester Labor Leader* thanked London on behalf of the English Independent Labor Party for his leadership. There was not, however, the writer concluded, any "responsible intimation that Mr. London's project, even if carried through, would lead the belligerents to accept mediation."[46]

London also received "decidedly friendly" messages from members of Congress. One such letter came from Democratic representative Warren Worth Bailey, an anti-preparedness leader and publisher of the *Johnstown* (Pennsylvania) *Democrat*, who wrote London that he had read the resolution with "much interest." Bailey said that although he had not given the matter thorough consideration, he was "in the main in sympathy" with London's position and "would be glad to see some step taken which might lead to a completion of the frightful struggle ... in Europe and to the acceptance of the principles of reason and justice along lines similar to those suggested by you."[47]

Gratified by the response to his proposal, London stated that at no other time in the history of this country had such an opportunity presented itself to the people and the president. Recent statements by the German chancellor von Bethmann-Hollweg and the British prime minister Herbert Asquith indicated that the belligerents would listen to mediation offers. A determined effort by a great neutral power such as the United States would end the "greatest agony the world has ever suffered."[48]

On December 18, 1915, the National Executive Committee of the Socialist Party, after a communication from London detailing the action he had taken, approved a motion expressing its pleasure with the introduction of London's peace resolution in Congress. The committee approved a plan for a nationwide campaign which included the passage of resolutions and the circulation of petitions at mass meetings, furnishing Socialist and labor papers with material for publication on the subject, requesting Socialist parties of the leading neutral countries to introduce similar resolutions in their respective parliaments, and the selection of a committee of three by the National Executive Committee to meet with President Wilson to request support for London's proposal. It also instructed the committee to protest emphatically, on behalf of the million Socialist voters, against the administration's preparedness program. Subsequently, the National Executive Committee appointed Eugene Debs, Morris Hillquit and James H. Maurer to see the president.[49]

On December 27, Walter Lanferseik, the executive secretary of the Socialist Party, wrote President Wilson requesting an early meeting with the committee to discuss London's peace resolution. Wilson agreed to a meeting on the morning of January 25.[50]

Although most Socialists endorsed the program adopted by the National Executive Committee, Victor Berger's *Milwaukee Leader* took exception. It referred to the mission of Debs, Hillquit, and Maurer as a "fool's errand." It criticized the National Executive Committee's faith in protests, petitions and resolutions as "childlike in its simplicity." Why, asked the *Leader*, should Wilson support a Socialist resolution when his supporters had flooded Congress with resolutions? "If capitalism is the cause of war, if capitalism creates conditions where war is one of its phases, as the Socialists contend, why expect the 'managing committee' of one of the greatest capitalistic governments in the world to strip its coasts of their defenses and leave itself naked to hostile forces, only in order to please a committee of the Socialist Party?" The *Leader* concluded that Debs, Hillquit and Maurer should not undertake such a "fool's errand."[51]

On January 25, Hillquit, Maurer and London met with the president for more than a half hour. London replaced Debs who declined to serve on the committee although he agreed with the resolution. Debs believed that a meeting with Wilson would prove "futile."[52]

During the meeting, the committee informed the president that the belligerents were ready to negotiate. They emphasized the main aspects of London's resolution which eliminated the possible objection that peace at this time favored the Central Powers. The peace proposal removed the seeds of future wars which lurked in heavy indemnities and forcible annexation of territories. By stressing gradual disarmament and an international court of justice, it would supplant the present "brutal method" for resolving international disputes.

The committee also called attention to the deplorable condition of Eastern European Jews. The civic and political status of the Jews, particularly in Russia, had not improved since the war began; they had, in fact, become more intolerable. Wilson expressed interest in the suggestion that an official statement from him would influence the Russian government. The president also told London that he would like to meet him again to further discuss the situation.[53] A few days later the House Committee on Foreign Affairs announced that it would hold hearings on London's peace resolution on February 24.[54] In preparation, London sent letters urging various interested groups and individuals to testify.[55] The *New York Call* also appealed to Socialists and humanitarians in the country to participate.[56]

During the next several weeks, the Socialist Party intensified its campaign on behalf of the resolution. The National Executive Committee asked Hillquit and Maurer to represent it at the hearings. Petitions in support of the resolution were circulated throughout the country.[57] Socialist papers urged their readers to send letters, postal cards and petitions to their congressman or to

6. The 64th Congress: The Specter of War   109

Left to right: James H. Maurer, Morris Hillquit and Meyer London at the White House after meeting with President Wilson on January 25, 1916. *New York Call.*

Henry D. Flood, chairman of the Committee on Foreign Affairs.[58] An appeal from London appeared in the *American Socialist*. "We need all the help we can muster," he wrote, "from within and without the party to make this hearing a big event."[59]

As the hearings approached, support for the resolution increased, London received numerous letters and petitions, as did the Foreign Affairs Committee.[60] The Socialist Party Convention of New York County endorsed London's efforts against "capitalist materialism."[61] It urged all Socialists to give him their loyal support. Many non–Socialist organizations endorsed the resolution. The Anti-Preparedness League, the Women's Peace Party, the United Peace Society and the National Workman's Committee on Jewish Rights indicated that they would send spokesmen to the hearings.[62]

London also received support from abroad. The National Executive Committee cabled Socialist leaders in Europe seeking their approval of the resolution. Socialist parties in Sweden, Holland, Norway and Denmark responded favorably. Halemar Branting, the Socialist leader in the Swedish Parliament, indicated his party's endorsement. In addition, he informed London that the Swedish Socialists had begun to canvass Socialist opinion in neutral European countries as to the possibility of combined effort to end the war.[63]

The committee hearings on London's resolution began on February 24.[64] London told the committee that he would take little time since he believed the resolution was self-explanatory. Three groups of speakers would testify: first, representatives of the American Socialist Party which had endorsed the entire measure; second, representatives from labor unions, the Society of Friends, the Women's Peace Party and several participants in the Ford peace expedition; and finally, members of various ethnic groups who favored evacuation of invaded territory and liberation of oppressed peoples.[65]

In his remarks to the committee, Morris Hillquit declared that the warring nations now realized the horror and futility of war, and the common people favored immediate peace. Their enthusiasm for war had lessened. Only the United States, he asserted, could promote a peace acceptable to both sides. "Is it conceivable," Hillquit asked "that if representatives of half the world's population through their governments ... addressed themselves to the belligerents with an offer of peace and mediation that such an address would remain unheeded?" Hillquit also emphasized the need to remove all political and civil disabilities imposed upon the Jewish people, the need for gradual disarmament, and the need for an international court of arbitration. The latter two, he declared, would reshape the world.[66]

The second session of the hearings began the next day with J. Hampton Rich, editor of *Our Rural Home and Carriers' Messenger*, the official publication of the Farmer's Educational and Cooperative Union. Rich told the committee it could best serve civilization by adopting a peace resolution.[67]

Many organizations urged adoption of the resolution in written statements. As the hearings drew to a close, London urged the committee to consider the resolution on its merits. "The Socialists," he noted, "have some sense ... on the subject of international peace. Had our advice been followed, there would have been no war in Europe."

London also noted with pride that at the very time "when we are considering this resolution, arguments to the same purport are being heard in the British Parliament."[68] The committee then adjourned without indicating any early action.

In the weeks following the hearings, Socialists agitated for a favorable report on the resolution by the committee. The *New York Call* urged Socialists to "bombard" Congress with demands to approve London's resolution.[69] "If acted upon," the *Call* declared, "there is every chance in the world that our country may be the final arbiter, and that it might be the one thing needed to lead to permanent disarmament.... If one country follows that course it is possible that the way will be cleared for the peace of the world for all time."[70] The peace terms proposed by London, the Socialist daily declared, were "sane to the last degree and they eliminated for all time that which is said to be the cause of this war—competitive armament." Why, the *Call* asked, is London's resolution not adopted immediately?[71]

On March 8, some two thousand people attended a Socialist rally at Cooper Union to support London's peace initiative. London, who arrived late from Washington, received the "biggest applause" of the meeting. Telegrams were sent to Wilson, leaders of the Congress and members of the House Committee on Foreign Affairs demanding action.[72]

London urged the National Executive Committee of the Socialist Party to organize meetings throughout the country. The committee responded favorably on March 11. It requested Executive Secretary Walter Lanferseik to publish a letter in the *American Socialist* urging Socialist branches and locals to conduct meetings on April 15 and 16 in conjunction with central labor organizations and to send letters to the House Committee on Foreign Affairs. In his call for the meetings, Lanferseik referred to the peace plan as the only sensible proposal. "We should back him [London] with every ounce of our energy, and call upon every organization that is sincerely interested in peace to aid our efforts."[73]

James Maurer, in a report to the National Executive Committee, stated that the resolution had accomplished much good and whether the committee acted favorably or not, it was one of the Socialist Party's great accomplishments in its struggle for world peace.[74] The New York Socialist Party, after reviewing a report from London, also "heartily" approved his resolution, his consistent opposition to preparedness agitation, and his fight against military expansion. The party called upon all Socialists to help rouse public opinion and pledged to return London to Congress.[75] Despite Socialist efforts, the House Committee on Foreign Affairs failed to act on London's proposal.

At the time that London pushed for his peace plan, the Wilson administration became embroiled in new difficulties with the Mexican and German governments. The United States had extended de facto recognition to the Carranza regime in October 1915, and during the next several months, relations improved between the two nations.

However, in early January 1916, the first in a series of events took place which brought the United States and Mexico to the brink of war. Francisco (Pancho) Villa, Carranza's archrival, resented the recognition of Carranza. Villa sought to provoke American intervention, discredit Carranza, and return to power as a national hero fighting to preserve independence. Villa turned against his former American friends and launched a ruthless campaign against American citizens in northern New Mexico. On March 10, Wilson announced an expedition to pursue Villa into Mexico with the sole purpose of capturing him and ending his raids.[76]

London sharply denounced Wilson's decision. The United States government, he stated, should patrol the border rather than order "working-class" soldiers into Mexico to capture or kill the Villistas. London asserted that the administration's statement that this did not constitute armed intervention in Mexico, but was intended to discipline Villa, was "nothing short of a subterfuge of phraseology." The term *punitive expedition* came from European military terminology. "It is armed intervention under another name. It is a diplomatic lie." The American "war lords," London charged, desired a war for business profit."[77]

The economic interests behind the president, London charged, who controlled nearly 50 percent of income-producing wealth of Mexico, would determine the deployment of American troops. American capitalists would do anything to impose their control over the Mexican people. Thus, London concluded, these capitalists would insist that troops remain in Mexico until political conditions made it possible to resume their exploitation of the Mexican people.[78]

On March 14, Representative John Hay introduced a joint resolution authorizing the president to increase and maintain the army at maximum strength during the Mexican emergency. London cast the only dissenting vote in the House.[79] The Senate passed the resolution unanimously on the following day.[80] London asserted that the punitive expedition was the forerunner of a general invasion of Mexico. Villa's raid at Columbus aimed at precipitating American intervention. "I do not impugn the motives of President Wilson," London remarked, "for he like every other man is impotent against the logic of events."[81]

Although alone in opposition to Wilson's Mexican policy, London spoke on March 28 against a bill to finance the expedition. "It was," he explained, "with a deep sense of responsibility and with an intense feeling of sadness that I did vote alone.... I believe, however, that I was right and you were wrong. The President now realized that in the blundering treatment of Mexico no more serious blunder has been committed than this so-called punitive expedition." The army, he warned, would move deeper and deeper into Mexico, and the Mexican people would rally around Villa as a patriot. "I fear that in spite of the pacific and honorable intentions of the President he will be forced by a dishonest press ... to maintain a larger army in Mexico and to spread the area of invasion. Then you will find yourselves at war, not with a bandit but the Mexican people." For that reason, London explained, he had voted against the Hay resolution.

Instead, he proposed that the National Guard and the army protect "every inch" of the border, and he suggested an appropriation of hundreds of millions of dollars for that purpose. However, no American soldier should enter another country, because that meant "laying the foundation for a long war, and war is a calamity." London's pleas went unheeded, and the House adopted the appropriation bill with the Socialist representative once again casting the only negative vote.[82]

As London had foreseen, Pershing's force grew and penetrated more than three hundred miles into Mexico. Alarmed at the size and strength of the American expedition, Carranza began a diplomatic campaign to compel Pershing to withdraw. Although neither Wilson nor Carranza desired war, a clash between American and Mexican soldiers occurred on April 2, at the town of Parral, 180 miles inside Mexico.

Wilson ordered an additional detachment to Mexico in order to pursue the raiders. Carranza, in a note to Secretary of State Lansing on May 22, demanded withdrawal of American troops under threat of war. Carranza also instructed his commanders to resist the American expeditionary force if it moved in any direction but north toward the border. On June 18, Wilson called out the National Guard to protect the American border, and the army prepared for a full-scale invasion of Mexico.[83]

During debate in the House several days later on a joint resolution federalizing the National Guard, London once again criticized Wilson's Mexican policy. He declared that the National Guard should be deployed only within the United States. This, he maintained, would avert war. The United States, moreover, should withdraw its troops from Mexico and protect its border. "There is no dishonor," he told the House, "in withdrawing from Mexico. You are a hundred million strong. Mexico is distracted, writhing in the agony of revolution. No one will doubt that you are powerful enough to defeat Mexico; you are not asked to retire before a stronger army power; ... but you do retire from Mexican soil because you are afraid to commit a wrong, to do an injustice; and I submit that to be afraid is not cowardly, but a manly thing."

Once the United States entered Mexico, London continued, it would not leave without annexing a large piece of its land. The same interests responsible for the Villa raid and punitive expedition would insist upon the retention of Mexican territory "in the name of American dignity, and as compensation for the blood which the American people will pour."[84] The resolution passed the House by a vote of 334 to 2, with George Huddleston, a Democrat from Alabama, joining London in opposition.[85]

Meanwhile, another clash between Mexican and American forces occurred on June 21 at Carrizal during which twelve Americans and twenty-nine Mexicans lost their lives and twenty-three Americans were captured. Wilson demanded the immediate release of the prisoners and prepared to ask Congress for authority to use the military to clear the northern states of "bandit groups."[86]

With war imminent, London returned to New York on June 24 to once again speak against American intervention in Mexico. London told an audience of more than 3,500 that he did not believe that the President was playing politics with the Mexican crisis. Wilson, he asserted, opposed war with Mexico, for it would prevent the United States from acting as the "great pacificator" for Europe. Moreover, the president knew that his efforts to avoid war would make him "irresistible" in November. London urged the American people to appeal to Wilson. "Heretofore, the President has always turned to the dictionary in time of trouble and found a way out. That's what he did when the *Lusitania* was sunk, and there were more lives lost there than were lost in the Columbus raid. It is not too late to prevent war with Mexico. We must demand that we want to know why the American boy should pierce the heart of the Mexican boy against whom he has no grudge." Wilson's intentions, London asserted, were still peaceful.[87]

London's assessment of Wilson's position proved correct. Neither he nor Carranza desired war. Wilson's primary concern was the European conflict. Carranza was preoccupied with domestic difficulties. Therefore, in July they agreed to appoint a joint commission to resolve their countries' differences. With war near in Europe, Wilson in January 1917 ordered Pershing's withdrawal from Mexico. In the meantime Mexico had drawn up a new constitution, and Carranza was elected president on March 11. Two days later the United States extended de jure recognition and sent an ambassador to Mexico.[88]

Meanwhile, a new crisis with Germany occurred when the German government announced on February 10, 1916, that after March 1 its submarines would sink armed merchant ships without warning. Two weeks later, Secretary of State Lansing notified the press that the United States would not warn its citizens against traveling on ships armed solely for defense. Many representatives and senators feared, however, that the president's insistence on the right of Americans to travel into the war zone would lead to war.

On February 23, the Democratic members of the House Foreign Affairs Committee met and agreed to support a resolution introduced by Jeff McLemore of Texas warning Americans against travel on armed belligerent ships. Senator Thomas P. Gore of Oklahoma introduced a similar resolution in the Senate two days later. Newspaper reports estimated that overwhelming majorities in both Houses would approve the Gore-McLemore resolutions.[89]

Wilson met this threat to his control of foreign policy in an open letter on February 24. He declared that he would seek to avoid war. However, he would not allow any abridgement of American rights. The following morning Wilson met with Democratic leaders and reaffirmed his determination to stand by his announced policy. Although some House Democrats still supported a warning resolution, they were unwilling to further challenge the

6. The 64th Congress: The Specter of War

president. A clarification on February 26 virtually ended congressional discontent.[90]

Although in sympathy with the McLemore resolution, London introduced his own resolution on March 2. It urged Congress to declare its unalterable opposition to war as a means of enforcing the claim that Americans may travel on armed belligerent merchantmen.[91] London warned that the United States was rapidly drifting toward war. However, the people, if aroused in time, could prevent the country from "being drawn in to the hopeless abyss of Europe's fate." The time had arrived, London exclaimed, for a showdown between the Congress and the president.[92]

This confrontation never materialized. The Senate responded to the president's request, and on March 3 voted to table the Gore resolution 68 to 14. The House Foreign Affairs Committee agreed the next day to recommend tabling the McLemore resolution.[93]

On March 6, the day before the House voted, a debate on the resolution suddenly erupted. Taking advantage of unanimous consent day, London spoke briefly on the armed ship question. He read his resolution which he said fully covered the situation. He then turned to the Foreign Affairs Committee's recommendation. If adopted, London declared, a matter of "unprecedented magnitude" would be disposed of without any discussion, a "dangerous mistake."

The president had asked the Congress for its opinion. London observed that President Wilson did not believe this request a command to agree with him. Congress should consider the president's proposal as an offer to cooperate in determining foreign policy. "Let us face this big problem as men should face a big problem," London implored. "The motion was a subterfuge." The House, he insisted should not follow the Senate which acted first and debated afterwards. Americans had no interest in quibbles over international law, but feared involvement in the war. A motion to table would dispel this fear.

London called for a full discussion of the entire question. Moreover, the House should declare that the United States had no quarrel with the people of any European country, that any disagreement between this country and a belligerent would be submitted to a board of arbitration, and finally, that although the United States would not waive its rights as a neutral, it would not use force to compel respect for them. In conclusion, London urged adoption of his resolution.[94] The House met the following morning, and debate lasted for seven hours. When the vote finally came, the motion to table the McLemore resolution carried by a majority of 276 to 142, as London voted with the minority.[95]

On the following evening, London told an audience at Cooper Union that the McLemore resolution was a side issue. The American people wanted an answer, not to the right to travel on belligerent merchantmen, but to whether or not this country was on the brink of war. "The American people want Congress to declare, armed merchantmen or unarmed merchantmen, that under no circumstances will this country be engulfed in the maelstrom of war."

London criticized the failure of Congress to respond to the president's request for a showdown. London explained that no principle of worth had governed his vote against tabling the resolution. The question had been whether Congress would choose to be a "fool" or "a damn fool," and it had chosen the latter.[96]

The German government continued its attacks against armed merchantmen, and American citizens continued to travel on belligerent ships. On March 24, 1916, a more crucial test of Wilson's policy occurred when a submarine torpedoed the French passenger steamer *Sussex*. After some hesitation, Wilson issued a virtual ultimatum to the German government. He warned the Imperial Government to immediately abandon its campaign against passenger and merchant ships, or the United States would sever diplomatic relations. Despite objections from the military, the German government announced on May 4 that henceforth its submarines would observe the rules of visit and search before sinking merchant ships. During the next nine months the German government kept its promise, and American opinion toward Germany "softened."[97]

Meanwhile, in early February, Wilson and the House Military Affairs Committee finally resolved their differences. The president, in order to get an army bill, abandoned the Continental Army scheme and accepted federalization of the National Guard. These actions cleared the air and made possible congressional action on his preparedness program. On March 6, the House Military Affairs Committee unanimously reported the Hay bill, which called for a substantial increase in the army and placed the National Guard under War Department control.[98]

Debate began in the House of Representatives on March 17. London told the House that although the Military Affairs Committee might have done much worse, he would oppose any increase in the military. He questioned whether an "extraordinary addition" to the army was essential for national defense. The unanimous report of the Military Affairs Committee indicated that the Democrats and Republicans had surrendered to the "clamor" of the press. They had allowed "two or three dozen individuals in the editorial rooms of the newspapers to fix the policy of the country."

Modern war, London maintained, involved the quest for commercial supremacy, for markets and for spheres of influence. Wars were "shopkeepers'

6. The 64th Congress: The Specter of War

quarrels." Unless this country desired to compete with other nations for markets and the extension of its colonial empire, no need existed for increasing the military. No reason for war existed unless there was a threat to a nation's existence. The United States, London insisted, had nothing to fear. "The very idea that any outside power could attack ... the United States is too preposterous to be entertained by a sane mind." The United States, he asserted, must remain free from militarist ideas. Any increase in the armed forces meant that Congress had yielded to the "false 'preparedness' campaign."[99]

On March 22, London, ever concerned about the use of the National Guard against strikers, and seeking to protect their rights, offered an amendment to the Hay bill, prohibiting the use of the National Guard to break strikes. Nothing, London told the House, undermined the American people's respect for their defenders than the use of the nation's military to suppress strikes. The chair ruled that London's amendment was not "germane," since no court or government agency had defined the word *strike*.

Undeterred, London introduced another amendment stating that the administration should not use the National Guard in connection with any controversy between capital and labor. Once again the chair ruled against him. An attempt by Edward Keating, a progressive Democrat and a member of the Labor Committee, to offer a modified form of London's amendment met a similar fate.[100]

On the following day, the House adopted the Hay bill 402 to 2.[101] London and Fred A. Britten of Illinois voted against the measure, but for different reasons. Britten believed the bill did not provide an adequate increase in the army; whereas London opposed any increase. London explained that he voted against the Hay bill as an American and as a Socialist. A large army threatened the welfare of the workers and obstructed world peace.[102]

During the weeks of controversy over the army bill, the House Naval Affairs Committee worked on a naval appropriations bill. As finally reported by the committee on May 18, 1916, the bill rejected the administration's five-year building program, but provided instead for five battle cruisers, four cruisers, ten destroyers, submarines and smaller craft. Large navy proponents in the House pressed for additional increases.[103] Once again London opposed military expansion.

In a brief speech on May 29, London sarcastically congratulated the National Security League, the Steel Trust and the munitions manufacturers for their success. They had created an irresistible state of hysteria, the Congress had yielded and his protests had fallen upon deaf ears. The Democrats, he charged, had played politics. "Were I in their place, I would have courageously defied the imperialist, the munition[s] maker, the Steel Trust, the war contractor. I would have trusted to the verdict of the American people." An adequate navy, he told the House, served the national interest only if it sought to defend the country against attack. If, however, the policy was one of aggression and imperialism, then the fleet was insufficient, "and you had better vote ... to treble and quadruple your present fleet."[104]

On June 2, London voted with the majority for an appropriation of eleven million dollars for a government armor-plate factory. He also voted with the majority against a Republican "big navy" amendment. The Democrats agreed to increase the number of submarines to fifty and to virtually double the naval aviation appropriation. Thus amended, the naval appropriations bill passed the House by 363 to 4, with London once again in opposition.[105] The Senate, however, passed a "big navy" bill on July 21. Wilson supported the Senate bill and brought heavy pressure to bear on the conference committee. The House conferees resisted for a time, but on August 15, the House gave in and accepted the Senate measure by a vote of 285 to 51.[106]

London remained steadfast in opposition. He called the measure a "waste of the people's money," and informed the House that the bill authorized the largest appropriation for a navy made by any country not at war. It meant that for the current fiscal year every man, woman and child would pay six dollars to support the army and navy while the per capita expenditure for education was only four dollars and fifty-six cents. Moreover, the burden would fall upon the poor people who worked for a living. The bill, London exclaimed, surrendered the United States Treasury to the munitions manufacturers.[107]

The administration also obtained a shipping bill as part of the general preparedness program. As passed in the House on May 20 and accepted by the Senate in mid-August, the bill created a United States Shipping Board which could spend up to fifty million dollars to purchase and construct merchant ships. The board also had authority to regulate rates and services of all vessels engaged in the interstate, coastal and foreign trade of the United States.[108] London supported the shipping bill because it provided for government ownership and control of the merchant marine.[109]

The defense appropriations of 1916 represented a huge outlay and forced Congress to seek additional revenue in an election year. In November 1915, Secretary of the Treasury William G. McAdoo presented a comprehensive tax program that would have placed the heaviest burden of taxation upon the lower and middle classes. It aroused bitter criticism and opposition from radicals and progressives who believed that the wealthy should pay for the preparedness program. Democratic southern and western progressives, who controlled the House Ways and Means Committee, pushed through a tax measure acceptable to labor and farm leaders.[110]

Although London had reservations about the bill, he supported it. Its passage, he believed, would represent an important victory for those favoring a progressive federal tax policy, one based upon the ability to pay. His criticized the inadequacy of the surtax on large incomes, the inheritance tax and the tax on munitions manufacturers. Other provisions of the bill, such as the anti-dumping clause, the Tariff Commission, and the dye stuff provision, London stated, also confirmed the Socialist contention that "no essential difference existed between Democrats and Republicans."[111]

On July 10, London defended the measure against its Republican critics. To the accompaniment of Democratic applause, he chided the Republicans for not openly opposing the income tax. "Afraid to disclose the real reason for their hostility to the measure ..., they argue in a roundabout way that because a small portion of the population in the country pays the larger share of the income tax, that the tax is unequal and unjust." It made sense, London pointed out, that New York and Chicago, the financial, industrial and commercial centers of the country, would pay a larger proportion of the income tax.[112] Shortly thereafter, the House approved the bill by 238 to 142.[113]

The Senate bill, as finally adopted on September 6, went further in taxing the wealthy. In addition to doubling the income tax, the Senate increased the surtax on incomes over twenty thousand dollars to 14 percent, the tax on estates to 10 percent, the tax on munitions manufacturers to 12.5 percent and levied a new tax on corporate capital and profits. The conference committee accepted the Senate bill with few changes, and both Houses adopted the conference report of September 7.[114]

By September 1916, the Wilson administration had largely achieved its preparedness program, despite strong opposition from progressives and peace groups. During the debates in Congress, Meyer London emerged as an outspoken critic of the president's program which he contended would lead the United States to militarism and war. London asserted that since no threat existed to American security, the United States should not prepare for war. It should pursue peace. Hence, he carried on a vigorous though unsuccessful fight for the Socialist Party's peace resolution. London also opposed American intervention in Mexico and demanded the immediate withdrawal of the Pershing expedition. During the armed ship controversy, he pointed out that Wilson's insistence on the rights of American citizens to travel as they pleased would lead to war.

The first session of the Sixty-Fourth Congress faced questions dealing with war and peace. Democrats also realized that this Congress would lead the nation into the presidential election of 1916. Although concerned with the nation's security, President Wilson looked ahead to Election Day and wooed Progressive votes he believed necessary to ensure his reelection. Wilson, who had opposed advanced progressive objectives, reversed himself and supported rural credits, child labor legislation, railroad legislation and other economic and social measures. From his vantage point on the Labor Committee, London vigorously supported bills beneficial to workers, and participated in "the most sweeping and significant progressive legislation in the history of the country up to that time."[115] By so doing, he won the respect of congressional progressives and leaders of the American union movement.

7

The Sixty-Fourth Congress: In Pursuit of Constructive Reform

> Workers should not be asked to assume all the burdens, all the risks, all the hazards of modern industry, with its accidents, occupational diseases, life-sapping intensity, with its sudden rushes and its long slacks, with its constant fears and anxieties.—Congressional Record, 64th Congress, 1st Session, 6,147.

During the first session of the Sixty-Fourth Congress, London proved as vocal on domestic matters as on questions relating to war and peace. He stressed the importance of social reform, and talked learnedly about national social insurance, child labor, the eight-hour day for railroad workers, and immigration. Few members of the House surpassed his insight on economic and social problems. Samuel Gompers counted him among the so-called labor group in the House which consisted of trade union members. He invited London to meet with these House members and representatives of labor to discuss issues of interest to American workers.[1] This afforded London the opportunity to establish a working relationship with colleagues on issues of import to him such as national social insurance.

Shortly after the session opened, London began work on a national social insurance bill.[2] Society, he believed, had a moral obligation to provide assistance to the unemployed worker.[3] On February 19, London introduced a resolution calling for the creation of a national insurance fund to mitigate sickness, disability and unemployment.[4] His primary goal, London asserted, was to prevent the Labor Committee from killing the resolution. He sought extensive public hearings to educate Congress, administrative officials and the general public to the necessity of such a plan. London deliberately omitted administrative details so the issue could be more clearly drawn and not bogged down in details. "I have done," he explained, "what I felt it my duty as a Socialist to do, namely, to bring before the old-party Congressmen not any pet scheme of mine for the development of the district which elected me, as others do, but to present to them the Socialist idea for national affairs."[5]

On March 9, 1916, the House Labor Committee announced that a hearing on London's resolution would occur on April 6.⁶ The National Executive Committee of the Socialist Party endorsed London's plan and appointed Dr. I.M. Rubinow to represent it at the hearing.⁷ Prior to the hearing, London received support from non–Socialists such as Dr. Miles M. Dawson, an authority on social insurance; Professor Irving Fisher, a noted economist and president of the American Association of Labor Legislation; and General W.C. Gorgas, the surgeon general.⁸

The hearing before the Labor Committee took place as scheduled on April 6. Among those who testified on behalf of the resolution were Dr. Rubinow, Dr. Dawson, Dr. John B. Andrews, secretary of the American Association for Labor Legislation, and several state insurance commissioners, insurance actuaries and research workers. They stressed the need for an investigation into the social insurance question, and urged Congress to adopt London's resolution without delay. At the conclusion of that day's testimony, the committee agreed to adjourn until April 11.⁹

On the second day of the hearings, Samuel Gompers testified for some six hours against the resolution. Gompers told the committee that he hoped Congress would investigate the need for social insurance, but he opposed London's resolution. He offered a substitute measure that called for an investigation of voluntary social insurance as contrasted to London's plan for national compulsory social insurance. "To inquire into a subject is one thing," Gompers declared, "but to commit the American government to declarations such as are contained in the London Resolution ... is quite another thing." If London's resolution had called for an investigation, Gompers asserted, he would have suggested changes and urged the committee to report it for favorable action by Congress. "But sirs, on last Thursday, in this committee room there was enacted a drama or a farce of such a tragic or ludicrous character that I cannot permit myself to remain silent or to let the matter go without protest." Not one trade unionist, Gompers charged, had been invited to testify. If the Legislative Committee of the American Federation of Labor had not called London's resolution to his attention, he would not have known of it at all. Gompers later admitted, when questioned by London, that he had, in fact, received a letter from London dated March 20, 1916, calling upon Gompers for suggestions on the measure.¹⁰

Gompers strongly disagreed with testimony that the cost of living had increased 15 percent more than wages in the last twelve years, and that despite trade union activities, the present condition of workers was worse than a decade ago. If true, Gompers declared, the trade union movement had failed, and he had wasted fifty years of service to the labor movement. It was not true, however, he asserted. Unusually high prices, he explained, resulted from abnormal conditions. "There has been, and is now, no force or group of people in the United States ... that have done so much..., with this fundamental problem of protecting and conserving the lives and the rights and the health and the interests ... of the workers, as the much misunderstood and misrepresented trade union movement."[11]

Gompers then discussed specific objections. No evidence, he said, supported London's statement about the employment of "millions of children." The labor movement took pride in its efforts to mitigate child labor and wanted Congress to enact a child labor bill. Gompers also disagreed with those, London included, who charged that methods used to relieve unemployment "had tended to degrade the unemployed into the unemployable." At this point an exasperated London interrupted. "Why," he asked Gompers, "do you try to say these things? I am so good-natured and kind toward the unions that I do not know why you say those things. Where do you find in my resolution an attack upon the trade unions?" Gompers replied that if London had said "whereas some of the methods heretofore employed," he would have made his meaning clearer. "I take it that he did not intend to say those things. I do not think he intended it as a trade union attack."

Section three, Gompers continued, did not provide that the commission should investigate and report so that Congress might take action, but that "it shall be the duty of the commission to prepare a detailed plan for the establishment and maintenance of a national insurance fund." It then stated that needy unemployed workers should receive aid. Thus, Gompers stated, someone would determine when the worker was in need. "The whole scheme, the whole fault, the whole philosophy represented by Dr. Rubinow ... and by Mr. London ... contemplate not individual development, not opportunity for initiatives for voluntary action, but regulation by the state." Although saddened by the illness, the maiming and killing of his fellow workers, Gompers declared that "he would rather see that go on for years and years, minimized by and mitigated by the organized labor movement, than give up one jot of freedom of the workers to strive and struggle for their own emancipation through their own efforts."

Section four, Gompers went on, required the commission to submit a report and recommendations for the relief of unemployment by the "regularization of industry." This meant that the government would not only regulate industry but the workers as well. Gompers also objected to the provision that requested the commission to submit recommendations for establishing industries to be maintained by the federal government.[12]

In conclusion, Gompers repeated that the American Federation of Labor wanted an investigation of the social insurance question. "But we ask that when you recommend an investigation..., it shall be with the understanding that the rights of the workers and the freedom secured by the workers shall not be frittered away by a patch upon our social system and that under the patch shall be a germ that shall devitalize the American citizenship and take away from them the vital principles of freedom of action."[13]

After the hearings, London on April 14 delivered a lengthy speech in the House on social insurance. He reminded his colleagues that until 1912 only the Socialist Party had recognized the problem of unemployment, health insurance and old age pensions on the national level. The time had arrived, he declared, to revise the doctrine of self-help. It had become increasingly difficult to cope with everyday problems single-handedly. While capitalists created corporations, workers joined unions, and the most intelligent elements of all classes joined the Socialist Party. "It is this new kind of self-help which seeks to accomplish the salvation of the great masses through cooperation on the economic and political field that is forcing to the front these new notions translatable into the phrases social legislation, social conscience and social insurance."

London then discussed the social insurance program advocated by Socialists. He divided the program into several categories: unemployment insurance, sickness and disability insurance, encompassing sickness, industrial accidents and occupational diseases; invalidity and old age insurance, and provision for widows and orphans.

Unemployment, he told the House, was neither accidental nor occasional, but an ever-present industrial hazard. Relief, temporary public works, the kindness of employers or vagrancy laws would not cure the problem. Instead, he proposed a national system of unemployment exchanges, a national insurance system and an extensive system of public works. Unemployment exchanges would not provide jobs but would give information to the worker, eliminate waste and centralize the labor market. European nations had developed programs to deal with unemployment on a permanent basis, although London admitted it would be unwise to adopt any European system of unemployment insurance. Such a system, he explained, had to reflect the higher standard of living in the United States, safeguard the individuality of the worker, and allow for the broadest possible cooperation with the labor movement. Moreover, it should be compulsory on employers but not employees. Unemployment insurance, London continued, was not a new theory, but an extension of the principle recognized in accident compensation, as adopted by thirty-one states. Both were risks and incidents of industry. Finally, to minimize and prevent the growth of unemployment, London proposed an extensive public works program.

London then turned to old age pensions and sickness benefits. These, too, did not involve a new principle. The American people, he pointed out, treated with reverence war veterans who required assistance. Workers in need should receive the same consideration. No good reason existed for distinguishing "between the man enfeebled by old age who has been rendering useful service to the country in industry or in agriculture and the former soldier."

Health insurance, he continued, which encompassed every type of disability whether attributable to industrial or non-industrial causes, required community action. "We have learned that society owes an obligation to compensate the worker against loss due to industrial accidents. We are slowly coming to understand that occupational diseases must also be brought within the purview of compensation laws." Health insurance, London asserted, should be organized on a national scale and accepted as a national function, especially since workers could not afford all forms of insurance. They "should not be asked to assume all the burdens, all the risks, all the hazards of modern industry, with its accidents, occupational diseases, life-sapping intensity, with its sudden rushes and its long slacks, with its constant fears and anxieties."[14] In conclusion, London called for a commission to plan a comprehensive national social insurance system.

On June 30, London introduced a modified version of his social insurance resolution.[15] On the following day, much to London's delight, the House Labor Committee unanimously approved the first Socialist measure ever to receive approval by a congressional committee.[16] It created a commission of five, consisting of two employers, two representatives of organized labor, and the secretary of labor as chairman, to "inquire into the causes of unemployment; to inquire into ... systems of insurance, voluntary or obligatory, contributory or non-contributory now in vogue to meet unemployment, invalidity, and sickness, and to what extent the Government of the United States may aid by establishing a Federal insurance system for the benefit of the wage earners ... when in need by reason of involuntary unemployment, whether the unemployment be due to a lack of work, to disability arising by reason of sickness, or to impairment or destruction of earning capacity because of old age."

If the commission found desirable a federal social insurance system or fund, it should prepare regulations for its successful administration, and report the amount of the fund and the method of working with existing insurance systems. The commission would report one year from its date of appointment, and would have fifty thousand dollars for its use.[17]

The resolution approved by the Labor Committee represented a compromise between London's original resolution and Gompers' proposal. Acceding to Gompers' objections, the proposal instructed the commission to investigate social insurance, but did not obligate it to recommend plans for a national insurance system. The committee eliminated references to unemployment relief by the "regularization of industry" and the creation and maintenance of industries by the United States as it did other passages that Gompers had found objectionable. On the other hand, London's proposal to investigate voluntary and involuntary systems was retained, along with provisions for the organization of a national system, if the commission found it desirable. Despite the Labor Committee's unanimous report, the House took no action on the resolution during the first session of the Sixty-Fourth Congress.

In the meantime, the House Labor Committee favorably reported the Keating-Owen child labor bill. This "forbade the shipment in interstate commerce of the products manufactured in whole or in part by children under fourteen, of the output of mines and quarries in which the labor of children under sixteen was involved, and of any products by children under sixteen working at night or more than eight hours a day."[18] London expressed dissatisfaction with the bill because it failed to meet his concept of an ideal child labor bill. He preferred a bill that absolutely prohibited the employment of all children under sixteen years of age. Nevertheless, he supported the bill because it represented a distinct improvement over present conditions.[19]

Debate on the Keating bill took place in the House on January 26. By arrangement, London spoke last on behalf of the measure. He told the House that he considered it merely a step forward. "When you regulate child labor you regulate a vice. By regulating a vice you retain it." Instead of regulating child labor, Congress should eliminate it. Constitutional arguments that the bill represented an encroachment upon states' rights received little sympathy from London.

He also questioned the sincerity of those who opposed the bill. The National Association of Manufacturers which insisted that such legislation lay within the exclusive power of the state argued in state legislatures that industry would be destroyed without uniform legislation throughout the country. The child, therefore, bore the brunt of the contest. "The child's life is being crushed, while the merry argument goes on. What shall it be, the State or the Nation, that is to save the child from perdition? The answer of the commercial soul is neither." London pointed out that the courts had sustained laws prohibiting the use of mails for sending lottery tickets and the transportation of women from state to state for immoral purposes. Why, therefore, should courts refuse to uphold a law which sought to protect the health and well-being of children?

The proposed measure, London repeated, merely scratched the surface of the "evil." It failed to adequately deal with the exploitation of children. "There is too much sham, too much hypocrisy, too many crocodile tears about our present child-labor legislation, and entirely too little constructive action. We must eliminate child labor. We must educate the child. We must help the parent in his struggle for existence."[20]

The House passed the Keating bill on February 2, 1916, by 337 to 46. The Senate Interstate Commerce Committee reported the bill favorably in April, but then sidetracked it primarily due to opposition from the National Association of Manufacturers and state's rights southern senators. The Democratic senatorial caucus, at the insistence of southerners, agreed on July 15 to set aside the child labor bill during the current session.[21]

The Kern-McGillicuddy bill, a model workmen's compensation measure for federal employees, faced a similar fate. It passed in the House on July 12 by an overwhelming majority.[22] During the debate, London attempted to broaden the coverage with an amendment stating, "The term personal injury shall include an injury resulting from an occupational disease." Representative Buchanan of Illinois called upon the House to support the amendment. He urged the greater importance of having compensation for occupational diseases than for accidents. Occupational diseases led to loss of time, an impairment of efficiency, and great doctor bills. The amendment failed 52 to 17,[23] and the bill passed shortly thereafter. Although no active opposition existed in the Senate, the press of other business delayed action.[24]

At this juncture, President Wilson, who had never actively supported the child labor bill or shown much interest in the Kern-McGillicuddy bill, heeded warnings that failure to pass the child labor and federal compensation bill would seriously hurt the Democrats in the 1916 campaign. He concluded that a Democratic victory might hinge upon social-justice progressives who had supported Theodore Roosevelt in 1912. On July 28, Wilson met with the Democratic senatorial steering committee and insisted upon the passage of the child labor and workmen's compensation bills.

The president's intervention proved decisive, as the Senate approved the child labor bill, despite continued southern opposition, on August 8 and the Kern-McGillicuddy bill on August 19.[25] London applauded the president's "judicious" action. Wilson, he said, had transformed the Democratic Party into a national party for the first time in its history. By getting the child labor bill passed, he had proved that the Democratic Party could legislate in the national interest without the approval of the South.[26]

The threat of a major railroad strike gave London yet another opportunity to champion the labor movement. In the early spring of 1916, the four railroad brotherhoods demanded an eight-hour day, with no wage reduction, and with time and a half for overtime. The railroad executives rejected these demands on June 15, but offered to submit them to federal arbitration. Further negotiations between the two sides proved futile. Faced with the disruption of rail service, Wilson invited both sides to the White House and reminded them of the serious consequences of a general strike. Neither would budge. Further attempts by the president to break the deadlock failed, and on August

27, the brotherhood presidents called a nationwide strike of four hundred thousand workers for September 4, 1916.

Two days later President Wilson appeared before a joint session of Congress and outlined legislation to prevent a strike. Congressional leaders balked and informed the president that Congress could not adopt all his proposals. On August 31, Wilson accepted an abbreviated measure drafted by Majority Leader Kitchin and William C. Adamson, chairman of the House Interstate Commerce Committee, imposing the eight-hour day beginning January 1, 1917, and creating a commission to study the railroad problem.[27]

When the House considered the Adamson bill on the following day, London urged approval of the measure because it solved a very serious and critical situation. He then offered an alternative, granting the president authority to nationalize the railroads. "If we legislate in panic now," London commented, "it is because most of us for years refused to recognize the existence of the irrepressible industrial conflict. Every voice has been heretofore heard in Congress except the voice of the great working masses."[28] The House adopted the bill shortly thereafter, 239 to 56, as London sided with the majority. The Senate approved the bill the next day.[29] The Wilson administration had narrowly averted a paralyzing railroad strike. Several days later, London

Meyer London walking on the Capitol grounds in Washington, D.C., 1916. Photographic Collection of Library of Congress.

took the floor to praise the Adamson Act. It ranked, he declared, as one of the greatest events in American history.[30]

Meanwhile, congressional leaders sought to push through a measure that London loathed — the immigration bill sponsored by Representative John L. Burnett of Alabama, supported by the American Federation of Labor, many social workers and anti–Catholic and anti–Jewish elements. This measure sought to exclude adult immigrants who could not pass a simple literacy test. President Wilson had vetoed the bill in 1915, but a bipartisan coalition made another attempt in 1916 to close the doors on immigration from southern and eastern Europe.[31]

In late January of 1916, London testified against the Burnett bill before the House Committee on Immigration. London told the committee that although he had devoted his life to the labor movement, he opposed the literacy test. Organized labor, he stated, had improved not only the working class, but all Americans. Its opposition to immigration was a great mistake. Instead of singling out the immigrant as its enemy, the labor movement should seek unemployment and child labor legislation. People, London asserted, had "the right to go to any part of the world and no man had the right to claim that any section of the globe had been especially set aside for him by the Almighty. God had never issued such a decree."

At this point, Congressman Albert Johnson of Washington, a conservative and restrictionist, asked London whether he included the Chinese. The Chinese, London replied, were also human beings. Chinese and Japanese immigration, however, would add to the existing race problem in this country. "It would be very unwise to create additional race problems."[32] The committee, London also noted, probably did not realize how seriously it would injure victims of religious persecution. He urged the committee to extend the principle of religious toleration to men and women born in other countries who now sought to escape persecution. If the committee reported the Burnett bill, he would fight against it on the House floor.[33]

Debate on the measure began in the House on March 24, and London received fifteen minutes to speak against it. He identified three principal sources of opposition to immigration. First were the nationalists in every country who feared contamination from foreigners. "This kind of human frailty might be excusable in old Asiatic or European nations, but it is utterly incomprehensible when found among the American people, full of the vigor of youth and absorbing unto itself all that is strong and virile in the human stock."

Second were congressmen who represented states that had child labor, undeveloped industry, and submissive workers. These states in fact suffered from the lack of immigration necessary to develop their natural resources.

"The white immigrant bringing with him the germs of discontent, coming here in quest of better opportunities, a rebel seeking a larger freedom is feared by these elements. And the strange thing about it is that it is these very States that have an illiteracy of distressing proportions among the native white population." One wondered, he commented, why those who opposed illiteracy did not end it in their own states.

The third and main source of opposition was organized labor. The working people, locked in battle with stronger capitalist forces, desperately sought to limit the labor supply. Organized labor thus played into the hands of the "unreasoning chauvinist and of the most reactionary labor-hating element in the vain hope that labor will improve its condition." London declared that he opposed immigration artificially stimulated in the interests of capital. Congress should adopt the most rigorous rules to prevent "greedy" employers from taking advantage of helpless immigrants. The use of imported foreign workers as strikebreakers, he asserted, must be prohibited.

Turning finally to the humanitarian aspect, he exclaimed, "I speak for the immigrant, who being a victim of religious, economic or political oppression, seeks access to the United States to improve his condition. If he is illiterate, it is so much more reason why an opportunity should be given to him to give his child the light which was denied to the parent.... As long as the schoolhouse exists there need be no fear of the illiterate."

The average member of organized labor, London concluded, unfortunately did not see beyond the narrow needs of the movement. Instead of viewing every immigrant as an enemy, union leaders should welcome him and teach him unionism. "I protest most solemnly against that narrowness of mind, against the lack of vision, against that absence of sympathy for our fellow men which refuses to a fellow human being a place of refuge." Only the end of all opportunity and the filling up of the land would justify the American people "before their own conscience and before history in adopting the philosophy of Cain, 'Am I my brother's keeper?'"[34]

On the following day, London joined those who opposed an amendment that excluded individuals convicted of or legally charged with a felony or other crime or misdemeanor involving moral turpitude, unless the accused showed to the satisfaction of the proper officials that the charge had no foundation. London argued that a helpless immigrant could not prove his innocence. "Surely, he cannot be expected to carry along with him witnesses who can prove his innocence. He cannot be expected to carry with him documentary proof of his innocence of a charge of which he may have no knowledge up to the moment he is confronted with the charge." The House rejected the amendment 78 to 68.[35]

On March 30, the House debate on the Burnett bill reached its climax.

London objected to Section 19 of the bill which stated that "at any time within five years after entry ... any alien who after entry shall be found advocating the teaching of anarchy, or the overthrow by force or violence the Government of the United States or of all forms of law or the assassination of public officials ... should be taken into custody and deported." He offered an amendment to strike out the words "advocating or teaching the unlawful destruction of all property" and "all forms of law" and substitute the expression "any alien who after entry shall be found by a court of competent jurisdiction guilty of the crime of advocating" and so on. The wording to which he objected, London stated, was meaningless. Moreover, the advocacy of unlawful destruction of property was a crime covered by subsequent provisions.

London expressed concern that some employers would fire strike leaders on the ground that they advocated or taught the unlawful destruction of property. In this way, without due process of law, employers would deprive strike leaders of a jury trial. They would be taken before a board of inquiry, comprised of laymen, without a right to representation by legal counsel, and would be denied the right of habeas corpus. London pointed out that he retained the expression "or the overthrow by force or violence the Government of the United States ... or the assassination of public officials" because that had meaning.

Representative Johnson of Washington asked London whether he endorsed the editorial views of certain foreign-born newspaper editors who advocated industrial sabotage? London replied that he opposed "everything that promoted violence in the labor movement. That is why I am a Socialist; that is why we seek to guide discontent into the intelligent channel of political action. That is why I despise the ... anarchist or any other kind of reactionary."

The most ridiculous and inflammatory statements, London continued, did not come from foreign editors, but from the western states where people spoke with "absolutely no control of their tongues by their brains." Johnson then asked whether or not a faction known as the Red Socialists or direct actionists advocated destruction of property. The term "direct action," London responded, meant nothing more than the right to strike. Proponents of direct action relied on strikes and not politicians. "I personally believe in the right to strike, provided it is conducted in an intelligent manner and provided it is a strike to improve conditions. At the same time I advocate the need of political action and the educational value of political activity." London pointed out that the anarchist movement had been crushed twenty years ago; it no longer existed.

Representative Burnett opposed London's amendment. He declared that "The contention of the gentleman is like anarchy itself. We cannot desire that anarchists ... should be allowed to continue to come here until by the long, slow process of courts we shall determine their rights, and that in the meanwhile anarchists can continue to ply their work." London's amendment was then rejected.³⁶ On the same day, the House passed the Burnett bill by 307 to 87.³⁷

London harshly criticized the bill. It was, he charged, a "dirty political game" arranged to enable congressmen to pose as friends of labor without rendering any service and thus win the labor vote in the coming election. London also doubted that the Senate would take action on the measure during the present session.³⁸ His assumption proved correct; President Wilson blocked Senate approval until after the election.³⁹

London's opposition to the Burnett bill and his criticism of labor's support of it rankled Samuel Gompers and the labor press. During the hearings on London's social insurance resolution, Gompers told the committee that immigration contributed greatly to unemployment in the United States. Yet, he stated, while London minimized the causes of unemployment, he worked to defeat legislation to restrict immigration.⁴⁰ Labor papers also took London to task for his position. They censured and upbraided him, but noted his services and sincere devotion to the labor movement.⁴¹ London also received critical letters. One accused him of lining up with the Catholic Church. "If that report is true, then the sooner you get out of the Socialist Party, the better it will be for the Party."⁴²

Although the House devoted much of its time to domestic matters, it also considered bills proposed by the Wilson administration to extend greater autonomy to the Filipinos and Puerto Ricans. A bill introduced by Representative William A. Jones of Virginia passed the Senate on February 4, 1916, with the so-called Clarke amendment promising independence to the Filipinos by March 4, 1921.

The Catholic hierarchy in the United States, however, fearful that an independent Philippines might expropriate church property, brought pressure upon Catholic House members to oppose the Clarke amendment.⁴³ Subsequently, thirty Democrats, mostly Irish Catholic, joined the Republicans to defeat the Clarke amendment on May 1 by 193 to 151, while London voted for it. The House then approved the original measure and instructed the House conferees to agree to no provision specifying a date for Philippine independence. London voted for the bill, but against the instructions to the conferees.⁴⁴

Several weeks later, in a report to his constituents, London criticized congressional action in regard to the Philippines. The Philippines were strategically vulnerable. From a military standpoint, he continued, the retention by force of ten million people thousands of miles away and near a possible enemy was suicidal. "Retention of the Philippines was a crime against America

7. The 64th Congress: In Pursuit of Reform

and the Philippine people." While Japan might attack the Philippines in case of war with the United States, the islands, if freed, would be safe, since the Filipinos were Christians, and Japan would not subjugate a Christian people.[45]

London expressed similar views in the House on May 29 during discussion of the Navy Appropriation bill. "The imperialist and the munitions maker and the politician," he charged, "have advised you to retain the Philippine Islands so that they may come out and argue that you want more battleships, more cruisers, a greater fleet on the Pacific."[46]

The House began consideration of a new organic bill for Puerto Rico on May 5. Although in sympathy with the measure, London objected to extending American citizenship to Puerto Ricans and to tying suffrage to literacy and property qualifications. Compulsory citizenship, he declared, was absurd. Some day he hoped that Puerto Rico would become an integral part of this country, but it should be its choice, and Congress should not force it upon them. Moreover, the imposition of literacy and property qualifications would disenfranchise 165,000 out of 200,000 voters in Puerto Rico. Congress would, he exclaimed, "assassinate" the rights of the Puerto Ricans to express their views through the ballot.[47] Those who were disenfranchised "will have the right to use the revolver, and will have the right to use violence.... Do you deny to a man the right to express his views through civilized means, through the medium of the ballot? He has the right to use every weapon at his command and every protection. The man whose vote you take away will have the right to put the knife of an assassin into the heart of any man who attempts to govern him against his will."[48]

At this point an unpleasant incident occurred. Representative Austin, a Republican from Tennessee, called London to order. Austin then asked that London's words be stricken from the record. "They were," he charged, "a disgrace to the American Congress." The chairman ordered London to stop speaking and requested that the stenographer strike his words. Still disgruntled, Austin remarked that he wished he could move to expel London from the House.

After several minutes of parliamentary discussion, a motion by Congressman J. Swagger Sherley, a Democrat from Kentucky, gave London an opportunity to clarify his remarks. London expressed his regret that his comments had caused displeasure. Two or three connecting words, he explained, would have removed the objectionable feature of his statement. "The substance of my remarks, the idea that I intended to convey to the House, was this, that in all democratic countries men are given an opportunity to express their ideas, their views, their political convictions by means of the ballot; that in those countries where men are deprived of the opportunity ... they have to use other means, and they do use other means."

London denied advocating the use of violence. As a Socialist, he believed in political activity, and had spent the greater part of his life fighting those who advocated violence. "You have heard me again and again on the floor denounce the use of violence. I am a great believer in intelligence and love. Love, intelligence and education are the great powers— the great force of the improvement of mankind." London repeated that if his remarks conveyed the thought that he espoused violence, he regretted that it was part of the record and agreed to withdraw the words complained of from the *Congressional Record.*

This explanation did not, however, satisfy Austin who demanded that London apologize. The Speaker said that he had done so, and London also stated that he had apologized. The House then approved a motion by Representative Garrett, a Democrat from Tennessee, to allow London to proceed with his statement. Apparently unshaken and undaunted, London repeated that the House would make a mistake in forcing American citizenship upon Puerto Ricans. All political parties on the island, he pointed out, objected to compulsory citizenship. Furthermore, the House would arouse discontent by depriving three-fourths of the Puerto Rican population of the right to express their displeasure through the ballot. "What other means will they possess of giving expression to their desires, to their wishes and political convictions? Why force upon Puerto Rico reactionary laws against which your own fathers contended for fifty years after the establishment of this Republic"[49]

The House discussed the Puerto Rican organic bill again on May 22, and London introduced amendments to eliminate the undemocratic features of the bill. The first sought to remove the requirement that members of the Puerto Rican Senate must own taxable property valued at not less than $1,000. If the Puerto Rican people, London argued, could manage their own affairs, why should Congress impose a property qualification on their senators? "It is a dangerous thing to do. You are giving the propertied class the right to rule the country." This bill, London declared, made a government of the people of Puerto Rico by Puerto Ricans inconceivable. The amendment was rejected without additional debate 42 to 4.[50]

London also tried to change the bill's suffrage provision. He offered an amendment to strike out the words that no person shall vote "who is not able to read and write or who is not a bona fide taxpayer in his own name in an amount not less than $3 per annum." London said that if adopted it would eliminate the most objectionable feature of the bill. The Puerto Rican people had voted for fourteen years and now Congress sought to end this right. "What the American States have freed themselves from, after long and painful effort, you now seek to foist upon Puerto Rico.... What a strange sort of democracy. What a peculiar kind of republicanism."[51]

At this point another heated exchange took place between London and Austin. Apparently disturbed by London's remarks, Austin reminded the House that the Committee on Insular Affairs had unanimously approved the bill. Moreover, the non-voting representative of Puerto Rico in the House supported it. If it was satisfactory to the Puerto Rican people and their representative, "the gentleman who represents the East Side of New York ought to hold his peace."

London immediately demanded that the expression "from the East Side" be stricken. "It is as if I said 'the gentleman from the mountainous regions of Tennessee.' I am a representative from New York." Edward Keating then asked that Austin's remarks be taken down, for he had understood him to say the "gentleman who misrepresents the East Side." Keating later withdrew his request, but insisted, despite Austin's denial, that he had made the statement. After a discussion of London's amendment, it was rejected 59 to 9.[52] The House, however, did not take final action as more important business crowded the calendar in the spring and summer of 1916.[53]

The first session of the Sixty-Fourth Congress ended on September 8, and London returned to New York to begin his campaign for reelection.[54] The National Executive Committee of the Socialist Party called for a vigorous campaign to return him to office and voted five hundred dollars for London's campaign.[55] The Executive Committee of Local New York had begun preparations for the fall election. It decided to concentrate its efforts in London's district and the Twentieth District where Morris Hillquit was the Socialist candidate for Congress.[56] Plans had also been made to coordinate activities in the two districts.[57] Louis Schaffer, who served as London's campaign manager in 1914, once more headed the Twelfth Congressional Campaign Committee.

Early in the campaign an unexpected development occurred. On September 5, the final day for filing nominations, the Democrats withdrew Henry M. Goldfogle in favor of ex-municipal judge Leon Sanders, an independent Democrat. Similar action took place in the Twentieth District. Sanders, head of two important Jewish organizations, the Order of B'rith Abraham and the Hebrew Immigrant Sheltering Home, was popular on the East Side, and Tammany politicians believed that he would cut into the Socialist vote. Julius Gerber, executive secretary of Local New York, charged that Tammany had probably made some "strong" promises in order to persuade Sanders to run. Two years earlier, he pointed out, Sanders had run as an independent for the New York Supreme Court. "He didn't want their support, and as a matter of fact didn't get it. His candidacy now is a sure indication that Tammany is desperate enough to do anything."[58] The *New York Call* viewed the eleventh-hour withdrawal of the "unspeakable" Goldfogle as the "last, expiring gasp of the two machines" in collusion to sacrifice Louis M. Block, the Republican candidate in the Twelfth.⁵⁹

Once again organized labor supported London's candidacy. The International Ladies' Garment Workers' Union, the Amalgamated Clothing Workers and the United Hebrew Trades, along with other unions that endorsed London and Hillquit, organized a Labor Conference to work on their behalf.⁶⁰ The Central Federated Union (CFU) of Greater New York unanimously endorsed London on October 13. It established a committee to coordinate activities with the East Side unions.⁶¹

Ernest Bohm, an official of the union, informed London that the CFU seldom took such unanimous action in a political matter, and "this in itself speaks volumes in its appreciation of your services rendered during the last Congress."⁶² In addition to the unions, a number of Socialist and non–Socialist organizations campaigned for London.⁶³ Like the unions, they opened campaign headquarters throughout the district, sponsored meetings, raised funds, distributed campaign literature, conducted canvasses, and served at the polls on Election Day.⁶⁴

As in previous congressional campaigns, London sought non–Socialist support, particularly Progressives. The *New Republic*, a progressive publication, endorsed London and urged former Progressives in the Twelfth Congressional District to vote for London. "There are not so many districts this year where the liberal can vote enthusiastically for a candidate who is positively good, rather than select the least distressing of two mediocrities. Although a solitary congressman in his first term is cramped under the machine methods which control the House, Mr. London was a noticeable figure in the sincerity and depth of feeling and in the intellectual distinction which he brought to debates on the floor and to committee work."⁶⁵ The National Voters' League also endorsed London in its publication *The Searchlight on Congress*. It described him as an independent with a "good" record."⁶⁶

London's chances of getting Progressive votes were further boosted when Solomon Sufrin, the Progressive candidate, withdrew from the campaign on October 17 and issued a neutral statement. A subsequent canvass by the Non-Partisan League indicated that 75 percent of Progressive Sufrin supporters planned to vote for London.⁶⁷ Theodore Roosevelt also rejected the Progressive Party nomination for president and returned to the Republican Party. This further weakened the Progressive Party and enhanced London's chances of winning Progressive support.

The Socialist congressman waged a vigorous, untiring campaign. Speaking at countless rallies, he proudly pointed to his record in Congress, a record well known on the East Side due to his monthly reports and extensive coverage in the Socialist press. The East Side, London told a rally on October 18, had

7. The 64th Congress: In Pursuit of Reform

Meyer London speaks at Union Square to a rally of striking Brooklyn streetcar workers, September 1916. Photograph Collection, Library of Congress.

through him voiced the cry against war. He had cast the only vote against war with Mexico. Two weeks later, but only after the president spoke out against war with Mexico, Congress did likewise.[68] In domestic matters, London stressed his efforts on behalf of a national social insurance system, his support for a child labor bill and his fight for unrestricted immigration. If reelected, he promised to continue his vigilance in Congress and to vote for peace rather than war, for a smaller military, for an open door to the immigrant, and for legislation to aid the workers in their struggle for a decent living.[69]

Prominent Socialists who campaigned for London in the Twelfth Congressional District lauded his record. Morris Hillquit urged the Twelfth District voters to reelect London so that he could continue his fight for the oppressed. Hillquit praised London's peace resolution and his opposition to militarism. "Re-elect Meyer London and a great cry of joy will go up from all over the country and you will secure the gratitude of millions of Socialists and progressive workers."[70] In a similar vein, James H. Maurer told a rally that people throughout the country were proud of London and his work in Congress, and they expected the voters of the Twelfth to send him back.[71]

Charles Edward Russell, before more than eight thousand people at two rallies, called London the "most respected, worthiest, and most brilliant Congressman that the House had seen in a lifetime." The question, Russell stated, was whether the voters of the Twelfth District would oust their faithful servant and replace him with a "slimy creature" of Tammany Hall. "I know London's career in Congress. I sit in the press gallery and look down on Meyer's head every day. Anyone who says London's record is not the most brilliant success we've had in Congress in our time is a dirty liar." No freshman congressman, Russell continued, had attained his influence and respect in such a short time. London's fellow congressmen might attack him as a socialist or accuse him of advocating anarchism, "but in their hearts they recognized him as the worthiest and most brilliant man in the crowd." The people of the East Side, Russell concluded, had declared their independence from Tammany two years ago; they should not allow anyone "to lie them out" of voting for London in this election.[72]

The *New York Call* and the *Daily Forward* echoed these sentiments. London, the *Call* declared, had made an "enviable" record in Congress from the worker's viewpoint.[73] Urging a large majority for London, the *Forward* stated that he had fulfilled his promises in Congress, and had not disappointed his constituents. Even the most ardent socialists were pleased with his performance.[74]

To discredit London, Judge Sanders and his supporters interjected the religious issue into the campaign.[75] London, they charged, did not believe in Judaism and had attacked God. A committee of Orthodox rabbis stated that London had told Congress that the American flag was nothing but a piece of cloth and that he was an atheist. On the other hand, they portrayed Sanders as a good American and a pious Jew.[76]

In an appeal to B'rith Abraham members for their support, Sanders said that he had accepted the nomination "because of the disgrace brought upon our people [Jews] by the tactics and speeches of the Socialist representative in Congress." Sanders denied that he opposed socialism. To the contrary, he favored many Socialist principles. Had London acted as a rational person, Sanders declared, he would not have entered the fight against him. "What I am doing is what I honestly believe to be necessary for the welfare of our people at home, as well as abroad."[77]

Angered by Sanders' charges and by the attempt to arouse religious bias, London called Sanders a "cheap, Kosher ham sandwich, Tammany Hall politician." He would not allow such a man to challenge his record. "I grew up with the East Side. Even in those early days when I came here ... there were two East Sides; the East Side of the gangsters, the poolroom, the dive, the houses of ill-fame — that is the East Side of Tammany Hall. There was the other East Side — the world of the dreamer, the student, the worker — whose soul was rich with all the virtues of the genius." However, the East Side in

7. The 64th Congress: In Pursuit of Reform

which he had grown up had changed since those days. Men and women no longer worked seven days a week and took work home. Who, London asked, gave the workers a six-day week? Religion had given the workers one rest day, but the Jewish contractor and manufacturer had taken it away. The Socialist Party gave it back to the Jewish worker. Tammany told the immigrant worker "to cringe and beg and accept charity and to look up to rich Jews for aid." The Socialist Party fought for their dignity. "They tell you that I fight God. I didn't go to Congress to fight God. I went there to fight the devil."[78]

London further commented about his opponents' charges in a letter to a constituent. Rumors, he stated, that he refused to attend a meeting with President Wilson to protest against the Burnett Bill were "a continuation of the underground methods of circulating absurd stories about attacking God, ridiculing the flag, or denying that I was a Jew, etc., ad nauseam." Attempts to discredit my work, he indignantly concluded, were "too contemptible" for further notice.[79]

In an article, "The Last Refuge of a Scandal," in the *New York Call*, William F. Feigenbaum wrote that working-class enemies had introduced the religious issue and "with the aid of their new ally, God, Tammany and all the forces of evil and corruption hoped to redeem the East Side from Socialism." Sanders, Feigenbaum charged, had violated his religion when he rode to the synagogue to pray on Yom Kippur. Sanders who lived on Riverside Drive, had appeared on the East Side and walked from synagogue to synagogue wearing his *tallit* (prayer shawl). "He could not have gotten to that section of the city without violating his religion, but he took a chance, in order to make his grandstand play." Sanders had made hundreds of votes for London rather than himself. Pious Jews resented having their religion ridiculed for political purposes. The real issue, Feigenbaum concluded, was not God, the synagogue or Sanders' false piety; it was the working class against capitalism.[80]

The Meyer London Non-Partisan League charged that Sanders had repudiated Tammany during his campaign two years earlier for the New York Supreme Court. Why, it asked, had Sanders changed his mind? "Is Tammany or [Boss] Murphy better today than they were two years ago or is Sanders worse?"[81] London, in a similar vein, told a meeting on October 23 that Sanders lacked the loyalty of a real Democrat. A man who "stabbed" his own party, he declared, could never be trusted.[82]

The *Daily Forward* and *New York Call* also stressed Sanders' connection with Tammany. Tammany, the *Forward* stated, had put on a *tallit*, *tefillin* and had pasted a Star of David on its forehead in order to campaign against London. Sanders represented the landlords, the cloak bosses, the upper classes and Tammany Hall, and would remain true to those interests.[83]

Amidst charges and countercharges, which marked one of the bitterest

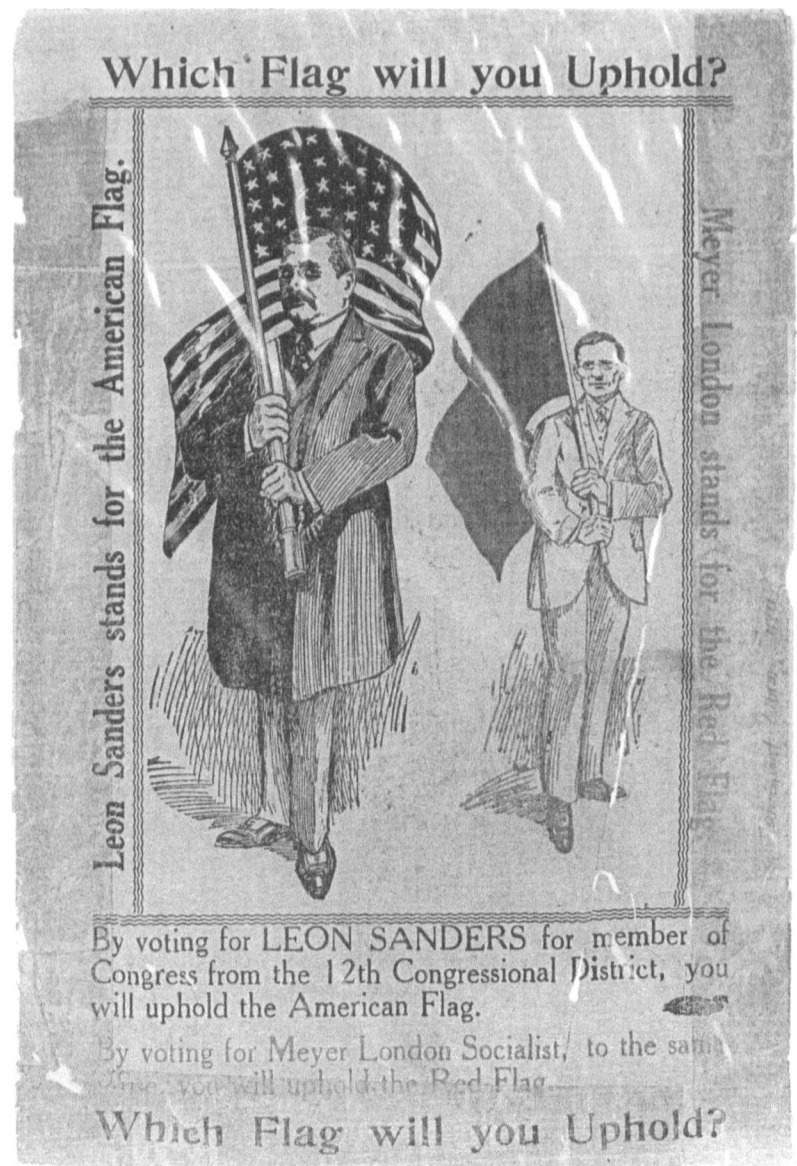

Judge Leon Sanders' campaign flyer circulated during the congressional election of 1916. Top: "Which Flag will you Uphold," Left: "Leon Sanders Stands for the American Flag." Right: "Meyer London stands for the Red Flag." Bottom: "By voting for Leon Sanders for member of Congress from the 12th Congressional District, you will uphold the American Flag. By voting for Meyer London Socialist to the same office, you will uphold the Red Flag. Which Flag will you Uphold?" London Papers, Tamiment Library, New York University.

7. The 64th Congress: In Pursuit of Reform 141

campaigns in the history of the East Side,[84] the voters went to the polls on November 7. Last-minute preparations were completed to man the polling places with Socialist watchers.[85] Fearful of irregularities at the polls, London, Charles Edward Russell and Henry Moskowitz met with Police Commissioner Woods and police captains in the Twelfth District. Woods assured them that he would have sufficient policemen in every election district to protect Socialist voters and the ballots. London told the *New York Call* that he had the votes to win. The rest, he said, was up to the watchers.[86]

Some twenty thousand excited East Siders gathered at the Forward Building on election night to await the returns[87] which were flashed from wooden booths to screens that covered the front of the building. London, who had rested during the day at his home, spent the night observing the canvass of votes and the transportation of ballot boxes from the polling places to the police stations.[88] Although the results appeared too close to call, his campaign headquarters claimed victory at midnight. At one o'clock in the morning, London also claimed victory. However, he cautioned that much work remained. "With Tammany in the field, it is not enough to cast the votes. You must see that the votes are recorded."[89]

The final count confirmed that London had defeated Sanders by a plurality well below that of 1914. London received 6,102 votes or 44.69 percent of the vote while Sanders garnered 5,759 votes, a percentage of 42.17. Louis Block, the Republican, ran a distant third with 968 votes or 7.08 percent of the vote.[90] Thus, although victorious, London's vote had increased by only 133 while his percentage had decreased from 47.98 to 44.69, a loss of 3.29 percent. Sanders gained 812 votes or 4.19 percent more than Goldfogle. As in 1914, London carried the Second, Sixth and Eighth assembly districts, but once again failed to capture Boss Ahearn's stronghold, the Fourth.

At six o'clock in the morning, London met with a large number of his jubilant supporters. He praised the watchers and others for their hard work on Election Day and during the campaign. "You did not," he told them, "make these sacrifices for me. You did not make these sacrifices because you hoped for favors from me. Everyone in this campaign worked for the ideal that spurs Socialists on to work against tremendous odds in the fight with capitalism." London viewed his reelection as a mandate against war, against imperialism, for unrestricted immigration, and for labor legislation. "It is a big honor for which I thank the voters of my district. It is more than an honor. It is a call from the people to continue work for them."[91]

In an interview, London told the *New York World* that the election had shown that East Side voters could not be "bamboozled" by religious issues. Block's small vote, he pointed out, indicated Republican support for Sanders. London also noted that the police commissioner had furnished ample protection to Socialist watchers, and had assisted a "great deal" in getting the vote counted.

Although pleased that he was the first Socialist reelected to Congress, London expressed regret that he would once again serve as the only Socialist.[92] Hillquit had lost in the Twentieth District by the slim margin of 459 votes. London attributed his defeat to the lack of competent watchers. Watchers so exhausted during the day could not prevent the theft of votes by Tammany at night. The Socialist organization, however, was better than in previous years. Six years ago, London asserted, Tammany would have produced a plurality of five thousand votes. Socialist organization would continue to improve until it would become impossible for Tammany to steal elections.[93]

Socialist and labor leaders around the country hailed London's reelection.[94] Eugene Debs, defeated in his bid for Congress in Indiana, extended his "heartiest" congratulations to London. "I wish," Debs wrote, "you were within arm's reach so that I might take you by the hand and express to you in person the pride and satisfaction I feel in your victory."[95] The *New York Call* proclaimed London's victory as a repudiation of Sanders' appeal to religious prejudice for votes. London and the Socialist Party had responded with a great campaign for socialism based on working-class grounds. The reelection of London and the election of two assemblymen proved locally that the Socialist Party was no longer a temporary political faction, but a permanent, fighting political party.[96]

Although reelected by a smaller plurality, London achieved a first for a Socialist — a second term in Congress. London's victory in 1916 was a vote of confidence for the beloved tribune of the Lower East Side. He had championed causes of major import to the working-class constituency. London had demonstrated his independent thinking and his willingness to confront his detractors. Moreover, his monthly meetings with constituents gave them insights into how Washington worked and helped educate them on issues important to them. London used the powers of incumbency with great effect.

Sanders refused to accept defeat. He charged that the Socialists had stolen the election, and challenged the results. On November 24, his attorneys appeared before Judge Clarence J. Shearn of the New York Supreme Court to secure an order restraining the Board of Elections from issuing London a certificate of election. Meyer London, his brother Horace and Alexander Levine, a law partner of Morris Hillquit, argued successfully against such an order, but agreed to an inspection of the void, blank and protested ballots.[97] Although this inspection produced more votes for London than himself, Sanders continued his efforts to procure a recount.[98] London stated that he welcomed a recount; it would show how many votes Tammany had rejected in violation of the law undetected by watchers. If a recount took place, London predicted that he would probably gain two hundred votes with Sanders losing that many.[99] On December 7, during further proceedings before Judge Shearn, Sanders' attorney withdrew his request for a recount after London gained additional votes. Horace London then requested and received a writ certifying his brother's election.[100]

In the meantime, London returned to Washington on December 3 for the second session of the Sixty-Fourth Congress which convened the following day. Deeply concerned by soaring food prices, as were many of his fellow congressmen,[101] London introduced a bill to create a federal food commission with authority to recommend legislation for federal food control. The commission could also authorize the president to prohibit food exports if it determined that the supply of food and food products did not meet the needs of the country.[102]

London maintained that only government control of the supply and distribution of food would alleviate the high cost of living. The European war had not created the problem, but had accentuated it. The problem, he contended, was inherent in a system which allowed private capital to control the food supply. London pointed out that the warring European nations had made some headway in eliminating speculation, waste and the middleman's profits. In this country, however, a number of profit makers existed between the farmer and the consumer.[103] London's bill was referred to the House Committee on Foreign and Interstate Commerce which planned to hold hearings on this and other food bills after the Christmas recess.[104]

The National Executive Committee of the Socialist Party endorsed London's bill and called upon Socialists and organized labor to back it with demonstrations and resolutions.[105] Additional support came from the Socialist press. The *Appeal to Reason* adopted the slogan "Feed America First" and pledged its power and resources on behalf of the measure.[106]

While prices continued to increase, wages barely kept pace and corporate profits boomed. By the end of 1916, real wages had risen 4 percent over 1914 levels, whereas the average price of farm products was 135 percent above the level of 1913. Profits reached new peaks with the more strategically placed corporations reaping the greatest windfall.[107] Relief authorities in New York City reported that prices of food had reached an unheard-of level. Over a few days in February 1917, basic foods such as eggs, bread, cabbage, potatoes and chickens jumped sharply. Hundreds of thousands of people in the city and throughout the country endured mounting hardship. Endurance reached the breaking point on New York's Lower East Side where wives found it increasingly difficult to feed their families on their husband's weekly wages of ten to fifteen dollars a week on average. Jewish women called for a citywide boycott which led to confrontations with grocers, butchers and food vendors, marches, and violence in late February.[108]

Greatly concerned by these events and by government inaction, London took the House floor on February 21 to demand immediate action. Prosperity, he said, seemed to have vanished. The wage increases which workers had received during the extraordinary prosperity produced by European conditions had been eaten up by rising food prices.

London approved President Wilson's request for an appropriation of four hundred thousand dollars to enable the Federal Trade Commission to investigate the food question, but he demanded immediate action. "'The people are now literally facing starvation, and do not forget that it is the men and women, if they have any fault, have the fault of working too hard..., that are in distress. These are not the wives of idlers who are now complaining of the lack of bread. I am wondering whether Congress will take the time now, when it is throwing away ... hundreds of millions of dollars, billions of dollars [for military expansion] to devote a couple of hours to the consideration of the national control of food." These bread riots, London continued, were not in European cities, but in New York, the richest city of the wealthiest country in the most prosperous period in American history.

London then referred to his food bill. He acknowledged that national control of food had no appeal to the average American. Would Congress, he asked, "by clinging to prevailing themes permit the food of the country, the social needs of the people, to be controlled by private capital, merciless, unscrupulous, lacking conscience, or would the question of food be taken up by the people as a national problem?"[109]

On the following day, London introduced a second measure to create a food emergency commission which would immediately purchase food, establish distribution centers, and sell food to the people or to municipal or state governments at reasonable prices. In a statement regarding the proposed commission, London insisted that Congress should not adjourn until it acted to alleviate the food crisis. He urged an appropriation of five million dollars for the purchase of food by a government commission. The bread riots, he stated, demonstrated the need to act without further delay.[110]

London took the floor again on February 24 to discuss an amendment to an appropriation bill that allocated four hundred thousand dollars to investigate the high cost of living. The present food emergency, he declared, indicated a distressing failure on the part of the government. "I am not a bit surprised that Congress which has been legislating for so many decades in the interests of certain economic groups finds itself unable to take a national outlook upon things and to legislate for the ... masses." Congress lacked both a basic knowledge of economic law and a social conscience. The food shortage

7. The 64th Congress: In Pursuit of Reform

convincingly demonstrated the economic and moral bankruptcy of capitalism. "Rich as never before — and bread riots! Surfeited with gold — and bread riots! A creditor of all the nations of the world — and bread riots! Such is capitalism. Such is the rule of private capital."

America had reached the height of industrial anarchy, London declared. The American people now faced the results of unregulated and uncontrolled individualism which permitted a minority to control the sustenance of the many. The remedy was democratic control of the food supply. London urged his colleagues, "Stop indulging in generalities. Stop talking of investigations. Stop recriminations and accusations."[111]

Representatives Sherley of Kentucky and Dies of Texas criticized London's proposal. The trouble with much of his position, Sherley stated, was the belief that every issue had a legislative remedy. He refused to permit the government to fix prices; he lacked confidence in its wisdom. "I would rather leave the competition of men with the natural law operating on all than trust to the social conscience of a Socialistic state."[112]

Dies launched a tirade against London and socialism. As a remedy for the high cost of living, he suggested that London and his constituents leave the crowded tenements and return to "God's open sunlight in the open country." Socialists wanted laws to control food prices, but few Socialists would go out and plow "old Beck" in order to grow corn to relieve the situation. "You know a Socialist can no more live in the open country amidst the growing grain, the lowing herd, and the grunting swine than germs can live in the sunlight."[113] On February 28, the House approved the amendment by a vote of 247 to 158.[114]

The Senate, meanwhile, had passed an amended Burnett immigration bill on December 14, 1916, and after both houses had approved the conference committee's report, the measure went to the president on January 16, 1917. Wilson, however, vetoed the bill. Opponents of restricted immigration in the House overrode the veto on February 1 by a nonpartisan vote of 287 to 106, and the Senate followed suit several days later.[115]

During the debate in the House, London joined those who upheld the presidential veto. In a brief speech, he denounced the bill as a "monstrosity," the result of ignorance, prejudice, sectionalism and narrow selfishness. "The nationalities, some of whose children will be excluded from the shores of America through this iniquitous measure, have contributed more than their share to the civilization of the world.... Give them the same opportunity which has been extended to the immigrant of the past, whether literate or illiterate, and they will all rise to the dignity of American citizenship and help you build and maintain a free and great Republic forever and ever more."[116]

Four days later, London sought unsuccessfully to secure passage of his national insurance resolution. Fearful that the House would not act upon it at the present session, he moved to suspend the rules and pass the resolution, a procedure which required a two-thirds vote.[117] Opposition came from the Republicans led by Minority Leader Mann and Representative Moore of Pennsylvania. Mann told the House that he was "sick and tired" of commissions. He could not recall any commission created by Congress which had any real service or value. The Constitution, Mann also argued, did not grant Congress the power to do what London's resolution proposed, and he doubted whether Congress should create a "one-sided" commission in order to get amendments made to the Constitution.[118]

Urging his colleagues to reject the measure, Moore declared that it struck at the "very foundation of existing insurance organizations of the United States whether they operate by authority from the State or upon the voluntary plan." London's proposal, he warned, marked the first step toward not only government ownership and control of insurance, but the introduction and adoption of a Socialistic program in the United States.[119]

Representatives Keating of Colorado and Sabbath of Illinois, both Democrats, and Gardner of Massachusetts, a Republican, spoke in favor of the resolution. Keating told his colleagues that he hoped they would not be influenced by Moore's charge of socialism. Although the lone Socialist in the House had introduced the resolution, the Committee on Labor, which consisted of both Democrats and Republicans, had unanimously reported it to the House. Social insurance was no longer the exclusive possession of the Socialist Party. "I hope," Keating said in conclusion, "this resolution will pass, not only by a party vote, but by the unanimous vote of the House."[120]

Sabbath and Gardner acknowledged that Mann's argument against commissions had some validity. Both maintained, however, that commissions occasionally produced valuable information which enabled Congress to enact beneficial legislation. The commission sought by London, Gardner asserted, would not sidetrack legislation, but would procure legislation. "Without a very thorough report we do not know what sort of legislation we need. Yet many of us think that social insurance ought to be instituted either by the States or by the United States or by a combination of the two, probably the latter."[121] Despite this bipartisan support, the motion to suspend the rules and pass the bill failed by twenty-nine votes with 189 for it and 139 against it.[122] Although placed on the House calendar, no further action occurred during the Sixty-Fourth Congress.

The international situation continued to preoccupy the Wilson administration during the fall and early winter of 1916–1917. While Wilson and a large segment of the American people strongly desired peace, events in Europe made it difficult, if not impossible, to maintain American neutrality. The belligerent powers in an effort to break the stalemate and achieve victory had decided to resort to their ultimate weapons. The Germans intensified submarine operations, and by so doing broke the *Sussex* pledge. The British increased economic warfare further aggravating Anglo-American tension. Faced with this potentially dangerous situation and strengthened by a mandate for peace from the American electorate, Wilson decided that the best way to avoid American intervention was to end the hostilities. During the election campaign, the German government indicated that it desired peace and informed Wilson that it would be receptive to an American peace initiative. However, Wilson refused to move until after the election. When November passed without action by the president, the German government took the initiative. On December 12, it announced that it would enter peace negotiations with its enemies. Six days later Wilson sent identical notes to all the belligerents calling upon them to state their war aims.[123]

Peace groups and non-interventionists hailed Wilson's appeal as the beginning of the end of the war. On New Year's Eve, London, Washington Gladden, and Dudley Field Malone spoke at a peace rally in Washington Square. London told several thousand people that although he had not voted for Wilson, it was the "greatest pleasure" of his life to support his efforts to end the war. Partisanship must be set aside to create public sentiment in support of the president's initiative. "I know," he stated, "what the response to President Wilson's appeal would be if it were to come, not from a diplomat, but from the men who are doing the fighting. Men who are manly enough to fight are manly enough to bear no malice against one another." London urged his listeners to stand with the president in his fight for peace.[124]

The Allies and the Central Powers, however, failed to reply satisfactorily to Wilson's note. Neither side stated their war aims. The Germans, instead, called for a conference of the belligerents only. The Allies publicly rejected the German proposal, but informed the president privately that they would discuss peace if the German terms were reasonable.

In order to clarify the American position as a result of these developments, Wilson addressed the Senate on January 22 and outlined the kind of peace he believed the United States would support in a league of nations. The president called for a "peace without victory," a peace based upon the equality of all nations, upon freedom of the seas, upon the limitation of armaments and upon the principle of self-determination.[125]

London praised Wilson's message. He commended the president for taking another step toward peace negotiations and for seeking to introduce a moral principle into international law — the principle that no nation should extend its control over any other nation or people. Although he endorsed the president's ideals, London warned against American participation in an international alliance using American military forces in the joint enterprises of the alliance. "I certainly favor a league of nations, but my contention is that as long as each member ... maintains an army and navy, and as long as the nations of the world have the power to use these forces, just so long will there be no opportunity for international peace."

A commercial boycott, as he had suggested in his peace resolution of December 6, 1915, rather than military force, should be used to punish offending nations. The primary cause of modern wars, London maintained, would be removed by establishing the principle that a larger nation should not trample upon the rights of any smaller nation. Coupled with arms reduction, international peace would be very close to realization. "I cannot agree, with the man who looks upon every effort in the direction of a brotherhood of nations as the effort of dreamers."[126]

Wilson's offer to use the good offices of the United States to end hostilities failed. His "peace without victory" address was followed by Germany's declaration of unrestricted submarine warfare on January 31, 1917. Three days later the president appeared before a joint session of Congress and announced the severance of diplomatic relations. Still hoping to avoid war, Wilson stated that the United States had no desire for a conflict with Germany. In the weeks immediately following the break in relations, the president and the American people continued to hope for peace, but developing events would compel the United States to abandon neutrality.[127]

Meanwhile, the House considered several appropriation measures that provided funds for preparedness. On January 31, London joined his anti-preparedness colleagues to oppose an emergency revenue bill to raise additional twenty million dollars annually for the army and navy and to extend fortifications. London told the House that he was not an obstructionist and that he would cheerfully help the party in power to enact necessary revenue legislation.

However, when he read the bill's title, he could not bring himself to vote for it. This bill, London protested, would tax every man, woman and child ten dollars a year for preparedness for which there was no "earthly use." The people requested bread, clothing and shelter, but Congress gave them weapons and fortifications. "War traffickers" would get one billion dollars from the pockets of the American people and the United States Treasury. This money would then be used, London declared, "to corrupt, to defile, to dictate the editorials of your newspapers to make and unmake men, and to shape public opinion. A new aristocracy, a new power, a new danger is being created by this ... appropriation."

Democrats as well as the Republicans, he charged, knew that the demand for preparedness was artificially stimulated by the munitions interests. His

7. The 64th Congress: In Pursuit of Reform 149

colleagues in both parties had to vote as their leaders instructed them. By doing this, they subordinated their reason and surrendered their independence.

London pleaded with his fellow congressmen to end the preparedness campaign and to devote the remainder of the session to the high cost of living. They should legislate for the people instead of the munitions interests.[128] The bill passed the following day by 211 to 196 with London in opposition.[129] London also opposed the Naval Appropriation bill. In a brief speech, he answered those congressmen who objected to submarines unless used exclusively to attack warships. Whether certain weapons should be used or whether their use should be restricted was less important than the justice of the war. "Were this country invaded, I would be in favor of shooting down the stars if the falling stars would crush the enemy. We would use any and all means—the more destructive the better.... That is why no sane mind can endorse the idea of war, unless it be a war to repel invasion."[130] The following day London and twenty-two others, including Majority Leader Kitchin, voted against the Naval bill as the House approved it by an overwhelming majority.[131]

On February 17, during the debate on the Army Appropriations bill, London again opposed American intervention. For two weeks, London told his colleagues, he had restrained himself. He now felt in complete self-control and could speak safely. The American people, London declared, had refused to go to war because Britain had denied freedom of the seas to American commerce. Should the United States go to war with Germany because it threatened the rest of our commerce? "In other words, shall we fight for the privilege of carrying on commerce with the belligerent nations? That commerce, so far as exports are concerned, is confined principally to the business of supplying the belligerents with munitions. He would rather vote hundreds of millions of dollars to the munitions traffickers than allow them to shed a single drop of American blood."

London denied that any vital American rights or interests were endangered, or that national honor was at stake. What, he asked, would the United States accomplish by going to war and winning? "It will have established the right of munitions makers to sell munitions. That is the only thing that will be established. It will be a war for cash, a war for commerce. It will be war for the right of the powder barrel, with the American flag on the barrel, giving it the sanctity of the flag and everything the flag represents." War was inconceivable if Congress honestly faced the question. London hoped that his colleagues would not succumb to the clamor for war.

Moreover, though he greatly admired the president, he feared the slogan "Stand by the President." When the president was right, the slogan had meaning, but not when he erred. The framers of the Constitution had not intended that Congress perfunctorily declare war upon somebody's suggestion. "The right to declare war means the right to refuse to declare war. It involves deliberation, study, analysis, the searching of one's conscience, the calling into action of all our mental powers. And if there ever was a time when every member of Congress should be free and strong and independent, this is the time."[132]

Representative Kelley asked London if he believed that the president had broken relations with Germany for commercial reasons. London replied that although he had opposed severing diplomatic relations with Germany during debate on the McLemore resolution, he had no desire to criticize the president for his recent action. He noted, however, that the president had not severed diplomatic relations with England for various violations of neutral rights.

London acknowledged a fundamental difference between the British and German methods of enforcing the blockade. The president broke relations with Germany because of this distinction. The wisdom of this decision was immaterial. The question which concerned most Americans, he stated, was whether this country would submit to the British blockade and not to the German blockade. "The method pursued by Germany threatens a small number of individuals who engage in that traffic and who find themselves within the war zone. So far as the right to freedom of seas is concerned, both belligerents disregard our rights." American lives, London declared, would be lost after warning had been given to stay out of the war zone. "If American lives are lost when you get within the range of the guns fired from the walls of a belligerent fortress, you have no complaint. That is what it amounts to. Germany has now surrounded the British Isles with guns which have a longer range than the guns she had before." If neutrals stayed out of the war zone, they had nothing to fear.[133]

During the three weeks following the break in diplomatic relations, no overt act occurred. Frightened American shippers kept their ships and cargoes in port. The demand for the arming and protection of American ships grew as goods began to pile high on wharves. At first Wilson hesitated to request congressional authority to arm American merchantmen. However, the Zimmerman Telegram, which proposed a German-Mexican-Japanese alliance in case of war, received by the president on February 25 from British intelligence, convinced him of Germany's hostile intentions and changed his mind.[134] On the following day, Wilson asked a joint session of Congress for authority to arm merchantmen and to "employ any other instrumentalities or methods" necessary to protect American ships and lives on the high seas.[135] He viewed his address as a final appeal to the German government to reverse course.

On the same day, Democratic leaders in the House drafted a bill which authorized Wilson to arm merchant ships and "employ such other instru-

7. The 64th Congress: In Pursuit of Reform   151

mentalities and methods" deemed necessary and adequate to protect American ships and citizens in their lawful pursuits on the high seas. It also empowered the President to spend one hundred million dollars for these purposes.

On February 28, the House Foreign Affairs Committee reported a compromise measure giving the president authority to arm merchant ships while eliminating reference to "other instrumentalities and methods" and prohibiting the War Risk Insurance Bureau from insuring ships carrying munitions. Publication of the Zimmerman Telegram prompted the House to approve the amended armed ship bill by 403 to 13 on March 1.[136]

During a lengthy session characterized by patriotic outbursts and denunciations of Germany, London opposed the bill. He realized, however, that he could not sway his colleagues. "After the distinguished minority leader has so suddenly shifted ground, and after the genial majority leader has announced that he will hereafter pray, I think that all opposition is about gone." The House had, unfortunately, reached the stage where sentiment ruled and reason had been suspended.

London chided his colleagues for their patriotic expressions. "When a man," he stated, "finds it necessary to proclaim how deeply he loves his flag and his country, he does not realize that he makes as much a fool of himself as if he should declare how deeply he loves his wife. It is taken for granted that a member of the American Congress loves the Republic and will give his life for it if necessary." All these patriotic exhortations were superfluous. Today, he went on, Congress was asked to defend American rights and commence within a war zone. Thus, the United States, which had neither developed a merchant marine nor had control of the seas in peacetime, now sought control of the sea at the point of a sword. "Was there ever anything more absurd, more indefensible, presented to an intelligent people?"[137]

Shortly before the final vote, anti-interventionists in the House introduced an amendment which forbade armed American merchantmen from carrying munitions or belligerent nationals to warring nations. The so-called Cooper amendment was rejected 293 to 125. London, who opposed arming American ships or allowing them to enter the war zone, voted present.[138] A group of twelve non-interventionist senators, led by Robert La Follette and George W. Norris, blocked passage of the armed ship bill by talking it to death as the Sixty-Fourth Congress ended.[139] On March 9, Wilson announced that he would put guns and naval crews on merchant ships on his own authority.[140]

During the Sixty-Fourth Congress, London had emerged as a leading spokesman for the labor movement. He supported progressive legislation to improve the plight of the working people. In addition, he waged a vigorous fight for his social insurance resolution which came within twenty-nine votes of passage. As the first Russian Jew in Congress, London championed the urban immigrant. Along with Adolph Sabbath of Chicago, he fought in the House against immigration restriction.

The question of American neutrality, however, overshadowed domestic matters in the fall and early winter of 1916–1917. Thus, London, elected for a second term in November of 1916, found his attention, like that of his colleagues, diverted to the international scene. Along with many of his House colleagues, he remained a vocal opponent of the administration's preparedness program, and repeatedly warned against American intervention in the European conflict. However, the inexorable course of events swept the United States into war.

8

The Sixty-Fifth Congress: War Declared

> War was wrong, inexcusable, indefensible.... Let us throw away our chances of reelection. The people will ultimately do right; they will ultimately stand by every man who will show courage in this moment of crisis.... Let us be free, strong men and do as men should do in momentous times like this.—*Meyer London,* Congressional Record, *65th Congress, Special Session, 109–11.*

London's second term in Congress proved the most difficult of his congressional career. The lone Socialist representative opposed the declarations of war against Germany and Austria-Hungary. He continued to express his displeasure by abstaining on important war measures. However, London rejected the militant anti-war position adopted by the Socialist Party. He believed that his oath of office bound him to defend his country against attack and not to undermine the war effort. Socialists, he maintained, should guide the forces released by the conflict to hasten the realization of the cooperative commonwealth. As a result of this position, London drew criticism from both those who supported "100 percent Americanism" and anti-war Socialists.

The Bolshevik Revolution created further difficulties for London since many of his congressional colleagues equated socialism with Bolshevism and left-wing Socialists resented his lukewarm support of the Bolsheviks. Nevertheless, London followed a course which he believed in accord with Socialist doctrine. His persistent defense of civil liberties in the face of growing war hysteria represents a high point in the struggle for the right to dissent in wartime.

March 1917 was a time of supreme crisis for the American peace movement as Socialists and non–Socialists rallied in one last desperate effort to stop American intervention in the European conflict. On March 4, the same day that the Sixty-Fourth Congress adjourned, Local New York asserted its "uncompromising opposition to war and militarism in all forms." In the event of war, the resolution declared, New York City Socialists must use every means to hasten the return of peace, to oppose war policies, to oppose censorship of the press and mails, to protest restrictions of speech and assembly, and to prevent the enactment of suppressive sedition and espionage laws. The local promised to assist workers in any mass action against conscription, martial law, and suspension or curtailment of their rights to organize and strike.[1] On March 7, Eugene Debs, before a cheering, overflow New York crowd urged the American labor movement to call a general strike in the eventuality of war.

London, who had returned to New York to continue his fight against intervention, took exception to both the position of Local New York and the statement by Debs. Before war was declared, London asserted, Socialists had the duty to oppose it and to prevent it, if possible. "But when war is an accomplished fact, then there must be unity. This has been the policy of Socialists throughout the world, and it should be the policy of Socialists in the United States. I would not advocate adding civil war to the crime of international war."

London's statement caused a stir within Local New York, and the Central Committee referred the matter to the National Executive Committee. In addition, on March 24, the Central Committee considered a motion that it send a letter to London requesting him to refrain from making such statements, and if he did, he should clearly indicate that it expressed his opinion. An amendment to the motion asked London to comment upon the truthfulness of the report appearing in the *New York Tribune*, but both the motion and amendment were defeated. The committee then approved a motion requesting London to attend a general meeting to be held on April 1. However, the executive secretary reported on March 30 that a meeting with London could not be arranged since he was on a lecture tour.[2]

Two days later London spoke at a mass meeting sponsored by the Emergency Peace Federation. He believed, he said, that the president still desired peace, but feared that "sinister" influences, including the press, would force Wilson's hand. "But there is something worse than war," London declared. "That is dishonor, and I contend that a war to carry on the trade in munitions, will be a war of dishonor."[3]

Further events propelled the country along the path to war. In mid-March, German submarines sank several unarmed merchantmen without warning. Meanwhile, events in Petrograd swept away a major moral obstacle to the United States joining the Allies. The Mensheviks overthrew Czar Nicholas II and established a provisional government.[4] Nevertheless, President Wilson hesitated to ask for war. On March 20, Wilson's cabinet unanimously agreed to war. The president, however, did not reveal his decision. The next day he summoned a special session of the new Congress for April 2, "to receive a communication concerning grave matters of national policy."[5]

8. The 65th Congress: War Declared

When the special session of the Sixty-Fifth Congress convened, the first business of the House was to organize. The congressional elections of 1916 had evenly distributed the seats between Democrats and Republicans, each having 215. It appeared that London and four other minor party representatives would determine control of the House.[6] London received much attention from both major parties and the press. On November 14, House Majority Leader Claude Kitchin and Thomas M. Bell, Democratic whip of the House, requested his support for the reelection of Speaker Champ Clark.[7] The *New York Call* predicted that London would be more important in the new House than in the old. It might find it necessary to draft measures to meet his approval in order to secure their adoption.[8] Hoping to take advantage of their position, the five so-called independents held several secret meetings. They agreed to act independently and not participate in the caucus of either party.[9]

The State Executive Committee of the New York Socialist Party passed a resolution on February 20 stating that London would best serve the party if he abstained from voting for Speaker of the House. The committee instructed the state secretary to inform London of the resolution and ascertain his intentions. If London planned to help either the Democrats or Republicans, the New York members would introduce a resolution in the National Executive Committee requesting that he refrain from voting.[10] Nevertheless, London continued to confer with his fellow independents. On March 4, they decided not to commit themselves presently to either party in organizing the House.[11]

When the House considered the question, on April 2, London ignored the State Executive Committee's instructions and voted for Champ Clark who was reelected Speaker.[12] He also supported the Democrats on the adoption of the House rules.[13] While it is impossible to determine whether London entered into an agreement with the Democratic House leadership, he received assignments to the Labor Committee, the Mines and Mining Committee and the Revision of the Laws Committee without amending the rules as in the previous Congress.[14] London had also established a good working relationship with the Democrats during the previous Congress, and no doubt he desired to maintain it for pragmatic reasons.

Still hoping to forestall American participation in the war, London introduced a resolution calling upon the president to initiate peace negotiations based upon the principles set forth in Wilson's speech to the Senate on January 22, 1917. The resolution took note of the recent revolution in Russia and the unanimous vote of the German Social Democrats against the military budget. These developments, since the severance of diplomatic relations with Germany, justified a new appeal for peace from the president. The resolution died in the Foreign Affairs Committee.[15]

London's hope that the United States could avoid involvement in Europe ended when Wilson appeared before Congress on April 2 to ask for a declaration of war. Debate began in the House on the morning of April 5.[16] London and some twenty representatives led by Majority Leader Kitchin spoke against the war resolution. Congress could best serve democracy, London declared, by rejecting the president's request for war. If Congress endorsed the idea of war, then all hope for peace vanished. The same men, London pointed out, who had argued during the debate on the armed ship bill that it excluded war, now stood ready to vote for war because the president asked for it. "You are invited to reverse a policy as old as this Republic; you are invited not only to defend the territory of the United States and the territorial water of the United States, ... but you are invited to fight for rights admitted to be disputable within the war zone thousands of miles away. You are invited ... to enter into all sorts of partnerships with kings, rulers by divine right, with monarchs of all sorts."

London then noted the democratic stirrings in Europe since the United States had severed diplomatic relations with Germany. The revolution in Russia, the unanimous vote of German Social Democracy against the war budget, the vote of the Austrian Social Democrats for peace, and the insistent demand in all other European countries for greater popular participation in determining international relations were hopeful signs. Moreover, London argued, the American people opposed war, and President Wilson's plan for compulsory military service indicated that the president realized this. "In order ... to get volunteers there must be a desire in the hearts of the people to fight, to fight for the things for which the President asks us now to fight. On April 2, he told the great mass of the American people that they should fight for a new idea, not to improve the Republic, ... but to change the forms of government in Turkey, in Austria, and Germany. No wonder he is compelled to recommend compulsory military service."

London recognized that most Americans sympathized with the Allies. He wondered, however, why this country resorted to the "last and most desperate method, the unspeakable method of war, before we have tried other expedients? Why has not the President ... again made his offer of peace? Why should we not suggest a truce?" London expressed fear that congressmen would vote not according to their own convictions and judgments, but as the president wanted them to vote.

He lashed out at those who argued that every vote against the war resolution helped the Germans. Such talk was "cheap, vulgar, nonsense." Elected representatives should speak their minds freely. London confessed the difficulty of his own position, but he would lose his self-respect unless he voted against the war resolution. The issue was between those who believed that this country had a mission "to influence the world for the better by being a free democracy, ... by marching unhindered on the road toward nobler and more beautiful ideals, and the group of men who believed that the United States must follow in the footsteps of the European countries and adopt the jargon of European diplomacy about national honor and dignity. There is no national honor in superior physical force, there is no national honor in a combination with other military and naval forces to crush a weaker military or naval force."

The German government, London acknowledged, had inflicted irreparable injury upon the United States. Was physical force, he reiterated, the only response available to this country "or shall we give to the world this splendid example of the humility of a great and free people, and say that we have been injured, ... but the loss is largely commercial, and that in the interests of humanity we shall refuse to add to the work of destruction?" The president, London concluded, had requested that the representatives of a free people embrace war, but every representative should respond, "No, I shall not kill; I shall not permit anyone to vote that my arm should be stretched to kill a fellow human being." War, London passionately pleaded, was "wrong, inexcusable, indefensible." He urged his colleagues to "throw away our chances of reelection. The people will ultimately do right; they will ultimately stand by every man who will show courage in this moment of crisis.... Let us be free, strong men and do as men should do in momentous times like this."[17] Debate proceeded throughout the day. The House finally approved the war resolution on April 6, 373 to 50. London was the only eastern congressman and the only Jew of the five in Congress to vote against the conflict.[18]

On April 7, the day after President Wilson signed the war resolution, the Emergency National Convention of the Socialist Party met in St. Louis to formulate a wartime program.[19] The majority resolution drafted by Morris Hillquit, Algernon Lee and Charles Ruthenberg, a leader of the left wing, declared the Socialist Party's unalterable opposition to the war and branded the declaration of war as a crime against the American people and the nations of the world. The resolution condemned the "false doctrine of national patriotism" and reaffirmed the adherence of the Socialist Party to the principles of internationalism and working-class solidarity. It pledged continuous opposition to the war and to conscription, as well as "vigorous resistance ... to censorship of the press and mails, restriction of free speech and assemblage ... and of the right to strike." It also opposed war appropriations or loans. The convention approved the majority resolution by a wide margin, and the party membership later ratified it by a vote of 21,639 to 2,752.[20] The convention also endorsed London's fight against war and militarism as consistent with Socialist loyalty.[21]

Adoption of the so-called St. Louis Manifesto led to defections from the party of many of its foremost national leaders and intellectuals, including Allan Benson, Charles Edward Russell, John Spargo, William English Walling, Algie M. Simons, William J. Ghent, Upton Sinclair and Winnfield Gaylord.[22]

Meyer London took exception to the extreme language of the St. Louis Manifesto. As the only Socialist congressman, he had vigorously opposed the preparedness movement and American intervention in the war. He believed, however, that his oath of office bound him to defend his country against attack and not to hamper or weaken its military position.[23]

London viewed the St. Louis Manifesto as a protest which did not offer a constructive policy for the party or a course of action for himself. Socialists, he said, could do one of two things. They could oppose the war as a matter of principle and obstruct the government's war effort, thereby inviting defeat for the United States. This he rejected as impractical, essentially wrong and immoral in a democratic nation. If the people lacked better representation, they were responsible, "and their rebellion would be a rebellion against themselves, and would add to the horror and calamities of a foreign war the still greater horrors and crimes, of a civil war."[24]

Socialists, London pointed out, could pursue a second approach — remain passive, and neither promote the war, nor obstruct it. This also did not appeal to London. "I hate anything," he declared, "that is passive, that requires no activity, that permits things to go on without our participation." Instead, London proposed that Socialists help direct the forces released by the war, "so that its sacrifices may be minimized..., the rights and liberties of the people retained and protected, and that some permanent contribution to the progress of the world may come even as a result of the war." In conclusion, London reiterated, "I must participate in the work of the world, although some of it may be the work of mischief."[25]

London further elaborated upon his position during a speech in the House on September 12, 1918. When asked whether he disagreed with the St. Louis platform, he told his colleagues that in a republic when a majority decided for war, their will should be carried out. Under such circumstances he could only allow himself to present his ideas on international peace in a way that would not obstruct the war effort, encourage the enemy or create dissension. "I must content myself during the war ... to analyzing the historical causes which led nations into war and to point out the basic principles upon which a lasting peace can be obtained when the war is concluded. That has been my rule. I have contented myself with that modest way of keeping alive my ideas of sticking by my higher religion, the religion of humanity."[26] London, like many pro-war Socialists and pro-war progressives, believed that the party should participate in guiding the forces released in wartime.

8. The 65th Congress: War Declared 159

Although aware that his course would incur the wrath of his comrades, London continued to follow the dictates of his conscience in voting on various war measures considered by the House of Representatives. The first of these, the War Loan Act of April 1917, authorized the Treasury to issue two billion in short-term notes and five billion in bonds, three billion designated as loans to the Allies. The House adopted the bond issue without a dissenting vote, on April 14, with London alone answering "present."[27] London later explained that, although still opposed the war, he voted for the bond issue because he sympathized with the Allies. The United States, he maintained, should give the Allies every type of non-combatant aid, not only billions of dollars, but food and war materials as well. London also believed that he had an obligation to those called to serve their country: to provide them with everything needed and to bring the conflict to a speedy conclusion.[28]

Shortly thereafter, the House began consideration of a new revenue bill to meet escalating war costs. Like most Socialists and progressives, London adhered to the belief that taxation should be based upon the ability to pay and that the wealthy class should bear the burden of the war through higher income, inheritance and excess profits taxes. London went even further and advocated the conscription of property as well as income. "Big issues of bonds and taxes upon food and upon small incomes," he maintained, "are only aggravated forms of taxes. All are finally paid by working people. That is why, in the face of war, our government ought to conscript property, and vast amounts of it."[29] London supported progressives such as Fiorello La Guardia of New York and Irvine Lenroot of Wisconsin who fought unsuccessfully to raise the income tax exemption figures of $1,000 for single men and $2,000 for married persons.[30] Once again London voted "present" as the House approved the bill 329 to 26.[31]

In the meantime, British and French war missions in Washington convinced Wilson that American money and material alone would not produce victory. The Allies also needed a large, well-equipped American army. The administration decided upon conscription as the best means to raise an expeditionary force. Shortly after the country declared war, Wilson presented a Selective Service bill which touched off a bitter struggle in the House. Democratic leaders such as Speaker Champ Clark, Majority Leaden Claude Kitchin and James Hay, chairman of the House Military Affairs Committee, opposed the bill, while southern Democrats sought to raise the proposed draft age.[32]

During the debate on April 25, London joined those who opposed conscription. Many Americans, he explained, refused to volunteer because they did not fully comprehend the president's new foreign policy. "Is not the very fact that up to the present moment only 1 out of 20,000 has volunteered, a conclusive argument against this policy of conscription? Is not an opportunity to volunteer a sort of referendum?" The House, London said, should not waste its time. The war would end before an army was raised. Moreover, how would this country transport a million and a half men to Europe? "You will have to build several dozen bridges," he remarked sarcastically, "or you will have to do what my ancestor did when he struck with his staff the Red Sea, and in that way permit your army to walk across the Atlantic Ocean."

When the conscription bill passed the House by a large majority on April 28, London voted with twenty-three other congressmen against it.[33] Despite his opposition to the draft, London refused repeated demands from the National Executive Committee and Socialist locals that he introduce a bill to repeal the conscription law; he believed it futile.[34]

In the months following the adoption of the St. Louis Manifesto, the Socialist Party continued to protest against conscription and American participation in the war. Since the Socialist Party was the only important national organization that opposed the war effort, its stand struck a responsive chord with many Americans, particularly those in northern industrial and foreign-language centers. Party membership increased by more than twelve thousand as Socialists campaigned vigorously to attract various anti-war groups to their banner.[35] As war fever grew in the country, public officials and organizations such as the National Security League clamored for the suppression of anti-war views in the name of national unity, and the Wilson administration responded with the Espionage bill.

The House began debate on this controversial measure in early May 1917. Defenders of free speech concentrated their attack on Section 4 which gave the president broad powers to prohibit the publication of any information relative to national defense.[36] On May 3, London spoke against the bill. He strenuously objected to the broad powers bestowed upon the president. Congress, he declared, should not allow one man to make the law. "I have a great deal of respect for the President, and because I consider him a man of extraordinary ability I am afraid of him. If he were a commonplace man, or a man below the commonplace he would not be as dangerous as he is."

Section Four, London continued, threatened freedom of the press, but Title XI endangered all, for it permitted any postmaster to exclude from the mails anything that he considered treasonable or anarchistic. "There is nothing," he exclaimed, "more oppressive in the world than a democracy gone mad, than a democracy which has surrendered its rights to an individual." Title XI constituted an attack on the liberties of the defenseless individual, not on powerful newspapers. London declared that he spoke on behalf of free speech. "Let us not surrender our individual rights at a time when we need enlist the cooperation of every man and woman. Let men speak freely. Do

8. The 65th Congress: War Declared 161

not drive them into the cellar of conspiracy.... Let us not, while we talk of fighting for liberty abroad, sacrifice and crush our liberties here."

London told the House that sentiment in favor of removing Section Four pleased him, and he hoped that Title XI would also be removed from the bill. He would support every measure to safeguard the military secrets of the country, but he would not go any further. He refused to surrender any of the liberties of the "humblest" citizen.[37]

When the bill came to a vote the next day, London supported a motion adopted by the House 221 to 167 to strike out Section Four, the so-called censorship provision.[38] Democratic leaders immediately introduced a compromise amendment that limited the powers sought by the president to certain specific violations and provided jury trials for offenders. Due to administration pressure, a sufficient number of Democrats reversed themselves as the amendment passed by the narrow margin of 191 to 185, with London in opposition.[39]

Representative Crosser, a Democrat from Ohio, then offered an amendment to Title XI to clarify what material should be barred from the mails. Crosser proposed to eliminate the word *anarchistic* and to substitute "or of a character advocating the destruction of or injury to the Government by violence." He explained that many individuals of high character, intellect and education advocated philosophic anarchy. "Their philosophy is of a very idealistic nature, and yet if this bill passes with the language in the section as it now stands, the writings of these men would be barred from the mails entirely." It was dangerous in a free society to say that a person should write or say only those things with which others agree.[40]

In supporting the Crosser amendment, London told the House that the ignorance of his fellow congressmen on the subject of socialism and anarchism was sufficient reason for removing the word "anarchistic" from the section. London pleaded with his colleagues to distinguish between a philosophy and the method used to achieve it. The Ku Klux Klan, he pointed out, resorted to violence, but it had no distinct philosophy about the reorganization of the world. Klan members were neither Socialists nor anarchists, but terrorists. By including the word *anarchistic*, London went on, every "little" postmaster could ban from the mail everything that advised the people to defend their rights, under the pretext that they advocated anarchy. "Make it clear that you are opposed to the use of the mail for the purpose of advocating the overthrow of government by violence. Make it clear so that there will be no mistake about it."

Representative Frank L. Greene of Vermont asked London whether he found the following language in a Socialist circular objectionable: "We call upon the working class ... to institute strikes against the mobilization of industry and military forces...; and we pledge ourselves to encourage and support these strikes and develop them into a general revolutionary movement against war and capitalism." People, London replied, had the right to oppose both capitalism and the war, but he rejected the policy of using revolutionary methods to oppose the war. Had he approved such a policy, he would not have continued his attendance in the House. War, London asserted, would be made impossible by educating the people. Greene then asked him to comment upon a Socialist anti-draft pledge. London stated that he did not endorse this pledge.[41]

The House adopted the Crosser amendment, and shortly thereafter approved the Espionage bill 260 to 106 as London voted with the minority.[42] The measure experienced further difficulty in the Senate where opponents of censorship eliminated the offensive provision. The Senate passed the bill on May 14 and sent it to conference where a deadlock ensued. On May 29, the conferees finally agreed to a modified form of censorship, but the House rejected the conference report and instructed its conferees to eliminate censorship of the press. Anxious to get the measure passed, the Wilson administration gave up the fight, and the president signed the bill on June 15.[43]

Despite removal of the censorship provision, the Espionage Act confirmed the worst apprehensions of its opponents. The government still had sufficient powers to move against offending newspapers. Postmaster General Albert S. Burleson seized Socialist papers under a provision in the act, which empowered the postmaster general to exclude from the mails any matter which in his opinion urged "treason, insurrection, or forcible resistance" to the laws of the United States.[44]

Suppression of Socialist publications made it increasingly difficult for Socialists to continue their anti-war agitation through normal channels. Alarmed by this, London introduced a resolution in the House on July 10 calling upon the postmaster general to provide the names of publications denied mailing privileges under the Espionage Act, the reason or reasons for their suppression, the instructions issued to local postmasters relevant to enforcement of the act, and correspondence between the Post Office Department and other departments relative to its enforcement.[45]

London hoped that this information would pave the way for amendments to the Espionage Act denying the Post Office Department censorship powers. In arguing on behalf of his proposal, London noted that Congress had not foreseen that every postmaster and assistant district attorney would regulate speech and censor the press. "The man has not yet been born upon whom the American people are ready to confer the power of determining what people shall think and what they shall say." One could not suspend freedom of speech and press. These constitutional rights were inseparable from civilized life. A country at war, he acknowledged, had the right to deny the enemy military information. However, the people could not surrender their right to disagree with the administration's policies. "The attempt to suppress by law all expressions of disapproval of the policies or methods of the government would result in a tyranny which no civilized nation can endure." Efforts to silence Socialist papers, London concluded, should arouse the American press and public. The people must act immediately to frustrate this attempt to censor opinion.[46]

In addition to London's resolution, the National Executive Committee of the Socialist Party appointed a committee consisting of Morris Hillquit, Clarence Darrow, Seymour Stedman, and Frank P. Walsh to meet with Justice and Post Office Department officials to discuss the use of the Espionage Act by federal grand juries to indict Socialists for anti-conscription and related activities, as well as the Post Office's banning of Socialist papers from the mail.[47]

On the evening of July 15, London met with Darrow; Stedman; J. Louis Engdahl, editor of the *American Socialist*; and Thomas A. Hickey, editor of the *Rebel*. He discussed the attitude of House members toward censorship of Socialist publications, and told them that he expected quick action by the House on his resolution.[48]

The House Committee on Post Offices and Post Roads held a hearing on London's resolution on July 23. In a letter to the committee, Postmaster General Burleson wrote that it was not in the public interest to furnish the House with the information requested by London, and urged the committee to reject the resolution. London denied Burleson's contention. He insisted that Socialists had the right to know the reasons for suppressing their papers.

Committee chairman John L. Moon indicated that the Congress had no power to compel the postmaster general to provide the requested information. Moreover, even if Burleson acceded, Congress lacked authority to correct the practices of the Post Office Department in such matters. Moon then suggested that the Socialists seek an injunction against Burleson. London immediately pointed out that most papers could not afford legal proceedings and that exclusion from the mails meant bankruptcy.

Despite his pleas, the committee adversely reported the resolution.[49] Undeterred, London took his fight to the floor of the House. On July 30 and again on the next day, he requested unanimous consent for consideration of the resolution. The chair, however, sustained parliamentary objections on each occasion.[50]

Attacks on the Socialist Party took place on many fronts during the summer and fall of 1917. In September federal agents raided party headquarters in Chicago. They also raided state party offices, seized files and checked membership lists. In many other areas proprietors pressured by vigilante groups refused Socialists the use of halls, while other places prohibited party meetings. In still other instances, Socialist speakers were attacked by self-styled patriots. Prior to the adoption of the Espionage Act, seven states passed laws limiting freedom of speech and press.[51]

The federal government also extended its control over speech and thought. The Trading with the Enemy Act of October 1917 authorized the president to censor all international communications and gave the postmaster general sweeping powers of censorship over the foreign-language press. Prior to final approval of the act, London threw the House into a "bitter" two-hour discussion when he made a point of order against the conference report.[52] The House conferees, he charged, had exceeded their authority and had violated the rules of the House by agreeing to Senate amendment number 127 in the report.[53]

London argued that the conferees could not go beyond the scope of the bill as passed by either house, that they could not assume to legislate, and that they had to limit themselves to areas of disagreement between the two houses.[54] Representatives Cooper, Stafford, Mondell, and Keating supported London's point of order. Although Speaker Clark questioned the wisdom of the proposed measure, he ruled that the conferees' substitute for Senate amendment 127 was germane, and they had not gone beyond their authority in that respect.[55]

On October 6 1917, the day that President Wilson signed the Trading with the Enemy Act, London took the floor to protest violations of civil liberties. Even in times of war, he declared, we should not suspend common sense. "We are working ourselves into a frenzy before a single shot has been fired at the enemy. What will we do later, when the crippled, wounded, and mutilated will return from the trenches?" The American people, London told the House, had shown great loyalty. Conscription was not popular, but the people ... had submitted to the law. "When you deal with a people of such profound loyalty, ... all attempts to suppress freedom of speech, freedom of thought, and a full discussion of vital issues are acts of unpardonable oppression."

In order "to make the world safe for democracy," London continued, Congress had allowed the deportation of twelve hundred men by a "lawless mob" in Bisbee, Arizona, and the lynching of Frank Little, a leader of the IWW, had gone unpunished.[56] At this point, Albert Johnson of Washington asked London if it was not true that Little had stated publicly that soldiers were "scabs" in uniform. "Yes," London replied, "but if the gentleman from Washington is willing to punish careless and foolish words by death nobody else would, particularly in the American Congress."

London then condemned other violations of civil liberties. Corporations had branded labor leaders as IWWs in order to suppress efforts by the workers to better themselves. Dozens of women had been imprisoned and held within the "shadow of the White House." The Post Office Department had suppressed Socialist literature. Congress had made the postmaster general "the main reservoir of wisdom" in the United States and every assistant district attorney an expert on politics, economics, and the people's liberties. Freedom of the press faced destruction in this country. The attempt to suppress the Socialist press, London declared, was particularly inexcusable in view of the importance of the Socialist movement as a permanent factor for international peace. "In all countries of the world they have been, and are now, the foremost champions of an enduring peace."[57]

Meanwhile, Wilson and Congress took steps to deal with a growing food problem. Food boycotts, parades and riots, led by Jewish women, occurred on New York's Lower East Side during late February 1917. Housewives found it increasingly difficult to afford staples such as eggs, beets, cabbage, potatoes and chickens as retail food prices soared by 20 to 30 percent in a few days. Their husbands made on average ten to fifteen dollars per week, and 40 to 60 percent was spent on food. Protests spread to Philadelphia, Boston and Chicago. New York Socialists sought to take advantage of the uprising. They organized protests and pressured Washington for relief from high food prices.[58]

On May 19, the president announced a food control program under Herbert Hoover, the former director of the Belgian Relief Commission. At first Hoover's agency acted without legal authority as a subcommittee of the Council of National Defense. Congress, however, began consideration of the Lever Act which provided for wartime controls over the production and distribution of food.[59] Samuel Gompers invited London to a meeting of labor officials and several other congressmen with President Wilson at the White House on the afternoon of June 11.

On June 20, London informed his colleagues that he favored the measure even though it did not protect the consumer against exploitation. The Socialist congressman disagreed with those who blamed food speculators for the high cost of living. He had no use for these "pirates," London exclaimed, but the real source of the problem was organized capital. A small number of people dictated prices, and so long as that continued, legislation directed at the effects rather than the cause would produce no permanent relief.

Six months ago, before the bread riots, London reminded his colleagues, he had directed their attention to escalating food prices. He had introduced a bill to provide for government food control and to authorize the president to halt food exports.[60] It took, however, a "formal declaration of war, famine, and pestilence before the Democrats or the Republicans get any sense in their heads." The Democrats had introduced a food control bill not because they understood the problem any better now, but because the president had proclaimed a slogan, "food control."

Although supportive of the bill, London asserted that it dealt "too tenderly" with the farmer. The measure not only gave farmers a guaranteed price for three years, but exempted them from the anti-hoarding clause. Nevertheless, he believed that some of its principles would have a lasting value. Food control, however, should become a permanent rather than a merely wartime policy. "My hope is that ... this assertion of the principle that the necessities of life must no longer be left to anarchy and general chaos, but must be taken under collective control of the people, contains a promise of more intelligent and more thorough going legislation in the near future."[61] The House adopted the Lever Act on June 23 by the overwhelming vote of 365 to 5.[62]

The *New York Call* applauded London's fight for food control. The Socialist congressman had spoken on the behalf of workers. He had shown that socialism alone could solve current problems and that capitalism could not get through a war without a "liberal dose" of collectivism. "Capitalism must steal the Socialist program, the Socialist method, the Socialist ideal for its own purposes." By so doing, capitalism had ensured its demise.[63]

Left-wing and right-wing Socialists alike, however, expressed dissatisfaction with London's unwillingness to follow the St. Louis Manifesto. His vote for Champ Clark as Speaker of the House, his "present" vote on the first War Loan Act of April 1917, and his refusal to introduce a bill to repeal conscription resulted in heavy criticism from anti-war publications and demands for his resignation and expulsion from the Party.

An editorial in *Advance*, the official organ of the Amalgamated Clothing Workers, which had endorsed the St. Louis Manifesto, noted that London was the only Socialist member of any parliament who had lacked the courage to commit himself on a measure such as the War Loan Act. Socialists would have preferred that London vote for the bill rather than "straddle."[64] By voting present, the *Radical Review* editorialized, London had "dismally failed" to advance Socialist principles. "He thus graphically illustrated to his political antagonists his unwillingness to draw the inexorable consequences flowing from a Socialist class position, and at the same time thereby exposed himself as a weak-kneed, gasconading imposter to unmerciful criticism the world over." London's "abominable and cowardly tactics" had also revealed the bankruptcy of "pure and simple political opportunism." Like all such pursuits, the political adventures of "this modern Don Quixote" had met with disaster, for they were not based upon "sound scientific perception of social phenomena, but upon boundless enthusiasm — wind."[65] The *American Socialist* pointed out London's lack of sympathy for the St. Louis Manifesto. He favored loaning billions of dollars to the Allies for the prosecution of the war, but the St. Louis convention had opposed giving a single life or dollar in support of a capitalist venture.[66]

Left-wing New York Socialists demanded that the State Executive Committee censure London. The committee, instead, provided a mild rebuke on May 16 when it expressed "deep regret" that London had voted for Champ Clark and "present" on the war loan bill. Although some of his actions did not meet with their full approval, a majority of the State Executive Committee refused to interfere with London's otherwise excellent work.[67]

London created a further furor within Socialist circles when party leaders learned that on April 18, 1917, he had cabled N.C. Tscheidse, a leading Menshevik member of the Duma, requesting him to deny disquieting rumors that Russian Socialists favored a separate peace with Germany.[68] London explained that his effort to forestall a separate peace was not made on behalf of the Allies, but in the interest of the Russian revolution and a universal and lasting peace.[69]

Nevertheless, Morris Hillquit considered London's opposition to a separate peace contrary to the position taken by the party at St. Louis. On April 20, Hillquit, international secretary of the American Socialist Party, sent a cable in the name of the National Executive Committee to Tscheidse: "Cables of Meyer London to you and those of Charles Edward Russell and others to Kenensky are not authorized by the Socialist Party. American Socialists have supreme faith in the ability of their Russian comrades to solve their own great problems in furtherance of peace, democracy and international Socialism."[70] Victor Berger agreed that the cables sent by London and other pro-war Socialists did not represent the sentiment of the American Socialist movement.[71]

On April 21, the Russian Socialist government informed London that it opposed a separate peace with Germany. It preferred an international peace without annexations or indemnities based upon the free development of all nations. The proletariat of every country should do its utmost to achieve peace on this basis.[72]

London broached the separate peace issue in a speech to the House on June 29. He analyzed the historical causes of the Russian revolution and its probable effect on the war. The Provisional Russian government had announced, London pointed out, that it desired a universal peace without annexations or punitive indemnities. The American press, however, had interpreted this as a demand for a separate peace with Germany. Yet the Russian government's proposal was "entirely in harmony" with President Wilson's principles, particularly those in his address to the Senate on January 22.

The Russian government had rejected a separate peace, London explained, because it realized the serious threat of a strong military power on its western frontier. In addition, Russia could not afford to see France defeated, Serbia destroyed, or any injustice to the peoples who formed a barrier against the eastward expansion of Germany. Perhaps the most important factor, he continued, was that Russian Socialists, like Socialists everywhere, embraced internationalism. London told his colleagues that the same thought animated him when he sent his cable expressing the hope that Russia would be a vital force in achieving a universal and lasting peace.[73]

Although criticized from all sides, London seems to have taken it in stride. In reply to Seymour Stedman, a prominent right-wing Chicago Socialist, London wrote that a Socialist who attempted to satisfy all Socialists would end up in an asylum, and while everyone might land there if the war lasted long enough, he hoped to retain his senses as long as possible. As for his failure to vote "no" on the first War Loan Act, London explained that Socialists in other parliaments had shown their disapproval in several ways, the refusal to vote among them. Socialists had also voted "no" or had walked out before the vote. He had refused to vote because he favored non-combatant aid to the Allies.

At a meeting of party members on June 24, London further elaborated his stance on the war and various war-related measures considered by Congress. He reiterated that it would be useless to introduce a bill for the repeal of conscription. During the question-and-answer period, members of the audience voiced their displeasure with London.[74]

Meanwhile, the American Socialist Party and the Dutch Socialist Party called for an international Socialist congress of neutrals and belligerents to consider peace plans. Originally set for May 15, 1917, in Stockholm, the conference was later postponed to June 10. The State Department, however, refused on May 23 to grant passports to the American Socialist delegation including Morris Hillquit, Victor Berger, and Algernon Lee. In so doing, Secretary of State Robert Lansing invoked the Logan Act of 1799 which prohibited private citizens from engaging in unauthorized diplomatic missions. Secretary Lansing characterized the conference as a "cleverly directed German war move" to bring about a separate peace between Germany and Russia.[75]

Meyer London expressed displeasure with the position of the State Department. The United States government, he said, "should encourage sending delegates anywhere, at any time to promote the cause of peace."[76] Even if the Stockholm Conference had been engineered by the Germans, London stated, it was "absurd" to prohibit American, British and French Socialists from participating in the conference. "Why cannot a conference of honest men meet ... whether at Stockholm on Petrograd or anywhere else?... It is highly important that the British and French and American Socialists should go to the Russian Socialists and say, 'Stand with us; hold on a little while longer, fight along with us, and we will settle this world trouble, and settle it on terms that will insure universal peace.'"[77] On May 25, London and Victor Berger met with Lansing, but the secretary refused to alter his decision.[78]

London continued to support the Socialist Party position in regard to Stockholm, and on at least two occasions, October 6, 1917, and May 1, 1918, he told the House that the Allied governments had committed a serious "blunder" by refusing to grant passports to the Socialist delegations. "Nothing," London declared, "had such a demoralizing effect upon the democratized army of Russia than this refusal."[79]

In addition to his support for the Stockholm Conference, London, on August 1, 1917, introduced a resolution calling for an inter-parliamentary conference to discuss terms for a lasting peace. The resolution called upon President Wilson to invite the Allied governments to elect delegations to meet in Washington in order to "promote democracy in international relations and to reach a common understanding upon which a lasting peace may be established."[80]

In an accompanying statement, London said that a growing demand existed throughout the world for clarification of the principal issues of the war. A declaration by representatives from the parliaments of Allied nations would appeal to the reason and conscience of the world. Moreover, it would have an immediate effect upon peace-loving peoples of the Central Powers. The United States, he continued, should take the initiative in such a conference, for it had not yet become embittered and was still capable of making objective decisions. An inter-parliamentary conference would neither weaken nor divide, but unite.[81] The resolution died in the House Foreign Relations Committee.

In the meantime, the municipal election campaign was in full swing in New York City. A four-corner race had developed with the incumbent mayor, John P. Mitchel, running as a fusion candidate after William M. Bennett upset him in the Republican primary. Tammany had nominated John F. Hyland, and Morris Hillquit headed the Socialist ticket. Mayor Mitchel disregarded his own record on municipal matters, and made support of the war the principal issue in the campaign. This gave the Socialist Party an opportunity to test the war issue. Hillquit took a strong anti-war stand and, in keeping with the St. Louis Manifesto, announced that he would not buy liberty bonds. He called for an international conference to end the conflict on Socialist principles of no annexation and no indemnities. Hillquit's campaign aroused popular support, and throughout September and October, Socialist rallies on the East Side attracted large and enthusiastic audiences.[82]

During September and early October, London's duties in Washington prevented him from taking an active part in the campaign. Scheduled to speak at the first important rally of the campaign on September 19, he failed to attend because of illness.[83] With the close of the first session of the Sixty-Fifth Congress on October 6, London returned to New York. However, during the following weeks, he remained conspicuous by his absence from the campaign. On October 20, the Socialist congressman stated that he was "worn out," but would soon campaign in the city. He hoped to report to the Congress that New York had elected a Socialist mayor and that Socialists had won victories throughout the country.[84]

London's failure to take an active role in the campaign probably stemmed from his opposition to Hillquit's antiwar position. Thus, on October 21, London told a crowd of some two thousand that Socialists could not be indifferent to the outcome of the conflict. At first Socialists had hoped that the war would end in a stalemate so that the people might turn on their rulers. Socialists now believed that the war should not end without the return of all occupied territory, and a way found to avoid future conflicts. "Let us be ... honest about it," London went on. "We do not want the Socialist vote to be interpreted as a vote for the Kaiser gang. But we want every Socialist to have the courage to speak the truth no matter at what cost." Socialists, London declared, should not be demagogues. It was nonsensical to believe that a significant Socialist vote would end the conflict. The war would not end until there was a "sound basis for a universal peace."

According to the *New York Times*, London received "strong" applause at the beginning and end of his speech, but none during his remarks on the war. One young man in the rear, the *Times* reported, shouted that London should be "read out" of the party like Charles Edward Russell. August Claessens, who followed London, observed that many Socialists disagreed with him. "He gave vent to certain sentiments that were not Socialistic, but they were his, and I want to say that he has a perfect right to say what he likes for no Socialist is controlled by the organization."[85]

Ironically, the pro-war *New York Times* defended London. What, the *Times* asked, was there in the teachings of Marx or any other Socialist that made London's statement "not Socialistic"? The New York Socialists had established a new brand of socialism. Indeed, was it socialism or had "they cut loose from the old moorings and adopted a new socialism which no great Socialist from Marx on down would recognize? What is the difference between socialism and pro–Germanism, and what is the difference between pro–Germanism and support of a militarist autocracy? Meyer London is a heretic not to socialism but to Kaiserism, but socialism today in New York means not socialism but Kaiserism, and, therefore, he is a heretic in truth."[86]

As the campaign closed, London spoke at a number of rallies on behalf of the Socialist ticket. Nevertheless, conservative Yiddish newspapers and Tammany politicians created the impression that London did not want Jews to vote for Hillquit.[87] To counteract this tactic, the *New York Call* published an interview in which London denounced the effort of Tammany Hall and Jewish politicians to confuse the voters. "It is a scandal that Tammany Hall and chauvinist politicians should attempt to use my name to injure the splendid prospects of the Socialist Party and its candidate for mayor. At every meeting I addressed, I called upon the citizens to vote a straight Socialist ticket." The only vote, London declared, that a "right thinking" person could cast was for the Socialist ticket from alderman up to Hillquit. During these perilous times, the people could not entrust the questions of bread and life to the rulers and servants of the "money bags" responsible for the high cost of living. Only working-class representatives could be trusted with the vital interest of the people.[88]

On Election Day, the voters repudiated Mayor Mitchel's militant prowar campaign by giving John F. Hylan the greatest plurality in the history of the city. The new mayor received 313,956 votes; Mitchel 155,497; Hillquit 145,332; and Bennett 55,483. Hillquit received 21.7 percent of the total vote or nearly five times as many votes as Charles Edward Russell in 1912. In addition, the Socialist Party elected seven aldermen, ten assemblymen and a municipal court judge.[89] Hillquit's great strength in the Jewish working-class districts on the Lower East Side indicated that London's war position did not reflect the mood of a considerable portion of his constituency.

The day following the November 1917 elections, the Bolshevik Revolution occurred in Russia. Unlike the majority of American socialists, London, who had expressed joy with the March Revolution, could find little to cheer about. He attributed the overthrow of the Mensheviks to general discontent with the incompetent Provisional Government. He predicted that the Bolshevik seizure of power would be temporary, for they represented a small faction of the Russian Socialists and had gained power by virtue of their great activity.

The Allies, London charged, had precipitated the crisis by failing to cooperate with the Provisional Government before the Bolsheviks had become so powerful. Nonetheless, socialism had not failed. The Socialist victory in Russia had never been equaled in the history of the world, and from this same socialism, London declared, would come the peace for which the world so deeply yearned.[90]

During the next few weeks, left-wing opposition to London intensified. More than likely, his perceived lukewarm support for Hillquit and his views on the Bolshevik Revolution contributed to this growing sentiment against him. Ludwig Lore, an editor of the new American left-wing publication, *The Class Struggle*, and a frequent critic of London, deplored his record in the

Sixty-Fifth Congress and demanded his expulsion from the party. "His whole activity during the momentous session," Lore wrote, "was of such inferior character, showed such an outstanding indifference to every fundamental question that arose and to practically every debate of importance that occurred that several of the more progressive Democrats and Republicans proved themselves of much higher value to the people at large. His voting record was equally as bad and not only justifies but demands his expulsion from the Socialist Party since he either voted in favor of or in many cases failed to record his vote against war measures and appropriations for military and naval purposes." If London was correct, Lore continued, those provisions of the party's constitution which provided for the expulsion of any elected official who voted for military or war appropriations should be eliminated. If wrong, however, as Lore believed, justice should be carried out as stipulated in the party laws.[91]

On November 24, the Central Committee of Local New York requested London to appear at a special meeting on December 1 to discuss his position on the international situation.[92] This meeting ranked as one of the worst he experienced due to his anti-war stance. Members of his own party attacked him and demanded that he give up his seat in Congress.

London remained steadfast. The St. Louis Manifesto, he reiterated, failed to provide an adequate program for active Socialists. It failed to recognize that war existed. In regard to his abstention on military measures, London pointed out that the party constitution specifically enjoined a Socialist office-holder from voting for such measures, but did not require him to vote against them. He had fulfilled his duty by abstaining. As for demands that he introduce a bill for the repeal of the conscription law, London stated that Socialists would be unable to agitate effectively for such a bill. Moreover, Congress would not adopt it. An unapologetic London rebuked his critics. "You wished to place yourself in a position where you could accomplish nothing. The country is at war and you act as if nothing had happened. You represent a tendency not a movement."

At the conclusion of his remarks, the Central Committee, aware that it could not get him to alter his stance, adopted a motion requesting that the National Executive Committee consult with London. It called upon them to develop a plan of action which would guide London during the second session of the Sixty-Fifth Congress.[93]

The next day London returned to Washington to await the opening of Congress on December 3. When asked by a reporter to discuss his meeting with the Central Committee, he declined to make a statement. "I shall follow," he said, "the traditions of my party and not discuss in the public prints what took place." London intimated, however, that he could safely follow his own dictates despite reports that party leaders had developed a course of action that they expected him to pursue in Congress.[94] Nevertheless, rumors persisted that London faced expulsion or had chosen to resign from the party. The rumors proved unfounded.

Although Meyer London opposed the war, he believed that German militarism represented a serious threat to democratic institutions and, therefore, refused to abide by the St. Louis Manifesto. As the lone Socialist representative, London, always the pragmatist, realized that an obstructionist position would arouse the hostility of his fellow congressmen, making it impossible for him to receive a fair hearing and to use the war as a means to further socialism. London opposed specific war measures such as conscription and censorship. At the same time, he urged the Wilson administration to take the lead in ending the war. His war position satisfied neither his congressional colleagues nor his more militant comrades. Nevertheless, he continued to follow the dictates of his conscience.

9

The Sixty-Fifth Congress: Champion of Civil Liberties

> To adopt the doctrine that once war is declared no act of the Government is to be challenged by the people and that all criticism should be suppressed would mean that an ambitious Government by plunging the country into war could destroy every vestige of democracy.—*Meyer London,* Congressional Record, *65th Congress, 2nd Session, 6,179.*

During the lengthy second session of the "War Congress," London continued as an outspoken critic of war. He refused, however, to do anything that would impede the country's military effort. At the same time, he urged Congress to take the initiative in creating an international league to secure peace, and he supported President Wilson's efforts in this direction. While critical of Bolshevik tactics, the Socialist congressman urged his colleagues to show understanding toward the Russian people. London advocated diplomatic recognition of Russia and opposed foreign intervention in her internal affairs. Russia, he insisted, should be free to decide her own destiny. In domestic matters, London once again called upon Congress to establish a national insurance system in order to ease the transition to a peacetime economy. He also supported a number of emergency measures aimed at extending government control over various areas of the economy, and in so doing, sought to make them permanent programs. However, his most important work of the session was his unflagging opposition to repressive wartime legislation and violations of civil liberties. London led the fight against those who sought to stamp out dissent in the name of patriotism.

The House convened on Monday, December 3, 1917, amidst a tense atmosphere attributable to the worsening conditions at home and abroad. The slow pace of the American war effort, the steady decline in Allied fortunes on the western front, plus setbacks in Italy and the Bolshevik seizure of power in Russia troubled Democrats and Republicans alike.[1]

The following day President Wilson appeared before the Congress to deliver his State of the Union address. Wilson took note of the dismal state of

9. The 65th Congress: Champion of Civil Liberties 175

the war in Europe as well as the low morale in the Allied countries. He referred to the growing clamor in this country of the "noisily thoughtless and troublesome," whose pessimistic predictions had raised doubts among the people as to the eventual outcome of the war. All this, however, had no significance in view of the high ideals to which the nation had dedicated itself. Humanity demanded, the president declared, "a just and righteous accounting from the enemy who in the end would be compelled to yield." In order to hasten the defeat of the Central Powers, Wilson asked Congress to declare war against Austria-Hungary.[2]

Debate on the war resolution began in the House on December 7. The high point came when London courageously announced that he could not support the measure. As a Socialist, he told his fellow congressmen, he had pledged to vote against the declaration of war. "In matters of war I am a teetotaler. I refuse to take the first intoxicating drink." Socialists, he asserted, in all parliaments, had opposed war until the last moment, and if there had been a Socialist majority in the European nations in 1914, war would not have occurred. Moreover, were there Socialist majorities in the parliaments of the belligerent nations today, the war would end tomorrow. A member of Congress, London continued, should not hesitate to express views which differed from those of the president. There was no reason why congressmen should not discuss international policies.

One should not interpret his vote against the war resolution, London explained, as an endorsement of the "infamous" attack by Austria-Hungary on Serbia. He would vote against the declaration of war because he felt obligated to give expression to Socialist thought and sentiment. He would do so although "anxious ... that the American people should appear unanimous and united in their longing for universal peace, to be based on no annexations, no punitive indemnities, upon aid to the weaker and smaller nations which have been invaded by the ruthless Central Powers, with disarmament and international arbitration as a means to prevent wars in the future."[3]

London's colleagues strongly condemned his statement. Adolph Sabbath, a Democrat from Illinois, stated that he too had an interest in the Russian people. However, his primary concern was the welfare of the United States. He reminded London that every person living under the American flag, whether a Socialist, a pacifist or anything else, had the duty to serve his country and thereby prove that he deserved to live in the United States and enjoy the benefits of liberty and democracy.[4]

Isaac Siegel, who had defeated Morris Hillquit in 1916, hastened to reassure the House that Socialists in both his district and London's supported the government and the American people in their determination to see the war successfully prosecuted. He hoped that London would change his mind so the House, like the Senate, could declare itself unanimously for war against Austria.[5]

The most vitriolic outburst against London came from Democrat Percy Quin of Mississippi. The Socialist representative, Quin admonished, did not represent the poor people of the country. To the contrary, if the argument that London had espoused since the beginning of the war was carried to its logical conclusion, the masters of Germany and Austria and those people who oppressed the poor in Europe would seek to come over here and oppress the poor people of this country. London represented "flannel-mouthed anarchy and those like him in high places, who pretended now to argue that this is a war of commerce and pelf and profit, are guilty of treason." Quin urged London's Socialist constituents to repudiate him.

In some sections of the country, Quin declared, a man in private life who uttered treasonable statements like those of London would be treated "rather harshly." In Mississippi, London would face danger for making such comments. The time had come, Quin concluded, for Congress to no longer tolerate treasonable remarks on the House floor. Representative Dyer of Missouri joined Quin in denouncing London. Any man, he exclaimed, who either opposed or refused to give the "utmost" aid in the House should have his citizenship taken away and be branded an enemy of the nation.[6] Shortly thereafter, the House adopted the war resolution by 365 to 1 as London cast the sole dissenting vote.[7] With the exception of the war resolution, the second session of the Sixty-Fifth Congress produced no major legislation during its first two months. There was very little important new legislation on the House calendar since it had enacted most of the essential war measures during the previous session. Much of this work, however, had been done hastily, and a number of problems arose which required attention and adjustment. In addition, dissatisfaction with the lagging war effort prompted several congressional investigations into the administration's policies.[8]

During this hiatus in legislative activity, London pressed ahead on a number of fronts. On December 6, he introduced a resolution calling upon the president to invite representatives of the parliaments of countries at war with the Central Powers to a conference in Washington for the purpose of organizing an international league to secure a lasting peace.[9] London explained that all the sacrifices of the war would be in vain unless some way other than war was found to resolve international disputes. The task of securing a permanent peace, of working out a code of international law, of providing for international arbitration, for gradual disarmament, and for guaranteeing the rights of the weak demanded immediate attention. If an international league had existed at the onset of the war, no nation would have dared defy the world.[10]

9. The 65th Congress: Champion of Civil Liberties   177

London took the House floor on January 11 to urge congressional support for his resolution. Only three days earlier, President Wilson had appeared before a joint session of Congress to deliver his Fourteen Point peace program in which he reaffirmed his support for a league of nations.[11] In his speech, London stated that the idea of an international league had always seemed inconceivable. Yet, during the last three years, twenty-one nations had engaged in a common effort against the Central Powers, and in effect had created such a league. The "dream of dreamers" had become reality. The problem, London continued, was whether the principle of international cooperation would be extended. Moreover, would it include other nations so that its primary and sole object would be to secure a lasting peace?

London pointed out that support had grown for the creation of a world organization. Former president Taft, Leon Trotsky, the French Chamber of Deputies, the British Labor Party, and Socialists throughout the world had recognized the need for a permanent league to secure peace. As his first act in the Sixty-Fourth Congress, he had introduced a peace resolution which included the creation of an international court, with the commercial boycott as a means of punishment. London stated that no nation had the right to intervene in the internal affairs of another. "It should be the very object and the very reason for existence of such a league to assure to each nation full scope to live its own life unmolested." Only questions affecting amicable relations between nations were a matter of international concern.

Representative Gordon of Ohio asked London whether he considered import duties to be such a question. Protective and punitive tariffs, London responded, acted as barriers among the nations of the world, and the entire world would benefit by eliminating them. It would, therefore, be in the interest of all nations to consider the tariff question. London also emphasized the need for disarmament. All treaties were mere scraps of paper as long as nations maintained large armies and navies. Elimination of armaments and militarism should be one of the principal goals of international cooperation.

President Wilson had repeatedly urged the creation of permanent international institutions to guarantee a lasting peace and arms reduction. Unfortunately, the American people and most of their representatives did not view these proposals as a practical solution for war. The people failed to realize that, even though the United States had not entered any treaties of alliance, isolationism had been abandoned. If this country did not initiate an international league, London asked, who would?

London then discussed the Soviet government's terms for peace which included evacuation of all Russian territory occupied by Germany, settlement of the question of Alsace-Loraine by plebiscite, the restoration of Belgium, the renunciation of indemnities by all the belligerents, gradual disarmament on land and sea, and a peace congress composed of delegates chosen by national representative bodies.

Representative Huddleston of Alabama asked London to compare the Russian terms with Wilson's Fourteen Points. London replied that most of the terms were identical to those enunciated by the President. Regarding the President's recent appearance before Congress, London stated that he had "instinctively" applauded him. As a rule, he admitted, he did not do that. On this occasion, however, he felt that a positive step was about to be taken. A clear statement of war aims was of immeasurable benefit to mankind. "Let the central powers and the democratic elements throughout the world say, what is there in that statement of demands, what are the things that we are going to continue to fight for." Had the Allies, London continued, made a definite declaration several months ago, Russia would not have withdrawn from the war. "And even today, Russia exhausted, bleeding at every pore, starving Russia, repudiates a selfish peace and pleads for the peace of the world."

Representative Miller of Minnesota then asked London whether he approved of efforts by the Russian government to negotiate a separate peace with Germany. London retorted that Miller knew that he had sent a cablegram to the Soldiers and Workmen's Council in April of 1917 suggesting that a separate peace was a danger to Russia and the world. Miller refused to accept this answer and asked London if he opposed the movement. London denied that such a movement existed. "On the contrary these men are today speaking for a universal peace. But one should have patience with a people who are in the agony of a revolution and of war." London urged the House to consider the basic principles upon which a permanent peace could be established.[12]

At the conclusion of London's remarks, Henry Rainey of Illinois took the floor to reply to him and to discuss socialism in the United States. Rainey stated that he could not agree with London's position that the principles enunciated in the president's message on January 8 had been discovered by Russian Socialists or for that matter by the Socialists of any other country. Moreover, the anti-war declaration of the American Socialist Party, Rainey declared, was as close to treason as any expression that he had heard from any one man or from any group of men. If the Democratic and Republican parties continued to debate "little" issues, he warned, they would find themselves confronted with the specter of socialism in this country and throughout the world. It was imperative, therefore, to return, when the war ended, to the "sane methods of holding land; to reestablish and maintain the methods of administering the affairs of the people of the Republic under which we have prospered and progressed — the methods which have prevailed since the birth of the modern state."[13]

9. The 65th Congress: Champion of Civil Liberties

Meanwhile, London had resumed his fight for a national social insurance system. On December 13, 1917, he introduced another resolution providing for unemployment, invalidity and sickness insurance. The House Committee on Labor, once again, unanimously reported the measure without amendment on December 15 and referred it to the House for consideration.[14] Socialist papers applauded London's initiative and reported that the Wilson administration seemed supportive.

In his remarks to the committee, London urged immediate action upon his proposal. The demobilization of industry at the conclusion of the conflict, he warned, would threaten the economic security of many workers who had adapted themselves to wartime conditions. In addition, the return of millions of veterans to civilian jobs made it imperative that preparations begin immediately for the return to a peacetime economy.[15]

Debate on the social insurance resolution began in the House on January 9, 1918. Edward Keating, who acted as floor manager for the measure, informed the House that the Labor Committee hoped to secure a vote on the resolution that evening. Keating then proceeded to discuss the history of the measure. He reminded the House that the Labor Committee had unanimously reported it after exhaustive hearings, during the preceding Congress. In the present Congress, the committee had once again unanimously reported the resolution. The United States, he pointed out, lagged behind virtually every European country in the area of social insurance. Experts who appeared before the committee stated that it would be impossible to apply one of these European systems in this country. As a first step, they suggested a commission to investigate the existing systems. If the commission decided favorably upon the need for social insurance in this country, it would then choose an appropriate system.

Following Keating's remarks, London argued on behalf of his resolution. A serious disarrangement of industry, he warned, would occur when the war ended. Many men would experience difficulty in finding employment. In addition, millions of veterans would seek their old jobs only to find them filled by women. Now, London insisted, was the time to prepare for that emergency. Information should be gathered so that when Congress finally enacted legislation it would be "based upon knowledge, systematized, sifted, analyzed and brought up to date." Unemployment was endemic to modern industry. A new system was needed to replace the unsatisfactory contemporary system of soup kitchens and vagrancy laws. The war must not, he continued, prevent Congress from dealing with the issue.

Turning to the question of old age pensions, London told his colleagues that the idea of an old person finding himself compelled to resort to charity after years of useful service to a community was "a negation of the most elementary principles of morality." The German people supported their government because it had established unemployment insurance, old age pensions and benefits for sickness and injury. If a feudalistic government, London exclaimed, could do such things in order to maintain support, it could be done by a free people in order to help build a strong nation. The problems of unemployment, old age pensions, and health insurance could not be solved on the county or even the state level. They were national problems and of national concern and required a national solution. At the conclusion of London's remarks, the House decided to postpone final action on the bill until January 16.[16]

At that time Representative Gard, a Democrat from Ohio, offered an amendment postponing creation of the commission until the war emergency had passed. Gard argued that the Labor Committee already possessed sufficient data. Moreover, abnormal conditions existed in the United States at this time, and the type of information that would benefit workers was information relative to the normal conditions which would exist when the war ended. Representatives Stafford and Sherley echoed Gard's sentiments.

McCormick and Keating joined London in answering critics of the resolution. McCormick opposed the Gard amendment countering that now was the time to begin the accumulation of preliminary information. Many nations, he observed, had begun preparations to deal with problems arising from the war. Congress would gravely err in delaying such a commission. The Labor Committee, Keating stated, believed that the commission could carry on its work at this time. Furthermore, the argument that the commission would run all over the world was not worthy of serious consideration. London argued that Sherley had failed to grasp the significance of the suggestion that Congress should prepare now, when there was no unemployment, for the dislocation in industry which would inevitably follow the end of the war. The commission would not promote unrest, but would make unrest unnecessary. The House, heeding London's pleas, rejected the Gard amendment 48 to 22.[17]

The debate continued with Moore of Pennsylvania and Rainey of Illinois speaking against the resolution. Moore repeated Sherley's arguments, but also charged that the commission's probe would create unrest in time of war. It would not succeed, however, in settling those problems. Rainey charged that the proposals were "purely and absolutely Socialistic." Sherley then moved to strike out the enacting clause. Keating made a point of order that this motion came too late, but the chair ruled that such a motion was in order at any time before the final reading of the bill. The House then voted 199 to 133 to strike out the enacting clause.[18]

Deeply disappointed by the rejection of the resolution, London took the floor on January 18 to express displeasure with his colleagues. The House, he complained, by failing to act, had shown its "utter incompetency" to deal with the unemployment insurance problem. Both parties had displayed "ignorance and darkness." Opponents of the resolution, he continued, had argued that the commission would be unable to obtain the proper information due to the war. But Congress now had the information. The Fuel Administration had issued an order depriving millions of men of employment for two weeks.[19]

Many congressmen, an outraged London charged, had not dared to vote for a study of the unemployment problem because a Socialist had introduced it. "Forty-seven treacherous Democrats, too cowardly to vote for a Socialist measure when it had a chance to pass, who voted for it last year refused to vote for it this year, the most contemptible political performance that any party could be guilty of. I just studied those 47 names, and I will memorize those names, and I will remember them." London declared that he felt like giving up his seat in the House to challenge them in their own districts. Now that millions of men would lose fourteen days employment, London continued, an investigation was inadequate to meet this emergency. He then proposed that Congress appropriate one hundred million dollars to be used by the Secretary of Labor to relieve unemployment.

Representative Walsh, a Republican from Massachusetts, rebuked London. It was fitting, he said, that "London should have the opportunity to run amuck amongst us and voice his rage against majority rule." London had failed to vote for several vital war measures, yet at this critical moment he asked the House to interrupt its deliberation of important war measures to consider a personal measure which would not contribute to the war effort but would increase already enormous expenditures. London, Walsh declared, should not encourage those who were halfhearted in their loyalty to the flag. Henceforth, he should "lend his voice and vote" in support of the president. When peace came, Walsh concluded, London might attain the praise which he desired. The "glory he apparently believes in above the glory and the destiny of his country."[20]

Despite this setback, London continued to fight for social insurance. On January 23, he introduced a resolution authorizing the Secretary of Labor to investigate and make a report to Congress on the advisability of establishing a system of unemployment, invalidity and old age insurance.[21] Shortly thereafter, James P. Maher, chairman of the House Labor Committee, referred the resolution to secretary of labor William B. Wilson for his consideration.

In his reply to Maher on March 5, Secretary Wilson endorsed London's proposal. An "alarming" increase in unemployment would occur, he stated, unless steps were taken to absorb returning veterans and those employed in war industries into the post-war labor force. He noted, however, that Congress, and not the secretary of labor, as London proposed, should determine the advisability of adopting a system of national insurance against unemployment, old age and invalidity. The secretary doubted that such a study could be adequately developed on an appropriation of fifty thousand dollars.[22]

London, encouraged by Wilson's position, revised the resolution and offered it as an amendment to the Legislative, Executive and Judicial Appropriations bill on March 13. The amendment called for an investigation by the secretary of labor "into the subject of insurance against unemployment." In arguing on behalf of the amendment, London pointed out that Secretary Wilson recognized the desirability of an immediate study of the entire social insurance issue. Every thinking person, he declared, realized that dislocation in industry would occur when the war ended. Now was the time to prepare for that eventuality. London noted that unlike his previous resolution, the secretary of labor, rather than a special commission to which many had objected, would investigate the subject. The Department of Labor, he declared, had been specifically created to deal with the issue. "It is the supreme duty of Congress to supply the Department of Labor with funds to make the necessary investigation. That will probably be the most important work in which the department has ever been engaged."

At the conclusion of London's remarks, Byrns of Tennessee made a point of order against the amendment. The amendment, he said, was legislation upon an appropriation bill, and even if it was in order on such a bill, it should have been made to the Civil Appropriation bill. The chair upheld the point of order. London then offered another amendment which authorized an appropriation of fifty thousand dollars to the secretary of labor to investigate the subject of unemployment insurance. Once again Byrns made a point of order. After a brief parliamentary debate, in which Sherley also stated that the amendment should be made to the Civil Appropriation bill, the chair sustained the point of order.[23]

London made one final effort to procure an investigation in the second session of the Sixty-Fifth Congress. During the consideration of the Sundry Civil Appropriations bill on June 17, 1918, he offered an amendment providing that the secretary of labor receive seventy-five thousand dollars to investigate unemployment insurance, with particular reference to securing jobs for soldiers discharged at the end of the war. London told the House that he offered the amendment in good faith. Sherley, he reminded his colleagues, had previously suggested that such an amendment would be in order on this bill. Once again, London emphasized the necessity to prepare immediately for the post-war period. Various European countries had already begun to study the question of reconstruction. The English had established a special reconstruction ministry in July 1917 to take up the entire problem of industrial rehabilitation. The United States, London asserted, should not be found "standing aghast and bewildered" when the war ended. Despite London's pleas, the House, once again, rejected the amendment.[24]

In other domestic legislation, London supported a number of measures aimed at extending government control over areas of the economy vital to the war effort. By December 1917, railroad transportation seemed near collapse as a result of increased war traffic, the lack of unified control and severe winter weather. Congress had received a report from the Interstate Commerce Commission early in December pointing out the need for strong unified control. On December 28, the president placed all railroad transportation under the control of a United States Railroad Administration headed by William G. McAdoo, who resigned as secretary of the treasury to become director general of the railroads.[25]

In an interview with the *New York Call*, London approved the president's action, but noted that it did not constitute socialism as critics charged. A great difference existed, he stated, between national management, which was limited to securing profits for the stockholders, and national ownership and control "for the people and by the people." As a Socialist he sought the latter. London hoped that this first attempt at national control of a public necessity would lead to the recognition of the fact that natural monopolies should belong to the people and be managed by them.

When asked if government management would assure better service, London replied, "Undoubtedly." During periods of national emergency the principle of competition breaks down as in the case of the railroads. "Concentration along national lines is inevitable when the nation acts as a unit. There is no place for competition in such a case." Unfortunately, nations had failed to take unified action except in wartime. The question, he concluded, was whether they would apply the same principle of efficiency in peacetime.[26]

Shortly thereafter, the House began consideration of a bill to fix the time and terms of government control of the railroads. On February 22, London opposed a provision in the bill limiting federal control to the duration of the war. "When you repudiate the idea that public utilities are ultimately to be owned and controlled and managed by the people," he declared, "you deny the very essence of democracy." If he had time, London told his colleagues, he could convince them that democracy could not endure without public ownership of public utilities. Congress had the responsibility to prepare for that "inevitable" event.[27] On February 28, the House defeated an amendment offered by London to extend federal control for ninety-nine years, by a large majority, as London could muster only four votes in its favor.[28]

London's remarks brought a sharp rejoinder on the following day from Martin Dies of Texas.[29] The conservative southern congressman not only objected to London's "Bolsheviki" speech, but to the fact that Speaker Clark had called upon the Socialist congressman to preside temporarily over the House on January 26.[30] In view of the fact, Dies remarked, that London considered this country the greatest failure in the world, it was outrageous that he was permitted to occupy the Speaker's chair under the American flag, near a portrait of George Washington.

Dies defended property rights, stating that without them there could be no liberty. London, he charged, wanted to transform the country into an industrial democracy similar to that in Russia. A national emergency, he continued, had necessitated government control of the railroads. Congress should ratify this action, not because it condoned government ownership of the railroads, but because in wartime power had to be concentrated in the president. Socialism, however, should not be tolerated. When the war ended Congress should restore all the power of the people. Dies urged the House to give the president all the power he sought, but to take it away when the war ended.[31]

London then requested and received unanimous consent to address the House. Dies, he stated, was no doubt unfamiliar with the body of American literature dealing with public ownership of the railroads. London suggested that in addition to the information Dies had received about the founders of this country he should enlighten himself by reading the works of economists who advocated national ownership of public utilities.

As for Dies' comments on socialism, London said that he could not take him seriously since Dies did not know what he was talking about. But when Dies talked about the greatness of the United States, he could agree with him. No man, London continued, loved this country more than himself. Democracy, however, was not a static condition, it had to be dynamic. "Lincoln, Washington [and] Jefferson were great because they met the problems of their day.... They did not point to the great men who preceded them centuries before. The gentleman looks to the grave all the time from his little village in Texas. He studies the past and points backward all of the time. I have my face to the sun." Socialism, London asserted, was a valid doctrine, a doctrine which sought to find a way to give people the product of their labor. Was it wrong to suggest industrial democracy as the means?

London then turned to Dies' attack upon the Bolsheviks. He did not try to justify their policies, but sought to put the unfolding events in Russia into proper historical perspective. The Russian people, he explained, had suffered oppression through the centuries, and had been led into a war not of their making. London recalled the long struggle of the United States to establish a sound government. In addition, it was unfair to talk of Russia's experiment as a Socialist experiment, for socialism was impossible in Russia under existing conditions.

9. The 65th Congress: Champion of Civil Liberties 185

The Socialist congressman told the House that he had tried to perform his duty as he construed it. He had thus invited attack from the "misinformed, the prejudiced and the vulgar," but there had been very little of it on the House floor. "I am doing my duty as well as any other member of Congress, and I am working as hard as any member ever did. I refuse to accept either the wisdom or the methods of the gentleman from Texas." London told his colleagues that he bore no ill feeling toward Dies, and he believed that Dies had not intended to be nasty to him. Dies had simply disagreed with his views. London and Dies later shook hands.[32]

The House also took up a bill to alleviate the acute housing shortage that had arisen in communities where shipyards and munitions plants were located. It authorized the secretary of labor to incorporate in New York a Housing Corporation in which the secretary held, as agent for the government, the entire hundred million dollars of its stock. This corporation would then provide housing and community facilities where needed.[33]

During debate in the House on April 1 and 2, London objected to those sections of the bill which limited the authority of the secretary of labor to the duration of the war and which provided for the eventual sale of this government-owned property. The House, however, rejected several amendments introduced by him to extend the secretary's authority over housing beyond the existing emergency.[34]

On behalf of these amendments, London argued that although the present bill dealt with an immediate need produced by the war emergency, the housing shortage would remain when the war concluded. Moreover, the provision to terminate the secretary's authority would prevent him from managing buildings constructed at the expense of the federal government. "Why," London asked, "should we ... now preclude the Government from utilizing the structures built at the expense of the United States? Why should we now compel the Government to sacrifice all the money invested in building these structures?" Would private real estate interests have precedence over the public interest?[35] Once again the view prevailed in the House that such government activity was necessitated by war conditions and should cease when those conditions no longer existed.

London also supported bills extending federal authority over agriculture, mining and rents in the District of Columbia.[36] During the consideration of an amendment to the Agriculture Appropriations bill which sought to establish the minimum price of wheat at $2.50 a bushel, London warned his colleagues that Congress could not fix the minimum price for an essential product like wheat and refuse to do so for other necessities. He suggested that Congress could do one of two things. It could authorize the federal government to regulate the prices of all essential articles or give up the effort to control the price of only one. European nations, he observed, had failed in their attempts to arbitrarily fix prices for a few products.

London then told his colleagues that he was amused when they talked about the evil of profiteering. Society was based on profiteering, and business was organized for profit. Yet Congress now asked the businessman not to be inspired by profit, but to be guided by the common welfare. Congress desired businessmen to acquire a "collective soul," but they had none. "Competition," London continued, "is your highest law. Individual against individual, group against group, class against class, all against everybody, everybody against all — such is the law of competition. To stop competition in one article and leave it unchecked in everything else is poor wisdom indeed." London denied that such legislation was socialism. It was not socialism to take a burden from the farmer and place it upon the consumer. This type of legislation was "socialism of the fool." The federal government, he insisted, should purchase all farm products. It should also have the authority to sell these products directly to the people at a price suitable to their purchasing power.[37]

The House rejected the Gore amendment, but then adopted an amendment setting the price at $2.40 per bushel with London in opposition.[38] The Senate balked at this reduction and refused to accept the lower House figure until early July. President Wilson, who believed that a price higher than $2.20 a bushel, the price established for the 1917 wheat crop, was inflationary, promptly vetoed the bill, and the House sustained the veto.[39]

As in the first session of the Sixty-Fifth Congress, London continued to speak against the suppression of Socialist newspapers and periodicals, the harassment and arrest of Socialist Party officials and numerous other violations of civil liberties which occurred as a result of the rising spirit of intolerant loyalty in the United States. On February 1, 1918, he rose in the House to protest the disruption of a convention of the South Dakota Socialist Party in Mitchell on January 23 by state authorities. The disruption of Socialist conventions, London declared, was a "dastardly act" perpetrated by "scoundrels." One could readily see, he continued, the danger in small groups of men who assumed the role of guardians of freedom. Congress should act to prevent a repetition of these abuses. The influence of the United States in the present conflict would be effective only if people respected it as a freedom-loving nation.[40]

One week later, Rainey, the self-appointed critic of socialism, took the floor to reply to London. As a result of evidence he had received, Rainey said, it was evident that the mayor and police officials of Mitchell had clearly exercised their duty. They were neither "scoundrels" nor "ignorant" merchants as London had described them. To the contrary, the citizens of Mitchell were "loyal, patriotic, law abiding citizens." Rainey charged that the platform adopted by the South Dakota Socialists called for the overthrow of the present industrial system in the United States. "Now, the little amenities, the tolerance extended in times of peace to the disturbers of peace and to disloyal elements — and in this country the Socialists are a disloyal element — no longer prevail in time of war."

No more "Socialistic" speeches in the House would go unanswered, Rainey asserted. He had not heard London disavow the St. Louis Platform which contained "the most disloyal utterances that ever came from any political party in the United States." It was insufficient to say that the platform had been adopted in the heat of passion and that it was ill considered. "Such a declaration, as the St. Louis declaration, especially on the part of Socialists who desire ... to pose as loyal Americans must be denounced and denounced in unsparing terms."[41]

At the conclusion of Rainey's remarks, the chair recognized London, and once again he proved more than a match for his conservative critics. The Socialist congressman told Rainey that he would be happy to hear a reply to his Socialist speeches. However, he hoped that the man who replied knew something about the subject. In his defense of the South Dakota "disturbers of the peace," London commented, Rainey had convicted the "petty little" mayor of Mitchell with the mayor's own words. Furthermore, the fact that Rainey had admitted he lacked familiarity with the subject had not prevented him from discussing it. He had also attempted to discuss socialism. "I am willing," London told the House, "for my part, to spend an hour each day in the next year in undertaking to teach him the principles of socialism." He expected to convince Rainey that American history taught the recurrent lesson "that the only country in which every man has an opportunity to live a full and free life ..., is a genuine democracy."

As for the plank in the South Dakota platform that called for the overthrow of the existing industrial system, London stated that it would happen peacefully by educating the people and by legislation. This was the basic difference between a Socialist and an anarchist. "The man who breaks up peaceful meetings, the man who abuses his authority as a public official to prevent an American from speaking is an anarchist and a violator of the law." London then quoted from a speech made by President Wilson to the American Federation of Labor convention in November 1917, in which Wilson voiced his disapproval of mob violence. The representative from Illinois, however, had not rejected mob rule. Instead, he had rejected the advice of the president, and accepted as authority the mayor of Mitchell.[42]

Spurred primarily by appeals from western states, where mounting war hysteria was directed against the IWW and German Americans, and to a lesser degree by Attorney General Gregory's request for broader authority to deal with "disloyal utterances," Congress adopted legislation against sabotage and sedition in the early spring of 1918. The Sabotage Act, signed by the president on April 20, made willful damage or destruction of war materials, utilities and transportation facilities a federal crime. The second of these measures, the Sedition Act, had passed the House in March.

Debate began in the Senate on April 4, and after heated discussions that body accepted an amended version of the House bill on April 10.[43] The Sedition Act, as amended in the Senate, prohibited a person, under pain of ten thousand dollars and twenty years imprisonment, to "utter, print, write, or publish any disloyal, profane, scurrilous, or abusive language about the form of government of the United States, or the Constitution of the United States, or the military or naval forces of the United States, or the flag of the United States or the uniform of the Army or Navy of the United States, or any language intended to obstruct the war effort in any way."[44]

The Senate also adopted a safeguard clause introduced by Senator Joseph I. France of Maryland providing "that nothing in this act shall be construed as limiting the liberty or impairing the right of any individual to publish or speak what is true, with good motives and for justifiable ends."[45] Another Senate amendment to the House bill empowered the postmaster general to deny use of the mails to any person who, "upon evidence satisfactory to him," used the mail service in violation of any provision of the act. The measure then went to the conference committee which agreed to strike out the France safeguard clause. The Senate accepted this action by the conferees.

Debate on the conference report began in the House on May 7.[46] At that time, London made a point of order against the report contending that the House conferees had exceeded their authority under House rules. They had completely altered the character of the bill, he argued, by striking out Senator France's clause. The bill was not drafted to punish free opinion, but to discourage those persons who sought to obstruct the sale of bonds, those who sought to encourage sedition and mutiny in the army and to interfere with the operation or success of the military or naval forces. The conferees, by deleting the safeguards, had "deprived the people of America of a right, because if a war cannot be conducted with the right of the people to hear the truth and speak the truth there must be something about it." Speaker Clark acknowledged that London had made a "very ingenious" argument, but denied his point of order.[47]

A few minutes later, London took the floor to oppose the bill. This measure as amended by the Senate, he exclaimed, was "one of the most mischievous pieces of legislation imposed upon a free people." Sufficient laws existed to punish the incitement of insurrection or resistance to the law. In addition, London disagreed with the argument that this "drastic" measure would elim-

9. The 65th Congress: Champion of Civil Liberties

inate lynching and mob rule. The evil of the bill, he continued, was that it "blindly" followed the Sedition Act of 1798. That law had attempted to protect government officials from indiscriminate abuse, whereas this measure sought to protect institutions. "See what an absurdity has been reached. It is made a criminal offense to utter abusive language about the Constitution. Can you abuse the Constitution? Can you use scurrilous language about the Constitution?" A constitution, London declared, was nothing more than a statement of the political and legal thought of a particular period.

London took exception to the theory that there should be no criticism of or changes in this country's institutions during war times. "We do not," he declared, "hesitate to change war implements proven to be inadequate. We should not hesitate, we should not flinch from making such changes in the economics and politics of the country as the needs of our time command." London also voiced opposition to the "unprecedented" powers bestowed upon the postmaster general; they were characteristic of the "vicious things" before the House.[48]

During the discussion that followed, several congressmen defended the bill and criticized London's remarks.[49] The intense feeling against London was perhaps best revealed in the remarks of Representative Quin. Why, he asked, did a man "come and spit on a bill and endeavor to make people believe it is horrible...?" The House did not expect anything better from London, who advocated Bolsheviki control of the United States government. "Is it possible that any man will talk against this sedition act and say that it should not be passed because it might deprive some man of an excuse or privilege to curse his Government, to abuse the Constitution, to spit on the flag, and to slap the soldier in the face? Is that the objective of the gentlemen who talk against this ... mild bill?"[50] The House then adopted the conference report 293 to 1, as London cast the sole dissenting vote.[51]

On June 5, London once again took the floor in defense of free speech. He attacked an order issued by Governor W. L. Harding of Iowa prohibiting residents of that state from using any language other than English in public places, in schools, in places of worship, on trains and over the telephones. Some public officials, London stated, evidently suffered from a "peculiar form of insanity" produced by the war. Several congressmen also expressed incredulity at the governor's actions. Representative Stafford of Wisconsin remarked that a governor who violated the Constitution by issuing such a proclamation had no authority to enforce it. Furthermore, if he attempted to do so, the courts would protect the rights of citizens.[52]

The *New York Call* and *The Public* applauded London's stand against the Sedition bill. History, the former declared, would justify London's position as it had justified Jefferson's fight against limitations placed on free speech during the administration of John Adams. *The Public* stated that insufficient recognition had been given to the role played by the Socialist member of Congress. "He has come through a most difficult year with the greatest of credit to himself. He is one of the few Socialist leaders who did not abandon his cause either for pacifism or patrioteering." The quality of his mind had been "well shown" during his fight against amendments to the Sedition bill. London upheld the right of American citizens to criticize the Constitution, even though such criticism might bring it into disrepute and thus violate the provisions of the bill.[53]

In the meantime the worst fears of the Allies had become reality; the Bolsheviks concluded a separate peace with Germany on March 3, 1918. London, who shared the disappointment of Allied statesmen over Russia's withdrawal from the war, characterized the Treaty of Brest-Litovsk as having been "dictated by the devil at the point of a sword."[54] In a report to his constituents, he strongly criticized the Lenin-Trotsky regime. Trotsky's order to demobilize the Russian army was a "crime." It invited the "German hordes to invade the soil of free Russia." Had Russia continued the struggle, London would have favored isolating Germany until the Russian people had forced the Germans to make peace. The Socialist congressman also criticized the Allies for having shown "abysmal stupidity" in dealing with the Russian situation. Although he disapproved of Bolshevik tactics, London stated that he hoped the United States would extend diplomatic recognition to Russia. "Why," he asked, "should we recognize the czar and then refuse to recognize a workingmen's government, mistaken though it may be in many ways?" London also condemned the possibility of Japanese intervention in Russia.[55]

On March 4, London offered a resolution in the House calling upon Congress to protest against any attempt to interfere in Russia's internal affairs and the suggested invasion of Russian territory by Japan or any other power. Such an invasion, it stated, would be tantamount to the "infamous attacks on Serbia and Belgium."[56] London attributed agitation for a Japanese invasion of Siberia to various corporations and individuals who had financial investments in Russia. Such a scheme, he declared, was contrary to the objectives that the United States hoped to gain by entering the war. If the Allies and the United States endorsed the Japanese plan, the Russian people would lose all their faith in the "heralded" democracy of the western nations.

London did not believe that President Wilson would support such a plan.[57] His faith in the president was borne out when, on March 5, the Japanese ambassador received a note from Wilson stating that the United States considered Siberian intervention unwise since it might play into the hands of Germany and "of the enemies of the Russian revolution, for which the government of the United States entertains the greatest sympathy."[58]

9. The 65th Congress: Champion of Civil Liberties

On March 11, Wilson sent a message to the Congress of Soviets in which he sought to allay the Russian government's fears of intervention. He expressed American interest in the "complete sovereignty and independence" of Russia as well as sympathy with the effort of the Russian people to free themselves from autocracy.[59] London praised the president's message, stating that it was unfortunate that he had not acted sooner. Nevertheless, Wilson's pledge of support to the Russian revolution was valuable to Russia and the world. The president had emphasized his support "of the right of Russia to be free of all foreign occupation of her territory and of his desire to prevent that occupation in so far as he is able to prevent it."[60]

During the next several months, Wilson resisted mounting Allied pressure for intervention. The United States, however, began to shift its position when Czechoslovakian forces in Russia broke with the Bolsheviks in late May 1918. The Czech hold on the Trans-Siberian Railroad and their strategic position in the Volga region provided the first real possibility of reopening an eastern front. The Wilson administration also overcame some of its qualms about intervention when the Supreme War Council decided, on June 1, to send a force, including American troops, to Murmansk and to occupy Archangel. A month later, on July 6, the United States finally agreed to a Siberian expedition with Japan in order to help the Czechs. Ostensibly, Wilson had accepted the idea that the Allies could not win on the western front unless the Germans maintained troops in the east.[61]

Several days earlier, the *New York Tribune* published an interview with London in which he purportedly supported American intervention in Russia to help the Russians save themselves from German aggression. The fact that the United States refused to recognize Lenin and Trotsky, London stated, had nothing to do with the necessity of taking action in Russia. Wilson must, however, seek their approval for American intervention.

This could be accomplished "with ease," for he did not believe that Lenin and Trotsky distrusted the United States. London, the *Tribune* said, had dismissed the possibility of military intervention in Siberia because it would require a million and a half troops to guard the six thousand miles of the Trans-Siberian Railroad. Moreover, in order to maintain an army of 1,000,000 men on the Russian front, via Siberia, it would be necessary to maintain 2,500,000 men, three-fifths of them engaged in guard work.

London also urged the Wilson administration to recognize the Russian government, although he did not expect the Lenin-Trotsky regime to last much longer. By failing to woo Russian intellectuals and professionals, the Bolsheviks had committed a "fatal" error which would cause their downfall. Intellectuals, London declared, had done more in the matter of social reform than any similar class in any other country. Under the present regime, however, only the workers, peasants, soldiers and sailors could elect members to the Congress of Soviets which had in turn elected Lenin and Trotsky. Intellectuals, professional men and landowners could not vote. "It is not really a democracy. It is a rule of the country by a majority of the people without giving the minority a voice." A government without the service of intellectuals and professionals could not succeed.[62]

This interview caused a stir within Socialist Party circles. The *New York Times* reported that London's associates within the local branch of the party expressed skepticism about the accuracy of the report that London favored sending several million troops to Russia. If quoted correctly, however, they observed, his position was contrary to that of the Socialist Party.

Morris Hillquit stated that he did not believe that the *Tribune* quoted London correctly. "I do not know Mr. London's views on intervention, but I hardly believe that he suggested landing a force of several millions in Russia." The fact that London was reported as stating that the consent of the Russian government was needed made it less credible, Hillquit continued, since it was common knowledge that the Russian government opposed intervention. "The entire thing seems so inconsistent that I am inclined to believe that he was incorrectly and not fully quoted."

Algernon Lee, spokesman for the Socialists on the Board of Aldermen, also expressed doubt that London had been accurately quoted. However, if this was London's position, he disagreed with it, and was confident that a majority of Socialists and all those who were well informed on international affairs agreed with him on this issue.

The State Executive Committee discussed the situation, and although some members urged action, the committee decided that it was an issue solely for Local New York. Rumors circulated after a meeting that the local, as a result of London's "heretical" views, might bring charges against him leading to expulsion from the party. Meanwhile, local Socialists sought to determine whether London had been accurately quoted.[63]

In Washington at the time, London immediately sent a telegram to the *New York Call* repudiating the statement attributed to him in the *Tribune*. He explained that when he had discussed the possibility of American military intervention in Russia it was in response to the academic question, what military aid could the United States give Russia if the Russian government requested it?[64]

London further elaborated upon the matter in interviews which appeared in the *New York World* and the *New York Call*. He told a *World* reporter that he opposed American intervention in Russia because it was wrong in principle, and not applicable to a people striving to govern themselves. London also denied having predicted that the Lenin-Trotsky regime would fall. When

9. The 65th Congress: Champion of Civil Liberties 193

asked what he would do about the Russian situation if he were president, London replied that he would recognize the present government in Russia and help it rebuild its economy. The United States, he asserted, should not choose a government for Russia or any other nation.[65]

In his *Call* interview, London stated that the Russian people would resent any attempt to send an army into Russia. It would be considered an invasion. The best response, London said, he could give to the *Call*'s query about the *Tribune* story was the joint resolution he had introduced in the House on March 4, protesting against the suggested invasion of Russia.[66]

The *New York World* further reported that some New York Socialists refused to accept London's denial. Left-wing Socialists, anxious to get rid of him, "gladly" welcomed friction between London and Local New York. They had criticized London at every party gathering for supporting the war and the Wilson administration. They now sought to exert pressure on London to refuse an appointment to a new commission that President Wilson planned to send to Russia.[67]

London had written a letter to Wilson on April 28, 1917, requesting an appointment to the Root Commission, a goodwill mission to Russia. If a Socialist was considered, they contended that the party should make the choice, and under this circumstance, London would not be selected. Socialists, the *World* noted, believed that London would be asked to serve on the mission. If he accepted the position in defiance of the Socialist Party, he would no doubt be expelled. Socialist assemblyman William Morris Feigenbaum explained that hostility to the rumored appointment was based upon the belief that any Socialist serving on the mission would be regarded as the representative of the American Socialist Party, and therefore should be chosen by the Socialists.[68]

London's left-wing opponents within Local New York also made a determined effort to block his nomination to Congress. The *Radical Review*, a left-wing publication, raised the question of London's candidacy. London's record in Congress, the writer declared, "was a poor if not disgusting one and certainly did not redound to the benefit of the Socialist Party." He had refused to accept the party's position on the war, and had declared that he represented all of his constituents and not only the Socialists residing in the Twelfth District. If the party repudiated London and refused to nominate him for a third term, it would lose the district. "This district is a pure and simple Meyer London bulwark and by no means can be classed as a Socialist stronghold." On the other hand, if the party renominated him, all their solutions and protests against the war were meaningless, and the prestige of the party would suffer immeasurably. "The blame for this vexatious, chaotic condition rests wholly with the Socialist Party. As long as campaigns are run in which the message of Socialism is relegated to the rear, so long will the Socialist Party be honeycombed with the Meyer Londons who are themselves the legitimate product of confused organization."[69]

On June 20, at a party meeting, a lengthy, acrimonious discussion took place on the situation in the Twelfth Congressional District. Many delegates expressed opposition to London's renomination and offered Judge Jacob Panken as a possible alternative. The more than six hundred party members in attendance decided to postpone the nomination until the next meeting at which London and Panken would appear.[70]

London's opponents, meanwhile, continued their efforts to prevent his nomination. In a statement issued to party members, they charged that London had disregarded the St. Louis Resolution, refused to introduce bills suggested by the National Executive Committee, and had neglected every opportunity to express the position of the Socialist Party. At the time, the statement concluded, when London had sent his cable to Russia, many believed that he should have been recalled from Congress. "If we had no courage to recall him then, let us have courage now to reconsider his nomination."[71]

On June 26, another meeting took place to consider the issue. After a "heated discussion" during which many objected to his nomination due to his independent stand on the war, Local New York renominated London by a vote of 509 to 119. Prior to the vote, London vigorously defended his position against his critics' attacks. He had sworn, he declared, to protect the Constitution of the United States. "We may like it or not like it — if I could sit down and amend it, I would do it from end to end — but as a Socialist I believe in standing by the law. That is the difference between Socialism and anarchism. We stand by the law as we find it, until we can change the law."

London pointed out that he had delivered fifteen to twenty speeches in his fight against war. But he had been in the minority, and the country had entered the conflict. London lashed out at those who held the "idiotic idea" that the workingman had no country. "I want to say this is my home, this is my country and I will fight for it, and, if need be, die for it." This, he defiantly declared, was his position, and he would not change it.[72]

However, London's statement on American intervention in Russia gave his left-wing Socialist enemies new hope that they might yet block his nomination. If charges were brought against him and sustained by Local New York, they believed his nomination would be revoked.[73] On July 13, they succeeded when the Central Committee adopted a motion not to concur in London's nomination by a close vote of 31 to 28. The committee then referred the matter of choosing another candidate to the City Executive Committee.[74]

That very day London delivered a lengthy speech in the House in which he sought to clarify his position on the Russian question, and perhaps silence his New York critics. The events which had occurred in Russia, he remarked, made the problem of assisting that country "the most complex one that has presented itself to thinking men." Few would deny that the czar's government had been an "abomination." It was unfortunate, London continued, that the upheaval resulting from the overthrow of the czar had occurred when the world was engaged in a "death grapple" with German militarism. "Revolutions are not Sunday-school picnics. They follow no prescribed code of good manners. A revolution means the upsetting of things."

The Russian revolution was more than a political uprising. The peasants sought an opportunity to earn their bread which meant access to land. Other countries, London noted, considered national ownership of land "extremely radical," but in Russia the collective ownership of land by the village community had prepared the people to accept the principle that freedom meant access to the land and that any system of government that denied access was fundamentally wrong. This doctrine had stirred fear among feudal lords and landowning classes everywhere.

This fear explained the Ukrainian peace, London explained. Collective ownership had been unknown in the Ukraine, and the revolution had threatened to extend it to all parts of Russia. Germany thus hastened to cut off the Ukraine from Russia by holding out the promise of self-determination, and the Ukrainian landlords accepted it as a means of checking the spread of revolutionary ideas. They had entrenched themselves with the help of their "kindred spirits" the Junkers. The Germans had established a dictatorship in the Ukraine, and some fifty thousand German troops were rooting out the revolutionary elements who desired to join the federated Russian Republic. The only people, London continued, who resisted these Germans and kept them from the western front were the very same Soviet elements whom some would repudiate as outlaws.

The industrial labor movement in Russia, he asserted, was necessarily more radical than that in other countries. The principle of democratic control and management of industry was not far from the principle of democratic control of the land. From the beginning of the revolution, London explained, a struggle had taken place between those who believed that Russia had to pass through the rise and development of modern industry and those who thought that Russia was ready to lay the basis for a cooperative industrial democracy. This latter group and the peasantry appeared to control Russia. "That the very attempt to establish such a government should bring down upon them the hatred of all who are discomforted in Russia and the implacable enmity by all elements everywhere similarly situated could have easily been foreseen."

London then discussed the Treaty of Brest-Litovsk. This treaty resulted from the complete economic and military collapse of Russia. With the overthrow of the czar, the Russian soldier saw no reason for continuing the czar's war, and soon thereafter the demand for peace became general. Farsighted persons in Russia realized, however, the disaster that would follow a separate peace. They understood that the only way to prevent a separate treaty with Germany was through a general resolution of the conflict.

The Kerensky government had promised an inter-allied conference to seek a general peace settlement. The Russian government, however, had delayed, and the allied governments issued a statement of war aims only after the Kerensky government had fallen. Moreover, when the Socialists, who had led the revolution, called for an international Socialist congress, the Allies had prevented it. As a result, conditions in Russia had continued to deteriorate and the Russian people lost their confidence in the Allies. Toward the conclusion of negotiations with Germany, Trotsky and Lenin proposed a general peace proposal, but the Western Allies failed to respond. Trotsky had sought to avoid signing any peace treaty, but Germany had insisted.

Had Germany refused to take advantage of Russia's distress and restored friendly relations with her, Germany would have been able to utilize the vast resources of Russia and could have defied the Allies forever. "But her rulers knew only the logic of the sword. She began a process of dismembering Russia." It was "inexcusable folly," London declared, for the Allies to treat Russia and those who made the "disastrous" peace as the villains. The Russian people wanted peace, and for eleven months promises had been made to them. Their government had hoped it would give them a breathing spell; Germany had refused to make it a real peace.

London then proposed that the United States should assist Russia. First it should extend economic and financial aid. The Russian government, he asserted, was no friend of Germany and would welcome aid from the Allies and particularly from the United States. Secondly, all talk of military intervention should stop. Finally, London urged recognition of the new government. "A government founded on the ruins of Czardom must be accepted as a Russian institution. We play into the hands of Germany by treating Russia as an outlaw." The United States should treat Russia as a temporarily disabled ally. Fortunately, London concluded, Russia had a friend in President Wilson.[75]

On July 15, the Executive Committee of Local New York discussed the action taken by the Central Committee in the Twelfth Congressional District. The Executive Committee considered the nomination too important and refused to take the responsibility for naming another candidate.[76] At a special Central Committee meeting two days later, the committee reversed its earlier

9. The 65th Congress: Champion of Civil Liberties 197

decision and renominated London narrowly by a vote of 42 to 38.[77] An air of secrecy surrounded the meeting. In keeping with the Socialist practice of refusing to discuss internal party matters publicly, all newspapermen, including Socialist ones, were excluded, and the chairman of the meeting requested all those in attendance not to discuss the matter with the press. Julius Gerber later announced that London had been confirmed by a majority, but refused to reveal the exact vote. When pressed for more information, Gerber retorted that it was not the public's business.

Nevertheless, fragmentary reports of the proceedings appeared the following day in the *New York Times* and the *New York World*. The meeting, they reported, which lasted until midnight, was acrimonious with a number of near fistfights. A considerable part of the opposition to London came from the Russian branches of the Socialist Party and young "hotheads" who argued that he had cooperated too readily with the Wilson administration, had supported the war too strongly, had done little or nothing to support the Bolshevik cause in Congress, and was not sufficiently international to represent the Socialist Party. During the meeting a member of the Central Committee had called London at his home to ask him to explain some of his actions in Congress. According to the *Times*, a feisty London had replied that he did not care what action the committee took, "but you can tell them this—that I'll wipe up the floor with anyone who gets in my way."[78]

The *New York World* attributed the Central Committee's decision to reverse itself to several factors. Firstly, more members attended. The July 13 meeting had lasted until 3:30 A.M., by which time many of the older men had left. Secondly, many believed that this was not the time to discipline London. Thirdly, London had the enthusiastic support of a large part of the Socialist Party. Finally, his constituents insisted that he was the choice of the district and that the Central Committee had no right to override the will of the East Side.

The *New York World* and the *New York Times* regarded the actions of the Central Committee as further proof of disloyalty and Bolshevik sympathy within the Socialist Party. The *World* declared sarcastically that London's belated endorsement by the "Bolsheviki" socialists might have been more spontaneous if he had managed to get himself indicted for sedition or something similar.[79]

The *New York Times* viewed London's nomination as the lesser of two evils. The Twelfth Congressional District, the *Times* stated, might have a better representative in Congress, but the possibility also existed that the district might send a worse man to Washington as evidenced by the arguments presented by those who opposed London at the meeting of the Party's Central Committee. "And the reasons curiously enough were all of them such as to make the ordinarily loyal and right-thinking American citizen contemplate with something of resignation, if not exactly with joy, the probability that Mr. London, instead of a man better loved by out-and-out pacifists and thinly disguised pro–Germans will carry the district again." If the accusations aimed at him were true, the *Times* stated facetiously, London was almost as bad as John Spargo and Charles Edward Russell in his opposition to "dear" Germany and not to be trusted in the cause to which more faithful leaders of the Socialist Party had devoted themselves, overthrowing the American government and replacing it with one similar to that established in Russia under the "wise" leadership of Lenin and Trotsky.[80]

Meanwhile, congressional leaders hoped that, with the November elections rapidly approaching, Congress might adjourn early so that members could return home to launch their reelection campaigns. However, President Wilson insisted upon a new tax bill to meet escalating military costs, and Congress remained in session during the summer months. In order to placate disgruntled congressmen, an arrangement was eventually reached to allow members to take short summer vacations while Congress remained technically in session.[81]

A request by the administration for additional manpower brought Congress back to Washington in late August from its intermittent recess. The proposed bill revised the Conscription Act by lowering the draft age from twenty-one to eighteen and raising it from thirty-one to forty-five. The House Military Affairs Committee amended the act delaying the call-up of those under twenty until the quotas of all other classes were reviewed and exhausted. Despite support by the House Democratic leadership, the amendment failed 167 to 120.[82]

During the debate on the bill, on August 24, London told his colleagues that they had failed to consider the most important question: whether Congress should take twenty-four million men and subject them to military rule. Room should be left for voluntary patriotism and sacrifices. "If we introduce the principle that there shall be no profits in war while the Nation bleeds and while men die, that all we produce shall go for the common good ... I would not object to the conscription of every man, every woman capable of rendering service." Later that day the House passed the bill by the overwhelming majority of 336 to 2, with London in opposition along with Gordon of Ohio.[83]

The House also finally acted upon the war revenue bill which President Wilson believed essential to the financial stability of the country. Initially, Democratic congressional leaders had opposed Treasury Department arguments for additional taxes on excess profits and luxuries to defray mounting war costs. They feared that businessmen would pass higher taxes along to the public in the form of higher prices, thus jeopardizing the chances for reelection

9. The 65th Congress: Champion of Civil Liberties 199

of the administration's tax program supporters. Despite pressure from the White House and charges of congressional irresponsibility by the press, the measure moved slowly in the House.[84]

On September 12, London took the floor to discuss the measure. He rebuked those Democrats and Republicans who had engaged in political harangues rather than discussing this important issue. "I can just imagine the soldier in the trenches reading of the cheap, vulgar, partisan nonsense with which we have been regaled here.... It is sickening." He accused both parties of playing politics in order to gain control of the next House. The war had necessitated the heavy burden of the revenue bill. The problem was not to find new articles to tax, but how to increase the productivity of the nation.

London warned his colleagues that the tax burden would grow even if the war ended in a few months due to the obligations the government had assumed toward veterans. The interest on the national debt would probably equal the entire government budget prior to the war. This unprecedented burden required new ways of thinking and new approaches. "Unrestrained individualism in industry is bankrupt. The Nation must undertake to guide industry along lines which will eliminate the waste of useless competition and do away with the profiteer."

In conclusion, London asserted that the country could increase productivity significantly by nationalizing its resources, by eliminating wasteful competition and by introducing democracy and cooperation in industry and agriculture.[85] The House passed the revenue bill unanimously on September 20.[86] London's decision to support this measure reflected his belief that he should pursue a constructive rather than obstructive role in relation to the war effort. The Senate, however, distracted by Wilson's peace negotiations in the closing days of the session, failed to act upon the bill.[87]

Meanwhile, London had renewed his efforts on behalf of an international league. On August 27, he urged congressional action. London reminded his colleagues that he had introduced a resolution on December 6, 1917, requesting that Congress support an international league, but the Committee on Foreign Affairs had failed to act upon it. The committee, he continued, seemed to believe that it had a limited role to foreign affairs.

London informed the House that he planned to reintroduce his resolution in a new form. He would ask Congress to appoint a joint commission to investigate the creation of an international league to secure peace. If President Wilson's message to the democratic and liberal elements of the world had meaning, Congress should immediately consider the question of organizing a permanent league to secure peace in the world after Germany's defeat. "How," London asked, "can we talk about democracy in international relations when the very members of Congress who have declared war refuse to consider any suggestion to study international relations?"

He urged the House to study the problem, to communicate with parliamentary representatives of other countries and to participate in an international conference. Every member of Congress, London stated, was important. He had the power to declare war, "to send millions of his fellow countrymen into carnage and death. He should have the courage to take a hand in shaping the foreign policies of the country."[88]

In yet another address to the House on September 12, London declared that if he could reach the people, he could convince them that the world's future depended upon adoption of the principles of the international league advocated by the Socialists. London pointed out that the resolution he had introduced on December 6, 1915, provided a solution to the "international evil" which afflicted the world. It called for the evacuation of Belgium, German withdrawal from all occupied territory, respect for the rights of smaller nationalities and the creation of an international court of arbitration.

Representative Norton asked London whether this league would include Germany and whether he would make peace with it at this time. London replied that he opposed dealing with the German government until it agreed to evacuate all territory seized during the war and to abrogate the Treaty of Brest-Litovsk. When Germany had taken those steps, the question of securing peace by establishing a permanent league should be considered. An international league to secure peace, London insisted, should include all nations.

Representative Focht inquired what prerogatives the United States would surrender to an international league. International order, London responded, involved the loss, to some extent, of what nations claimed now as absolute sovereign rights just as the individual had surrendered his sovereign rights in order to live as a member of the community. "If every nation is to insist that whatever it desires is right and that the opinion of the world is not to be consulted, there can be no lasting or any other kind of peace among nations."[89]

On October 17, 1918, during the pre-armistice negotiations between the United States and Germany, London introduced a resolution declaring that the recent peace offers of the Central Powers had produced a flood of "noisy and boastful statements" reeking with hatred and vengeance which misrepresented the true spirit of the American people and their government. Moreover, these representations of vindictiveness and ultra-nationalism in Allied countries tended to retard rather than encourage the efforts of revolutionary forces within the Central Powers for peace and for the democratization of their political institutions. Therefore be it "Resolved by the House of Representatives ... that it is the sense of the American Congress that the American people are not inspired by a vindictive desire to destroy the German people.

9. The 65th Congress: Champion of Civil Liberties   201

That in seeking a complete victory the American people crave for a permanent victory for humanity through the organization of an international league to secure peace; that the people whom the Allies and the United States are now arraigned against shall be welcomed to membership in such a league on an equality with all other peoples."[90]

London explained that he not only wanted to make the world safe for democracy, but for social democracy as well. A peace treaty, he warned, that excluded any people from an international league would lead to future wars. Germany's defeat, he predicted, was inevitable, and even though capitalist newspapers would not admit it, the German Socialist movement had contributed to the present situation. London also emphasized the work of the Socialist parties of the world on behalf of peace. Their repeated efforts to promote an international Socialist conference had not been without effect, for although an international conference had been prevented, the inter-allied Socialist conference had presented to the world the basis for a democratic settlement of the war. It seemed unbelievable, London declared, that the German people should continue the monarchy.[91]

As the second session of the Sixty-Fifth Congress drew to a close and with the possibility of a cessation of hostilities imminent, London once again urged his colleagues to prepare for post-war reconstruction. On October 4, 1918, he introduced a resolution calling for the creation of a joint congressional committee on reconstruction to prepare and recommend legislation to provide employment at the conclusion of hostilities; for the nationalization of railroads, telegraph and telephone lines, steamships and all other public means of transportation; the acquisition and retention of agricultural lands which may be needed for returning soldiers; the reclamation of arid and swamp lands; the acquisition, retention and exploration of natural resources; the encouragement of agricultural cooperation and collective aid to farmers; and the creation of a national system of compulsory education. The committee should report to Congress no later than January 1, 1919.[92]

On October 18, London presented his resolution as an amendment to the Deficiency Appropriation bill then under discussion. He told the House that although the country was on the "threshold of peace," it was unprepared for peace. Plans had not been made for the economic dislocation which would occur when millions of veterans returned to civilian life. London reminded his colleagues that he had pleaded with them to prepare for the reconstruction period, but his pleas had fallen on deaf ears. London, however, withdrew the amendment when it appeared that it would be ruled out of order.[93]

Despite the anti-war position of the Socialist Party, Meyer London voted for various measures essential to the country's military effort. He remained, however, an outspoken critic of those who sought to suppress dissent. Looking forward to a speedy conclusion of the war, London addressed himself to post-war problems. He urged the House to prepare for the economic difficulties that would accompany the conversion from a wartime to a peacetime economy. In order to ensure future peace, he advocated a league of nations.

Due to his position on the war and the Bolshevik Revolution, London aroused the ire of his conservative colleagues in the House as well as his more militant comrades in the Socialist Party. Nevertheless, he never wavered in his beliefs. He was willing to allow the people of the Twelfth Congressional District to determine, in the coming congressional election, whether he had acted in their and the country's best interests.

10

The Elections of 1918 and 1920

> I fail to see how any upright and honest citizen or any patriotic American citizen can vote for him. Mr. London's votes show that he has a right to the support of the Germanized Socialists. He has no right to the vote of patriotic American citizens.—*Theodore Roosevelt,* New York Call, *November 3, 1918, 1.*

London faced a difficult uphill fight for reelection to Congress for a third term in 1918. Arrayed against him were left-wing Socialists who had sought unsuccessfully to block his nomination, elements within the Jewish community antagonistic to him for his lack of religious orthodoxy and his attitude toward Zionism, and a united Democratic and Republican opposition. Furthermore, the late adjournment of Congress, the Fourth Liberty Bond Drive, the influenza epidemic, and the weakened state of the Socialist Party, due to harassment by federal, state and local authorities, reduced the effectiveness of his campaign. This combination of factors led to his defeat by a narrow margin, in an election marred once again by voting irregularities.

The Socialist congressman returned to Congress for the lame duck session of the Sixty-Fifth Congress and continued to speak out on both domestic and international affairs. With the conclusion of the Congress, he resumed his private law practice and served as counsel to the Cloakmakers, the Furriers and other labor organizations, all the while looking forward to the 1918 congressional elections.

In an effort to defeat London and other Socialist congressional candidates in New York City, the National Security League urged the Democrats and Republicans to run fusion candidates on a loyalty platform. Charles F. Murphy, the Tammany Hall chieftain, in an enthusiastic acceptance declared, "Sink all partisanship. Name only one hundred percent Americans to Congress. Elect them to win the war and a victorious peace. America first." Charles D. Orth, the chairman of the National Security League, suggested in letters to Murphy, and Samuel S. Koenig, chairman of the Republican County Committee, that the Democrats and Republicans nominate former ambassador Oscar S. Straus to oppose London.¹ Straus had announced in June 1918 his willingness to run for Congress, if nominated by both the Democrats and the Republicans. "I am not seeking office," Straus wrote Orth, "and don't propose to, I would not accept a nomination for Congress on a partisan platform, but only on the platform of patriotism."²

Straus refused, however, to accept a fusion nomination in the Twelfth Congressional District. He informed Orth that the population in this district was largely Jewish, and if he sought the nomination there, it would expose him to the charge of appealing to ethnic prejudices. "In all my private and public life," Straus stated, "I have always been an American, first and last, and I would not run in a district where it could be ... said I was appealing to a racial or religious class instead of to an electorate on purely patriotic grounds."³

Although Straus refused to run against London, the National Security League secured the cooperation of the Republicans and Democrats in four Manhattan districts. The Republicans agreed not to nominate candidates in the Twelfth and Thirteenth congressional districts, while the Democrats announced they would not contest the Republicans in the Fourteenth and Twentieth congressional districts.⁴ Several weeks later, Tammany announced that former congressman Henry M. Goldfogle would once again oppose London. President Wilson endorsed the strategy.⁵

Despite the unified efforts of the Democrats and Republicans, New York Socialists viewed the coming election with cautious optimism. The Democratic-Republican fusion in the four congressional districts, the *New York Call* declared, indicated Socialist Party strength. In 1916, the Socialist daily noted, London had received 6,103 votes against a combined vote of 6,731. However, Judge Jacob Panken, the Socialist candidate running for municipal judge in the same territory the following year, received a majority of the total vote. Based upon Panken's success, the *Call* predicted London's election by a comfortable majority.⁶

In an editorial on August 2, the *Call* further commented that Socialists should thank their political adversaries for drawing the lines so sharply. For more than a generation little difference had existed between the Democrats and Republicans, each serving the same capitalist interests. Now, however, both parties would "sail together under the fraudulent issue of 'loyalty,' the criminal elements of the slum being joined in a fraternal bond with the reaction of the boulevard."⁷

London, in a more realistic assessment, condemned the fusion against him. The fact that the two political machines had combined, he declared, provided an unanswerable argument in his favor. He represented a well-defined political philosophy. Millions of people throughout the world believed in socialism, in the doctrine that cooperation should replace international conflict. To deny American Socialists the opportunity to present their philosophy was to deny the basic principle of representation. "The combination of the two gangs of politicians to defeat me is nothing short of a political crime."[8]

He also criticized the National Security League which had been instrumental in promoting the fusion against him. The League, in order to help voters return only loyal congressmen that fall, prepared a chart which showed the voting records of all congressmen on eight important wartime measures. Some 1,800 newspapers carried it during the summer of 1918. London was one of the seven members of the House who voted wrong on all of the measures. Only forty-seven members of the House were deemed 100 percent loyal. The "National Obscurity League," London told the House on August 27, probably had a larger percentage of war profiteers than any other organization in the world. "Every self-respecting Representative should rejoice at being repudiated by that crowd. It is not a misfortune to anybody."[9]

In addition to the united opposition of the Democrats and Republicans, left-wing Socialists and Poale (labor) Zionists either remained inactive or worked against him in the 1918 campaign.[10] The newly emerging left wing of the Socialist Party opposed London because he had failed to support the St. Louis Manifesto and the Bolshevik cause in Russia. The Poale Zionists, as well as other Zionists, criticized London's position regarding the creation of a Jewish homeland in Palestine.[11] In a letter to the secretary of the Poale Zion shortly after the campaign began, London wrote that he favored presenting to the international peace conference, with due regard to the principles of self-determination and no forcible annexation, the question of securing a free state "to which such of the Jewish people as desire to do so may return and may work out their own salvation free from interference by those of [an] alien race or religion." Moreover, every type of restriction against Jews should be removed. London stated that he would view an appropriate resolution dealing with the matter with the utmost sympathy.[12]

Dissatisfied with London's position, the Poale Zion demanded that London introduce a resolution in Congress supporting the Balfour Declaration which had been endorsed by the American Federation of Labor, the International Ladies' Garment Workers' Union and the Amalgamated Clothing Workers of America.[13] In his reply to the Poale Zion, London repeated substantially anti–Zionist arguments to a Jewish homeland in Palestine. American Jews, he stated, considered the United States their homeland where they could pursue their religious beliefs without persecution. London also declared that America should not allow itself to be divided along ethnic, religious or racial lines. "No matter what a man's religion, or former nationality, or racial origin may be, unless he is willing to be part of the American people he is a stranger." Jews who desired their own homeland, London maintained, were welcome to it. So long as they did not presume to speak in the name of all Jews, they were within their rights. Zionists also had a right to present their position to the international Socialist movement and to the peace conference. If they achieved their goals without violating the Socialist principle which forbade forcible annexation of territory, then no Socialist, himself included, would object. "It is in this light that I would treat any resolution that may come up in the American Congress."[14] His position angered the Poale Zionists and cost him their support. Subsequent efforts by London's friends to placate the Zionists on his behalf failed when London refused to compromise his principles.[15]

Faced with the defection of left-wing Socialists, Poale Zionists, and the fusion candidacy of Henry M. Goldfogle, London depended more than ever upon the East Side labor movement. Once again the unions did not disappoint him. On the evening of September 27, representatives of some seventy-five unions organized the Meyer London Trade Union Conference.[16] In addition to their participation in the Trade Union Conference, the Cloakmakers, the Fur Workers and the Amalgamated Clothing Workers conducted independent campaigns for London.[17]

A number of Socialist and non–Socialist organizations also endorsed his candidacy and worked on his behalf. The Workmen's Circle, as in previous campaigns, formed the Workmen's Circle Meyer London Campaign Committee. The Young Socialists and the Socialist Consumers' League, the latter numbering some twelve thousand women, also aided in the campaign.[18] Among the non–Socialist organizations were the East Side Galicians, the Merchants and Professional Mens' League, the Madison Street Independent Citizens' League and the Nonpartisan Businessmen's League.[19]

Prominent Socialist leaders such as Eugene Debs, Charles Irwin and Max Eastman urged London's election.[20] Debs, in prison at the time, endorsed the candidacies of seven New York City Socialist congressional hopefuls. "I take it," Debs stated, "that Comrade London will be returned to his seat by an increased majority and I hope our Comrades will bring all their energies to the task."[21]

London also received the support of progressives such as Cyrus Sulzberger and Amos Pinchot. Sulzberger, in a letter to the Meyer London Professional League, stated that London should be elected for the "courage and intelligence" he had displayed in Congress. Socialist principles should be studied closely in reconstructing the world after the war. This required Socialist representation in Congress. London's election, he concluded, went beyond his district; it would benefit the country.[22]

The Socialist campaign in the Twelfth Congressional District began on Labor Day, September 2, with a series of rallies featuring London. Speaking in both English and Yiddish, he told an audience of several thousand gathered in Rutgers Square that the American people were living through the greatest crisis in history. "If ever there was a time when all the strength and all the wisdom that man can muster is to lead the world aright, this is the day." London denounced the "cheap politicians" who sought to teach Socialists the meaning of patriotism. Socialists, he declared, were the sworn enemy of oppression. Throughout the world, they had courageously defended their ideas and had fought for them when they had few listeners and even fewer supporters. Now these ideas influenced men responsible for the policies of nations.

In Congress, London continued, he alone had spoken on behalf of a new and better world. An effort was being made to silence his voice, but it would fail. With his critics in mind, London asserted, "There is no Socialist in America and for that matter there is not a Socialist in the world, including Germany, that would not like to see the defeat of German Kaiserism." Even German Socialists opposed the kaiser, and looked forward to a democratic Germany. War, London concluded, produced the noblest forms of sacrifice, but it was also during wartime "that every reptile and every unclean creature and every scoundrel, resorts to the flag, to conceal his smallness and his rascality."[23]

In the following weeks, the campaign in the Twelfth Congressional District moved at a relatively slow pace. The Fourth Liberty Loan Drive began on September 18 and lasted for the next four weeks. The Democrats and the Republicans limited their political activities and energies to raising money for the war. London, who actively supported the drive, also suspended his campaigning until October 21, when the drive concluded.[24] Other factors hampering London's campaign were the epidemic of Spanish influenza,[25] the decision of school authorities to enforce a law prohibiting the use of schools for political rallies[26] and the lengthy Sixty-Fifth Congress.[27]

As in the 1916 campaign, London ran on his record. He reminded the voters of the Twelfth District of his efforts on their behalf, and requested them to determine whether he had represented them fairly and honestly. In a letter to the *New York American*, London proudly asserted that he was not a "rubber-stamp" congressman and that he had not been afraid to speak his mind. He had voted alone and against the entire House when duty demanded it. "I stand on my record. I have made my district known in Congress, and I have introduced Congress to my district by frequent reports to my constituents." During his two terms, London continued, he had protested against existing and attempted wrongs, but he had never failed to point out the "beautiful" things about American life. He had never forgotten that this country was the land of opportunity and was worth fighting and dying for.

London pointed out that he had worked and voted against every measure that might have led the United States to war. Nonetheless, he had accepted the decision of the country. "I wonder whether I am to be punished for having had the courage to vote against war or for standing by my country's decision when the country chose war?" As the only Socialist in Congress, he had explained President Wilson's international policies. "Where others looked upon the suggestion of a league for a durable peace as a mere high-sounding phrase, I took it to be the principal object of America's participation in the world's contest." Would voters repudiate him because he had fought for social insurance, for freedom of speech and the press, for open diplomacy, and against mob violence?

Furthermore, would he be denied the opportunity to serve the people during the reconstruction period? "Shall I be prevented from urging public and democratic control of public utilities, the curbing of the profiteer, national enfranchisement of women, the limitation of the power of the courts to declare acts of Congress unconstitutional? Shall I no longer be able to plead for the poor and the helpless?" Would his political career be curtailed because he had attended congressional sessions more regularly than any New York City Democrat, and because he had probably attended more sessions of Congress than all the Tammany congressmen together?

In conclusion, London facetiously remarked that the question for East Side voters would be "whether they desired to be represented in Congress by the Socialist Party whose propaganda is un-American; or a candidate of both the Republican and Democratic parties whose hundred percent Americanism is established beyond the slightest doubt. I do not fear the result. I fully believe the East Side has awakened to the necessity of the hour, and will send me as a one hundred percent American to Congress."[28]

London and his supporters, as in previous campaigns, hammered away at Goldfogle's lackluster record in Congress. Goldfogle, London declared, was "an ordinary Tammany jade, a zero without a circumference," whose political career could be described in one word — "nothing." Goldfogle's failure to vote on the child labor bill and women's suffrage was dramatized in widely distributed posters. In addition, canvassers distributed literature dealing with Goldfogle's voting record and absenteeism in the House.[29]

London also dwelt upon the problem of post-war reconstruction. The United States, he declared, had not prepared to help returning veterans and the millions of workers employed in war plants. A federal program was necessary. He urged support for his reconstruction resolution and the Socialist Party, the only party capable of offering new insights on the issue.[30] Pointing to federal wheat regulation, London called for control over essential food commodities. Such regulation, however, needed the cooperation of the American people. Otherwise, he warned, it would result in a "disastrous form of concentrated paternalism."[31]

Regarding an international league, London noted the similarity between President Wilson's position and that of the inter-allied socialist movement. Both maintained that a league of nations should be an integral part of the peace treaty. Only the election of Socialists to Congress, London declared, would ensure that Wilson's plan would become reality.[32]

London's opponent, former congressman Henry M. Goldfogle, made "one hundred percent Americanism" the principal issue in his campaign. In a letter which also appeared in the *New York American*, he wrote that his election would show Congress, the Wilson administration and the American people that the East Side supported loyalty to the country and measured up to "one hundred percent Americanism." He pledged his unqualified support for the president and for all war measures. Goldfogle noted that the Democrats and Republicans had united to nominate "one hundred percent" candidates in other districts as well. When London described those parties as "gangs," he failed to remember that "our great president" stands at the head of the Democratic Party, and ex-presidents Taft and Roosevelt at the head of the Republican Party.

The people, Goldfogle continued, regarded the Socialist Party as un–American, and pro–German. London did not represent himself in Congress, but the Socialist Party, and must be judged in that light. The Socialist Party, he charged, had adopted resolutions favoring the Bolsheviks, and had opposed American intervention in Russia. In addition, London admitted that he had not purchased bonds during the liberty loan drives in 1917. Moreover, the Socialist Party opposed loans necessary to finance the war. Due to the activities of this party and its representative in Congress, the American people believed that the East Side was unpatriotic. "Many thousands of excellent, upright, patriotic, and loyal American citizens on the East Side have suffered because of this, and as a result of the Socialist propaganda, which in these war times is harmful to the country and a menace to its welfare."[33]

As in previous campaigns, Goldfogle and his supporters sought to woo the Orthodox Jewish vote by interjecting the religious issue. Shortly before the election, the *Morning Journal*, an Orthodox Yiddish daily, charged that London had attended a session of the House on Yom Kippur. London's action, it exclaimed, had disgraced Judaism, and had insulted the sensibilities of every Orthodox Jew in the country. His presence in the House, on this holy day, had even shocked Christian congressmen.[34]

In response, London did not deny the charge, but accused Tammany of shaming Judaism by dragging religion into the campaign. At a meeting on November 3, London proclaimed that Boss Murphy's servants insulted Orthodox Jews when they spoke about the Jewish faith. London called attention to the fact that he had intervened on behalf of Jewish postal workers in the District of Columbia so they could remain home for two days instead of one on Rosh Hashana. He had not, however, bragged about this. He had not done it as a personal favor, but to help those who wanted to be Orthodox and celebrate the holiday.[35]

The *Daily Forward* rallied to London's support. In an Election Day editorial, Abraham Cahan charged London's political opponents with using the Jewish issue for political gain. The lowest elements on the East Side had covered themselves with prayer shawls to hide the "degradation of their souls." Among these "holy people" of Tammany, one could find the owners of houses of prostitution who were not permitted to enter a synagogue. Such people offered hundreds of dollars for an *aliyah*,[36] but such dirty money was not accepted.

In the present campaign in New York City, Cahan wrote, these creatures had the gall to oppose the Socialists in the name of Jewishness. Although the Londons and Hillquits did not speak like Orthodox Jews, they worked for the Jewish people and knew how to support the feelings of religious Jews. In conclusion, Cahan urged Jewish voters not be misled by Tammany. They should vote for London and other Socialist candidates who truly represented their interests.[37]

As the campaign drew to a close, Theodore Roosevelt, as well as a number of prominent "uptown" German Jewish leaders including Samuel Untermeyer, Abram I. Elkus, Rabbi Stephen A. Wise, Jacob H. Schiff, Louis Marshall and Nathan Straus, who feared an anti–Semitic backlash, appealed to the voters of the Twelfth District to elect Goldfogle.[38] London's actions in Congress, Roosevelt proclaimed, clearly indicated that he supported the anti-war program of the Socialist Party. "Under these circumstances I fail to see how any upright and honest citizen or any patriotic American can vote for him. Mr. London's votes show that he has a right to the support of the Germanized Socialists. He has no right to the vote of patriotic American citizens."[39]

On election eve, November 4, Samuel Untermeyer told an audience of some two thousand, "what a seditious thing you are asked to do at a moment when our country is about to reap the fruits of the world prestige our President has built up.... You are asked to convey to our allies and our enemies the message that his own people no longer share the confidence in his judgment and the accomplishments that have brought us to the verge of this great triumph." Elkus urged the audience to heed the president's appeal to elect a Democratic Congress.[40]

London lashed back at his critics. At a rally on October 24, he declared, "What the Roosevelts and Louis Marshalls say in New York is what the Bismarks and the von Bethmann-Hollwegs used to say in Germany."⁴¹ In an Election Day appeal, London stated that Socialists were not nihilists, but sought to to eliminate only those things that were bad. Old party politicians had failed in their efforts to "terrorize" the Socialists. They had dressed themselves in patriotism, and had attempted to shame the Socialists for the thousands of comrades fighting in Europe. They had tried to use the Jewish issue. The intelligent voter, however, realized that a Socialist candidate would protect the right of a Jew to be a Jew. London called upon the voters to cast a straight Socialist ticket.⁴²

Swelled by the participation of women for the first time in a New York general election, a record number of voters went to the polls in the Twelfth Congressional District on November 5.⁴³ Throughout the day London's headquarters received disquieting reports of intimidation and fraud by Tammany and Republican workers at polling places. Nevertheless, London's supporters continued to express optimism.

As evening approached some fifty thousand people gathered on East Broadway to await election results. Early returns indicated that London had taken a small lead.⁴⁴ Later returns, however, showed that Goldfogle had forged ahead, and the final vote revealed that London had lost by 827 votes out of a total of 15,231. Goldfogle polled 7,452 votes or 48.61 percent of the vote while London received 6,625 votes or 42.45 percent of the vote. London carried the First, Second and Sixth assembly districts. Goldfogle won the all-important Fourth Assembly District by 1,202 votes, thus ensuring his election. A further examination of the results indicates that Goldfogle gained 1,693 votes or 6.44 percent more than Sanders in 1916. London's total vote increased by 523 votes, but his percentage of the vote decreased from 44.69 percent to 42.45 percent, a loss of 2.24 percent.⁴⁵

The New York press applauded London's defeat and other Socialist reversals in New York City as a repudiation of socialism. The Socialists, the *New York World* proclaimed, had been thoroughly defeated and discredited by the election results. "Their pro–German attitude generally and the disintegration of their forces under false leaders landed them once more among the negligible quantities in politics."⁴⁶ The *New York Times* enthusiastically proclaimed the defeat of London and Morris Hillquit. "In both districts a combination of Republicans and Democrats, that is of loyal men, was made against the Socialists, who like the majority of so-called American Socialists are German Socialists, adversaries of war, friends of Germany."⁴⁷ The *New York Evening Mail* interpreted the election as a "sweeping repudiation" of socialism by the American people. By defeating London and other Socialist congressional candidates, New York City had completely cleansed itself of the "Socialistic taint" in Congress.⁴⁸

The left-wing publication *Class Struggle*, for different reasons, joined the capitalist press in applauding London's defeat. London had been much worse than opportunistic. "He created the impression that he stood in with the enemies of the Russian revolution.... He joined the capitalist politicians and the capitalist press by denouncing the Bolsheviks and their regime." Moreover, London had failed to condemn foreign intervention in Russia when the party had instructed him to do so. In the fight against the Espionage Act, he had been "content to play the role of tail to the Republican kite."[49]

London and his supporters charged that the Democrats and Republicans had stolen the election, and made plans to challenge the results. In a statement to the *New York World* on November 6, London asserted that a large number of ballots were defaced and not counted. "They are all our ballots. They bear the evidence of mutilation by the same person in each election district." London also charged that election officials had insisted that a Republican or Democratic election official accompany women when they voted in booths. Socialist watchers had protested, but to no avail.[50]

Alexander Kahan, chairman of the Watchers' Committee, claimed that some one thousand Socialist ballots were voided in the Twelfth District. He had complained to the Board of Elections that Socialists were not getting a fair count, but the board told him that it could do nothing. Board officials had promised to investigate the matter. Max Danish also reported that in larger election districts officials had voided upwards of 150 London ballots.

There were reports of assaults against Socialist watchers. Mitchell Loeb, London's campaign manager, charged that a policeman and a Tammany election board chairman had beaten him unconscious after he had protested irregularities at a polling place in Public School 160 at Broome and Suffolk streets. Loeb and other Socialist officials also complained about defaced ballots; bought votes; the ejection of Socialist watchers and lawyers from polling places when they endeavored to call the attention of the police to irregularities; lights turned out in the polling places to permit the defacing of Socialist ballots, and voters intimidated by Tammany thugs.[51]

The Socialist press demanded a recount. London, the *Daily Forward* commented, had apparently received a large majority, but it was destroyed by fraud unsurpassed in Tammany's history.[52] The Democrats, the *New York Call* declared, had "raped democracy at home in a manner that will bring down upon them the contempt of future historians." London had increased his 1916 vote, but "such a wholesale stealing of votes took place that the recorded figures show nothing but the outrageous thievery on the part of the corrupt interests." The results in London's district should be challenged in the courts.[53] The *Advance* also charged that London was defeated by the "worst thefts" seen at the polls in twenty years.[54]

10. The Elections of 1918 and 1920

At a meeting sponsored by Local New York on the evening of November 9, London, Socialist campaign managers and members of the Executive Committee of Local New York appointed a committee to coordinate legal action. It also invited representatives of the unions, the Socialist Party and other organizations to attend a conference on November 13 to consider a course of action.[55] At this meeting, Socialist officials announced that they would seek a recount in the Twelfth Congressional District. They requested that Socialist watchers and voters who had knowledge of election law violations report such information to the legal committee.[56]

On November 22, Horace London, counsel for his brother, appeared before Justice Eugene A. Philbin of the New York Supreme Court to argue on behalf of a petition for examination of the void, defective, and protested ballots in the Twelfth Congressional District. London pointed out that the petition with attached affidavits revealed the existence of void and defective ballots in every one of the forty election districts comprising the Twelfth Congressional District. In one district, he stated, there had been 113 defective ballots out of a total of 400 votes. In another district, out of a total of 300 votes, 100 had had been declared defective. London claimed that the greater portion of 1,147 ballots reported void, defective and blank were Meyer London votes.

Four attorneys appeared on behalf of Goldfogle to oppose the motion, including Louis Marshall and Senator James A. Foley, the son-in-law of Tammany boss Charles F. Murphy. Arguing against the motion, Marshall said that the matter should be resolved by the House of Representatives to which Congressman London had resort for redress. Horace London replied that this privilege was not jeopardized, but the immediate recourse was to the courts. Justice Philbin reserved his decision and requested that attorneys on both sides submit briefs the following day.[57]

On December 6, Justice Philbin issued an order requiring the Board of Elections, Henry M. Goldfogle and others to show why the ballots of the Twelfth Congressional District should not be opened and inspected.[58] Subsequently, a hearing took place before Justice Donnelly of the Supreme Court on December 17, at which time he granted London's petition for a recount.

The court, however, ordered the examination by the Board of Elections to take place after a certificate of election was granted to Goldfogle.[59] This meant that if the recount favored Goldfogle, London would have to take the fight to retain his seat to the House of Representatives. The recount began on January 3 and lasted for twelve days.

Horace London and Herman Volk represented the interests of London and the Socialist Party respectively, while Goldfogle and the Board of Elections each had two representatives at the proceedings.[60] On January 8, Horace London told the *New York Call* that the outlook appeared "very bright." His brother had gained 376 votes with the votes of six election districts, with the void and protested ballots remaining to be examined.[61]

When the recount finished on January 15, Horace London announced that a notice would be served on Goldfogle contesting his seat. The charges specified that there was a miscount, that hundreds of ballots were improperly declared void and that numerous ballots were improperly marked for Goldfogle. The action would involve an investigation by the House Committee on Elections and a vote by the House. "In order to insure just and democratic elections," Horace London declared, "the instances of fraud must be prosecuted to the utmost. We intend to see that every election inspector who signed a false tally sheet is put behind bars."[62]

In a report to the Executive Committee of Local New York on January 15, Julius Gerber, the executive secretary, reiterated that the recount had revealed "gross violations" and that he believed the matter should be pursued in order to make an official record of the findings, either in court or the House of Representatives. In order to do this properly, Gerber pointed out, additional funds were needed. The Executive Committee endorsed Gerber's recommendations, and agreed to conduct a financial appeal in order to continue the fight.[63] After further consideration, however, London and the party decided not to pursue the contest. The lack of adequate time due to the delay in obtaining the recount, insufficient funds, and the belief that a Socialist would not get a fair hearing in Congress influenced the decision.[64]

Although fraud was a constant in the Twelfth District, the fusion of Democrats and Republicans proved the decisive factor in London's defeat. If the parties had fused in the 1914 and 1916 campaigns, London would have lost in both elections. Despite the fact that women voted for the first time in 1918, the Socialist vote had not increased dramatically from 1914 to 1918. The movement of Jews to other parts of the city, their failure to become citizens and to register to vote contributed significantly to this phenomenon.

One final consideration is the large vote, 7,452, for Goldfogle. Although London's vote also increased, Tammany proved more successful in getting out the vote. The candidacy for governor and election of the popular Al Smith, a son of the Lower East Side and a Tammany star, plus the "one hundred percent Americanism" theme, no doubt resonated with the Irish and immigrant communities, especially among new citizens who voted for the first time.

Undaunted by his defeat for reelection, London returned to Washington for the final session of the Sixty-Fifth Congress. The war had ended suddenly, and the country, as London had predicted, found itself without any plan for orderly military demobilization and reconstruction (reconversion of the economy).[65]

The War Industries Board relinquished its control over industry and abruptly began to cancel war contracts. Subsequently, many industries faced the necessity of making a rapid conversion to peacetime production without having given any real thought to the problem. Nevertheless, industry managed to effect a substantial reconversion by the middle of 1919, but in the process many workers were left jobless. The rapid demobilization of American military forces exacerbated the unemployment situation. Succumbing to the demand to bring the boys home, the Wilson administration released some six hundred thousand men almost immediately, and by November, 1919, nearly the entire force of four million had been demobilized.[66]

In a speech to the House on January 2, 1919, London addressed problems of post-war reconstruction. London reminded his colleagues that long before the United States had entered the war, and on several occasions thereafter, he had urged the House to consider the unemployment question. Again and again, he had asked for a study of social insurance, but Congress refused to act. Discontent would grow, London warned. "You cannot stifle the craving for a change, you cannot suppress the desire on the part of those who have faced danger to get some genuine reward, not in the form of a humiliating gift, but a reward in seeing the world get better." Congress should treat the problem of veterans as part of the effort to improve the economic situation of all Americans. Consideration should be given not only to returning soldiers, but to those whose jobs they will take.

The problem, London continued, was how to provide employment for all. He suggested that the government agencies created to promote war industries be utilized in this transition period to provide unemployment insurance to the returning veteran and to require him to find employment. If, however, he could not find a job, the government should undertake public works projects and take control of some privately owned industries.

Government control of industries, London admitted, was not the most economic or efficient way of doing things, but a beginning had to be made. The people had to learn to control and operate their own industries. "Let the Government take up one industry after another, taking up first the most suitable industries, so that the worker will know that he owes a duty to society to work and to be useful, that in return society owes him the duty of a wage which will enable him to live a man's life."[67]

As in the first two sessions of the Sixty-Fifth Congress, London continued his fight against repressive wartime legislation. Major Socialist Party officials, including Eugene Debs and Victor Berger, had been indicted and along with some two thousand other persons brought to trial and convicted under the Espionage Act.[68] Popular passion did not subside with the Armistice. By 1919, the Bolshevist menace appeared to have become more serious. The Bolshevists had strengthened their position in Russia, and their influence had spread elsewhere in Europe. Labor unrest and violence raised fear among many Americans that revolution was imminent in the United States. The fear of radicalism replaced the war as the excuse for repression. Bolshevism became the new devil, and to many Americans, Bolshevism and treason were synonymous.[69]

Against this background of growing intolerance, London delivered a series of speeches to the House in which he demanded the immediate repeal of the Espionage and Sedition acts, the release of political prisoners and an end to the deportation of radical aliens. No country, he told the House on January 22, 1919, could survive when men feared to speak the truth. Yet, in various parts of this country, public officials continued to commit a variety of "outrages" against the law in the name of the law. "Let us forget," London pleaded, "the hatred and the bitterness of the war. Let us begin ... [to] build anew; not only ... the rest of the world, but ... a better America. We can only build well upon the foundations of freedom of the press, freedom of thought, and freedom of speech, and upon respect for the rights of the minority."

In the same speech, London voiced opposition to an amendment introduced by the Immigration Committee to eliminate exemptions for political refugees. There was no excuse for such a radical departure from American tradition. The great majority of the men who helped build this country fled from some form of oppression. Unsettled conditions in Europe would produce a large number of political offenders, thus making this the "worst" possible time to shut the doors of America.

London took exception to the Immigration Committee's argument that it had a duty to the country to protect it against the influx of Bolshevik ideas and propagandists. "I need not dwell," he told his colleagues, "on the futility of legislating against the spread of an idea. If there is anything sound about an idea, if it can in any way be adapted to the needs of the people, if it can hold out any hope for the future, it cannot be shut out by an artificial rule. You cannot bar an idea by restrictive immigration laws." Bolshevism frightened the Immigration Committee, London declared.

In an effort to explain events in Russia and the Bolshevist movement, he pointed out that no one had made a real effort to understand the meaning of the word or the significance of the movement which it supposedly represented. The term *Bolshevism*, he explained, had originated during a factional struggle over methods and policies at a Social Democratic Convention held in 1903. The groups whose views had prevailed became known as the Bolsheviks, meaning "those in the majority." The Bolsheviks had taken control of the government of a country ruined by a disastrous war, in the midst of revolution, and confronted with numerous complex problems. Like the word

Bolshevism, the government's methods were peculiarly Russian. The American people had nothing to fear for "it is impossible to apply the methods used in the desperate moments of a revolution in a country ruled for a thousand years by an absolute monarchy to a country with nearly 300 years of development of political institutions."[70]

A persistent London raised the question of civil liberties again on February 12. Rather than investigating Bolshevism, Congress should seek to determine whether a conspiracy existed in the United States to suppress freedom of speech, freedom of the press, and freedom of assembly. The war had ended, yet Congress did not repeal the Espionage or the Sedition acts. The Espionage Act, he charged, had not been designed to stop spying, but to regulate and control speech, the press and thought. Thousands of men still remained in jail because they had expressed views unpopular in wartime.

London then compared the present Sedition Act to the sedition law of 1789. Under that law only eleven persons had been tried and the maximum penalty was two years imprisonment and a fine of one thousand dollars. Under the present law, Congress had fixed the penalty at twenty years imprisonment and a fine of ten thousand dollars. "I can understand," he remarked sarcastically, "why the fine was fixed at $10,000 instead of $1,000; we are now ten times as rich; but why should it be 20 years instead of 2 except that we appreciate liberty to only one-tenth the extent it was appreciated then."

In addition, the trials had taken place in a hostile atmosphere. It was difficult, London declared, to try a political case before a jury in wartime. At this point, Representative Black asked him whether a legal remedy existed for dealing with those who advocated the violent overthrow of the American government. London replied that individuals who advocated the overthrow of government by violence placed themselves outside of the law. Socialism opposed the overthrow of anything by violence. That is why, London pointed out, he had voted against the war. "As a Socialist I oppose the use of physical violence, and that is why I condemn those slanderers and ignoramuses who seek to confuse the life-giving philosophy of Socialism ... with the theory of violence."

Returning again to the question of Bolshevism, London explained that it was a phase in a revolution that would probably last for several years. The present form of government was not the last and final form. "It is a stage in a struggle incident to Russian life. No other nation in the world has or has had similar conditions." Thus, while collective ownership of land might appear to be subversive in a country where individualism prevailed, in most of European Russia the peasants viewed collective ownership as the only proper form of land ownership.

Black then asked London if he approved a provision in the Soviet constitution stipulating that a land owner could be deprived of his property without compensation. London replied that he would allow compensation to private landowners, but he would break up large estates. However, the question was not whether Congress approved of the Russian constitution or methods of revolutionary government. The United States, London pointed out, had taken four years to establish a constitution. Moreover, it was adopted in secret and many delegates had left the constitutional convention in disgust. Therefore, the American people should sympathize with the "groping" of the Russians for freedom and a better society. The question, he reiterated, was not whether their constitution was good or bad, but whether other nations would permit the Russian people to solve their problems.

In conclusion, London urged his colleagues to repeal the "obnoxious" Espionage Act and to end the unfair attack upon socialism. "We are the advocates of the theory of evolution, and we do not want those who happen to be in power to use the coercive, brutal power of the majority to suppress freedom of thought, freedom of the press, and freedom of assembly."[71]

Representative Walsh of Massachusetts took the floor to answer London. He noted that London's term of service in the House would end shortly. Although London would not have the privilege of participating in the Paris Peace Conference, he would, Walsh sarcastically observed, have the opportunity to visit Russia to introduce some of his recommendations. "With him as an assistant to the leaders of that element [the Bolshevists] in Russia, with the experience he has had in legislation here, I doubt not that he will be able to give great aid in bringing peace and quiet once more amidst those troublous and troubled people." As for London's demand for the repeal of the Espionage Act, Walsh stated that this would happen with the drafting of a peace treaty. "So I submit that the gentleman from New York might well wait until the turmoil resulting from the struggle has somewhat abated."[72]

Despite such hostile reactions, London continued with his one-man campaign to repeal the Espionage and Sedition Acts. On February 21, and again on the following day, London took the floor to denounce these measures. He compared the "wave of dark reaction" engulfing the world to conditions in Europe after the collapse of the French Revolution. The Espionage Act, London asserted, was the most oppressive law, not only in the history of this country, but in the history of modern times. Congress had conferred upon every law official the right to suppress the written and spoken word. "Now in war time the people are insane, but there is no earthly excuse for retaining the espionage law today."[73]

In his final address of the session on the question of civil liberties, London told the House, on February 22, that not only had no attempt been made to repeal the "hysterical" wartime legislation, but some favored continuing the restrictions and making them more stringent. London referred to the report that thousands of radicals faced deportation without due process of law. He reminded the House that he had opposed the deportation of aliens who advocated the forcible overthrow of the United States government; it deprived a person of trial by jury and the opportunity to confront his accusers and to cross-examine them. One needed only to convince a labor department official that grounds existed for the charge and the accused was helpless. Labor unions would suffer most seriously, London warned, unless Congress repealed the law and abandoned the policy of deportation. Alien radicals, he explained, had played an important role in organizing immigrants, and without the organization of the immigrant, labor unions could not survive.[74]

Despite London's pleas for the repeal of the Espionage and Sedition acts and the release of political prisoners, Congress failed to act, and President Wilson refused to grant amnesty to those who had opposed the war. In addition, London's efforts to allay fears of Bolshevism and social upheaval went for naught, as the Wilson administration launched a campaign against civil liberties such as the country had not witnessed in peacetime since 1799.[75]

As the session drew to a close, London took the opportunity to express his opinions on the Versailles peace negotiations. In a speech on February 6, 1919, London wished the president success in his work. "I believe that he is right in being where he is now, trying to get the best he can for America and humanity out of this crisis. I would readily give my life to promote the things he has announced he stands for." President Wilson, London continued, had more loyal support from the Socialists than from the "tories and plutocrats and munitions manufacturers of Europe and America."

Many statesmen, who had hailed Wilson's Fourteen Points, now opposed the very things that the president had informed the world this country supported. Disarmament, the abolition of conscription, and a league of nations have been rejected as visionary. Although a league of nations might prove impractical and impossible of immediate realization, thoughtful individuals must make the effort. "The moral appeal of the president to the world is strong," London continued, "and yet in this country the big moral principle, that new ethical code he proclaims to the world is ridiculed as nebulous and absurd." President Wilson represented those people who desire disarmament and a league of nations, but he lacked support. Moreover, the president had encountered numerous difficulties at the peace conference, including the secret treaties. In closing, London decried the fact that the United States had no definite international policy prior to the war and that a similar situation presently existed.[76]

With the adjournment of the Sixty-Fifth Congress on March 4, 1919, London returned to New York. He looked forward to the election of 1920, confident that the people of the Lower East Side would return him to Congress once the war hysteria had passed. During the next two years, he devoted himself to his law practice which, as in the years prior to his congressional service, consisted primarily of labor litigation. London also served as legal counsel to the Cloakmakers, the Furworkers, the Suit Case and Bagmakers' Union and the Workmen's Circle.[77]

London, in January 1920, represented the Cloakmakers in a dispute with the Suit and Shirt Manufacturers' Association arising out of the union's demand for a 30 percent increase in their weekly wages. The Manufacturers' Association rejected the demand, but agreed, as did the Cloakmakers, to arbitration when Governor Alfred E. Smith offered his good offices.[78] On January 8, 1920, London appeared before the board appointed by the governor to settle the dispute. In his opening remarks, London argued that the existing agreement with the Manufacturers' Association did not prohibit the workers from seeking higher wages or from striking if the manufacturers refused their demands. He would advise his clients, London stated, that they had this right. Aroused by London's remarks, the manufacturers threatened to leave the hearing until board chairman Edward M. Boyle, chairman of the State Industrial Commission, declared that, if necessary, the meeting would proceed without them.[79]

In presenting the Cloakmakers' case to the Board of Arbitration on January 14, London emphasized the rising cost of living. A union member, he stated, needed $2,500 to support his family in "reasonable comfort." This was based upon a War Labor Board report which had placed the minimum wage at $1,900. London noted that the cost of living had risen 23 percent since that time. With the conclusion of the arguments of both parties on January 21, the Board of Arbitration took the matter under advisement.[80]

On January 27, the board granted the Cloakmakers a 15 percent increase. The award raised the minimum wage in every craft in the cloak and suit trade in New York to between thirty and forty dollars per week for the less skilled and to between forty and fifty dollars for the more skilled workers.[81] Officials of the Cloakmakers and the ILGWU expressed pleasure with the settlement. London and Klein thanked Governor Smith and the Board of Arbitration for their impartial handling of the matter.[82]

London also served as counsel to the International Furriers' Union during its disastrous thirty-week strike in 1920.[83] The fur industry had prospered during and immediately following the war, but in 1920, it experienced a depressed period. As unemployment grew, the union decided to strike for equal distribution of work. The walkout began on May 27. Morris Kaufman, the president of the union, assured the workers that it would not last long since the manufacturers could not afford a prolonged strike. The employers, however, in order to break the strike, established shops outside of New York, employed scabs and gave work to unorganized Greek shops in the city.[84]

As the strike dragged on, London spoke at numerous rallies on behalf of the striking workers, and was instrumental in procuring financial assistance from the cloak makers and the Amalgamated Clothing Workers for the beleaguered union.[85] In addition, London argued in court unsuccessfully against an anti-picketing injunction sought by the Associated Fur Manufacturers which was granted on October 11.[86]

London also presented the union's argument on November 17 against an application by the Associated Fur Manufacturers to restrain the International Furriers' Union and its members from striking against members of the Association.[87] However, before the court's decision, the strike ended on December 20, 1920, on the terms proposed by the Association. As a result of the settlement, the fur workers were forced to work fifty hours a week, to accept wage reductions ranging from 20 to 50 percent, and to do unlimited overtime work at the regular hourly basis. The loss of this strike seriously weakened the union and led to a shakeup in union leadership.[88]

The two years between London's defeat in 1918 and his congressional campaign in 1920 were troublesome ones for the Socialist Party. Most American socialists sympathized with the Bolsheviks' effort to eliminate the vestiges of czarist autocracy. But the right wing of the Socialist Party, led by Victor Berger and Morris Hillquit, did not approve their methods or advocate a similar course of action in this country. On the other hand, the left wing of the party, strengthened by the Bolshevik Revolution, enthusiastically embraced their program.

Early in 1919 the revolutionists began to organize a left-wing section within the Socialist Party, with its own press, dues and membership cards. It formulated a plan for immediate revolution and issued a manifesto similar to that of the Third International created in Moscow in March 1919. By May, there were approximately thirty thousand Socialists who supported the left-wing program. Moreover, the left-wingers had gained control of many local organizations of the party and had isolated their moderate members.

This growth of left-wing strength caused serious concern among moderate party leaders. Thus, when the spring election of new members to the National Executive Committee resulted in the choice of a left-wing majority, the old National Executive Committee invalidated the results. In addition, it suspended the seven foreign-language federations affiliated with the left wing and expelled the entire state organization of Michigan. The National Executive Committee later expelled the state organizations of Massachusetts and Ohio. All in all, the Socialist leadership expelled or suspended some seventy thousand members.

Thwarted in its effort to gain control of the party, the left wing met in New York City on June 21, 1919, to determine a course of action. The delegates rejected by a vote of 55 to 38 the proposal, supported by the representatives of the foreign-language federations, to immediately form a new party. The majority of the delegates favored remaining within the Socialist Party and making a concerted effort to capture control of the old party organization at its emergency convention in Chicago on August 30. Angered by this decision, some thirty-one delegates, led by Isaac Hourwich, withdrew from the meeting and issued a call for a convention to establish a communist party.[89]

The remnants of the Socialist Party assembled at the end of August in Chicago to formulate a program. The left-wing delegates, led by John Reed and Benjamin Gitlow, never had an opportunity to capture the party machinery since they were excluded from the convention. They then proceeded to organize the Communist Labor Party. The remaining Socialist delegates adopted a manifesto rejecting "drastic measures" to achieve the transition from capitalism to socialism, and endorsed the methods utilized prior to the war. The manifesto strongly supported the Soviet government of Russia, denounced the League of Nations and approved industrial unionism and industrial representation in parliamentary bodies.

One of the most important questions confronting the convention was the relationship of the American Socialist Party to the international Socialist movement. The majority of the delegates opposed affiliation with the Third International and favored the creation of a new international. A minority report urged affiliation with the Third International. In a referendum submitted to the party membership, the minority report carried by better than two to one.[90]

During these eventful spring and summer months, London refrained from making public statements on these important developments. He remained true to his practice of remaining aloof from doctrinal disputes within the party. Nevertheless, previous utterances on the Bolshevik Revolution and his attitude toward revolutionary methods revealed that he had no sympathy for the left-wing movement. The feeling was mutual. Left-wingers were extremely critical of London's position regarding the war and the revolution, and had opposed both his nomination and election in 1918. They would also work against him in the 1920 campaign.

With the approach of the fall elections of 1919, London took to the political hustings on behalf of Socialist candidates for state and municipal offices. The campaign opened with a meeting at Forward Hall on September 30 at which London was one of the principal speakers. He warned the audience that the party was threatened by extremists who desired to destroy it. He urged them to put aside their grievances and to work for the party's best interests.[91]

10. The Elections of 1918 and 1920

During the following week, London spoke at rallies on the East Side, the Bronx and Harlem. He criticized the Harding administration for failing to deal with the unemployment problem, but he leveled his strongest attacks on the Tammany-Republican machines which had organized fusion tickets to defeat Socialist candidates.[92] Despite the weakened condition of the party, coupled with fusion tickets, New York City Socialists elected five members to the lower house of the state legislature.[93]

On January 7, after the five Socialist assemblymen had taken the oath of office, Speaker Thadeus C. Sweet suspended them until an investigation of charges against them was completed. A resolution was then introduced in the legislature charging them with adherence to the principles of the Third International, abdicating their legislative independence to the Socialist Party and opposition to the war. It also provided for their suspension. After the Speaker ruled all discussion of the resolution out of order, the Assembly adopted it by a vote of 140 to 6.[94]

London condemned these proceedings in no uncertain terms. "There seems to be a great rivalry," he told the *New York Times*, "among various reactionaries as to which will do the greatest damage to the Constitution." In this instance, it was the Socialists who championed the fundamental principles of Americanism. The Socialists, he continued, advocated peaceful methods, and sought to convince "impatient" party members that under a republican system of government the Socialist Party might become the majority and control the government. Democracy ceased to exist, London declared, when the minority was oppressed. Constitutions were designed to protect the minority against "hasty and unreasonable" action by the majority.[95]

Meanwhile, the New York Assembly's Judiciary Committee conducted an investigation into the qualifications of the suspended Socialists. As a result of its probe, seven of the thirteen members of the committee signed a report that substantiated all charges against the Socialists. The committee recommended permanent expulsion. The Assembly debated the issue on March 31, and on the following day voted to expel the five Socialists.[96]

A disgusted Meyer London called the expulsion "an act of treason." Businessmen, he charged, desired a government that would protect their interests. They wanted the legislature open to the representatives of business but closed to those of labor. "In short, this is government by anarchy."[97]

On April 14, at an amnesty rally on behalf of Eugene Debs and other political prisoners, London lashed out against the reactionary wave sweeping the United States. Five years of war had made the world "savage and brutal." He urged his comrades to keep calm during this reactionary period. As the builders of a new social order, they should follow the path of intelligent progress.[98]

One month after the expulsion of the socialist assemblymen, the Eighth National Convention of the Socialist Party convened in New York City to nominate a presidential ticket and to adopt a platform for the coming election.[99] Elected as a delegate by Local New York, London participated in his first party convention since 1912. The former congressman did not play an important role during the proceedings dominated by Morris Hillquit and his associates.

The major issue in the 1920 convention, which lasted from May 8 to May 15, was the question of affiliation with the Third International. As in the Chicago convention of 1919, the Committee on International Affairs divided on this issue. The majority report presented by Hillquit recommended affiliation with the International, but only if Moscow modified its insistence on the dictatorship of the proletariat. There were two minority reports. The first, submitted by John Louis Engdahl and William F. Kruse, leaders of the left wing, urged the American Socialist Party to reaffirm its affiliation with the Third International. The second, submitted by Victor Berger, opposed joining the Moscow organization under any condition. During the debate that followed, London remained silent.[100] When the delegates finally voted, they overwhelmingly rejected Berger's report. In a roll-call vote on the Engdahl report, the delegates also rejected it 90 to 40, with London recorded against the report. The majority report then carried by a voice vote.[101]

Of equal importance were discussions of the platform and declaration of principles. The declaration, considered by the convention on May 11, stated that the Socialist Party had the responsibility to educate the workers as to their present condition and their potential power. The party would seek power for the workers through political action and by supporting class-conscious labor organizations. The declaration stressed the party's dedication to constitutional methods and to religious freedom.

Engdahl offered a substitute for the proposed declaration. It emphasized the class struggle and played down political action while stressing the need for industrial organization. It also called for the dictatorship of the proletariat during the workers' final struggle for political supremacy to ensure the success of the revolution. Once again London did not participate in the debate dominated by Hillquit, Engdahl and Berger. After five hours of discussion the delegates defeated the Engdahl substitute 103 to 33 as London voted with the majority.[102]

Section 9 of the declaration, which stated that the party favored complete separation of church and state and recognized the right of religious freedom, also caused much discussion. London moved for the elimination of this language. In arguing on behalf of his motion, London emphasized the danger of mentioning religion in the platform of a political party. It was unnecessary to mention it because the Constitution had resolved the struggle between church and state in this country.

Judge Jacob Panken spoke against London's motion.[103] The party, he stated, needed a position on the issue to which members could refer. The state organization of Michigan was suspended because it adopted a resolution that denied party members the right to speak in that state unless they attacked the church. The delegates subsequently rejected London's motion.[104]

The convention considered the platform on May 13. As with the declaration of principles, the left wing introduced a substitute proposal which the delegates rejected. They then approved the first seven planks with a minimum of discussion.[105] The plank dealing with foreign relations engendered a lively debate. Meyer London objected to the second paragraph of the plank which called upon the United States government to disband the League of Nations and to create an international parliament of democratically elected representatives from all nations.

The former congressman, who supported the League concept, offered an amendment which read, "The Government of the United States should negotiate ... to reorganize the League of Nations into an International Parliament." Taking issue with most American Socialists, London argued that although the League "today is not what we desire," it was nevertheless a beginning. The present League, he continued, should be "reorganized on a more democratic basis." The convention should not repudiate the League. British and French socialists believe, he pointed out, that the existing organization could significantly improve international relations in a way that would benefit all nations. The delegates rejected the amendment by a voice vote.[106]

London then proposed a second amendment to the effect that "the Government of the United States negotiate a movement to erect an International Parliament of Democratically elected representatives." London stated that it was unrealistic to urge the United States to initiate action to disband the League since it was not a member. His proposal would clarify the plank.

Hillquit took the floor to oppose London's proposal. The amendment, he stated, would not improve the plank for it already called for the creation of a parliament of the world. At his request, the amendment was defeated and the committee's plank accepted without change.[107] Shortly thereafter, the convention completed its discussion of the platform and approved it, as amended, by a voice vote.[108] The convention then proceeded to nominate Eugene V. Debs and Seymour Stedman as the party's candidates for the presidency and vice presidency respectively.

The convention held its last regular session on the evening of May 14. A number of left-wing delegates from Chicago caused a stir when they introduced a resolution condemning the position taken by Morris Hillquit in his defense of the expelled New York assemblymen at the hearing in Albany. They were particularly disturbed by Hillquit's comment that the American Socialists would resist an invasion even if it came from Soviet Russia.

London immediately came to Hillquit's defense. He moved that the resolution be expunged from the record of the convention. London condemned the resolution as a "painful and disgraceful thing, aimed at a man who had given all the years of his life to the Socialist movement." The fact that he had differences with Hillquit did not affect his recognition of his service. The whole world, London continued, was "crazy," and Socialists were no exception.

London told the delegates that he had originally opposed dignifying the Albany hearings with a defense. He had changed his mind because the "brilliant" performance of the Socialists at the hearings had served the cause of Socialist propaganda. With a "roar of yeas," the delegates voted to expunge the resolution from the record.[109] The delegates returned to communities around the nation to begin preparations for the coming political campaign.

The 1920 Socialist campaign in New York began when the state convention of the party convened on July 3. The more than one hundred delegates in attendance adopted a "moderate" platform similar to that of the national convention and nominated a full slate of candidates for the statewide offices.[110]

On July 8, a committee of the Socialist Party of New York County selected candidates for Congress and the New York Legislature. After considerable discussion, the committee chose London as the party's standard-bearer in the Twelfth Congressional District. Opposition to his nomination came from the Jewish branch of the Second Assembly District which, although refusing to endorse his candidacy, failed to propose another candidate. In addition to London, the committee designated Charles W. Ervin, Algernon Lee, and Morris Hillquit to run for Congress in the Thirteenth, Fourteenth and Twentieth congressional districts respectively.[111]

The *New York Call* observed that the campaign of 1920 appeared brighter as a result of the strong ticket selected by the New York County Committee. It not only predicted a London victory[112] in the coming election, but declared that Socialist congressmen would triumph in the Twelfth, Thirteenth, Fourteenth and Twentieth congressional districts and possibly in the Eighteenth, Twenty-Second, Twenty-Third and Twenty-Fourth districts unless the old parties united behind fusion candidates.[113]

Charles D. Orth, president of the National Security League, subsequently appealed to the voters of the major parties to encourage their leaders to consider fusion. The Socialist Party, Orth declared, "is international and not national. It is destructive and not constructive. It does not stand, as should all political parties, for the people, but is a class party. Its tenets and principles were conceived in hate and envy."¹¹⁴ The pleas of the National Security League bore fruit, early in August, when the Democratic and Republican organizations in New York City agreed to run fusion candidates in districts where the Socialists posed a serious threat. Thus, as in 1918, the two old parties fused in the name of patriotism and supported Henry M. Goldfogle in the Twelfth Congressional District.¹¹⁵

In late August and early September, London subordinated his campaign to the drive to reelect the five ousted Socialist assemblymen in the special election on September 16.¹¹⁶ London agreed to campaign in the five assembly districts on their behalf. At a rally in Brownsville on August 27 for Charles Solomon of the Twenty-Third Assembly District, London denounced the "blind, reactionary tactics" of the Wilson administration. Nations, he said, were judged by how they treated minorities, and if they oppressed minorities, they should be regarded as repressive. Washington should clean its own house by ending deportations and lynchings, before it criticized Russia.¹¹⁷

On the following evening, London addressed some two thousand people at a rally on behalf of Louis Waldman in the Eighth Assembly District. The expulsion of the five assemblymen, he asserted, represented an attempt to force Socialists to resort to violence. "It was a trap to put us outside the law and crush us. It failed. But let them think twice," London warned, "before attempting it again. We have plenty of patience, but there is a limit even to our patience."¹¹⁸

At yet another rally for Waldman on September 1, London exclaimed that state voters had the legal right to ignore every law passed by the New York Assembly during the 1920 session. The suspension of duly elected and qualified members of the legislature meant the legislature had been improperly organized, it was a "rump" legislature, and its enactments were not binding in a court of law. London declared that he would like to face the "scoundrels" responsible for the expulsion on the same platform, and have them explain the reasoning behind their action. Every "clean" man and woman, regardless of party, would vote to return the five Socialists.¹¹⁹

As London predicted, the five assemblymen won by increased margins in the special election.¹²⁰ On September 21, the New York Assembly voted to seat Orr and Dewitt, but once again refused to seat Claessens, Waldman and Solomon. Orr and Dewitt denounced those voting against their colleagues and then walked out of the Assembly.¹²¹

London, in Albany at the time to testify before a legislative committee on behalf of the United Tenants' Organization, refused to appear, in protest of the Assembly's action. He sharply rebuked the Assembly, declaring that it had completely rejected the principle of representative government.¹²²

In addition to his efforts on behalf of the Socialist assemblymen, London continued his amnesty campaign. The National Executive Committee of the Socialist Party had designated September 13, the second anniversary of the Debs trial, as Amnesty Day, and had elicited the support of labor and liberal groups.[123]

On the morning of that day, a delegation of twenty-five headed by Samuel Gompers and London, representing the United Hebrew Trades, met with Attorney General Mitchell Palmer in Washington to demand general amnesty. London told the attorney general, "Whatever may be said to excuse the imprisonment of such persons during the war, it is ridiculous to pretend that they are still enemies of mankind who must be shut up from the world." He branded the Espionage Act as a "stupid and vicious law." Eugene Debs "is a prophet, an artist, a passionate lover of his fellow men who would endure any fate rather than retreat from his labor of love for others." London demanded the pardon and release of Debs and of all his fellow prisoners. Palmer rejected the delegation's plea for general amnesty, but promised to discuss the matter with the president and to review each case individually.[124]

Meanwhile, preparations had begun for a vigorous campaign in the Twelfth Congressional District. Socialist leaders planned to concentrate their efforts in the all-important Fourth Assembly District which Goldfogle had carried in 1918 by 1,202 votes. They attributed his success there to irregularities at the polls and inadequate organization.[125] On September 27, the New York County Executive Committee appointed Charles Grossman, party organizer in New York County, to manage London's campaign. In a statement to the *Call*, Grossman announced that the campaign in the Twelfth District would open with a rally on Sunday, October 3. Grossman stressed the significance of the Fourth Assembly District and the need to procure an honest count of Socialist ballots. He urged volunteers to report to campaign headquarters at Clinton Hall.[126]

Organized labor also joined the campaign to reelect "their friend and legal advisor." On August 25, a conference took place at Beethoven Hall to organize trade unionists. London urged the unionists to forget revolutions for the present and to concentrate on the struggle at home. "They have their troubles there [Russia] while we have ours and must meet them. The great revolution will be the revolution of the mind. Not revolutions brought by bombs, nor even the revolutions sustained by armies and wars."[127]

As in previous elections, the ILGWU, the International Furriers' Union and the Amalgamated Clothing Workers, the Cloakmakers and the Workmen's Circle organized campaign committees and collected money in the shops for London.[128] The ILGWU announced that it would make a special effort in the Twelfth and Twentieth congressional districts. Once again the union designated Saul Metz to manage the campaign in the Twelfth District and opened

10. The Elections of 1918 and 1920

campaign headquarters at Clinton Hall.[129] *Justice*, the official publication of the ILGWU, declared that the Cloakmakers' Union of New York had never before taken such an active part in a socialist campaign. The Cloakmakers' motto was "Hillquit and London must receive the vote, get it honestly counted and go to Washington next November!"[130]

The fur workers also worked vigorously on London's behalf. Morris Kaufman, manager of the Furriers' Union, in a letter to some one thousand furriers residing in the Twelfth District, urged them to throw their entire support into the campaign for London's election. "This year we want to give Meyer London such a tremendous majority that all the crookedness and thievery of which the old party politicians are capable will be of no avail," Kaufman declared. "London deserves your support. He is with you. Are you with him?"[131]

London's candidacy received an additional boost from the Farmer-Labor Party. Newly organized in July 1920 by Socialist trade unionists, the railroad brotherhoods and other unions, liberals and ex–Bull Moosers, and a number of agrarian radicals, the party agreed not to run a congressional candidate in the Twelfth Congressional District. The Farmer-Labor Party adopted this policy in those places where a radical candidate appeared to have a good chance of being elected if the radical vote was not split.[132]

The campaign in the Twelfth District began on October 3 with a rally at Clinton Hall. In his speech, London touched upon the issues which he planned to emphasize during the ensuing weeks: civil liberties, his record in Congress, Tammany corruption in the 1918 election, and foreign policy. London told a cheering crowd that there were very few people on the East Side who could not distinguish between the Tammany "clique," which had succeeded in dominating the district by purely Tammany methods, and the Socialist Party. Two years before, he explained, the old party politicians had resorted to intimidation and fraud. "This year it is our purpose to increase the vote so that the majority will be so big that, no matter how much they steal, there will be a majority left for me." London stressed the need for better organization than previously. Socialists had the votes, he declared. The problem was to get them counted.

Reviewing his work in Congress, London stated that he had spoken more frequently than most of his colleagues, delivering over one hundred speeches. Moreover, he had always had an attentive audience. Many Democrats and Republicans in the House desired that he speak because they realized that he could speak freely whereas they were bound to their party machine and could not. The Democratic platform, he noted, sought to win liberal support. How, he asked, could the Democrats make an appeal to liberalism after their "shameful record" over the last four years? London reminded his audience

Meyer London campaign flyer, 1920. Photographic Collection, Tamiment Library, New York University.

that a few weeks earlier he had accompanied a delegation that met with Attorney General Palmer to request amnesty for individuals imprisoned for the "crime" of belonging to a minority party.

In reference to foreign policy, London criticized the Republican and Democratic presidential candidates for their position on the League of

10. The Elections of 1918 and 1920

Nations. He did not understand, London stated, Harding's position on the League, and he doubted, for that matter, if Harding knew where he stood on it. On the other hand, Cox claimed that he favored the League with interpretations and reservations that would not destroy its effectiveness. London asked his listeners if they understood what that meant, for he did not.

He criticized the League of Nations for being used to destroy Jews in Central and Eastern Europe as well as revolutionary Russia. The United States government found no difficulty in dealing with that "great democrat," the Emperor of Japan, but would not recognize the Soviet Union because it did not like Russia's form of government. London suggested that before the United States attempted to dictate to Moscow, "our great leaders" should reform Tammany Hall.

London urged his audience to vote for the entire Socialist ticket and not him alone. The growing Socialist vote on the East Side, he stated, showed that what had once been a personal vote for him had become a Socialist vote. London noted that every two years certain political groups demanded consideration for their views in return for their support. "I have told them all to go to hell," he exclaimed. "I am a Socialist.... I won't change my platform for any political consideration." If elected to Congress, London pledged, he would once again represent the thoughts and aspirations of workers everywhere.[133]

As in the 1918 campaign, Goldfogle's main issue remained "one hundred percent Americanism" versus socialism. In addition to the National Security League, major newspapers such as the *New York Times*, the *New York World* and the *New York Tribune* endorsed his candidacy. The *New York Times* declared on October 30 that Goldfogle deserved the support of the voters in the Twelfth District. During his eight terms in the House, he had been a "faithful" public servant and had done "good" work, particularly on behalf of the postal employees. "It would be ... to the disadvantage of the Twelfth Congressional District to give to a Socialist the seat so long occupied by Mr. Goldfogle, who was born in this city and who is a man of American convictions and American understanding."[134]

The *New York World* stated that Goldfogle, as a member of Congress for sixteen years, was one of its oldest members, the dean of the New York delegation and an influential legislator. Goldfogle had the support of the postal civil service employees, and several southern congressmen had spoken out on his behalf. Through the years, Goldfogle had served the interest of organized labor. He favored a reduction in the high cost of living, repeal of various war measures and liberal immigration laws.[135]

The *New York Tribune* noted that the Socialists were making a concerted effort in the Twelfth, Thirteenth, Fourteenth and Twentieth congressional districts. Voters should not allow these districts to drift to an anti-nationalistic party which stood for "slackerism and defeatism" during the war.[136]

The *Tageblatt*, an Orthodox Yiddish daily, in calling for Goldfogle's election, pointed out that he favored free immigration, defended the Jews and protested against pogroms in Poland.[137] This appeal to ethnic interests brought an immediate and sharp rejoinder from London and his supporters. Goldfogle's support of free immigration, London told an overflow crowd at Clinton Hall on October 17, was not surprising. No New York congressman opposed free immigration. It did not require courage to champion such a policy. Socialists favored unrestricted immigration, London observed, because they wanted people from other nations to come to the United States and fight for freedom, whereas capitalists and their representatives supported free immigration because they wanted to exploit the new arrivals.

Goldfogle, London continued, went to the synagogue on Jewish holidays and wore a green necktie on St. Patrick's Day. Devotion to the Jew did not consist of giving lip service to Jewish greatness, but in a readiness to fight for the Jew's economic, political and moral advancement. Goldfogle's record was empty in this respect. "If he really wanted to help the Jews, he would have urged, as I have urged, that the Russian revolutionary government be recognized. It is in Russia, where the Jew has been massacred and tortured for centuries, that the Jew is at last able to live without fear of religious persecution." The collapse of the revolutionary government would result in the greatest era of persecution in Russia that the Jews have ever faced. The Jewish problem, London stated, was part of the world problem, and the solution for both lay in the application of Socialist principles.[138]

At a meeting on October 27, several Orthodox rabbis endorsed London's candidacy. Although not Socialists, they noted that the Socialists had stood by the Jews. London had done more for the Jews than "thousands" of his opponents put together.[139]

The *Daily Forward* declared that anti–Semites and Jewish politicians were making "wild" charges about London. Abraham Cahan called upon the Jewish voters of the Lower East Side to elect congressmen who would speak against Polish oppression. Send Hillquit, London and others to Congress, he pleaded, so they could arouse America, so they could tell the American people what the newspapers were suppressing.[140]

As Election Day approached, the Socialists intensified their efforts in the Twelfth District. Volunteer campaign workers distributed literature, conducted canvasses and performed other essential tasks. The Socialist Party Campaign Committee, the Cloakmakers' Campaign Committee, the Furriers' Union, the Amalgamated Clothing Workers, and the Workmen's Circle sponsored numerous well-attended rallies nightly. Many of the leading Socialists in the city appeared on London's behalf. Among them were Judge Jacob Panken, Alderman B. Charney Vladek and Abraham Cahan.[141]

Eugene Debs, in an eleventh-hour appeal from his prison cell in Atlanta, urged the voters to return London to Congress. "Several years ago," Debs said, "the East Side was judged by the representative it chose to go to the House of Representatives, and of their choice I was proud. Your representative Meyer London did his duty honestly, honorably, and he fought for your — and our — interests as a true Socialist. Your representative spoke in Congress and your voice rang out clearly, unmistakably. Send Comrade London back to Congress so that your voice of protest should again be heard."[142]

Voters of the Twelfth District went to the polls in record numbers on November 2. During the day, Clinton Hall was a beehive of activity as hundreds of workers rushed to and from London's campaign headquarters. London spent the day traveling from one voting place to another in order to deal with irregularities.

Excitement gripped the East Side as the polls neared closing. As in previous campaigns, movie picture screens had been set up in front of the Forward Building where large crowds gathered to await the results. The count proceeded slowly. The first scattered returns did not come in until close to midnight. A heavy rain added to the confusion and several thousand people sought shelter on the upper floor of Clinton Hall. Returns from seven districts gave London a small lead, but by five o'clock in the morning, with only sixteen election districts unreported, his margin had increased by two thousand votes. By nine o'clock, it had become certain that London would once again represent the Twelfth Congressional District.

The large crowd, which had maintained an all-night vigil, called for London who still watched the count. Shortly thereafter, he appeared. A band struck up the *International*, the *Marseillaise* and the *Star Spangled Banner*. Members of the crowd lifted London to their shoulders and carried him to the platform. "This is your victory and that is why I consider it my victory, an elated London shouted to the roaring crowd. "You put up the fight, you supplied the enthusiasm, the spirit, the material assistance that has made this possible. To you belongs the credit for what has been achieved." He had found it difficult, he continued, to serve as the only Socialist in Congress during the war. He would also face obstacles in the new Congress. "But with your assistance and cooperation and good cheer to sustain me, I shall endeavor to fight for the workers of this city, state, and nation."[143]

Initially, the *New York Tribune* and the *New York World* prematurely reported Goldfogle's reelection.[144] An elated Goldfogle issued a victory statement in which he declared that East Side citizens who had reelected him stood for "100 percent Americanism."[145] However, on the next day, the *Tribune* and the *World* reported London's victory.¹⁴⁶ Complete returns showed that London had defeated Goldfogle by a majority of 1,558 votes, the largest margin in his three congressional victories. London received 10,212 votes or 54.06 percent of the vote as compared to Goldfogle's 8,654 votes or 45.81 percent. London carried the Second, Sixth and Eighth assembly districts, and although he failed to carry the Fourth Assembly District, Goldfogle's majority fell from 1,202 votes in 1918 to a mere 90.¹⁴⁷

Other Socialist congressional candidates in New York City lost, amidst charges of election irregularities. The Socialists succeeded, however, in electing Samuel Orr of the Bronx, and Charles Solomon and Henry Jaeger of Brooklyn, to the Assembly, the latter two being the only ones among the ousted Socialist assemblymen who succeeded in winning. Samuel De Witt, Louis Waldman, and August Claessens lost to fusion candidates in close races. Moreover, for the first time, New York Socialists elected a member to the New York Senate.¹⁴⁸ London expressed disappointment in the result; he had hoped for more Socialist congressmen. The Democrats and Republicans, London charged, had stolen many Socialist votes. In many districts Socialist watchers did not have a chance. "But this much is certain. This is the opening wedge for the Socialists in Congress, and soon, I know, I will be joined by other comrades."¹⁴⁹

In an analysis of the election results, London attributed his large majority to the determined effort on the part of the people of the Twelfth District to "avenge" themselves for the "theft" of the 1918 election. They wanted to make it so great this time that it would be impossible to steal enough." The desire to punish the Democrats for their "maladministration" was the decisive factor in the Republican landslide. It also contributed to the defeat of Berger, Hillquit and the relatively poor showing of Socialists elsewhere. Inadequate organization and "wholesale" fraud were also factors in the Socialist setback in New York. London charged that his majority represented only about half of those votes actually cast for him. Hillquit and he had needed a majority of at least one thousand in order to break even in the count. That number represented about the number of stolen votes despite considerable effort to prevent it.¹⁵⁰

Socialist and labor papers applauded London's victory. *Justice* attributed London's success to the support given him by the ILGWU. London, it commented, could never have won, if his election had hinged solely on the activity of the Socialist Party. "Fortunately, the entire Cloakmakers' Union in New York City ... threw itself into the campaign, and it was due to their efforts in the pre-election canvass and vigilant watch on Election Day that London's vote was not stolen from him as two years ago."¹⁵¹

The *Fur Worker* declared that "amid the wide desert of reaction a green oasis is visible in the twelfth congressional district." By their action the voters of the district had proved that London had been defeated in 1918 with the aid of stolen ballots. The Twelfth District, The *Fur Worker* declared, "had the best representative elected this year."[152] For the third time in six years, the *New York Call* stated, Socialist and labor forces in the Twelfth District had succeeded in sending "their champion" to Congress. London's victory represented a "victory of clean, liberal, working-class forces over Tammany and reactionary elements."[153] The *Daily Forward* hailed London's election as a triumph for the Jewish workers who had worked so zealously in his behalf.[154]

London's victory in 1920 occurred against the background of labor unrest, the Red Scare of 1919- 1920 and the Harding landslide. Although the Republicans swept every borough in New York and defeated Al Smith in his reelection bid, voters in the Twelfth District in record numbers voted for Meyer London. Alarmed by the arrest and deportation of alien residents and the violation of civil liberties, the renewed threat of immigration restriction and a stagnant economy, East Siders, Socialist and non–Socialist alike, supported London who had a proven record on these vital issues. He had consistently championed the cause of the worker and the urban immigrant.

Although disappointed with Socialist results elsewhere in the country, party leaders expressed pleasure at the size of the vote in New York. Otto Branstetter, the National Executive secretary, congratulated the Local New York organization "for the perseverance, courage and loyalty" to Socialist principles which had enabled it to grow steadily during three years of persecution. This "splendid" showing served as "an inspiration to the Comrades ... in all sections of the national organization."[155]

The East Side celebrated London's victory in the weeks following the election. Several thousand people gathered at Thomashefsky Theater on November 13 for a benefit performance in London's honor. The Socialist congressman-elect described the "dark forces of reaction, dishonesty and bigotry" which confronted an honest man who fought for an ideal in Congress. The war had ended, London stated, but the next Congress would not be a pleasant place to serve. These reactionary forces wanted to destroy the Socialist Party and to stamp out idealism. "Were they to destroy every Socialist organization in the country, were they to arrest and jail every Socialist leader, from out of the ground would emerge new men and powers to defend our cause." They spent millions of dollars on the war, and now hundreds of thousands are unemployed. "Yet they are the diplomats, they are the wise men and we are the traitors. We deny," London exclaimed, "that we are the traitors, we throw the accusation back in their faces."[156] Socialists and trade unionists also honored London at a banquet at Beethoven Hall on the evening of December 21. They praised his lifelong devotion to the cause of socialism and the labor movement.[157]

In the meantime, London had begun to prepare for the next Congress. He met with the National Executive Committee of the Socialist Party on December 4, 5 and 6 to discuss his congressional program.[158] The National Executive Committee announced that London would introduce a resolution in Congress calling for immediate peace with, and recognition of Russia. London would also support the repeal of wartime legislation, general amnesty for political prisoners and peace with Germany.[159]

During the next several months, London discussed what he considered the most pressing issues: the Russian situation, immigration, unemployment and amnesty for political prisoners. London urged the United States government to extend diplomatic recognition to Russia and to resume commercial relations with her. Putting aside humanitarian reasons for helping Russia, London suggested that it served American interests to cultivate her friendship. A friendly Russia, London declared, could help counter Japanese military ambitions. "We have no interest in helping British, French, Italian or Japanese imperialism. We have an interest in helping the Russian people rebuild their country. Our national policy should be framed with that view in mind." The United States, he pointed out, had traded with Czarist Russia and with Japan and had recognized both. It could consistently recognize and trade with Russia regardless of its government.[160]

As for immigration, London continued to criticize those who proposed a restrictive policy. London told the Order of the Lions, a Jewish fraternal order, at a meeting on December 9, that the gates of this country should be kept open for the persecuted people of Europe. "If America is to be what its founders intended it to be, a place for sovereign citizens to live in, the policy of repression, suppression, deportation, exclusion and imprisonment which has characterized the reactionary wave must be substituted by a policy to encourage those who have ideas and plans to submit to make this a better place for mankind."[161]

On the afternoon of January 30, in Cooper Union, London and Congressman William N. Vaile of Colorado, a member of the House Immigration Committee and a proponent of immigration restriction, debated the resolution that the "future welfare of the United States required free and unrestricted immigration." Vaile, who took the negative position, argued that continued immigration threatened existing institutions and would threaten the standard of living in the United States. This country, Vaile stated, consisted of much more than territory. It was a land of ideals, traditions and a people who had developed a national consciousness. This growth needed to proceed unhindered. Thus, Vaile implied that racial purity was one of the reasons for restricting immigration.

In arguing in support of free immigration, London declared that unemployment did not result from immigration or surplus population, but by a defective industrial system. Immigration during the last half century had in fact stimulated economic growth. In the United States, London observed, there were five million unemployed, although immigration had been reduced to a trickle over the past five years. The Socialist congressman-elect also dismissed the contention that the so-called "new immigrants" had proved less desirable than those who came to this country fifty years ago.

London then dealt with the Americanization issue which he characterized as an "absurd" term. Americanization was defined as an attempt to force people to accept a particular way of life instead of teaching them through kindness, love and consideration to follow it. Americanization through coercion would not succeed. "You cannot advance Americanism except by teaching the immigrant the ideals of America." London declared that no such thing as pure racial stock existed. Sweden, Switzerland and other nations had assimilated diverse ethnic groups, lived in peace, and had attained a level of prosperity equal to those who feared contamination. The United States government had become great because it provided for peaceable change. This principle faced destruction, however, by those who maintained that there was something eternal about the Constitution.[162]

London also addressed the unemployment problem. Once again he called for unemployment insurance and promised to continue his fight for it in Congress. London suggested that the government could solve the problem by providing employment in the construction of homes, public schools and public works.[163]

In the months following the election, the Socialist Party, organized labor, and various liberal groups continued to urge the Wilson administration to grant amnesty to political prisoners. The National Executive Committee approved a new nationwide amnesty campaign to coincide with the second anniversary of Eugene Debs' imprisonment. It announced that London would request Congress to help obtain general amnesty, and would present a petition containing some two million signatures to Congress with a plea for the repeal of the Espionage and Sedition Acts.[164]

Shortly before Amnesty Day, Samuel Gompers invited London to join the American Federation of Labor Committee on Amnesty for Political Prisoners at a meeting with President Harding on April 4.[165] At the appointed hour, Gompers, London, Benjamin Schlesinger of the ILGWU, Max Pine of the United Hebrew Trades and other labor officials met with the president and "pleaded" with him to grant a general amnesty to all political prisoners. Harding promised his "earnest consideration" of the cases of those in prison and assured the delegation of his desire to "do justice." Following the interview, London stated that he believed the president would not grant a general amnesty. Instead, the administration would decide each case individually and would release "all or practically all."[166] One week later, the Sixty-Seventh Congress met in a special session.

The years between his defeat in 1918 and his return to Congress in 1920 were busy ones for Meyer London. Following his return to New York, he immersed himself in his law practice and the East Side labor movement. As counsel for the cloak makers and the fur workers, he represented them during their strikes in 1920. He continued to speak out against the reactionary wave sweeping the country, particularly the New York Legislature. London did not play an important role in the struggle between right- and left-wing Socialists for control of the party. However, he opposed the left-wing movement and supported the Hillquit faction at the 1920 Socialist Party Convention. Once again, the party nominated London in the Twelfth Congressional District. Despite Communist opposition and a concerted effort by Tammany to steal the election, the voters returned him to Congress with his greatest margin of victory. For the third time, London was the lone Socialist member of Congress and the voice of the urban worker.

11

The Sixty-Seventh Congress: The Struggle Against Reaction

> Just now we hear nothing but hatred, nothing but the ravings of the exaggerated ... I am the best stock. I do not want to be contaminated; I have produced the greatest literature; my intellect is the biggest...—and this is repeated in every country, by every fool all over the world.—*Meyer London,* Congressional Record, *67th Congress, 1st Session, 515–16.*

Unlike the previous Congresses in which Meyer London served, the landslide victory of 1920 gave the Republicans control of the White House and the new Congress. The business community, which had contributed heavily to the Republican campaign, hoped that a Republican president and Congress would pursue a program of economy, drastic tax reductions, sound financing, tariff protection, less control by federal regulatory agencies, and, in brief, turn away from the quasi–Socialistic experiments launched during the war.[1] President Harding characterized it as a "return to normalcy."

Despite the prevailing conservative mood, London refused to become despondent, and continued his struggle against economic injustice and the forces of reaction. He opposed the Fordney-McCumber tariff bill, the unfair attempt to shift the burden of taxation to middle- and low-income groups, and introduced resolutions to investigate unemployment and unrest in the coal mining industry. However, London's main achievement in the area of economic legislation was the passage of his bankruptcy bill which provided additional protection for workers' wages. In the vital struggle for civil liberties, he pressed for the passage of the Dyer anti-lynching bill and the release of all remaining political prisoners. He also continued his fight against immigration restriction. London called for diplomatic recognition of Russia and presented a Socialist resolution to end the war.

Two days after the new Congress convened on April 13,[2] London participated in the Socialist-sponsored Amnesty Day demonstration held in Washington in conjunction with meetings across the country. London led a delegation which met with House Speaker Gillett to plead the case for amnesty.³ Other delegations called upon President Harding, Vice President Coolidge and Attorney General Daugherty. In addition, a petition for amnesty, signed by some three hundred thousand citizens, was presented to the Congress.⁴

On April 19, London introduced a joint resolution in the House recommending amnesty and pardons for political prisoners in the United States.⁵ This resolution was identical with a Senate resolution introduced on March 10 by Joseph I. France, a Republican from Maryland. It declared that the "further prosecution and imprisonment in the United States of such a body of political offenders is contrary to the democratic idealism and traditions of freedom to which our country is committed." London believed that amnesty should apply to individuals who had come into conflict with wartime legislation as a result of their "sincere and disinterested advocacy" of an economic theory, a political philosophy, or a religious belief that did not constitute an offense in peacetime. The resolution, he noted, represented the sentiment of several million people who demanded amnesty at legislative hearings and mass meetings throughout the country.⁶

London took the floor on July 1 to discuss his proposal. The Socialist congressman pointed out that since the armistice, the Socialist Party, the American Federation of Labor and numerous other groups had urged the restoration of liberty and full civic rights to political offenders. However, these appeals had been in vain. Virtually every country in the world, London told his colleagues, had granted amnesty since the war ended. "Some of these amnesties cover not only military and political offenses, but even cases involving stolen military material."

London then attacked the Espionage Act. Unreasoning fear had prompted its enactment. The law was based upon the indefensible theory that any criticism in wartime was treasonable. "To adopt the doctrine that once war is declared no act of the Government is to be challenged by the people and that all criticism should be suppressed ... would mean that a government could destroy every vestige of democracy."

Due to the war hysteria, London further argued, courts and juries had found it impossible to administer justice impartially. Congressional hearings on the amnesty question had produced "overwhelming" evidence of violations of due process and the imposition of severe sentences. London reiterated that it had become the practice of "civilized" governments to grant amnesty to the victims of war legislation. The United States had followed this policy from its inception. The continued imprisonment of men because they espoused unpopular political and economic theories was intolerable in a free country.

The Harding administration, he acknowledged, had taken a positive step with the restoration of mailing privileges of numerous Socialist publications.

It should now release and restore full civic rights to the men and women on whose behalf he was speaking. The war had ended, London concluded. "A democracy cannot afford to be vengeful."[7]

On December 23, 1921, President Harding announced that he would free Debs and twenty-three other political prisoners on Christmas Day.[8] Socialists, labor leaders and liberals applauded the president's action, and urged renewed efforts in behalf of remaining prisoners. London declared that it was not enough to release these prisoners. They must also have full citizenship restored.

He called for the release of jailed members of the Industrial Workers of the World. The doctrine that workers should form industrial unions rather than craft organizations was "neither inherently illegal nor logically indefensible." So long as they did not resort to violence, the government should not respond similarly. London called for renewed effort for a general and complete amnesty.[9]

On January 21, 1922, a persistent London once again reminded his colleagues that some 118 political offenders languished behind prison bars. The administration had released Debs because he was a national figure. But London indicated that he was also concerned about the person who had distributed a flyer and was imprisoned for ten years because some "fool reactionary judge" wanted to intimidate dissenters. No "earthly" reason existed for keeping political prisoners in jail.[10]

Support for London's amnesty resolution had grown within labor and liberal circles. The House Judiciary Committee, after a meeting with representatives of the American Civil Liberties Union, agreed to conduct hearings on the resolution on March 16.[11] In presenting the general case, Albert De Silver, director of the American Civil Liberties Union, emphasized that remaining political prisoners had never been directly or indirectly linked with any act of obstruction to the war. However, the president had released six prisoners who had committed overt acts against the war while continuing to hold members of the IWW and the Working Class Union of Oklahoma for no other offense than exercising their constitutional right of free speech. Moreover, the attorney general had never reviewed the records of their trials.

Due to a lack of time, London spoke briefly and reiterated that members of the IWW were imprisoned not because they interfered with the war effort, but because they were IWW. While several members of the committee expressed sympathy toward the prisoners, the Judiciary Committee refused to act upon London's resolution.[12]

Nevertheless, efforts intensified to free the prisoners. On May 11, 1922, London; Representative Anthony Griffin, a Democrat from New York; and Senator Edwin F. Ladd, a Republican from North Dakota, introduced identical resolutions calling upon Congress, rather than the president, to grant a general amnesty.[13] A few days later, London urged his colleagues to adopt this resolution. While the House, he stated, was "singing the praises of those who love peace, of those who advocate international concord, of those who seek the abolition of war," it should address the question of amnesty for those who had the courage to express their true convictions about war during the conflict.

President Harding, London charged, had refused to meet with the political prisoners' children. "It is very likely that he could not have seen the children without granting their request, and his advisers, the Wall Street clique, the open-shop supporters, the enemies of every progressive thought, see to it that the president should not be influenced by the plea of the children, and that the appeal of the victims of the espionage law should not reach his heart."[14]

On June 7, Representative Hersey of Maine, a member of the Judiciary Committee, rose to oppose London's amnesty resolution. Hersey declared that there had been much "propaganda and ridiculous agitation" on behalf of "Socialist draft evaders," and others who opposed the Espionage Act. Congress might overlook agitation and propaganda from socialist groups and "cheap" newspapers, but it could not ignore the statements made by London in the House. "Socialism, the father of bolshevism, can never ascend to power in the United States through the efforts of the gentlemen from New York or the picketing of the White House by children of convicts." Members of Congress should accept London's challenge and confront the issue of socialism.[15]

In reply, London noted that fifty-one congressmen had signed a petition that requested the president to grant amnesty to 113 political prisoners. He expressed surprise that Hersey would "resort to the cheap and vulgar method of denouncing the amnesty movement as socialism, Bolshevism, and anarchism, instead of employing argument." A careful examination of the hearing conducted on his resolution, London asserted, would lead the reader "to the inescapable conclusion that the victims of the espionage act now in prison or under indictment should be immediately relieved of all penalties and restored to full civic rights."[16] London made his final appeal for amnesty during the Sixty-Seventh Congress on September 22, 1922. Once again he implored his colleagues to grant freedom to some fifty-two prisoners who refused to seek amnesty on grounds of principle.[17]

Pressure in favor of amnesty continued to grow in late 1922 and 1923 as religious leaders, governors, college presidents, journalists and various organizations gave their support to the amnesty campaign. However, no action occurred until December 15, 1923, when President Coolidge commuted the sentences of the last thirty-one political prisoners.[18] Although no longer in

Congress at the time, Meyer London no doubt experienced a sense of gratification.

The Dyer anti-lynching bill also received London's support. In a speech to the House on January 18, 1922, he argued that neither a state nor an individual nor a mob had the right to take a human life. "Every manifestation of passion, hatred, or violence which results in the destruction of human life is abhorrent to every civilized man." London attributed the spread of mob violence to the war. No longer was it a sectional question or limited solely to "colored" people. "As a Socialist ... I repudiate every form of mob violence."

London disagreed with those who opposed the measure on the basis of states' rights. The federal government, he argued, could exercise its police power to implement those things for which it had been created and for which it existed. The federal government could punish murder and, if it desired, could also punish mob action. London called for the enforcement of the Fourteenth and Fifteenth amendments to protect the Negro. The "colored" man was defenseless and needed protection from unruly elements.

In areas where Negro workers constituted a majority of the workforce, London continued, white employers desired to keep the workers subservient. The illiterate white worker did not realize that the entire labor force suffered when a "colored" worker was deprived of his political and economic rights. "I want a real anti-mob bill. I want an effective anti-lynching bill. No local sentiment, passion or prejudice should be permitted to defy the legal rights of the humblest citizen."[19] The House passed the bill on January 26 by a vote of 231 to 119, as London voted with the majority.[20] Due to a southern filibuster, the Senate failed to vote on the measure.[21]

In the meantime, the House had begun to consider three bills that the previous Congress had passed, but which President Wilson had vetoed. The first of these was the Johnson-Dillingham immigration bill. The war had slowed immigration to a trickle, but after the armistice, it rapidly increased. From June 1920 to June 1921, some eight hundred thousand persons came into the country, and reports from Europe indicated that millions more planned to leave. The Johnson-Dillingham bill reflected organized labor's growing concern that increased immigration would further depress the domestic labor market.

Other Americans feared that many of the immigrants, particularly those from Southern and Eastern Europe, were Bolshevists or adherents to some other radical doctrine. Johnson reintroduced the bill in the House in virtually the same form to which Wilson had objected. It limited the number of immigrants to 3 percent of the various foreign-born nationalities in the United States in 1910.[22]

London, along with Adolph Sabbath of Illinois and Isaac Siegel of New

York, led the fight against the measure. During the debate on April 21, 1921, London stated that the United States had sent two million men abroad to make the world "safe for democracy," and to liberate the very people whom Congress now sought to exclude. He rejected the idea that immigration restriction would stop the flow of radical thought. Immigration, London further argued, would not depress the nation's economy. On the contrary, a restrictive policy would "cripple" the United States. The unprecedented growth and prosperity of this country, he asserted, was as much a cause as the effect of immigration.

London also rejected the racist argument that the so-called new immigrants from Southern and Eastern Europe were inferior to the old immigrants who came prior to 1900. It was indeed strange, he pointed out, that at no time in history had any nation progressed so rapidly in industry, science and social legislation as this country since 1900. The new immigration was neither different nor worse, and furthermore, similar arguments had been used against the old immigration.

London repudiated organized labor's contention that unrestricted immigration would seriously affect the labor market. Unemployment was endemic to the present industrial system. "Unemployment does not depend on the number of persons.... Unemployment shows a state of chaos in industry, a lack of relation between the job and the job seeker, between the worker and his job." In conclusion, London declared, freedom-loving people must assert themselves. "Just now we hear nothing but hatred, nothing but the ravings of the exaggerated... 'I am the best stock. I do not want to be contaminated; I have produced the greatest literature; my intellect is the biggest ...' — and this is repeated in every country, by every fool all over the world."[23]

On the following day, London opposed an amendment offered by James Husted of New York to strike out a provision in the bill exempting immigrants against whom there was by law or regulation any discrimination because of religious faith or belief. The Jewish people, London stated, were still subjected to religious persecution in many lands. No government should adopt any law which discriminated against a group of people because of their religion. "The state of civilization of a country, London told the House, "could be measured by the degree of tolerance, the degree of kindness, with which the minority is treated.... With the world in confusion, it is the minority, whether it was religious, racial or social, that is always the victim. Please do not propose anything that will weaken the effect of the provision calculated to protect religious dissentients."[24]

The House rejected the Husted amendment and passed the bill without a roll call.[25] On May 13, the House approved the conference report by a vote of 276 to 33, as London voted with the minority.[26] President Harding signed the bill on May 19. Although designed to last for one year, the Emergency Quota Act, as London feared, was later extended until 1924.[27]

The second measure passed during the lame duck session of the Sixty-Sixth Congress, but vetoed by President Wilson, was the Fordney emergency agricultural tariff which imposed high duties on meat and farm staples in an effort to halt declining farm prices. Wilson had pointed out in his veto message that the bill would not provide the desired relief. Immediately after the new Congress convened, the Farm Bloc reintroduced the emergency tariff bill.[28] The House approved it on April 15 by a vote of 269 to 110, with London voting "nay."[29]

London criticized the bill on the basis that it levied duties on products when farm exports by the United States exceeded imports. Such a tariff could not help the farmers, but would leave them worse off than before.[30] The Emergency Agricultural Tariff bill received President Harding's signature on May 27, 1921, and although intended for only six months, it remained in effect until replaced by a permanent tariff.[31]

The House Ways and Means Committee led by Chairman Joseph W. Fordney of Michigan had already started work on a new general tariff. The committee completed its work by the end of June, and discussion of the bill began in the House on July 17 under a special rule imposed by the Republicans limiting amendments from the floor and requiring a final vote on July 21.[32]

London took the floor to sharply denounce the proposed measure. "A more reckless, a more arrogant, a bolder steal has never been attempted in the history of plunder by legislation than this protective tariff bill," he began. The Republicans had only one remedy for the ills of the world, the tariff. If the United States adopted a protectionist policy, London warned, other nations would retaliate. Tariff barriers produced international conflict, and unless governments trade in a spirit of cooperation, "the clashes of hostile tariffs would lead to the clash of arms." Fordney, London noted, had admitted during the debate that the proposed schedules did not seek to correct weaknesses in the Underwood tariff.

The Socialist congressman took exception to the Democratic argument that a prohibitive tariff would prevent European countries from paying their debts to the United States. London told his colleagues that he seriously doubted that these debts would ever be paid. However, the issue went beyond the collection of debts. The real issue was whether the United States would engage in business with the rest of the world and thereby promote the economic growth of all nations. The proposed tariff would make this impossible.

Taking up the main arguments of the protectionists, he rejected the view that the lower wages paid European workers made it impossible for American manufacturers to compete with cheaper goods produced by European industries. Everywhere in Europe the standard of living had improved. Furthermore, the claim that farmers and workers would benefit from the tariff was erroneous. They would pay more for construction materials, food, clothing, and other items upon which the bill levied high duties.

Congress, London closed, had enacted more than fifty tariff laws since the founding of the nation. There were high tariffs and low tariffs, but economic crises and unemployment had followed each. "The worker then will only come into his own when the sordid profit system ... will be replaced by the cooperation of men for the benefit of all, by democracy in industry and concord among nations."[33]

In an effort to circumvent the House rule on amendments to the measure, London, on July 16, introduced a bill that he hoped the Ways and Means Committee would accept as an amendment to the tariff bill. This proposal made duties on imports conditional upon the maintenance of certain minimum labor standards in the industry or branch of agriculture producing similar products in the United States. Protected American industries would be required to recognize the principle of collective bargaining, to grant an eight-hour day and forty-four-hour week to their employees with at least one and one half days of continuous rest each week, and to eliminate the employment of children under the age of sixteen.[34]

Several days later, London discussed his proposal. He had introduced it, he explained, as a test for the advocates of protection who always claimed to speak on behalf of labor. "With the onslaught which the triumphant swine of plutocracy are now making upon organized labor, the refusal to grant protection to an industry unless it concedes to the toilers the right to organize and to deal collectively" is absolutely necessary. London urged his colleagues to adopt his bill in part if they would not approve all of it.[35] Despite his plea, the committee failed to act. The House voted on the Fordney bill as scheduled on July 21, and passed it by a vote of 288 to 127.[36]

Final action on the measure did not take place until late in the summer of 1922.[37] On August 22, 1922, and again on September 13, London denounced the measure. Rather than creating new barriers, London said, the Congress should endeavor to open and broaden communication between the peoples of the world. To the accompaniment of applause from Democrats, London urged the House to "bury" the tariff bill. "There is already a reaction against it. There is distrust. Nobody is for it. Forget about it. Let it die the ignominious death which it deserves."[38]

In his speech on September 13, London joined the Democrats in condemning the embargo on dye stuffs and chemicals included in the conference report. The House, he said, "was about to become the victim of an infamous legislative swindle." He reminded his colleagues that during the debate on the bill they had rejected the embargo, as had the Senate.[39]

When the conference report finally came to a vote, a number of Republicans joined with the Democrats and London to reject it. In so doing, they instructed the House conferees to eliminate the dye and chemical embargo.[40] On September 15, the House voted 210 to 91, with London in opposition, to approve the conference report which in accord with House wishes excluded the embargo.[41] The Fordney-McCumber Tariff received President Harding's signature on September 21, 1922. It had the distinction of being the highest protective tariff in American history.[42]

The House Ways and Means Committee had also begun work on a tax bill aimed at fulfilling Republican campaign promises to repeal the excess profits tax and to reduce the high surtaxes still in effect under the War Revenue Act of 1918–1919. The committee reported the new revenue bill on August 17, 1921, with the request that debate on the measure be limited to four days.[43]

London took the floor that very day to denounce the bill. The bill sought, he declared, to shift the burden of taxation to those who worked and performed useful service and who could not afford to have a substantial part of their wages taken for taxes. The poor worker ultimately paid all the taxes because the wealthy always managed to shift the burden of taxation to the poor. The government had drafted young men during the war and sent them to the trenches. It should now make the wealthy pay for the war. Rather than repeal the surtax and excess profits tax, Congress, London asserted, should increase them. In addition, Congress should enact an inheritance tax. Through taxation, large fortunes should be taken by the government and used to promote the country's welfare.[44]

Two days later, London rose to speak against an amendment exempting foreign investments from taxation. The tax bill, he declared, provided for plutocracy as a whole, while the proposed amendment took care of a particular kind of plutocrat. Was this Congress, he asked, "to become openly and avowedly a soviet plutocracy? Are the directors of railroads and the attorneys of railroad companies to be permitted to lay down the law to the American people? Is there any limit to their arrogance?"[45] Despite opposition from London and other progressive-minded representatives, the House passed, on August 20, a measure embracing the tax program of Treasury Secretary Andrew Mellon by an overwhelming majority of 274 to 125.[46]

In the Senate, however, midwestern Republicans and Democrats united to form a solid majority to oppose the House bill. The Senate adopted 837 amendments, and yielded on only 7 in the conference committee. Therefore, the bill, signed by President Harding on November 23, 1921, failed to embody all of the changes advocated by Secretary Mellon and business interests.[47]

As in the Sixty-Fourth and Sixty-Fifth Congresses, London vigorously supported the cause of labor. Shortly after Congress convened, Samuel Gompers invited London and several other members of the House to attend a meeting on April 28 at the American Federation of Labor headquarters in Washington to discuss matters pertinent to the labor movement.[48] This so-called labor group, however, did not have a significant impact on an administration generally indifferent to the plight of labor.

Undeterred, London pressed ahead on the behalf of labor in the House. On May 11, 1921, he discussed the unemployment situation exacerbated by the short but severe post-war depression of 1921–1922. The Republican and Democratic Parties, he charged, lacked the knowledge and ability to deal with important social and economic problems. "They repeat the old slogans, slogans a century old. We hear 'protection,' 'free trade;' again 'protection' and again 'free trade,' as if unemployment had anything to do with it." Unemployment, he pointed out, existed in countries which had protective tariffs and in those with free trade. It resulted from maladjustment in industry.

The Republicans and the Democrats, he continued, had failed to consider the problem. No one knew the number of unemployed since no reliable statistical information existed on the subject. Most of his fellow representatives, London stated, did not know and did not care to know about the issue. They ignored the labor problem and denounced every new idea as bolshevisim.

As in previous Congresses, London proposed a program to alleviate hardship caused by unemployment. It included a national system of unemployment insurance, the elimination of child labor, reduction of the hours of labor, public works projects, the authorization of loans to municipalities, cooperative building loan societies and labor organizations for the construction of 1.5 million homes, and the creation of a commission to study the problem of the regularization of industry in order to reduce unemployment.[49]

Undeterred by a lack of support for his unemployment plan, London, on May 27, introduced a resolution calling for a congressional investigation into the problem.[50] London declared that the unemployment question was much more important than either the tariff or taxation. The administration, however, had devoted its attention to business, the tariff and the budget, while the unemployment of some five million men and women, and the hardship it produced, received little attention.[51] The resolution, despite London's efforts, died in the Labor Committee.

London made one final effort during the first session to get Congress to deal with the issue. On August 22, two days before the House recessed for its summer vacation, he introduced a resolution authorizing an appropriation of five billion dollars to be utilized to alleviate distress caused by involuntary unemployment.[52] In seeking support, London pointed out that since Congress had voted subsidies to the railroads and to exporters, it should appropriate funds to help the unemployed.[53]

The Socialist representative sought Samuel Gompers' support, but he refused. The resolution, he maintained, did not specify its objective. "Whether the $500,000,000 to be appropriated is to be given in charity to the unemployed or to be expended in constructive work is not stated," Gompers wrote London. The American Federation of Labor desired a "practical reclamation bill," national in scope and of value to the country.[54]

Although Congress failed to heed London's pleas to address the unemployment problem, President Harding, faced with violence in the West Virginian coalfields and the threat of a nationwide railroad strike, announced in early September that he would call a conference on unemployment.[55] London told the *New York Call* that the conference would end in failure; the Republican Party was incapable of doing anything worthwhile for the people. If the Harding administration, he continued, was serious, it would have acted five months ago and spared millions of suffering people. The time for investigations had passed. Relief was needed immediately.

London once again suggested several steps to solve unemployment. First, he called for the reduction of working hours to help spread work in industries with high unemployment. Second, the government should appropriate funds to cooperative societies and other organizations to stimulate manufacturing. Finally, federal, state, and municipal agencies should launch public works projects.

Many expected that the reconversion of industry to peacetime production and the demobilization of the armed forces would increase the number of unemployed into the millions. During the Sixty-Fifth Congress, London told the *Call*, he had made numerous attempts to get the House to consider the matter. However, it had failed to act on his proposals because congressmen found it easier to denounce the kaiser. London stated that he was making every effort to obtain action on his most recent resolution. He had contacted unions and other progressive organizations nationwide for support. In addition, the House Labor Committee would probably hold hearings on the resolution during the summer recess so that it could be submitted to the House shortly after it reconvened.[56]

As London had predicted, President Harding's unemployment conference failed to propose permanent measures to remedy the problem or to provide relief to the unemployed.[57] Limited ideologically by its opposition to any national expenditure or national legislation to resolve the problem, the conference instead called for readjustment of railway rates, reduction of taxes, and settlement of tariff legislation to bring about recovery rather than unemployment insurance and a federal program of public works.[58]

On October 18, London once again took the House floor to discuss unemployment. The Republican Congress, he sarcastically commented, had accomplished one thing: the number of unemployed had increased by some three million. The statesmanship of the Republican Party was bankrupt; the Democrats offered nothing constructive. "We hear again the same old nonsense about protection and free trade. It is sickening." During the war, he had asked for the creation of a commission to study the problem. He had wanted the country to prepare for the economic dislocation which would occur when the war ended. He had based his argument upon incontestable facts, and subsequent events justified his warning. The unemployment conference had accomplished nothing. Under Secretary of Commerce Hoover's leadership the commission reached unanimous agreement on unimportant matters and adjourned when essential issues arose. London implored his colleagues to abandon the idea that they had no responsibility to consider the unemployment question.[59] But once again the House failed to act.

Undeterred by the resistance of the Harding administration and the Congress, London continued to implore his colleagues for congressional action.[60] On February 23, London introduced an amendment to the Department of Labor appropriation bill increasing the $225,000 allotted to the Employment Bureau to $100,000,000, but the House rejected it 51 to 3.[61]

During consideration of the Bonus bill on March 23, he criticized the measure on the ground that it failed to deal with the issue most vital to veterans, the right to a job. Of the six million unemployed in the country, London said, seven hundred thousand were ex-servicemen. If one-fourth of the $4.5 million required by the bill was invested in industrial expansion, loans to cooperatives, furnishing aid to unions and housing construction, it would be of much greater help to war veterans than doling out cash gratuities or insurance certificates as proposed in the Bonus bill.

Once more, London called upon the Harding administration to create employment opportunities. On numerous occasions during the war, workers were urged to fight for a new and better world. "Neither a cash bonus nor an 'adjusted service certificate' gave any promise of anything new or better."[62] Although London had reservations about the bill, he voted with the majority as the House passed it 337 to 70 on the following day.[63]

Unstable conditions in the coal mining industry also attracted London's attention. During the post-war years, the coal industry suffered from cutthroat competition and overproduction. Miners received low wages and were frequently without work. In good times they worked three or four days a week; in bad times, two days.

The United Mine Workers' Union attempt to organize miners in West Virginia's bituminous fields in 1919–1920 brought strong resistance. Fighting broke out between striking miners and company guards. State and federal troops restored order, but violence flared up again in May 1921. At the end of August, President Harding, in order to prevent fighting between armed miners and sheriff deputies, issued a proclamation directing the miners to disband and ordered federal troops to the area. The uprising collapsed, and state authorities arrested the strike leaders.[64]

On January 19, 1922, London introduced a resolution calling upon the Mines and Mining Committee to investigate conditions in the coal industry with particular reference to the condition of the workers and the state of unemployment therein and to recommend legislation based upon his resolution.[65] London stated that he wanted to give the miners an opportunity to present their grievances to the American people. Representative Philip P. Campbell, chairman of the Rules Committee, informed London that he would consider the advisability of holding a hearing on the resolution. Subsequently, the Rules Committee failed to act.[66]

Early in 1922, another crisis developed when negotiations for a new contract with the bituminous and anthracite operators failed. On April 1, 1922, some 500,000 bituminous miners walked out, followed shortly thereafter by 150,000 anthracite miners.[67]

On May 2 and again on May 5, London took the floor to urge nationalization of the mines. The situation in the coal industry, he asserted, clearly illustrated the "chaos and anarchy" of private ownership of public resources. Some two thousand owners controlled approximately ten thousand mines and employed seven hundred thousand miners irregularly. As a result, the miner had been unable to maintain a decent standard of living.

London rejected the argument that irregular employment was due to the seasonal nature of the industry. Long periods of idleness, he argued, occurred because of insufficient planning. Only the United Mine Workers of America had offered a proposal for the regularization of employment. While the union had failed to achieve all its objectives, it had succeeded in establishing certain minimum standards in the industry. On the other hand, the operators had no regard for the present or future interests of the country, but were solely interested in making money.

London then criticized the Harding administration for failing to pressure the operators to reach an agreement with the miners. The administration, he insisted, could not afford to be indifferent. "It is apparent that it is unsafe for the people of the United States to permit their greatest natural resource to be wasted, mismanaged and exploited by a crowd of profit seekers. The irregularity of employment, the overdevelopment of the industry, the high prices forced upon the consumer, the army of useless middlemen, ... the menace to democracy by the prevalence of industrial absolutism in the nonunion fields make it imperative that ... the mines be brought under the control of the Nation."⁶⁸

As the strike dragged on, the Harding administration refused to intervene. However, when violence erupted on June 21 in southern Illinois, the president finally acted. Negotiations with John L. Lewis, the president of the United Mine Workers, and bituminous and anthracite operators resulted in an agreement to reopen the mines under the terms of the expired contract and with the understanding that a federal coal commission would investigate the industry. On August 19, Harding sent a message to Congress asking for legislation to establish the commission.⁶⁹

The president's message, London observed, offered little of value. It was an excuse for having done nothing. Nevertheless, he would support the measure provided that labor had "adequate" representation on the commission.⁷⁰ The bill reported to the House did not, as London feared, provide for labor representation. In fact, it excluded anyone with an interest in the coal industry.

On August 23, London offered an amendment to the bill to allow commission members to file minority reports. In arguing for his amendment, he criticized the bill for failing to give representation to organized labor and for excluding persons who had knowledge about the industry. London doubted that the president would find nine persons to serve on the commission who had no interest in the coal industry. At the conclusion of his remarks, the House rejected the amendment 112 to 60. A few moments later, the House also defeated a motion by London to recommit the bill. It then passed the measure, 219 to 55, with London in opposition.⁷¹

On September 11, London moved that the House accept the Senate version of the Coal Commission bill. The Senate had included, he pointed out, a provision that the commission report upon the "advisability and wisdom" of the nationalization of the coal industry. It had also changed the provision that no person interested in coal could serve on the commission. The House rejected the motion 117 to 7.⁷² Final action on the bill took place on September 20 when the House adopted the conference report.

London facetiously congratulated the House conferees for substituting other language for the word "nationalization." London stated that he had no quarrel with the new language, for it probably meant the same thing. He expressed pleasure that the conferees had receded from their original position on the makeup of the commission. Once again, however, he called for the inclusion of representatives of labor and coal operators.

He then moved to recommit the conference report with instructions to the House conferees to insist on the amendment providing that the commission consist of seven members, two to be appointed by the president on the

United Mine Workers meet in Washington during the coal strike of 1922. From left, Congressmen William J. Burke; Oscar E. Bland; John I. Nolan; John L. Lewis, president of the United Mine Workers of America; Frank Morrison; Sam Gompers, president of the AFL; Meyer London; William O. Atkeson. Photograph Collection, Library of Congress.

recommendation of the United Mine Workers, two upon the recommendation of the Coal Operators Association, and three to be appointed by the president. After several minutes of parliamentary maneuvering, the chair overruled a point of order and called the question on London's motion. It was defeated 156 to 106. The House then adopted the conference report 183 to 87.[73]

After the passage of this act and the restoration of peace in the coal industry, Congress showed little further interest in the matter. It ignored the Coal Commission' report. In the ensuing years, the position of the coal miner continued to deteriorate as did the industry.[74]

London's most successful effort on behalf of labor was a bill he introduced on June 9, 1921, to amend section 17 of the United States Bankruptcy Act of 1898.[75] His amendment aimed to protect workers who had wages due them at the time their employers were pronounced bankrupt. London's proposal stipulated that wages earned during the six months prior to bankruptcy and deposits placed by workers with employers as security for the faithful performance of a contract of employment would not be dischargeable as other debts in bankruptcy proceedings. Employers would still be obligated to pay wages due their employees.

In a statement urging its passage, London declared that losses suffered by employees under existing bankruptcy acts constituted a serious problem. In competitive industries, small employers seeking to remain in business withheld employees' wages for weeks and subsequently found it impossible to pay the wages when faced with bankruptcy. Small employers also obtained large sums of money as security from employees. Such deposits did not, however, even enjoy priority. His proposal, London said, would deter prospective bankrupts from defaulting in the payment of wages and from speculating with their employees' money.[76]

The House Judiciary Committee favorably reported London's bill on October 21 with only one significant change. It reduced the six-month period to three months in regard to wages earned by workers prior to the beginning of bankruptcy proceedings. On October 31, the House passed the bill after a brief discussion without a roll call.[77] The Senate passed the bill unanimously on December 22, and on January 12, 1922, President Harding signed the first bill enacted by Congress introduced by a Socialist representative.[78]

In other domestic matters, London opposed the Harding administration's plan to complete and enlarge the naval construction program of 1916.[79] London's demands for curtailing armaments reflected the growing clamor for arms reduction in the country. In determining the navy's size, the only consideration, London maintained, should be whether it was adequate to carry out the country's foreign policy. If "our policy is to lead by example, ... to help perpetuate ideals of liberty, we need no big navies. All we need is to live up to the high ideals which have given birth to America, and America will be an irresistible force for good and for all time."[80]

The United States had promised the world disarmament, and then proceeded to increase its armaments. Nobody, he declared, would believe a word this country said. London doubted that governments would ever disarm. "The only way disarmament will be accomplished will be when the men who are called upon to die at the behest of statesmen will go to jail for opposing war and will refuse to manufacture weapons of war."[81] House Republicans overrode scattered support for various disarmament proposals and passed a bill appropriating $396 million for the navy by a vote of 212 to 15, with London in opposition.[82]

London also criticized a proposed $220 million military appropriations bill providing for an army of 115,000 men. American soldiers, he asserted, would never go to Europe or Asia in our lifetime. No president would ever dare again to involve the United States in a European war. The fact that the Republicans enjoyed a large majority in the present Congress clearly showed that the American people opposed intervention in the last war. The Congress, however, still possessed a militaristic mentality. Against whom, he asked the proponents of the measure, did they plan to conduct military operations?

11. The Sixty-Seventh Congress

The founding fathers had shown distrust of standing armies when they included a provision in the Constitution that no appropriation for the army could be made beyond two years. "The less money taken from the Treasury ... for the development of military ideals, the fewer men in uniform, the better." London urged his colleagues to make the country bigger and stronger "by raising it to a nobler sphere of endeavor. Every cent," he exclaimed, "appropriated for the army was a 'criminal waste.'"[83]

Although London devoted much time to the amnesty, unemployment and disarmament issues, he did not ignore foreign affairs. Of particular concern to the Socialist congressman was a formal peace with Germany and diplomatic recognition of Russia. Having failed to ratify the Treaty of Versailles, the United States was not a party to the peace which had become effective on January 10, 1920.

Congress had attempted to end the war unilaterally by joint resolution, but President Wilson vetoed it in May 1920. Harding approved the reintroduction of the Knox resolution in the special session of the Sixty-Seventh Congress shortly after it convened. The Senate Foreign Relations Committee broadened it to include Austria-Hungary, and on April 30, the Senate adopted it by a vote of 49 to 23. However, the House refused to accept the Knox resolution and approved a substitute resolution introduced by Stephen Porter of Pennsylvania, chairman of the Committee on Foreign Relations. The House and Senate resolutions differed in details, but were similar in their effort to claim for the United States all the advantages that it would have enjoyed had it signed the Treaty of Versailles.

Debate on the resolutions began in the House on June 11. In order to expedite passage of the peace resolution, the Republican leadership introduced a special rule limiting debate to two days and also limiting the House to a choice between the Knox and Porter resolutions without amendments.[84]

London argued that no reason or justification existed for the rule. House Republicans had repudiated the resolution adopted by the Senate, but were now so confident in their substitute that they sought to prevent changes. "Any fool," London said, "could enter war. It is hard to make peace." House members should have the opportunity to propose adoption of the Versailles Treaty, amendments to the treaty, amendments to scrap the treaty or for a league of nations. The entire procedure, he concluded, was indefensible.[85] Despite objections from London and the Democrats, the Republicans pushed through the special rule.

Shortly thereafter, London once again rose to discuss the peace resolution and to offer the Socialist Party's program for peace. The Socialist congressman indicated that he preferred the Porter resolution because it declared an end to the war, whereas the Senate version merely repealed the war resolution.

This was a technicality most Americans would not understand. London, however, criticized a provision in the Porter resolution which reserved certain rights for the United States under the Versailles Treaty. It should have reserved all rights to which the United States may have become entitled due to its participation in the war. Was this country, London asked, prepared to adopt isolationism as a policy? Had not modern communications brought the world closer together and made the concern of one nation the concern of all? "We drifted into the war. We do not know how to drift out of it. Our statesmen did not know how to avoid war. They do not know how to make peace."

London then outlined the Socialist program for peace. It included the cancellation of the allied war debts, the revision or scrapping of the Versailles Treaty, the organization of an association of nations founded on democratic principles, the summoning of an international parliamentary conference to discuss the basic principles of world peace, the creation of an international fund to aid people in need of food, raw materials and machinery, universal disarmament and recognition of Russia.[86]

Shortly before the vote on the Porter resolution, London offered a resolution embodying the views of the American Socialist Party on international affairs. It declared the state of war between the United States, Germany and the Austro-Hungarian governments at an end, and called for an international inter-parliamentary conference to meet in Washington to develop a plan for world peace. His proposal, London pointed out, fulfilled the program adopted by the 1920 convention of the Socialist Party.[87] The House Foreign Relations Committee ignored London's proposal, and on June 13, the House overwhelmingly adopted the Porter peace resolution by a vote of 304 to 61. London voted with the majority. He did not explain his vote.

Meanwhile, London introduced a resolution on June 10, 1921, which urged the president to recognize and establish friendly relations with the Russian government.[88] Time had come, he declared, to abandon "the game of hide and seek." The United States should either support the various groups of "political adventurers who organize abortive insurrections" in Russia or recognize the fact that a government existed there and that the administration's current policy denied opportunity for American business interests. London noted that the present Russian government had existed for three years. Like all revolutionary governments, it had been charged with many excesses. However, the overthrow of this government would lead to even greater chaos and the possible restoration of czarism.

In extending diplomatic recognition, the United States had never bothered to inquire whether the form of the government conformed to American ideals. This nation had done business with the czar, the kaiser, the sultan of Turkey and the mikado of Japan. It was to the vital interest of the United

States that Russia, which occupied one-third of Asia, and which was a neighbor of Japan, be restored to her former position.[89]

On December 15, 1921, London once again defended the Russian government while supporting a resolution appropriating twenty million dollars to aid famine-stricken people of the Volga region. The Russian people, he maintained, had suffered severely both as a result of the war and foreign intervention. The Wilson administration, without the approval of Congress, and against the will of the American people, had waged war upon the Russian people. This appropriation represented "a very poor atonement indeed for the sins we have committed and are committing against the Russian people."

As for his colleagues who blamed existing conditions in Russia on the Bolsheviks, London once again pointed out that the Russian people had a right to seek change in their own way. The present government was the best that Russia had ever had. London reiterated his belief that Bolshevism represented the "exuberance of revolution." "Three or four years is not by any means too long a term for a people of 150,000,000 souls to get on their feet after suffering a thousand years of oppression under a coercive government."

London asked his colleagues why they had not protested against the czarist government which had made Russia a vast prison? "Why do you speak now with such hatred of the effort of a people groping toward the light, struggling in their own agony, toward the broad road ... which will lead them into permanent and lasting democracy?" The House passed the bill 237 to 44.[90] On June 28, he again implored the House to adopt his resolution calling for the restoration of diplomatic relations with Russia, but without success.[91]

The second session of the Sixty-Seventh Congress ended on September 23, and London now focused on his bid for reelection. In an effort to unseat the Socialist congressman and to weaken Socialist strength on the East Side, the Republican and Democratic leaders in the New York Legislature pushed through a bill, in March 1922, "gerrymandering" the Eleventh, Twelfth, Thirteenth and Fourteenth congressional districts.[92] The thirty-nine other New York congressional districts remained intact.[93]

Passage of the measure surprised Local New York Socialist leaders. According to Assemblyman August Claessens, the Senate acted first on a bill sponsored by Republican Senator Ward V. Tolbert. Republican Assemblyman Sol Ullman of the Sixth Assembly District in Manhattan sponsored the measure in the Assembly, where it was passed in the last-minute rush to complete unfinished business before the session ended. Members of the Assembly, Claessens said, had not received copies of the bill, and had no idea what it contained.[94]

Senator Tolbert later admitted, the *New York Call* reported, that party leaders, since 1918, had discussed rearranging the boundaries of the congressional districts below Fourteenth Street in Manhattan. Population changes, Tolbert claimed, had made the old districts unwieldy and out of proportion to the number of voters in them. However, he denied responsibility for the bill. "I did not draw the bill. I do not know its provisions. I introduced the bill after it was drawn up by the Democrats and the Republicans. They both agreed on it. I do not remember who gave it to me. I think it was a messenger."[95]

The Socialist Party, labor unions and various civic organizations protested immediately to Republican Governor Nathan Miller. In a telegram to the governor, S. John Block, state chairman of the Socialist Party, requested a hearing on the bill. "The bill," he charged, "is an obvious attempt by a Republican controlled legislature to insure the election of a Tammany Hall member of Congress in place of the Socialist member from the Twelfth Congressional District."[96] On March 27, Governor Miller agreed to a hearing.[97] In the meantime, Socialists prepared to deluge the governor with telegrams and petitions signed by thousands of residents of the Twelfth District.[98]

On April 11, a delegation, including union leaders and Socialist officials, met with the governor.[99] In arguing against redistricting, Block maintained that the Tolbert-Ullman bill "ruthlessly" disregarded a federal law requiring congressional districts to be "composed of a contiguous and compact territory, and containing as nearly as practicable an equal number of inhabitants." The federal census of 1920 showed that the four districts had a total population of 725,358 which, if evenly divided, would have meant 181,339 people for each district. The pending measure, Block noted, made no attempt to apportion the total population equally. The Twelfth Congressional District received 147,476 people, far below the average of 181,339.

The inequalities established by the bill, Block insisted, were "so shockingly apparent that they hardly require any argument to show that the Legislature has utterly abused its powers, and has completely disregarded the constitutional and statutory mandates." The "lawless" politicians and the legislators who assisted them in carrying out their scheme, Block charged, sought to take from the Twelfth District a substantial portion of the people who supported the Socialist Party and place them in the Eleventh District or in the other two districts where their votes would not harm the old parties.[100]

A.S. Gilbert, the attorney for the New York County Republican organization, maintained that the figures presented by Block did not agree with the ones he had received. In response to questions from Governor Miller, Gilbert admitted that if the Socialist Party's population figures were accurate, it justified criticism of the bill. He insisted, however, that the Socialists could still carry the Twelfth Congressional District. The *New York Call*, in its report of the hearing, stated that the governor appeared impressed by the arguments presented against the bill.[101] But whatever hopes London's supporters had that the governor would veto the bill were dashed when he signed it on April 14.[102]

Faced with the fact that thousands of Jewish garment workers, who had made possible his earlier victories, had been taken from his district and replaced with loyal Tammany supporters, London decided against a fourth term. Other factors also contributed to his decision. Many London supporters and potential supporters had moved to other parts of the city. Thousands had never bothered to become citizens and could not vote. In addition, the Socialist Party had continued to lose strength while the Communists, who opposed London, had become more active in the Jewish unions upon whom he relied for support. Finally, the Socialist congressman had tired of his lone fight in the House. He had hoped that other Socialists or progressives would join him in Congress, but his expectations had not been fulfilled.[103]

Socialist leaders in Local New York and London's supporters in the labor movement refused to accept his decision. A nominating convention held by East Side Socialists on July 7 declined, after a "heated discussion," to accept London's decision. The convention appointed a committee to confer with Socialist Party officials of New York County to persuade London to withdraw his declination.[104]

In the ensuing weeks, Socialist Party officials, labor leaders and other progressives deluged London with appeals to reconsider. They appealed to him in the name of the Socialist Party, the trade unions and progressivism. His enemies, they declared, on the right and the left, regarded his refusal to run as a victory for themselves. London's supporters predicted that he would be reelected despite the gerrymander, and promised to redouble their efforts to achieve victory. Late in August, London finally succumbed to the pressure and accepted the nomination. In explaining his change of mind, London told his wife that he could not let the "boys" down.[105]

In addition to the Socialist Party nomination, London also had the support of the Farmer-Labor Party. Abandoning its traditional policy of aloofness, the Socialist Party, at its May 1922 convention, altered the party's constitution so that state organizations could cooperate politically with various labor, farmer and progressive organizations.[106] Hoping to strengthen its chances in the coming election, the New York Socialist Party convention in early July unanimously approved a resolution favoring collaboration with the Farmer-Labor Party and other working-class organizations.[107] The Farmer-Labor Party, in return, agreed to fuse with the New York Socialists, making it possible for London to run on a Socialist Party-Farmer-Labor Party ticket.

Another important development in the campaign occurred when a joint convention consisting of Socialists, Farmer-Laborites and trade unionists formed the American Labor Party in New York City on July 16. This party was established in order to present a united front for independent political action by uniting all labor and progressive elements not included in the Socialist or Farmer-Labor parties. The new organization adopted a platform and nominated a full slate of candidates including Meyer London.

The American Labor Party did not, however, have a place on the ballot. Its candidates appeared under the label of the Socialist Party–Farmer-Labor Party.[108] London hailed the creation of the new party. A coalition of industrial and farm workers into one political organization represented the best hope for the American people. "A small minority now, it is destined to shape the future policy of the country."[109]

Confronted with this formidable labor–progressive coalition, the Democrats and Republicans sought to fuse in the Twelfth and Twentieth congressional districts. The Republican candidates in both districts withdrew on August 25. The *New York Times* reported that fusion plans had not been completed, but it appeared that the Republicans would endorse Assemblyman Samuel Dickstein as the Democratic candidate in the Twelfth Congressional District, leaving the Twentieth District for future agreement.[110] Tammany, convinced that it could carry these districts without making a deal for Republican support, rejected the offered fusion.[111] Thus, on August 29, the last day for filing, the Republican Party designated Louis Zeltner as its candidate in the Twelfth District.[112]

London's campaign opened with a rally on October 4. During his remarks, the Socialist congressman discussed the principal issues in the campaign: the gerrymander and his record in Congress. The "infamous" gerrymander of the Twelfth District, he declared, would be the most important issue. "The attempt to defeat me at the polls this coming November is a desperate one, as evidenced by the fact that, in splitting up the district, Tammany took out of it strong Socialist and Jewish neighborhoods and substituted Chinatown, the Bowery and Little Italy." Despite this, London pledged to carry the campaign into those districts with "unabated fervor."[113]

In nightly rallies at Clinton Hall, London reviewed his work in Congress, and noted his advocacy of unpopular causes including the fight against militarism, his appeals for free speech and amnesty for political prisoners and his demand for free immigration.[114] He criticized the Sixty-Seventh Congress for ignoring important problems facing the country, such as labor unrest and world peace. In these fields, the Republicans and the Democrats proved "intellectually impotent." The remedy they offered for industrial unrest was force. The Democrats and Republicans planned to pass anti-strike legislation after the election. A conspiracy, London charged, existed among the "leaders of the plutocracy" against working men and women.[115]

London and his supporters also attacked the record of Democrat Samuel

Dickstein.[116] They ridiculed Dickstein's claim that he had pushed through the New York Assembly several bills providing for the inspection of Kosher meat. London pointed out that old party politicians had first passed the Kosher bills and then proceeded to gerrymander the Twelfth District. They had shown their devotion to the Jews by giving them Kosher meat and by taking twenty-five thousand Jews out of the district so that they could not reelect their congressman.[117]

The *New York Call* declared that Dickstein had not served the interests of either city or state workers. London, on the other hand, had given years of loyal service to the trade unions of the city. In Congress, he was the prominent spokesman for labor against the "open shoppers" and their designs. "To even suggest that Dickstein may be paired with London as a labor representative is to do violence to what is common knowledge in labor history." The only candidate for Congress in the Twelfth District who truly represented labor's interests was Meyer London who deserved every worker's vote.[118]

As in his previous campaigns, London had the support of organized labor. The ILGWU, the Amalgamated Clothing Workers of America, the International Furriers' Union, the Cloakmakers and the United Hebrew Trades were among the more important unions who endorsed his campaign and worked vigorously for his reelection.[119] London also had the support of the Workmen's Circle, the Poale Zion, the Jewish Socialist Venband and the Young People's Socialist League.[120] The Cloakmakers and the Workmen's Circle once again established campaign committees in the Twelfth District.[121]

Toward the close of the campaign, London received a boost when Samuel Gompers called for his return to Congress. In a telegram to the New York Joint Board of the Cloakmakers, Gompers stated that as a member of the House, London had consistently worked "for justice, freedom, democracy and humanity." The people of the Twelfth Congressional District were justified in having confidence in London, and should reelect him by a large majority.[122]

In order to offset the gerrymander, the Socialist Party–Farmer-Labor Party concentrated its efforts in the Twelfth District. Local New York requested candidates in other districts and prominent New York Socialists to spend at least one evening a week in London's district. Among those who campaigned on London's behalf were John Block, B. Channey Vladek, Judge Jacob Panken, Abraham Cahan, Louis Waldman, Assemblyman Henry Jager, Morris Hillquit, and Edward Cassidy, the Socialist Party Farmer–Labor Party candidate for governor.

To further emphasize the gerrymander issue, large trucks bearing maps of the district, indicating the sections that had been added to the district and those that had been taken away, were driven through the Lower East Side.

Circulars, letters and canvasses were also utilized to make voters understand the gerrymander.[123]

London's campaign received an unexpected boost when the Communist Party withdrew its candidate in the Twelfth District shortly before the election. Resentment had grown among Jewish workers who believed the Communist candidate would take votes from London. The Communists did not want to give the Socialists the opportunity to accuse them of helping to defeat a candidate of the working class.[124]

The Socialist press also gave London invaluable support. The *Daily Forward* and the *New York Call* sought to thwart voting fraud. The *Forward*, for the first time since his successful 1914 campaign, printed the names and addresses of the district's registered voters. It urged readers to examine the list for false registrants.[125] The *Forward* and the *Call* also warned against Tammany's effort to colonize the Fourth Assembly District. Fear of such activity had been raised by an increase in the number of registered voters in the Fourth Assembly District while registration elsewhere in the city had declined. "The reaction is desperate and determined to prevent London's return to Congress." Socialists, the *Call* declared, should make certain that the "election crooks' dirty work" is nullified as much as possible."[126] On October 29, the *Daily Forward* offered a ten thousand dollar reward for the first twenty arrests and convictions of illegal registrants and voters in the Twelfth Congressional District.[127]

Abraham S. Gilbert, special state attorney general in charge of the Election Bureau, reassured Socialist Party officials that everything possible would be done to prevent fraud and that the police would cooperate to make this a clean election. He promised to have state inspectors visit those polling places where past trouble had occurred. Inspectors would cover most of the First, Second, and Eighth assembly districts and all of the Fourth Assembly District.[128]

The worst fears of Socialists were borne out when on October 27, Gilbert revealed that investigations by his office had uncovered numerous election frauds. He described conditions on the Lower East Side as "indescribably rotten." False registration, perjury and neglect of duty by public officials were common.[129]

Jurisdictional differences, however, occurred between Gilbert and the district attorney of New York County Joab H. Banton, a Democrat. Banton agreed to cooperate in preventing fraud, but insisted that his office prosecute all alleged irregularities. The *Call* accused Banton of dragging his feet, and questioned his motives, as did the conservative *New York Tribune*.[130]

In addition to Gilbert's efforts to ensure a clean election, London's campaign committee conducted canvasses to root out "colonizers." An incomplete

Socialist investigation produced some two hundred illegal registrants, with predictions that as many as one thousand would be uncovered.[131]

London appealed for vigilance at the polls. Polling places had to be adequately manned in order to win the election. "In addition to the fraudulent registration," he warned, "an attempt will be made to count us out on Election Day. If we can get a decent count, and we can if each Socialist and trade unionist will take his or her place on the firing line next Tuesday — we cannot lose." The election would be decided, he stated, between the time the polls closed and the following morning.[132]

As the campaign drew to a close, Socialist leaders viewed London's chances with increased optimism. Canvassers had revealed that Socialist strength was equal to that in 1920, and perhaps even stronger, due to resentment against the gerrymander and the weakness of Samuel Dickstein.[133]

In the last major address of the campaign, London told some two thousand cheering people that socialism had given meaning to his life. "Without Socialism, I would have been nothing. My campaign does not end tomorrow. My campaign against capitalism will not end so long as there is life in my body."[134]

With last-minute appeals from the *New York Call* and the *Daily Forward* urging East Siders to cast a straight Socialist ticket, the voters of the Twelfth Congressional District went to the polls on November 7.[135] Despite a vigorous campaign, London lost by 5,127 votes. Samuel Dickstein received 11,027 votes or 60.08 percent of the vote, London polled 5,900 votes or 32.55 percent of the vote, and Louis Zeltner ran a poor third, with 1,183 votes or 6.51 percent of the vote.[136]

The gerrymander proved decisive as London's percent of the total vote dropped from 54.06 in 1920 to 32.55, a decrease of 21.51 percent. London also failed, for the first time since 1910, to carry any of the four assembly districts comprising the Twelfth District. The impact of the gerrymander was most obvious in the Fourth Assembly District which London lost by a mere ninety-five votes in 1920. Dickstein carried this Tammany bastion by 3,452 votes. The newly redrawn congressional district included Chinatown, Little Italy and the Bowery, all Tammany strongholds. In addition, First, Second, Third and Fourth streets, the heart of Socialist and Jewish strength, were removed. Furthermore, Al Smith rebounded from his defeat in 1920 with a large majority on the East Side, thus helping Dickstein and Democrats throughout New York. Of the Socialist candidates for office in the city, only August Claessens managed to survive what Socialists characterized as the "worst debacle" in recent party history.[137]

In election postmortems, the *Daily Forward* attributed London's defeat to the gerrymander and to widespread fraud in the district.[138] Socialist leaders, the *New York World* reported, considered the landslide victory of Al Smith, the Democratic gubernatorial candidate, as the principal factor in their poor showing. Smith, who championed the cause of the urban worker, won their support at the polls in increasing numbers. This further weakened London's political base and support for Socialist candidates.[139] Widespread fraud had also occurred on the East Side, but had not played a significant role in the outcome of the election.[140] The *New York Call* editorialized that the American Labor Party could have conducted a more thorough campaign had it organized earlier. In addition, prolonged unemployment, particularly in the needle trades, limited these workers' contribution to the campaign.[141]

London did not have long to reflect on his defeat. On November 10, President Harding summoned Congress back into a special session to pass a subsidy bill to assist the merchant marine.[142] During the weeklong debate, London joined with the Democrats to demand nationalization of the merchant marine.

In a speech on November 24, London referred to Republican losses at the polls. He commented sarcastically, "The Republican Party, under a sentence of death, proceeds to steal from the Treasury of the United States. They call it a subsidy."[143] The bill not only proposed to give away the merchant marine to private shipping interests, but would also subsidize them for years. Finally, London dismissed the argument that the subsidy would save the government money.

No real effort, he continued, had been exerted to develop a government merchant marine. Government operation could not succeed when the administration announced that it would sell the ships to private interests and when the Shipping Board refused to compete with privately owned vessels. "This attempt to artificially develop a merchant marine at the expense of the taxpayers, with the avowed object of supplanting the merchant fleets of other countries is but a continuation of the imperialistic policy we launched ... in 1898, when we took possession of the Philippine Islands." He would not vote for the appropriation of the taxpayer's money to support a private monopoly.[144]

The House passed the bill on November 29 by a vote of 208 to 184.[145] The Senate, however, bogged down by a southern filibuster of the anti-lynching bill, failed to act before the special session ended at noon on Monday, December 4, 1922.[146] Shortly thereafter, the Sixty-Seventh Congress convened for its final session.

Meyer London's final three months in Congress were anti-climactic, but he continued to address a variety of matters including prohibition, workmen's compensation in the District of Columbia, the nationalization of industry, war debts and the invasion of the Ruhr.[147] In his most important speech of the session, on January 20, London strongly condemned the French occupation of the Ruhr. Congress, he asserted, must not remain silent. "The voice of America should be heard.... There is no other voice that can speak with authority." London criticized the Versailles Treaty. Germany, London pointed out, had lost much of its territory in Europe, a large segment of its population, its merchant marine, its iron and coal producing center and its colonies. In addition, the victorious nations had imposed an indemnity which Germany could not pay. By occupying the Ruhr, France sought to prevent German industrial and commercial recovery and to enable French steel manufacturers to add to their acquisition of the iron region of Lorraine, the coal regions of Germany. The invasion of German territory, London declared, would ultimately lead to a resurgence of militarism. France had played into the hands of the German military clique.

Representative Garner of Texas asked London what the United States should do. As a first step London suggested that Congress request France "in solemn but kind words" to evacuate the occupied territory. Secondly, the president should be instructed to mediate, and finally, an international economic conference should be called. France, he stated, owed a respectable hearing to the American Congress. Garner then asked London what he would do if France failed to heed this country's appeal. In that eventuality, London replied, the United States should morally isolate France and refuse to do business with her.[148]

London experienced great difficulties in the Sixty-Seventh Congress Conditions differed from those he had first encountered in the House in 1915. At that time the atmosphere in Washington was more liberal and tolerant. The Democrats had controlled Congress, and President Wilson pushed through a progressive reform program. Republicans, however, now dominated the Congress, and the prevailing mood was pro-business, conservative and nationalistic. The Red Scare had fostered xenophobia, hostility to reformers and distrust of the labor movement.

Nevertheless, London continued to espouse the cause of the urban immigrant, the working class and political dissenters. In an effort to silence this radical voice and to weaken the Socialist Party in New York City, the New York Legislature gerrymandered the Twelfth Congressional District. This cynical political maneuver along with Al Smith's landslide victory in the gubernatorial race proved decisive in London's defeat. Although he lost, London could take comfort in the fact that the Socialists would still have representation in the House due to Victor Berger's victory in Wisconsin.

12

Meyer London: The Final Years

> A man of rare and noble parts has gone from amongst us, a faithful champion of the workers, a loyal comrade within the Socialist movement, a warm hearted friend of all suffering humanity.... His loss is irretrievable.—*Morris Hillquit,* New York Times, *June 27, 1926, 1.*

The lame duck session of the Sixty-Seventh Congress ended on March 4, 1923, and with it Meyer London's congressional career. During the last three years of his life, he opposed communist efforts to gain control of Socialist-led unions that he had helped build. The ILGWU managed to fight off the communists, but they gained control of the Furriers' Union. London, however, helped prevent them from gaining control of the Workmen's Circle.[1]

In the political arena, London supported the candidacy of Senator Robert La Follette on the Progressive Party ticket. In a heated debate with Scott Nearing, a left-wing Socialist, on October 5, 1924, London outraged communists in the audience when he urged "class conscious Socialists and workers" to support La Follette. He warned against seeking to imitate the communists in Russia. What worked in Russia might be "poison to Great Britain and death to the United States." Much in America, London insisted, was worth preserving. Once again, he rejected the dictatorship of the proletariat. "They tried it in Italy. What is Mussolini? He is Lenin upside down. We were making more progress in the United States than any country in the world when the war stopped anything progressive. It is false that America is devoted only to the dollar. There is more idealism here ... than in any other country on earth."[2] By supporting La Follette's candidacy in 1924, London reaffirmed a belief which guided his career: Socialist goals were attainable in the United States through the ballot box and education rather than revolutionary methods.

London made his last bid for elective office in 1925, when he ran unsuccessfully for the New York Supreme Court in the First Judicial District, comprising New York County and the Bronx. He received 30,882 votes, but trailed the lowest major party candidate by some 90,000 votes.[3]

One final question remains: why did the popular London fail to run for Congress in 1924? The lack of evidence requires a speculative answer. A number of factors need to be considered: the gerrymander and changing demographics on the Lower East Side; the continued decline in the Socialist Party; Jews, particularly workers, found Governor Al Smith appealing, and began to vote Democratic; and finally, a realistic London had tired of tilting against the Tammany machine. His decisive defeat in 1922 no doubt convinced him that he lacked the support necessary to win in the Twelfth District.

Unlike Eugene Debs, Victor Berger and Morris Hillquit, London never became a major Socialist Party leader. Throughout his association with the Socialist movement, he held no important office in either the national, state or local organizations. Nor does he appear to have had any ambition in that direction. He attended party conventions infrequently, and generally refrained from taking an active role. Moreover, London had little time for party matters, and refused to become involved in doctrinal disputes that plagued the American Socialist movement in the first two decades of the twentieth century. Socialists, he believed, could not afford to fight each other for it exposed their weaknesses and strengthened the enemies of the working class.

Philosophically, London belonged to the so-called right or conservative wing of the Socialist Party. He believed that the final objective of the Socialists, an industrial democracy, would occur through evolutionary rather than revolutionary means. He rejected the use of violence and sabotage and supported political action and trade unionism. Although critical of capitalism, London believed that it had served an important historical mission. The next step was the democratization of industry. Ultimately, the people would control the nation's industry and natural resources.

He accepted many of the basic principles of Marxism, but refused to be doctrinaire and dogmatic, contending that the difficulty with many American Socialists was their tendency to imitate their European comrades. American Socialist had to adapt to their American environment, London maintained. They should study America and American history before studying Marx, Lenin and other European Socialists. Moreover, London recognized the need to modify Socialist principles in the light of experience and changing conditions.

Elected to Congress for three terms, London never created a lasting political organization as did Victor Berger in Milwaukee. London disliked the routine of organizational work and lacked interest in political leadership. His success rested on his popularity on the Lower East Side. Jewish workers, deeply grateful for his unselfish service to them and their unions and his position on ethnic matters, showed appreciation by taking an active part in his campaigns and by voting for him on Election Day. London's victories over the entrenched Tammany machine were also made possible by the strong support he received from the unions, particularly the ILGWU, which buttressed the Socialist Party. London, however, had broad appeal. He wooed and willingly accepted non–Socialist support among professionals and within the business community much to the dismay of his more doctrinaire comrades.

In Congress, London championed the cause of working men and women. He introduced legislation to improve the plight of the workers and defended organized labor against its critics. A minority of one, he realized that his legislative achievements would be limited. Nonetheless, London believed it his duty to make the American people and Congress aware of existing economic and social problems. He used the House as a sounding board, and aroused interest in his theories as well as admiration for himself personally. His fight for national social insurance is an important chapter in the history of this movement.[4]

The first Russian-Jewish immigrant in the House of Representatives, London became a leading spokesman for the urban immigrant. He voiced continued opposition to restrictive immigration legislation, arguing that the United States should not abandon its traditional role as a haven for the oppressed of the world. He also sought to safeguard the rights of aliens already in the country.

As a legislator London took a pragmatic approach. He introduced measures which he believed had a chance of passage, and proved willing to compromise when necessary. In so doing, he won the support of progressive Democrats and Republicans who shared his interest in economic and social justice. They judged London's proposals on their merits rather than on their ideological source. Thus, London succeeded in winning hearings for several of his bills. Moreover, the House Labor Committee unanimously reported his national social insurance resolution after London agreed to modifications proposed by Samuel Gompers. His proposal came within twenty-nine votes of passage. The Sixty-Seventh Congress adopted London's bill to alter the Bankruptcy Act, the first Socialist-sponsored measure enacted by Congress.

During his three terms in Congress, London established a good working relationship with his colleagues—Democrats and Republicans alike. Occasionally, they gave London the opportunity to close a debate. House Speaker Champ Clark also gave him the honor of presiding over the House, much to the chagrin of his critics. Attacked by ultra-conservatives in both parties, London held his own during acrimonious exchanges, and progressive congressmen, such as Edward Keating, a Democrat from Colorado and Joseph Medill McCormick, a Republican from Illinois and the owner-publisher of the *Chicago Tribune*, rose to defend him. London was considered a good fel-

12. Meyer London

Chess match between House champion Meyer London, seated on left, and Roy Fitzgerald, Republican, Michigan. Standing next to Fitzgerald is London's brother Lewis, circa 1923. Photographic Collection of Library of Congress.

low with a ready wit. An avid chess player, he won the House championship in 1923.

London had the misfortune to serve in Congress at a time when foreign affairs began to take precedence over domestic concerns. The Socialist congressman voiced his party's opposition to war and militarism. An outspoken critic of Wilson's preparedness program, he feared it would lead the United States to war. Rather than prepare for war, London insisted that America should bring peace to the world. He introduced and carried on a vigorous fight for a resolution that called upon the president to summon a conference of neutral nations for the purpose of offering mediation to the belligerent nations. London voted against the declarations of war on Germany and Austria-Hungary, and in so doing, antagonized many of his congressional colleagues. He refused, however, to abide by the anti-war position taken by the emergency convention of the Socialist Party, and incurred the wrath of his left-wing comrades.

Under attack from all sides, London showed that independence of mind and pugnacity that characterized his three terms in Congress. He followed the dictates of his conscience which he believed in accord with Socialist principles. At first, London refused to vote on important war measures. But his belief that German militarism constituted a serious menace to democratic institutions throughout the world, plus his love for America, led him to actively support the war effort. Another factor, which undoubtedly played a role in London's decision to support the war, was his recognition that failure to do so would completely alienate the House and make it impossible for him to further the socialist agenda.

London sought to make the best of the war. Like many Socialists and progressives who reluctantly supported the war, he believed that it could advance the cause of reform. He supported emergency measures extending government control over various areas of the economy. In so doing, he sought to convince his colleagues that these measures should be established on a permanent basis.

Perhaps his most important contribution during the war was his unflagging opposition to repressive wartime legislation, violations of civil liberties and his support for a league of nations. Despite charges of disloyalty from his colleagues, London led the fight against those who sought to stamp out dissent in the name of "100 percent Americanism." With the conclusion of the conflict, London campaigned for the release of all political prisoners and repeal of the Espionage and Sedition acts. He was one of the first members of Congress to call for the organization of a league of nations. On December 6, 1917, he presented a resolution proposing that Congress initiate the organization of an international league to secure a durable peace. In addition, London proved to be one of Wilson's most loyal supporters on this matter.

The Bolshevik Revolution in Russia made London's task in Congress even more difficult. Like most Russian-Jewish immigrants, he expressed delight with the overthrow of the czar. He was less enthusiastic about the Bolshevik seizure of power, and openly opposed the Treaty of Brest-Litovsk. Called upon in the House to explain the events taking place in Russia, London became one of the first important Socialists to express reservations about the Lenin-Trotsky regime. He refused to accept its undemocratic features such as the dictatorship of the proletariat. Nevertheless, London defended the right of the Russian people to work out their own future, called for diplomatic recognition of the new regime and opposed foreign military intervention. Once again London's position proved unsatisfactory to both left-wing Socialists, many of whom later became communists, and his conservative congressional colleagues who viewed socialism, bolshevism and anarchism as one and the same.

Throughout Meyer London's years of service to the trade unions, and while in Congress, he devoted himself to the cause of the poor and needy with never a thought of personal gain. His pleasures were few: a good cigar, a good book and the challenge of a chess game. According to his brother Horace, London had a substantial law practice, but frequently refused fees. Moreover, much of his income went to help unions and strikers, the Socialist Party and a variety of charitable causes.[5]

With the utmost courage, he served the Socialist Party and organized labor. A person of great character and ideals, he refused to compromise on matters of principle, and was fearless in adhering to his convictions. An intellectual at heart, London mastered six languages and enjoyed reading Russian, French and Italian literature. One of the best-read men in the House, he immersed himself in history and economics, and his colleagues considered him an authority in these fields.

An untiring worker, London seldom missed a congressional session and frequently worked late into the night on legislative matters. He rarely wrote out a speech, usually speaking with sheaves of notes and statistics before him. His well-reasoned arguments won the attention of the House, and his colleagues frequently plied him with questions. London proved a masterful debater, and many a congressman found himself bested in exchanges with the Socialist representative.

A basically modest man, he disliked praise. At his fiftieth birthday celebration, while labor and Socialist leaders heaped praise on him, London remained backstage muttering to himself, "What damn fools, making such a fuss over nothing at all!"[6]

For almost forty years Meyer London worked on behalf of the immigrant masses and the labor movement. But his career ended abruptly when a taxi struck him down on Sunday morning, June 6, 1926, while he was crossing First Avenue at Eighteenth Street with his wife Anna. Rushed to Bellevue Hospital by the taxi driver, London died at ten o'clock that night from internal injuries.[7] London's sudden death came as a great shock to the East Side, as well as the Socialist and labor movements. Some twenty-five thousand people viewed his body which lay in state at the Forward Building from two o'clock Tuesday afternoon until the building closed at midnight. The funeral, a non-religious affair, took place the following day with two thousand people crowding into Forward Hall to hear eulogies delivered by Morris Hillquit, B. Charney Vladek, Abraham Cahan, Jacob Panken and Norman Thomas. Police estimated that fifty thousand mourners took part in the funeral procession which passed through the streets of New York's Lower East Side while another five hundred thousand people watched — the largest outpouring of East Siders since the funeral of the beloved Yiddish writer Sholom Aleichem in 1916. Indicative of the esteem in which London was held, he was interred in Mount Carmel Cemetery, Brooklyn, in the Poets' Corner, near Sholom Aleichem.[8]

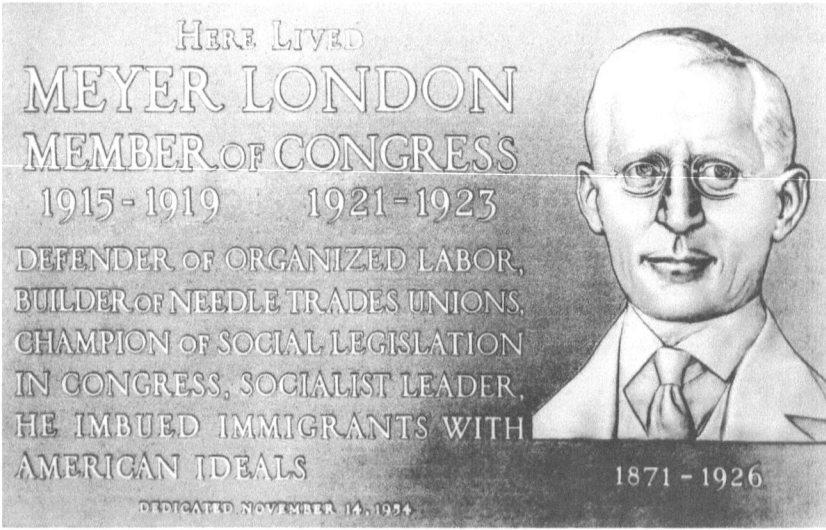

Top: Abraham Cahan addressing a large crowd in Mount Carmel cemetery on the tenth commemoration of London's death, July 1926. Photographic Collection, Tamiment Library, New York University. *Bottom:* Historical marker placed by the Meyer London Memorial Committee on London's residence, 274 East Broadway, on November 14, 1954. Photographic Collection. Tamiment Library, New York University.

12. Meyer London

Meyer London's funeral procession moving uptown from the Forward Building on East Broadway, July 1926. Photographic Collection, Tamiment Library, New York University.

In the years following London's death, he became a folk hero. His idealism, his strong sense of commitment to the poor, to struggling workers, and his love for America were not forgotten. His friends and associates in the Socialist and labor movements created the Meyer London Memorial Committee which erected a monument to London at his grave site. The committee sponsored well attended memorial services there on the tenth and twenty-fifth anniversaries of his death. It commissioned the biography written by Harry Rogoff. The library at the Rand School of Social Sciences on Fourteenth Street near Union Square was renamed the Meyer London Library. During World War II, the navy commissioned a Liberty ship USS *Meyer London*. A newly constructed school, PS#2 on the Lower East Side, was named in his honor. Finally, a plaque was placed on a building located at 274 East Broadway where Meyer and his family shared a modest apartment at the time of his election to Congress.

Morris Hillquit expressed the feelings of the East Side and London's comrades within the Socialist and labor movements when he said, "A man of rare and noble parts has gone from amongst us, a faithful champion of the workers, a loyal comrade within the Socialist movement, a warm hearted friend of all suffering humanity. The terrible void which his sudden death has left in our ranks will never be filled. His loss is irretrievable."9

Newspaper clipping announcing the tenth anniversary of London's death. Photographic Collection, Tamiment Library, New York University.

Epilogue:
Failure of a Dream

By the time Meyer London died in 1926, the Socialist Party of America had declined significantly both in membership and influence. At its height in 1912, party membership totaled 127,984, and in the presidential election of that year Eugene Debs received 897,000 votes, about 6 percent of the total vote. Many believed that the party represented a serious challenge to the two older parties. However, by 1918 membership had declined to 74,519 and would continue to plummet during the 1920s, reaching a low of 7,798 in 1928. During the early Depression years, a brief revival occurred when Norman Thomas emerged as the party's standard bearer. In 1932 party membership rose to 16,863 and Thomas polled 884,781 votes. The following year party membership grew to 20,950, but thereafter it declined to 11,902 in 1936, with party membership in New York falling from 3,153 in February 1933 to 1,856 in February 1937. Historians have differed as to why the decline occurred. They have emphasized either internal or external reasons or a combination of both. I agree with the latter. Certainly continued internal bickering, along with the emergence of the Communist Party, and government repression during and after the war, were major factors. The hostile attitude toward labor in the post-war years was yet another reason. While in Congress and thereafter, London in his capacity of counsel for the ILGWU, the Furriers' Union and the Workmen's Circle confronted these issues with mixed results.

Had he lived into the late 1920s and 1930s and experienced the Great Depression and the tumult it created, London, like many right-wing Socialists, would have endorsed Franklin Roosevelt. London had shown his willingness to support non–Socialists when he supported Senator Robert La Follette as the Progressive Party presidential candidate in 1924. By the mid-1920s, London, Abraham Cahan and other right-wing Socialists had abandoned the goal of transforming American society and now sought to reform it. Cahan and the *Forward* had drifted away from socialism. In 1936, the *Forward* endorsed Franklin Roosevelt.

Shortly before the 1936 presidential election, the ILGWU and the Amalgamated Clothing Workers, traditionally Socialist, created the American Labor Party (ALP). They sought to give New York Socialists sympathetic to the New Deal, but reluctant to vote Democratic, another alternative to support Roosevelt. The ALP served as a "halfway house between the Socialist Party and the regular Democratic organization."

No doubt, London, closely allied with Cahan, would also have approved the New Deal. The enactment of the Social Security Act would have particularly pleased him. London had championed the cause of national social insurance during his three terms in Congress. He brought the subject into the public arena and helped educate his colleagues on the issue. David J. Lewis, a Democrat from Maryland, chairman of the House Labor committee on which London served during the Sixty-Fourth Congress, introduced the Social Security bill and served as its floor manager in the Seventy-Fourth Congress. A number of congressmen who supported London's proposal in the House and who assumed leadership roles in the Seventy-Fourth Congress voted for the Social Security Act in 1935. New Deal measures such as the National Labor Relations Act, the Hours and Wages Act, and others would have won London's hearty approval.

Meyer London and his fellow Socialists failed to achieve their ultimate goal — the cooperative commonwealth with its promise of a more just, equitable and humane society. However, their efforts, both successful and unsuccessful, helped shape the great social struggles of twentieth-century America. As Tony Michels writes in *A Fire in Their Hearts* "the questions they posed..., What is a just society? How might we achieve it? ...remain forceful and relevant ... for all Americans" to this very day.

Chapter Notes

Chapter 1

1. The Pale of Settlement encompassed Congress Poland, Lithuania, Byelorussia and the Ukraine, excluding Kiev. Moses Rischin, *The Promised City: New York's Jews, 1870–1914*, rev. ed. (Cambridge, MA: Harvard University Press, 1977), 21–22.
2. Ibid., 20–30; Salo W. Baron, *The Russian Jew Under Tsars and Soviets* (New York: Macmillan Company, 1964), 5.
3. Harry Rogoff, *An East Side Epic: The Life and Work of Meyer London* (New York: Vanguard Press, 1930), 8–9; Melech Epstein, *Profiles of Eleven* (Detroit: Wayne State University Press, 1965), 162–63; Algernon Lee, "Meyer London," in *Dictionary of American Biography*, ed. Dumas Malone, 11 (New York: Scribner's Sons, 1928), 372.
4. H. Rogoff, 8–9; Epstein, *Profiles*, 163.
5. Rischin, 24.
6. The Hebrew term *cheder*, meaning "room," has been applied since the sixteenth century or possibly earlier to the traditional school. The principal objective of the "cheder," a Jewish primary school, was the preparation for individual study of the Talmud and its commentaries.
7. H. Rogoff, 8; Epstein, *Profiles*, 163; Tattler, "The Solitary Socialist," *The Nation* 102 (May 1916): 478.
8. H. Rogoff, 9; Epstein, *Profiles*, 163.
9. Joseph Rappaport, "Jewish Immigrants and World War I: A Study of American Yiddish Press Reactions" (PhD diss., Columbia University, 1951), 16; Baron, 57.
10. "The Representative with a Million Constituents," *Independent* 80 (November 1914): 281; *New York Post*, November 4, 1914, 2.
11. H. Rogoff, 9; Epstein, *Profiles*, 163.
12. Irving Weinzweig, "The Life of a Fighter," *Advance* 10–11 (June 1926): 8.
13. H. Rogoff, 9–10; Epstein, *Profiles*, 163; Abraham Rogoff, "Formative Years of the Jewish Labor Movement in the United States, 1890–1900" (PhD diss., Columbia University, 1945), 34; Ronald Sanders, *The Downtown Jews: Portraits of an Immigrant Generation* (New York: Harper and Row, 1969), 111; Herz Burgin, *Di Geschichte fun der Idisher Arbeiter Bewegung in Amerika, Rusland und England* (New York: United Hebrew Trades, 1915), 180. Unfortunately, very little is known about London's life in Russia.
14. H. Rogoff, 10–11; Epstein, *Profiles*, 163–64; "The Representative with a Million Constituents," 281; Tattler, 478; Weinzweig, 8; William F. Feigenbaum, "Child of the Workers," *New Leader*, June 12, 1926, 1.
15. Tony Michels, *A Fire in Their Hearts: Yiddish Socialists in New York* (Cambridge, MA: Harvard University Press, 2005), 3–4, 50–68.
16. Thousands of New York Jewish workers, cloak workers in particular, struck for improved working conditions. H. Rogoff, 11; Epstein, *Profiles*, 164. London did not keep a diary, and unlike some of his Jewish contemporaries, he did not write an autobiography in his later years.
17. Ibid., 164; Feigenbaum, 1.
18. German socialists organized the Socialist Labor Party in 1877, but it achieved little success until Daniel De Leon came upon the scene. Attracted by the logic of Marxist scientific determinism, De Leon had joined the SLP in October 1890 and quickly won a place within the top councils of the party. In August 1891, he assumed the editorship of the *People*, the party's official English language weekly, and within the next year De Leon became the unquestioned leader of the Socialist Labor Party. Rischin, 225; Howard Quint, *The Forging of American Socialism: Origins of the Modern Movement* (New York: Bobbs-Merrill, 1953), 14–15, 142–46.
19. Ibid., 152–66. De Leon believed that the key to emancipating the proletariat was the creation of a trade union movement organized on an industrial basis and closely linked to the SLP. Although De Leon advocated the overthrow of capitalism, he hoped to achieve this through the ballot box rather than violence. Daniel Bell, "The Background and Development of Marxian Socialism in the United States," in *Socialism and American Life*, ed. Donald Drew Egbert and Stow Persons, 1:246–48 (Princeton, NJ: Princeton University Press, 1952).
20. Quint, 164.
21. Ibid., 171–72; Sanders, 174–80; Jacob S. Hertz, *History of the International Ladies' Garment Workers' Union* (New York: Der Wecker, 1924), 72.

22. Burgin, 422–23; H. Rogoff, 13–14; Epstein, *Profiles*, 164; Louis Levine, *The Women's Garment Workers: A History of the International Ladies Garment Workers' Union* (New York: B.W. Huebsch, 1924), 86; Robert William Iversen, "Morris Hillquit: American Social Democrat, A Study of the American Left from Haymarket to the New Deal" (PhD diss., University of Iowa, 1951), 51–53, 85; Bell, 263–64; Quint, 1.
23. Ira Kipnis, *The American Socialist Movement, 1897–1912* (New York: Columbia University Press), 289–94.
24. H. Rogoff, 13–14; Epstein, *Profiles*, 164.
25. *Social Democrat*, February 17, 1898, 1.
26. Quint, 300–301.
27. *Social Democrat*, August 12, 1897, 4; Nathan Fine, *Labor and Farmer Parties in the United States, 1828–1928* (New York: Rand School of Social Science, 1928), 191–92; Quint, 301.
28. Kipnis, 58.
29. Quint, 310–11.
30. *Ibid.*, 314, 317. London did not participate in the convention.
31. *Ibid.*, 314–15.
32. Quint, 321–23. Additional provisions called for public ownership of all monopolistic industries, all means of transportation and communication and all mines; reduction of hours of labor; and adoption of political reforms such as the initiative, referendum and proportional representation.
33. In the fall of 1898, the town of Haverhill, a center of shoe manufacturing, elected two Social Democrats to the state legislature and a Social Democratic mayor. *Ibid.*, 323.
34. The Social Democratic Executive Board feared that political cooperation with non-Social Democrats would jeopardize the party's political independence. Kipnis, 78–79.
35. . Among the labor organizations that participated in forming the new party were the Socialist-oriented Central Labor Federation and the Central Labor Union. Quint, 326.
36. *Social Democratic Herald*, September 16, 1899, 3.
37. *Ibid.*, September 30, 1899, 3; October 7, 1899, 3; Kipnis, 79.
38. Quint, 327.
39. Kipnis, 79.
40. *People* (Anti-De Leon), March 18, 1900, 1.
41. Kipnis, 25–42; Quint, 332–43; Philip S. Foner, *History of the Labor Movement in the United States* (New York: Nordan Press, 1955), 2:401.
42. Quint, 339.
43. Edward John Muzik, "Victor L. Berger: A Biography" (PhD diss., Northwestern University, 1960), 95.
44. Bell, 274.
45. *People* (Anti-De Leon), March 18, 1900, 3; *Social Democratic Herald*, March 17, 1900, 1.
46. Quint, 345.
47. *Social Democratic Herald*, March 17, 1900, 1.
48. Quint, 346.
49. *People* (Anti-De Leon), March 18, 1900, 3.
50. *Ibid.*
51. Quint, 348–49.
52. For a detailed discussion of unity discussions in this period, see Quint, 351–59.
53. Muzik, 103–4; Quint, 361–64.
54. *Ibid.*, 372, 374–76.
55. *Ibid.*, 377–87; Raymond S. Ginger, *The Bending Cross: A Biography of Eugene Victor Debs* (New Brunswick, NJ: Rutgers University Press, 1949), 212–13.

Chapter 2

1. Rischin, 175–94. Also see Aaron Antonovsky, *The Early Jewish Labor Movement in the United States* (New York: YIVO, 1961) and A. Rogoff, "Formative Years of the Jewish Labor Movement."
2. ILGWU, *Proceedings of the Twelfth Annual Convention*, June 1–13, 1914, 137.
3. Tattler, 478.
4. B. Hoffman, *Fuftsig Yor mit di Clokemacher Union 1888–1936* (New York: Local 17, 1936), 126. According to Hoffman, the United Brotherhood retained London to fight injunctions granted to two firms in 1899. The following year the United Brotherhood created the ILGWU. Sanders, 396–97.
5. H. Rogoff, 37–38; Isabel London, *Meyer London: An Appreciation*, London Papers, Bobst Library, NYU.
6. *Meyer London's Address*, Ladies Garment Worker (July 1914): 8; Hyman Berman, "Era of the Protocol: A Chapter in the History of the International Ladies' Garment Workers' Union" (PhD diss., Columbia University, 1955), 28; Levine, 103–4.
7. Berman, 107.
8. Berman, 50; H. Rogoff, 29–30.
9. The workers in this branch of the ladies' garment industry were known as reefer makers because they made short, thick double-breasted jackets for women and children, called reefers.
10. Among the conditions were a fifty-nine-hour work week, inside sub-contracting, and payments by workers for needles, straps, and shuttles. In addition, workers had to provide their own sewing machines. Levine, 128–29.
11. Joel Seidman, *The Needle Trades* (New York: Farrar and Reinhart, 1942), 234–36.
12. *Ibid.*, 101–2; Levine, 128–33; Rischin, 246–47; Berman, 42–47. Sub-contracting was the system whereby an employer in a particular shop would contract with a few operators and pressers to make all the garments in the shop and these contractors would hire helpers at low wages to do the work. Some sub-contracting pressers made as much as $150 a week; whereas, the workers who helped them made as little as $6 a week. Levine, 174–75.
13. Rischin, 247.

14. Berman, 50.
15. Levine, 146–51.
16. The term *general strike* as used in the needle trades meant a strike by all workers in one branch, such as cloaks or dresses, in a particular city. Seidman, 97.
17. *New York Times*, November 23, 1909, 16; Levine, 154–155; Berman, 65; *New York Call*, November 23, 1909, 2; November 29, 1909, 2; November 30, 1909, 2; December 2, 1909, 3; London spoke at several rallies to encourage the strikers.
18. Berman, 90.
19. Levine, 154–67; Rischin, 248–49; Seidman, 103–4.
20. Levine, 172–80.
21. Melech Epstein, *Jewish Labor in the U.S.A., 1914–1952* (New York: Trade Union Sponsoring Committee, 1953), 2:359.
22. *New York Call*, June 30, 1910, 1; *New York Times*, June 30, 1910, 11.
23. *New York Call*, July 5, 1910, 1.
24. Berman, 114–15; Seidman, 105. For a more recent account of the cloak makers' strike, the Protocol of Peace and its significance see Richard A. Greenwald, *The Triangle Fire, the Protocols of Peace, and Industrial Democracy in Progressive Era New York* (Philadelphia: Temple University Press, 2005).
25. *New York Call*, August 6, 1.
26. I. London, *Meyer London*.
27. *Ibid.*; H. Rogoff, 33–34.
28. *New York Call*, July 5, 1910, 1.
29. Berman, 117–18; Levine, 184, 186.
30. Berman, 120–23; Levine, 184–85.
31. *New York Call*, July 21, 1910, 1.
32. Berman, 123–24; Levine, 186; Alpheus Thomas Mason, *Brandeis: A Free Man's Life* (New York: Viking, 1956), 291–92.
33. Mason, 292–93; Berman, 294; Levine, 186–87; *New York Call*, July 28, 1910, 1.
34. *New York Call*, July 27, 1910, 1. On the previous day union leaders denied a statement by the manufacturers that Brandeis had agreed to act as attorney for the cloak makers. They praised Meyer London's work stating that his "thorough knowledge of the situation makes his services indispensible."
35. *Ibid.*, July 28, 1910, 1; Mason, 292. It was London, however, who was mistaken. Although sympathetic toward the workers, Brandeis did not accept the closed shop and considered it "unAmerican and unfair to both sides."
36. *New York Call*, July 29, 1910, 2; Berman, 128; Levine, 187–88; Mason, 294.
37. Rischin, 251.
38. *New York Call*, July 29, 1910, 2; Berman, 129; Mason, 294.
39. Levine, 189–91; Mason, 292–97.
40. Max Danish and Leo Stein, eds., *ILGWU News History, 1910–1911* (New York: International Ladies' Garment Workers' Union, 1950), 34.
41. *Ibid.*
42. Levine, 190.
43. *New York Call*, July 31, 1910, 1.

44. *Ibid.*, August 3, 1910, 1–2.
45. *Ibid.*, August 5, 1910, 1.
46. *Ibid.*
47. The two principal papers supporting the strikers were the *Daily Forward* and the *New York Call*.
48. Berman, 139; Levine, 191.
49. *New York Call*, August 11, 1910, 1.
50. *Ibid.*, August 15, 1910, 2; see also August 13, 1910, 1–2, for report of the hearing.
51. *Ibid.*, August 15, 1910; 2.
52. *Ibid.*
53. *Ibid.*, August 13, 1910, 1–2.
54. *Ibid.*; Levine, 151.
55. *New York Call*, August 8, 1910, 2. In this article London is referred to as "the oracle, the prophet, the pillar of fire which lights the way for the 75,000 cloak makers."
56. Berman, 143–44; Levine, 192–93; Melvyn Dubofsky, "New York City Labor in the Progressive Era 1910–1918: A Study of Organized Labor in an Era of Reform" (PhD diss., University of Rochester, 1960), 164; *New York Call*, August 27, 1910, 1; August 29, 1910, 1.
57. *New York Times*, August 28, 1910, 1; Berman, 148; Levine, 193.
58. *New York Times*, August 31, 1910, 5; *New York Call*, September 1, 1910, 1–2. Judge Alton P. Parker, the Democratic presidential candidate in 1904, consulted with London on the appeal.
59. *Ibid.*, 2.
60. Berman, 150.
61. *New York Call*, September 2, 1910, 2.
62. *Ibid.*, September 3, 1910, 1; *New York Times*, September 3, 1910, 1; Berman, 150–51.
63. Julius Henry Cohen, *They Builded Better Than They Knew* (New York: Messner, 1946), 221. When London and Cohen could not agree upon an appropriate name for the new agreement, Marshal suggested that it be called the "Protocol." Mason, 300.
64. *New York Call*, September 3, 1910, 1; Mason, 300–301; Levine, 194; Berman, 151.
65. *New York Call*, September 3, 1910, 1.
66. *Ibid.*, September 8, 1910, 1.
67. *Ibid.*, September 9, 1910, 2.
68. Berman, 211–16.
69. *Ibid.*, 217–18. As quoted in a letter from London to Moskowitz, January 26, 1911, London Papers, Bobst Library, New York University; hereafter referred to as London Papers.
70. *Ibid.*, 219–20; *New York Call*, October 7, 1910, 2. Brandeis had previously agreed to chair the Board of Arbitration.
71. As quoted in Jesse Thomas Carpenter, *Competiveness and Collective Bargaining in the Needle Trades 1910–1967* (Ithaca, NY: Cornell University Press, 1972), 191; *Ibid.*; Levine, 200–204; Mason, 301–2.
72. Mason, 227. More than half of the cloak industry, the dress industry and other minor branches of the ladies' garment industry were covered by a Protocol agreement at one time or another.

73. Berman, 243–48; Mason, 303.
74. Berman, 248–51.
75. *Ibid.*, 252.
76. *Ibid.*, 253.
77. *Ibid.*, 254–55.
78. *Ibid.*, 266–67.
79. *Ibid.*, 285; Mason, 304.
80. *Ibid.*, 305; Levine, 254; Berman, 295.
81. Greenwald, 103–14.
82. Levine, 254; Berman, 295. For a critique of the Protocol, see Greenwald, 76–79; also see 103–15 for the "Hourwich affair."
83. B. Hoffman, 243.
84. Mason, 298; Berman, 305; Levine, 254–55.
85. Mason, 306; Levine, 254–55.
86. Mason, 306–7; Berman, 303–9.
87. Berman, 310–13; Levine, 257–58; Mason, 307.
88. Berman, 314–17.
89. *Ibid.*, 318; Levine, 258.
90. Berman, 319–20; Levine, 260.
91. Mason, 308–9; Levine, 261; Berman, 321–22.
92. Berman, 322–25; Levine, 295.
93. Levine, 263; Mason, 309; Berman, 329–30.
94. Berman, 331; Levine, 263.
95. Berman, 331–33; Levine, 264.
96. Levine, 265–67; Berman, 334–35; *New York Call*, December 12, 1913, 3.
97. Levine, 266–67.
98. Berman, 337–38; Mason, 309; Levine, 267. Levine states that London "declared bitterly that he 'had been driven out.'"
99. ILGWU, *Proceedings 1914*, 138.
100. Mason, 310.
101. *New York Call*, January 19, 1914, 2. Greenwald, 112–13.
102. David Von Drehle, *Triangle: The Fire That Changed America* (New York: Atlantic Monthly Press, 2003), 171. It should be noted that London served as the ILGWU representative on the Joint Sanitary Board, which was charged with overseeing shop conditions.
103. Greenwald, 161. Greenwald maintains that the FIC, led by Al Smith and Robert F. Wagner, helped Tammany Hall demonstrate its support for working-class voters and eventually woo them away from the Socialist Party.
104. Philip S. Foner, *The Fur and Leather Workers Union* (Newark, NJ: Nordan Press, 1950). The first four chapters contain the early history of the fur workers. A. Rogoff, 96–99; Seidman, 169–70.
105. H. Rogoff, 49.
106. *New York Call*, June 15, 1912, 1; June 16, 1912, 1; Foner, *The Fur and Leather Workers*, 41–43; *New York Times*, June 22, 1912, 15. By the end of the fifth week, some nine thousand fur workers were out on strike.
107. *New York Times*, June 22, 1912, 15; *New York Call*, June 22, 1912, 1–2.
108. *New York Call*, August 23, 1912, 1.
109. Foner, *The Fur and Leather Workers*, 44.
110. H. Rogoff, 50–51.
111. *New York Call*, August 22, 1912, 2.
112. *Ibid.*, August 23, 1912, 1.
113. *Ibid.*, August 24, 1912, 1; August 25, 1912, 4.
114. *New York Times*, September 9, 1912, 20; *New York Call*, September 9, 1912, 1–2. Provisions of the agreement were as follows: a forty-nine-hour week, half holiday on Saturday all year round, overtime at time and a half, ten paid legal holidays, prohibition of homework, weekly wages to be paid in cash, a Joint Board of Sanitary Control, and a Joint Arbitration Board. The agreement was for two years.
115. Foner, *The Fur and Leather Makers*, 51; Seidman, 136. London replaced R. Fulton Cutting on March 11, 1913, as a member of the Arbitration Commission in the men's clothing industry. The commission was created by the settlement ending a tailors' general strike which had lasted from December 1912 to March 1913.
116. Seidman, 195.
117. *New York Times*, February 21, 1915, 19–20.
118. *New York Call*, August 23, 1912, 1.

Chapter 3

1. Within this great Jewish quarter, five types of Eastern European Jews crowded together in their "separate Jewries." The Russians were the most numerous and heterogeneous. The Galicians, the Romanians, the Levantines, and the Hungarians constituted the other four. Rischin, 76–78.
2. *Ibid.*, 93–94. Congestion peaked in 1910 when 542,061 people lived on the Lower East Side.
3. *Ibid.*, 61–69.
4. *Ibid.*, 81–85. Most of New York's office buildings and factories, which employed over half of the city's industrial workers, were located on the Lower East Side.
5. *Ibid.*, 81–85, 92.
6. Morris Hillquit, *Loose Leaves from a Busy Life* (New York: Macmillan, 1934), 107.
7. Rischin, 222.
8. H. Rogoff, 18; *New York Call*, November 5, 1914, 2; Michels, 5, 28–29.
9. *New York Call*, June 12, 1926, 1; H. Rogoff, 21. Rogoff states incorrectly that London was a candidate in the Fourth Assembly District.
10. *New Yorker Volkszeitung*, November 5, 1896, 1; November 14, 1896, 3; New York Secretary of State, *Manual for the Use of the Legislature of the State of New York* (Albany, 1896), 905, hereafter referred to as the *Legislative Manual*. The *Legislative Manual* gives the vote in the Sixteenth Assembly District of the Socialist Labor Party but does not list the candidate.
11. See chapter 1.
12. *Social Democratic Herald*, October 1, 1898, 3; Burgin, 443–44.

13. Epstein, *Jewish Labor*, 2:269.
14. *Social Democratic Herald*, November 2, 1898, 1; *New Yorker Volkszeitung*, November 18, 1898, 3.
15. *Social Democratic Herald*, November 26, 1898, 1.
16. *Ibid.*, September 30, 1898, 1; *Legislative Manual State of New York, 1898*, 939.
17. See chapter 1.
18. H. Rogoff, 21–22.
19. The results of the 1904 election for assemblyman of the Fourth Assembly District were as follows:
Samuel Cohen (Democrat) 2,403
William H. Burns (Republican) 3,658
Meyer London (Socialist) 1,196
See *The City Record, Official Canvass of the Votes Cast in the Counties of New York, Bronx, Kings, Queens and Richmond*, December 14, 1904, 8591, hereafter referred to as *Official Canvass of the Votes Cast in New York County*.
20. See chapter 2.
21. Rischin, 43–46.
22. As a result of mounting tsarist repression in the 1800s, Russian reformers recognized the need to organize the large Jewish working classes emerging in the cities. In 1897, in the city of Vilna, a small group of Jewish intellectuals and craftsmen formed the General League of Jewish Workers in Russia, Poland, and Lithuania, better known as the Bund. This represented the first attempt to organize Jews for secular, independent political action. The Bund organized and conducted strikes throughout the Pale of Settlement. *Ibid.*
23. H. Rogoff, 115–16; Hertz, 139.
24. Meyer London to S. Sematzky, n.d., London Papers. See Michels, *A Fire in Their Hearts*, for a full discussion of Yiddish-speaking Socialists in New York.
25. H. Rogoff, 24; Hertz, 24.
26. Meyer London to Bernstein, April 5, 1916, London Papers.
27. H. Rogoff, 25.
28. *Ibid.*, 24–28; Epstein, *Profiles*, 166–67; Rischin, 162–65.
29. London received 7,573 votes. *New York Call*, November 4, 1909, 1.
30. *Ibid.*, May 2, 1910, 1. The *American Socialist* wrote, however, that Hillquit's health failed and that the Socialists could not get him to run again. *American Socialist*, December 15, 1910, 2.
31. Arthur Gorenstein, "A Portrait of Ethnic Politics: The Socialists and the 1908–1910 Congressional Elections on the East Side," *Publication of the American Jewish Historical Society* 50 (March 1961): 202.
32. *Ibid.*, 207.
33. *Ibid.*, 207–8.
34. *New York Call*, September 12, 1908, 3.
35. Gorenstein, 214, 218.
36. *Ibid.*, 219–21.
37. *Ibid.*
38. H. Rogoff, 18.

39. The Workmen's Circle is a Jewish fraternal order organized in 1892 to protect working immigrants in the United States and assist them in time of illness and unemployment. By 1915 it had a membership of fifty-two thousand and assets of $625,000. London served as its counsel from 1905 until his death in 1926; Bell, 310; H. Rogoff, 52–55; Maximillian Hurwitz, *The Workmen's Circle: Its History, Ideals, Organization and Institutions* (New York: Workmen's Circle, 1936).
40. The majority resolution declared that Orientals represented a menace to "the most aggressive, militant and intelligent elements of our working population." Refusal to exclude certain races and nationalities "would place the Socialist Party in opposition to the most militant and intelligent portion of the organized workers of the United States." Socialist Party, *Proceedings of the First National Congress*, 1910, 75–77.
41. Hillquit's resolution stated that the Socialist Party "favored all legislative measures tending to prevent the immigration of strikebreakers and the mass immigration of workers ... brought about by the employing class for the weakening of American labor, and of lowering the standard of life of American workers." The United States, however, must remain at all times "a free asylum" for the persecuted. *Ibid.*, 98.
42. The Stuttgart Congress passed a resolution which condemned all measures restricting immigration on racial or ethnic grounds "as reactionary and of no benefit to the working class." The Congress opposed, however, "artificial" immigration, such as contract labor. Kipnis, 277; David Shannon, *The Socialist Party of America* (New York: Macmillan, 1955), 84–89.
43. Socialist Party, *Proceedings 1910 Congress*, 127.
44. *Ibid.*
45. *Ibid.*, 128.
46. Kipnis, 287. Hillquit sought to placate Sam Gompers and the AFL which supported immigration restriction.
47. *New York Call*, July 30, 1910, 2.
48. *Ibid.*, September 27, 1910, 1.
49. *Ibid.*, October 6, 1910, 4.
50. *Ibid.*
51. *Ibid.*, October 17, 1910, 2.
52. *Ibid.*, October 31, 1910, 1.
53. *Ibid.*, October 6, 1910, 4.
54. *Ibid.*, October 25, 1910, 1.
55. *Ibid.*, October 13, 1910, 1.
56. *Ibid.*, September 1, 1910, 2; October 29, 1910, 1.
57. *Ibid.*, October 12, 1910, 1.
58. *Ibid.* November 5, 1910, 2. Hillquit did not campaign actively on London's behalf. Due to a lack of evidence, one can only speculate on Hillquit's failure to assist in the campaign. It is possible that Hillquit, displeased with the decision to bypass him in favor of London, decided to sit out the election. Over the years, a strained relationship developed between the two men over party policy and leadership of the ILGWU.

59. *Ibid.*, September 27, 1910, 1; October 6, 1910, 4.
60. The Poale Zion platform stated that both socialism and Zionism were reactions to the intolerable conditions in Jewish life. Its program included trade union and mutual aid activities, and affiliation with the World Zionist organization. Zhitlowsky was a leading intellectual revolutionary and proponent of Jewish nationalism. See chapter 3 in Michels.
61. *New York Call*, September 23, 1910, 1.
62. Gorenstein, 224.
63. *Daily Forward*, November 1, 1910, 4–6.
64. Louis B. Boudin, "Milwaukee and New York," *New York Call*, November 24, 1910, 6.
65. *New York Call*, October 25, 1910, 1. William Travers Jerome served as district attorney in the first decade of the twentieth century; William Randolph Hearst was the publisher of the *New York Journal* and *American* and candidate for mayor in 1905 and governor in 1906; William J. Gaynor was elected mayor of New York in 1909. At this time, London lived at 274 East Broadway.
66. *Ibid.*, October 29, 1910, 2; November 7, 1910, 1.
67. *Ibid.*, October 29, 1910, 1.
68. *Ibid.*, November 7, 1910, 2.
69. *Ibid.*, October 31, 1910, 4.
70. *Ibid.*, September 1, 1910, 2.
71. *Ibid.*, October 31, 1910, 1. Born in the United States, Goldfogle, a German Reform Jew and lawyer, was the protégé of John F. Ahearn, the Tammany boss in the Fourth Assembly District. First elected to Congress in 1901, he served seven terms. Ahearn sought to woo Jewish voters in the predominately Jewish Fourth District running Jewish candidates and making them part of the organization. Thomas M. Henderson. *Tammany Hall and the New Immigrant* (New York: Arno Press, 1976). For a biographical sketch of Goldfogle, see Jacob Magidoff, *Der Spiegle fun der East Side* (New York: Author, 1923), 117–25.
72. *Daily Forward*, November 3, 1910, 4.
73. *Ibid.*, November 2, 1910, 4; November 3, 1910, 4; *New York Call*, November 8, 1910, 6. See also the *Appeal to Reason*, October 22, 1910, 2, a Socialist weekly for similar criticism of Goldfogle's record. The *New York Evening Post*, a nonsocialist paper, called Goldfogle a typical Tammany Hall officeholder, useless in Washington. As quoted in the *New York Call*, November 7, 1910, 2. The *New York Evening Journal* during the 1904 campaign asked "What impression is such a man apt to make upon his fellow citizens in Congress? How can a Congressman deficient mentally and physically be of use in fighting the battle that requires brain, character, and the respect of other men?" As quoted in Hillquit, 114.
74. The Independent League was a reformist organization.
75. H. Rogoff, 57.
76. *New York Call*, October 25, 1910, 1.
77. *Ibid.*, November 9, 1910, 2.
78. *Daily Forward*, November 2, 1910, 1; November 3, 1910, 1; November 7, 1910, 1; *New York Call*, November 7, 1910, 1.
79. *New York Call*, October 25, 1910, 1; *Daily Forward*, November 4, 1910, 1; November 5, 1910, 1.
80. *New York Call*, November 5, 1910, 1.
81. *Ibid.*, October 25, 1910, 1.
82. *Ibid.*, November 2, 1910, 1; November 5, 1910, 1; November 7, 1910, 1; *Daily Forward*, November 2, 1910, 1. According to the *Forward*'s canvass, a majority of the voters supported London.
83. *New York Call*, November 5, 1910, 1.
84. *New York Call*, November 8, 1910, 1. The *Call*'s headline, on November 8, was "Tammany Uses Money to Beat Meyer London."
85. *Ibid.*, November 1, 1910, 5; November 2, 1910, 5; November 3, 1910, 5; November 4, 1910, 6; November 5, 1910, 5; November 7, 1910, 1. Detailed instructions were issued to those serving as watchers in the *Call* on November 8, 1910, 2.
86. *Daily Forward*, November 2, 1910, 1.
87. *Ibid.*, November 1, 1910.
88. *Ibid.*, November 5, 1910, 5.
89. *New York Call*, November 8, 1910, 6.
90. Henry M. Goldfogle (Democrat) 4,606, 45.89 percent of the whole vote
Jacob W. Block (Republican) 1,850, 18.43 percent of the whole vote
Meyer London (Socialist) 3,322, 33.09 percent of the whole vote
Official Canvass of the Votes Cast in New York County, December 31, 1910, 57–58. The Socialist Labor Party did not have a candidate. See Hertz, 136.
91. *New York Call*, November 9, 1910, 1–2.
92. *Ibid., Daily Forward*, November 9, 1910, 1; November 10, 1910, 4. The *Forward* criticized the "kosher" Jews who allied themselves with Tammany. Thus, the Jewish quarter could not blame anti-Semites for London's defeat.
93. Boudin, "Milwaukee and New York," 6.
94. Danish, Max H., "The Campaign in the Ninth," *New York Call*, November 29, 1910, 6.
95. Muzik, "Victor L. Berger: A Biography" (PhD Diss., Northwestern University, 1960), 206.
96. *Official Canvass of the Votes Cast in New York County*, December 31, 1911, 17–18.
97. Kipnis, 358.
98. *Ibid.*, 346; Bell, 283.
99. *New York Call*, August 27, 1912, 2.
100. *Ibid.*, November 9, 1910, 1. The legislature enlarged the district by including all of the Fourth and parts of the Second, Sixth and Eighth assembly districts. The Ninth now became the Twelfth Congressional District. Epstein, *Profiles*, 172; Peter Kenneth Ewald, "Congressional Apportionment and New York State" (PhD. diss., New York University, 1955), 268; see the *Legislative Manual of the State of New York, 1912*, 355–56, for a description of the district.
101. *New York Call*, October 8, 1912, 3. Dr. Henry Moskowitz was the head worker at the Madison House Settlement. He played an important role during the Cloakmakers' Strike of 1910.

See chapter 2. For a more detailed account of Moskowitz, see J. Salwyn Schapiro, "Henry Moskowitz: A Social Reformer in Politics," *Outlook* 102 (October 26, 1912), 446–49.

102. *New York Call*, October 12, 1912, 5.

103. *Ibid.*, October 16, 1912, 3.

104. London used a campaign leaflet containing a facsimile of Gompers' letter of endorsement. "Campaign Leaflets," London Papers. See chapter 3 for discussion of Gompers' letter.

105. Editorial in the *Ladies' Garment Worker* 3 (November 1912), 1–2.

106. *New York Call*, October 12, 1912, 5. Other labor organizations that endorsed and enthusiastically supported London's campaign were the United Hebrew Trades, the Children's Jacket Makers' Union, the Brotherhood of Tailors, the Reefer Makers' Union, the Singer Sewing Machine Agents' Union, Bakers' Union Local 100, the United Garment Workers, the Mineral Workers' Union, the Ladies' Waist Makers' Union, the Women's Trade Union League, the International Painters' and Paperhangers' Union, the Vest Makers' Union, the Neckwear Makers' Union, the Dry Good Clerks' Union and the Workmen's Circle. *Ibid.*, October 13, 1912, 3; October 15, 1912, 3; October 16, 1912, 3; October 18, 1912, 5; October 19, 1912, 2; October 26, 1912, 2.

107. *Ibid.*, October 19, 1912, 4; October 24, 1912, 2; October 28, 1912, 1; October 31, 1912, 1; November 1, 1912, 3.

108. See chapter 3.

109. *New York Call*, September 27, 1912, 5. A Dr. James had been appointed by the City Executive Committee as its representative to the East Side Campaign Committee. He was later replaced by I. Sackin. *Ibid.*, October 12, 1912, 5.

110. *Ibid.*, October 28, 1912, 5.

111. *Ibid.*, October 16, 1912, 3. London repeated this theme on other occasions. See the *New York Call*, September 17, 1912, 3, and October 19, 1912, 2.

112. H. Wayne Morgan, *Eugene V. Debs: Socialist for President* (Syracuse, NY: Syracuse University Press, 1962), 129.

113. *New York Call*, October 28, 1912, 1.

114. *Ibid.*, October 15, 1912, 1.

115. *Ibid.*, October 17, 1912, 2; October 19, 1912, 2; October 28, 1912, 1.

116. *New York Call*, October 24, 1912, 2.

117. *Ibid.*, October 22, 1912, 1.

118. *Ibid.*, October 28, 1912, 2; October 29, 1912, 2.

119. October 28, 1912, 1.

120. *Daily Forward*, November 1, 1912, 12–15; November 2, 1912, 15; November 3, 1912, 10.

121. *Ibid.*, October 30, 1912, 1. Appeals of a similar vein appeared in the *Daily Forward*, November 3, 1912, 1, and November 4, 1912, 4.

122. *New York Call*, October 29, 1912, 1. The headline in the *Call* read "Politicians in Midnight Session Prepare to Combine against London."

123. Henry Goldfogle (Democrat) 4,592, 39.42 percent of the whole vote

Alexander Wolf (Republican) 839, 7.18 percent of the whole vote

Meyer London (Socialist) 3,646, 31.22 percent of the whole vote

Henry Moskowitz (Progressive) 2,602, 22.18 percent of the whole vote

See *Official Canvass of the Votes Cast in New York County*, December 31, 1912, 57.

124. *New York Call*, November 6, 1912, 1–2; November 7, 1912, 2; *Daily Forward*, November 6, 1912, 1; November 6, 1912, 4; November 7, 1912, 1. See also John Wall, "Meyer London Elected!" *New York Call*, November 11, 1912, 6; letter to the editor from Saul Horowitz, ibid., November 18, 1912, 4; Affidavit of Morris Schuman, November 12, 1912, London Papers; Emanuel Julius, "Fair Count of Votes," *New York Call*, October 17, 1914, 1; and the *American Socialist*, December 4, 1915, 2, for descriptions of election irregularities.

125. *New York Call*, November 7, 1912, 2.

126. *Socialist Party Minute Books, Executive Committee Local New York*, November 6, 1912, MB 43, Folder 1, 63.

127. *New York Sun*, November 5, 1914, 6.

128. *New York Call*, June 9, 1913, 1.

129. *New York Call*, October 8, 1913, 1; October 25, 1913, 2.

130. *Ibid.* It was at this time that the Protocol was under attack. See chapter 2.

131. *Official Canvass of the Votes Cast in New York County*, December 31, 1911, 17–18.

132. Bell, 310.

Chapter 4

1. See chapter 2 for discussion of the "Hourwich affair."

2. ILGWU, *Proceedings of the Thirteenth Annual Convention*, October 16–28, 1916, 5, 132.

3. Epstein, *Profiles of Eleven*, 149.

4. Rischin, 235.

5. ILGWU, *Proceedings 1914*, 186. No one was allowed in the hall during the debate except the delegates. London was allowed to remain since he was an officer of the International.

6. *Ibid.*, 204–5.

7. Louis Levine states that they declined on the ground that they needed a rest. Criticism of their role in the Hourwich struggle, however, was probably the decisive factor in the decision. Levine, 273.

8. ILGWU, *Proceedings 1914*, 234.

9. The exact date of Hillquit's appointment is uncertain. In the report of the General Executive Board to the convention in 1916, there is reference to Hillquit serving as counsel for the International during the two years from the last convention. See ILGWU, *Proceedings 1916*, 5.

10. ILGWU, *Minutes of the Executive Board of the International Ladies' Garment Workers' Union*, July 1, 1914, 146.

11. *New York Call*, July 4, 1914, 1.

12. *Ibid.*, July 6, 1914, 1.

13. *Ibid.*, July 13, 1914, 2.
14. *Ibid.*, July 4, 1914, 1.
15. *Ibid.*, July 13, 1914, 1.
16. ILGWU, *Proceedings 1914*, 227–29; *Minutes of the Executive Board*, July 1, 1914, 146.
17. Sally Miller, *Victor L. Berger and the Promise of Constructive Socialism, 1910–1920* (Westport, CT: Greenwood, 1973); 152; Oscar Ameringer, *If You Don't Weaken* (New York: Henry Holt, 1940), 300. Ameringer states incorrectly that London left the day before the others for Europe. It was Russell and not London who preceded the others.
18. *Socialist Party Minute Books, Executive Committee of Local New York*, July 10, 1914, MB 47, Folder 1, 3. The committee also planned to secure Eugene Debs for two meetings at Carnegie Hall and in the Twelfth District.
19. *Socialist Party Minute Books, Central Committee of Local New York*, September 26, 1914, MB 44, Folder 1, 128. The campaign committee reported on October 24 "that the work is going splendidly" and London would be elected. *Ibid.*, October 24, 1914, MB 44, Folder 1, 131.
20. The members were Benjamin Schlesinger, president of the ILGWU; Max Pine, a former secretary of the United Hebrew Trades; Dr. B. Rosenblatt, secretary of the Workmen's Circle; J. B. Salutsky of the Jewish Socialist Federation; and Meyer Gillis who had handled funds in earlier campaigns. *New York Call*, October 1, 1914, 4. The Socialists opened campaign headquarters at 175 East Broadway on October 9. Additional branches were opened at 52 Pine Street, 48 Jefferson Street, 285 Madison Street, and 243 East Broadway. *Ibid.*, October 9, 1914, 1.
21. *Ibid.*, October 3, 1914, 1.
22. *Ibid.*, November 2, 1914, 1; Epstein, *Jewish Labor*, 59.
23. ILGWU *Proceedings of Annual Convention 1916*, 59. Metz drew his full salary while on leave from his union duties. *New York Call*, October 19, 1914, 1.
24. *New York Call*, October 13, 1914, 3; October 17, 1914, 3. Among the other unions which endorsed London's candidacy were the United Garment Workers, the Reefer Makers, the Brotherhood of Tailors, the Iron Workers, Ladies' Tailors Local 38, the Neckwear Makers, Shirtmakers Local 23, the International Painters' and Paperhangers' Union, Pressers' Local 35, the Capmakers and Blockers, Bakers' Union Local 100, Vest Makers, and the White Goods Workers. *Ibid.*, November 2, 1914, 1; *Daily Forward*, November 1, 1914, 1.
25. London ads appealed to voters of all parties. Rischin, 235. See also *Daily Forward* for October 1914.
26. *New York Post*, November 4, 1914, 1; *New York Tribune*, November 5, 1914, 6.
27. *New York Call*, October 30, 1914.
28. *Ibid.*, October 21, 1914, 1; October 24, 1914, 1; October 29, 1914, 1; November 2, 1914, 1; *Daily Forward*, October 27, 1914, 4; October 29, 1914, 4; October 31, 1914, 1; A. Liesin, "Der kongressional campayn oifn New Yorker east side," *Zukunft* 19 (November 1914): 1082–88.
29. *New York Evening Journal*, November 2, 1914, 16. Both the *Call* and the *Forward* printed this editorial. *New York Call*, November 3, 1914, 2; *Daily Forward*, November 3, 1914, 8.
30. *Daily Forward*, October 27, 1914, 4; H. Rogoff, 174–75.
31. *New York Call*, October 29, 1914, 1; November 3, 1914, 1; *Daily Forward*, October 29, 1914, 1.
32. *Daily Forward*, October 27, 1914, 4; October 29, 1914, 1; October 30, 1914, 1; November 1, 1914, 1; November 2, 1914, 1.
33. *Socialist Party Minute Books, Executive Committee Local New York*, October 12, 1914, MB 7, Folder 1, 41–43.
34. *New York Call*, October 17, 1914, 1.
35. *Ibid.*, October 19, 1914, 1.
36. *Ibid.*, October 28, 1914, 3; October 29, 1914, 1; November 3, 1914, 1.
37. *Ibid.*, October 29, 1914, 1.
38. *New York Tribune*, November 2, 1914, 12; November 3, 1914, 6.
39. *New York Call*, October 31, 1914, 6; November 3, 1914, 1; Charles Edward Russell, "The Great Duty of the Day," *New York Call*, November 2, 1914, 3.
40. *Daily Forward*, November 2, 1914, 1; November 4, 1914, 4.
41. *New York Call*, October 31, 1910, 1.
42. *Ibid.*, November 2, 1914, 2; November 3, 1914, 2.
43. *Daily Forward*, November 4, 1914, 4.
44. *New York Call*, November 2, 1914, 2.
45. *Daily Forward*, October 24, 1914, 2; October 25, 1914, 2; October 26, 1914, 2; October 27, 1914, 6–7; October 29, 1914, 7–8; October 30, 1914, 7; October 31, 1914, 4; November 1, 1914, 1.
46. *New York Call*, November 3, 1914, 1. Among the unions which planned to participate were the Moving Van Drivers, Paper Cigarette Makers, Brass Bed Workers, Iron Workers, Reefer Makers, Butchers, Cabinet Makers, Bakers' Local Union 100, Cloak Operators, Neckwear Makers, Furriers, Children's Jacket Makers, Cloak Pressers, Skirt Makers, Seltzer Workers, Basters' Union and Ladies' Tailors' Union Local 33.
47. *Daily Forward*, November 4, 1914, 4.
48. *New York World*, November 4, 1914, 2.
49. *New York Call*, November 4, 1914, 2. *Tageblatt* (1885–1928) supported the Tammany organization.
50. *New York Call*, November 5, 1914, 1; H. Rogoff, 58–59; Sanders, 353.
51. *Daily Forward*, November 4, 1914, 1.
52. *New York Call*, November 5, 1914, 2.
53. *Ibid.*, November 5, 1914, 1; *Daily Forward*, November 4, 1914, 1; H. Rogoff, 59; *American Socialist*, December 4, 1915, 2.
54. *American Socialist*, November 4, 1914, 1.
55. *New York Call*, November 4, 1914, 1; November 5, 1914, 1.
56. *Ibid.*, November 4, 1914, 1.
57. *Ibid.*, November 5, 1914, 1. London later

stated that the count was not completed until 8:30 in the morning. *New York Post*, November 4, 1914, 1.

58. *New York Sun*, November 5, 1914, 6; *Milwaukee Leader*, November 4, 1914, 1; Epstein, *Profiles*, 173.

59. *New York World*, November 4, 1914, 2; *New York Press*, November 4, 1914, 2; *New York Sun*, November 4, 1914, 2; *New York American*, November 4, 1914, 3.

60. *New York Times*, November 5, 1914, 6. The *Call* described how newspapermen obtained returns. Some three hundred newspapermen gathered at Police Headquarters where the vote was tabulated. Policemen received the returns by telephone from each police precinct in the city. The returns were written on slips, then copied on charts and finally sent out on the ticker service. These slips, however, did not include the votes of Socialist candidates. Thus city newspapermen paid no attention to Socialist candidates. *New York Call*, November 5, 1914, 2.

61. *Daily Forward*, November 4, 1914, 1, 4.

62. *New York Post*, November 4, 1914, 1.

63. *New York Times*, November 5, 1914, 4–5; *New York World*, November 5, 1914, 1; *New York Press*, November 5, 1914, 1, 6; *New York Tribune*, November 5, 1914, 1, 4.

64. Henry Goldfogle (Democrat) 4,947, 37.98 percent of the whole vote
Meyer London (Socialist) 5,969, 47.98 percent of the whole vote
Benjamin Borowsky (Republican) 1,133, 8.67 percent of the whole vote
See *Official Canvass of the Votes Cast in New York County*, December 31, 1914, 58–59.

65. Fine, 228.

66. *New York Post*, November 4, 1914, 1. See also the *Appeal to Reason*, November 14, 1914, 1; *New York Press*, November 5, 1914, 5.

67. *New York Call*, November 6, 1914, 1. Goldfogle told the *New York World*, "It was all a matter of who got the most votes. London got more than I." *New York World*, November 5, 1914, 6. Charles F. Murphy expressed displeasure with the defeat of Goldfogle. The Socialists, he stated, had moved into the Twelfth in order to accomplish it. *New York Tribune*, November 5, 1914, 6.

68. *New York Tribune*, November 5, 1914, 1; *New York Tribune*, November 5, 1914, 6.

69. *New York Times*, November 5, 1914, 6; *New York Tribune*, November 5, 1914, 6.

70. As quoted in H. Rogoff, 296.

71. *New York Call*, November 5, 1914, 1; November 7, 1914, 6.

72. *Daily Forward*, November 4, 1914, 1, 4; November 6, 1914, 4.

73. "A Victory for Socialism and the Worker," *Ladies' Garment Worker* 5 (December 1914), 12–13. *Appeal to Reason* declared that American Socialists were "exceedingly fortunate" with London's election. Although he would not do much as one Socialist against 434 "defenders of capitalism," what he attempted to accomplish would "undoubtedly result in a sweeping victory" in the congressional elections of 1916. *Appeal to Reason*, November 14, 1914, 1; November 21, 1914, 3. Victor Berger's paper, the *Milwaukee Leader*, commented that London's election was highly encouraging particularly in view of the reactionary wave sweeping the country. Editorial from the *Milwaukee Leader* reprinted in the *American Socialist*, November 14, 1914, 2.

74. *New York Tribune*, November 5, 1914, 8; November 6, 1914, 6; *New York Post*, November 5, 1914, 8.

75. *New York Times*, November 6, 1914, 10. For further editorial comment see the *New York American*, November 6, 1914, 18; *New York Sun*, November 6, 1914, 8; *Der Tag*, November 11, 1914, 4.

76. *Ibid.*, November 5, 1914, 2.

77. *New York Call*, November 6, 1914, 1; *New York Times*, November 5, 1914, 6; *New York World*, November 5, 1914, 6; *New York Post*, November 4, 1914, 1; *New York American*, November 5, 1914, 4. London's interview with the *Call* also appeared in the *Milwaukee Leader*, November 5, 1914, 1; the *American Socialist*, November 14, 1914, 2, and the *Appeal to Reason*, November 14, 1914, 1.

78. *New York Post*, November 4, 1914, 1.

79. *New York American*, November 5, 1914, 4; *New York Call*, November 6, 1914, 1.

80. *Der Tag*, November 5, 1914, 2; *New York American*, November 4, 1914, 4.

81. *New York World*, November 8, 1914, E6.

82. *New York Call*, November 5, 1914, 2; *American Socialist*, November 14, 1914, 2; *Appeal to Reason*, November 14, 1914, 1; *New York Times*, November 5, 1914, 6.

83. *New York Times*, November 9, 1914, 1.

84. *New York Call*, November 9, 1914, 1. See also the *New York World*, November 9, 1914, 4; *New York Post*, November 9, 1914, 14.

85. *New York Call*, November 9, 1914, 1. Claude G. Bowers, a columnist for the *Terre Haute Tribune*, in a letter to his friend Eugene Debs, described the meeting as the largest, most enthusiastic, and impressive political gathering he ever attended." An enthused Debs warmly praised London and described him "as bright and interesting chap as you have met in many a day." Eugene V. Debs to Claude G. Bowers, December 15, 1914, *Letters of Eugene V. Debs*, ed. by J. Robert Constantine (Urbana: University of Illinois, 1990), 2:115.

86. During a speech to the White Good Workers' Union at Cooper Union on November 6, London, the *Call* reported, brought laughter from three thousand girls when he remarked "jokingly" that when he entered Congress he would seek a law prohibiting union men from marrying working girls who could not show a union card. The *New York World Record* failed to see any humor in London's statement. The *World's* headline read "None But Union Girls May Wed. Meyer London, America's Only Socialist Tells 'Em So." In an editorial, the *World*

declared that if London's remarks "were a fair measure of his intelligence, the Socialist party would have less to congratulate itself on Meyer London's election." In an editorial directed to London on November 12, the *New York Call* defended London, but warned him that Socialists who had been elected to office should not engage in "hasty speech." See *New York Call*, November 7, 1914, 3; "A Warning to Meyer London," 1914, 6; *New York World*, November 7, 1914, 1; November 8, 1914, E7.

87. *New York World*, November 10, 1914, 8. The reception "immensely pleased" London. It impressed him with the magnitude of his task. "I fervently hope," he told the *Call*, "that I will be physically capable of handling the tremendous job." *New York Call*, November 10, 1914, 3.

88. *Ibid.*, November 6, 1914, 2.

Chapter 5

1. Quoted in William English Walling, ed., *Socialists and the War* (New York: Rand School of Social Sciences, 1915), 212–13.

2. Bell, 313.

3. *Congressional Record*, 64th Congress, 1st Sess., 1, 216. Other than fragmentary statements, this is the only detailed discussion of the war by London that this writer could find for the period from August 1914 to January 1916.

4. James Weinstein in *The Decline of Socialism in America, 1912–1925* (New York: Monthly Review Press, 1967), 120–21, points out that at first American Socialists tended to "excuse" European Socialists for their support of the war. This tendency, he notes, continued among the leaders of the right and center, although the party eventually associated itself with anti-war leaders in Europe, such as Karl Liebknecht.

5. Among these were Liebknecht and Kier Hardie, the founder of the British Labor Party.

6. Meyer London, "There Must Be an End," *The Masses*, May 18, 1915, 18.

7. *New York Call*, June 22, 1915.

8. *Congressional Record*, 64th Congress, 1st Sess., 1, 216.

9. London, "There Must Be an End," 18.

10. *New York Call*, February 15, 1915, 3, 11.

11. *Ibid.*, December 8, 1914, 3.

12. *Ibid.*, February 21, 1915, 2:1.

13. The National Executive Committee had also worked out a comprehensive peace plan. See Weinstein, 121, and Austin Van der Slice, *International Labor, Diplomacy, and Peace, 1914–1919* (Philadelphia: University of Pennsylvania Press, 1941), 142–44.

14. Shannon, 85–86.

15. *New York Call*, February 21, 1915, 2:9.

16. Shannon, 88; H. Rogoff, 63.

17. London, "There Must Be an End," 18.

18. *New York World*, November 8, 1914, 6.

19. *New York Call*, February 21, 1915, 2:9; June 6, 1915, 3; Shannon, 87.

20. Rappaport, 150.

21. Arthur S. Link, *Woodrow Wilson and the Progressive Era, 1910–1917* (New York: Harper and Row, 1954), 174–79.

22. *New York Call*, April 16, 1915, 1.

23. *New York Times*, April 16, 1915, 4.

24. The resolution called upon organized labor in the United States to consider immediately a general strike in those industries producing munitions and food supplies. It also called for the creation of a labor delegation which would visit the labor centers of the belligerents to discuss with them the best method of ending the war. *New York Call*, April 16, 1915, 1.

25. Shannon, 89.

26. Link, *Woodrow Wilson and the Progressive Era*, 179.

27. *New York Times*, January 31, 1916, 4.

28. *New York Call*, June 6, 1915, 3.

29. *Ibid.*, June 10, 1915, 3.

30. The National Security League was organized by 150 public leaders who met in New York on December 1, 1914. Its avowed objective was to prepare the United States for a possible war with Germany. Link, *Woodrow Wilson and the Progressive Era*, 177.

31. *New York Times*, June 16, 1915, 4.

32. *New York Call*, June 20, 1915, 1.

33. *Ibid.*, June 22, 1915, 2; *New York Times*, June 22, 1915, 8.

34. *New York Call*, July 1, 1915, 1.

35. *American Socialist*, July 31, 1915, 1.

36. *Ibid.*, July 10, 1915, 1.

37. London's busy schedule forced him to inform Local New York that he could not speak at an anti-war meeting. He wrote the local that he was "doing more than his share of the work." *Socialist Party Minute Books, Third and Tenth assembly districts of Local New York*, July 1, 1915, MB 46.

38. *New York Call*, October 17, 1915, 8.

39. Arthur S. Link, *Wilson: Confusions and Crises, 1915–1916* (Princeton, NJ: Princeton University Press, 1964), 4: 20–25.

40. *New York Call*, November 17, 1915, 3.

41. *American Socialist*, December 4, 1915, 4.

42. Meyer London, "*Di Vahl Resultaten un di Brenendste Frage oif der Tagsordenung,*" *Zukunft* 20 (December 1915), 1067–73.

43. *American Socialist*, December 4, 1915, 1.

44. *New York Call*, November 29, 1915, 1–2.

45. Alexander Trachtenberg, *American Socialists and the War* (New York: Rand School of Social Sciences, 1917), 21.

46. *New York Times*, April 19, 1915.

47. *Ibid.*, September 5, 1915, 2:3. The Jewish Workers National Conference also urged London to support a resolution in the House demanding that the belligerents grant Jews equal rights with other citizens at the conclusion of the war. *New York Call*, September 2, 1915, 3.

48. Rappaport, 239.

49. *New York Call*, January 20, 1915, 1; January 21, 1915, 2. London met with Frank P. Walsh,

chairman of the United States Commission on Industrial Relations, who informed him that a federal investigation had already started. Due to a busy schedule London could not go to Chrome, but he sent one of his congressional secretaries as his personal representative.

50. *New York Times*, May 14, 1915, 22. The eight were accused of the murder of Herman Leibovitz, a strikebreaker, during the garment strike of 1910. *Ibid.*, October 6, 1915, 8. See also Levine, 287–88.

51. *New York Call*, June 13, 1915, 5; M. H. Danish, "Monthly News and Events," *Ladies' Garment Worker* 6 (July 1915), 11. The eight union officials were acquitted after a trial in the Criminal Branch of the Supreme Court of New York. See *New York Times*, October 6, 1915, 8; October 8, 1915, 20; October 9, 1915, 15.

52. Paul H. Douglas and Aaron Director, *The Problem of Unemployment* (New York: Houghton, 1934), 26–33. London stated that estimates of unemployment varied from one million to five million. *New York Times*, February 21, 1915, 5:19.

53. The American Association for Labor Legislation was founded in 1906 to promote better labor legislation and stricter enforcement of existing laws. It played a major role in the campaigns for unemployment reform and health insurance. Irwin Yellowitz, "The Origins of Unemployment Reform in the United States," *Labor History* 9, no. 3 (Fall 1968): 338–60.

54. *New York Call*, December 29, 1914, 1.

55. *Ibid.* See also Ibid., January 10, 1915, 5, and Meyer London, "The Nation and the Problem of Unemployment," *American Labor Legislative Review* 5 (June 1915), 446–49.

56. *New York Call*, January 19, 1915, 1.

57. *Ibid.*, January 21, 1915, 1.

58. *Ibid.*, February 9, 1915, 1–2.

59. *Ibid.*, February 12, 1915, 2; *American Socialist*, February 20, 1915, 1.

60. *New York Times*, February 13, 1915, 11.

61. *New York Call*, February 13, 1915, 1. The *New York Call* and the *New York Times* gave slightly different versions of the events at this point. The *Times*, which gave a fuller report, stated that London was "heckled" from the crowd by a group of Wobblies who stood near the platform. Socialists in the crowd, the *Times* went on, shouted that he should ignore them. But London replied that he was elected to represent them along with the other people in Congress and would therefore answer them. *New York Times*, February 13, 1915, 11. The *Call* reported that London was interrupted by a young man in the audience "who suffered from anarchistic views." *New York Call*, February 13, 1915, 1.

62. *New York Times*, February 13, 1915, 11.

63. *Ibid.*, February 21, 1915, 5, 19. London expressed virtually the same views in an article in *The Masses*. Meyer London, "The Unemployed," *The Masses*, (April 1915): 20–21.

64. Weinstein, 60–61.

65. *New York Times*, March 1, 1915, 4; *New York Call*, March 1, 1915, 2.

66. *Ibid.*, March 8, 1915, 2; *American Socialist*, March 20, 1915, 1. London spoke in Rochester, New York on April 14. *New York Call*, April 14, 1915, 2.

67. *Ibid.*, June 8, 1915, 1.

68. *Ibid.*, July 19, 1915, 2; *New York Times*, July 19, 1915, 6.

69. *Ibid.*, August 17, 1915, 20.

70. Meyer London, "The Federal Suffrage Amendment," ibid., October 17, 1915, 2:14.

71. See *New York Call*, October 1915.

72. *Ibid.*, October 18, 1915, 1; October 23, 1915, 8. London also shared the platform with Debs on October 18, 20, and 23. *Socialist Party Minute Books, Executive Committee Local New York*, September 22, 1915, MB 47, Folder 1, 232.

73. *New York Times*, November 3, 1915, 1; November 4, 1915, 1.

74. *New York Call*, November 4, 1915, 1.

75. London, "Di Vahl Resultaten," 1,067.

Chapter 6

1. It is not exactly clear when London arrived in Washington. He did, however, speak to a group of Washington Socialists on Saturday, December 4. *New York Call*, December 9, 1915, 2; *American Socialist*, December 18, 1915, 2. London received an annual congressional salary of $7,500, the equivalent of $50,000 in current dollars. This represented a boost to the family's financial situation.

2. *New York Call*, December 1, 1915, 2. Shortly after London's election, the *Call* had speculated about London's committee assignments. The socialist daily predicted that the Democrats would not give London a seat on any important committee. They would "bury" him on a committee where he would not be able to speak out on behalf of the workers or the Socialist Party. He would be placed on the Committee of Disposition of Useless Executive Papers. *New York Call*, February 4, 1915, 3.

3. *Ibid.*, December 9, 1915, 1; *American Socialist*, December 18, 1915, 2.

4. *New York Call*, December 9, 1915, 1; May 1, 1916, 9; *Congressional Record*, 64th Congress, 1st Sess., 12. The motion calling for adoption of the rules was amended without objection.

5. The *New York Call* reported later that a "powerful section" of Democrats in the House, fearful of giving a Socialist the prestige which went with membership on the Immigration Committee, had defeated efforts to place London there. *New York Call*, May 1, 1916, 9.

6. *Congressional Record*, 64th Congress, 1st Sess., 241; *American Socialist*, December 18, 1915, 2.

7. *New York Call*, December 9, 1915, 1. Melech Epstein states that for tactical reasons London agreed to follow the Democratic caucus

Notes — Chapter 6

in minor matters. Otherwise, he would not have been recognized by the Speaker of the House or congressional committees. Epstein, *Profiles*, 74. This writer has been unable to discover any evidence that would substantiate Epstein's statement. London did not, for example, support Champ Clark for Speaker nor did he vote with the Democrats on the adoption of the House rules.

8. "The Representative with a Million Constituents," 281; Tattler, 478; Laurence Todd, "The Lone Congressman," *Advance* 10–11 (June 1926): 2; Epstein, *Profiles*, 80. See Muzik, 210–11, for a description of Victor Berger's work schedule.

9. *New York Call*, November 29, 1915, 2. There seems to have been some opposition within Local New York in regard to providing secretarial help for London. The Executive Committee, therefore, decided shortly after the election to combine the office of the East Side organizer and secretary to London. *Socialist Party Minute Books, Executive Committee*, November 30, 1914, MB 47, Folder 1, 58–60.

10. *New York Call*, December 25, 1916, 6.

11. *Ibid.*, February 21, 1916, 1.

12. *Congressional Record*, 64th Congress, 1st Sess., 32.

13. *Ibid.*, 6. A contest developed, however, over adoption of the House rules. Representative Mann moved to commit the resolution to a select committee chosen by the Speaker. The Republicans sought to take political advantage of an attempt by several Democrats led by Charles A. Lindbergh of Minnesota to restrict the power of the Rules Committee. London voted with these progressive Democrats and Republicans, but Mann's motion was defeated 209 to 194. A motion to accept the rules was then adopted. *Ibid.*, 9–12; *New York Call*, December 9, 1915, 1; *American Socialist*, December 18, 1915, 2.

14. Link, *Wilson: Confusions and Crises*, 4:34–37.

15. *New York Call*, December 8, 1915, 1; December 12, 1915, 1; *American Socialist*, December 18, 1915, 1.

16. Meyer London, "Democrats Join Republicans in Betrayal of Nation to Militarism," *American Socialist*, December 1915, 1.

17. Link, *Wilson: Confusions and Crises*, 4:17–40.

18. Arthur S. Link, *Wilson: Campaigns for Progressivism and Peace, 1916–1917* (Princeton, NJ: Princeton University Press, 1965), 5:102–4.

19. *New York Evening World*, December 17, 1915, 7.

20. *Congressional Record*, 64th Congress, 1st Sess., 358; *New York Call*, December 17, 1915, 1.

21. *New York Times*, December 17, 1915, 6. London's decision to support the war tax measure brought sharp criticism from the Socialist Labor Party's official organ, the *New Yorker Volkszeitung*. The *Volkszeitung* accused London of having committed a "grave error" in voting for the bill. His vote was contrary to the constitutional amendment adopted by the Socialist Party making mandatory the expulsion of any elected Socialist who voted for either war or war credits. Louis B. Boudin, "Socialist Congressional Responsibility," *New Review* 4 (January 1916): 26–27.

22. *New York Call*, December 20, 1915, 1. The *Call* reported that although Congress had been in session for only about two weeks, London had obtained the reputation in the House and "its official and semi-official world" as a student of history and economics. In addition, his fellow congressmen frequently sought information from him on labor legislation, the international situation and numerous other issues.

23. *Ibid.*, December 22, 1915, 1.

24. London made a similar statement during an interview with a reporter from the *Chicago Tribune* shortly after the congressional session opened. See *Milwaukee Leader*, December 15, 1915, 3; *New York Call*, December 19, 1915, 14; *Appeal to Reason*, December 18, 1915, 1.

25. *New York Times*, December 23, 1915, 14; *New York Call*, December 23, 1915, 1. *Appeal to Reason*, January 15, 1916, 5.

26. *New York Call*, December 24, 1915, 2.

27. The *Brooklyn Eagle* and the *New York World* praised London for his reports. The *Eagle* stated, "On behalf of the calm thinkers of the United States we are inclined to congratulate London. It is not a bad thing to have in the House ... one man standing for a considerable minority of American thought and of the American electorate. And though we may never agree with London again, his courage and poise have to be conceded by all fair minded persons." As quoted in the *New York Call*, December 31, 1915, 4. The *World* stated London's desire to meet his constituents once a month "must be commended." Perhaps more remarkable "than the plan of the Congressman, who is said to be first to institute regular conferences of this kind, is the interest and intelligence manifested by the voters of the East Side." The *World* noted that it was not feasible for all members of Congress to emulate London's example, but if a third did, "we should have fewer complaints of the failure of representative government." As quoted in the *American Socialist*, January 8, 1916, 1. The *American Socialist* also noted that London's colleagues were "much impressed" by his meetings. The fact that almost every newspaper in New York City published accounts of the two meetings impressed congressmen who had remained unnoticed in the House for many years.

28. *New York Call*, December 23, 1915, 2.

29. See chapter 6.

30. Although the American Socialist Party had officially taken an unequivocal position against war, disagreement existed beneath the surface. Marxist tradition was unclear on the question of war. According to Theodore Draper, Marxism was neither pro-war nor anti-war. "It began militantly pro-war; then it became anti-war; but in the event of actual war, it made the guilt of aggression, the danger to national independence,

and the relative 'progressiveness' of the opposing sides the decisive factors in determining a concrete policy." The Second International, Draper points out, had adopted resolutions against war, but had failed to agree upon a course of action in the eventuality of war. Theodore Draper, *The Roots of American Communism* (New York: Viking, 1957), 50–57.

31. *Ibid.*, 56, 59.
32. *Appeal to Reason*, December 11, 1915, 5; "A Socialist Digest," *New Review* 3 (December 15, 1915): 368–69.
33. *Milwaukee Leader*, January 20, 1916, 10.
34. Rappaport, 194–95. The *Daily Forward* had declared on December 8, 1914, that if a European monarchy attacked the United States, "we all would fight for America with ... our hearts and souls ... not out of blind patriotism, but because America has the freest institutions in the world." *Ibid.*, 178.
35. *New York Call*, January 29, 1916, 6. A letter printed in the *American Socialist* accused London of a "vicious lie." It was not true, the writer declared, that all Socialists or even a majority of Socialists would rally to their country's defense. Only the Londons and the Russells would fall for the "defense gag" when the country entered the war. The Londons in the Socialist Party "elected for any reason ... rather than because his electors are Socialists are doing more to fill that electorate with puerile and dangerous ideas than we can hope to undo." *American Socialist*, February 5, 1916, 3.
36. H. Rogoff, 102–3.
37. *New York Times*, January 31, 1916, 4.
38. *Congressional Record*, 64th Congress, 1st Sess., 3638.
39. *New York Call*, March 27, 1916, 4.
40. *Congressional Record*, 64th Congress, 1st Sess., 5021.
41. *Ibid.*, 32, 90, 228. *New York Call*, December 15, 1915, 1.
42. H. Rogoff, 66; Weinstein, 121–24.
43. *New York Call*, December 16, 1915, 1.
44. *Milwaukee Leader*, December 20, 1915, 10.
45. Louis B. Boudin, "Socialist Terms of Peace," *New Review* 4 (January 1916): 1–2. In yet another article, Boudin questioned party responsibility in conjunction with London's peace terms. There was a tendency, he wrote, due to the enthusiastic response to London's resolution, to overlook its shortcomings. London, he continued, "unceremoniously set aside" the peace program adopted by the National Committee in May 1915 and then approved in a referendum by the party membership. The question was not which peace program was the better one, but whether London could "disregard the party's solemn expression of opinion on so tremendously important a subject." This in turn was part of the greater question: "On whose responsibility does our representative in Congress act?" Boudin, "Socialist Congressional Responsibility," 4 (January 1916): 26–27.

46. *New York Call*, December 13, 1915, 1; December 23, 1915, 3; *New York Times*, December 13, 1915, 4; *American Socialist*, January 1, 1916, 2; *Appeal to Reason*, January 8, 1916, 4. London's resolution also received favorable comment in the British Parliament. *Milwaukee Leader*, December 20, 1915, 10.
47. *New York Call*, December 20, 1915, 1.
48. *Ibid.*, December 13, 1915; December 10, 1915; *New York Times*, December 13, 1915, 4.
49. *American Socialist*, December 25, 1915, 1–2; *New York Call*, December 21, 1915, 1; *Milwaukee Leader*, December 21, 1915, 1; *New York Times*, December 21, 1915, 2.
50. Walter Lanfersiek to Woodrow Wilson, December 27, 1915, 298, Woodrow Wilson Papers, Library of Congress; *New York Call*, January 20, 1916, 1; *Milwaukee Leader*, January 20, 1916, 1.
51. *Milwaukee Leader*, December 22, 1915, 8. Charles A. Maurer, the brother of James H. Maurer, sent a letter to the *Leader* in which he noted several examples where Socialists including Berger had approached the "capitalist" government in an attempt to resolve specific problems. Maurer asked if they also were "fools' errands." *New York Call*, January 24, 1916, 6.
52. Eugene V. Debs to Walter Lanfersiek, December 24, 1915, Constantine, 2:1.
53. *American Socialist*, February 5, 1916, 1; *New York Call*, January 26, 1916, 1; *Appeal to Reason*, February 5, 1916, 3. In reflecting upon the meeting some years later, Hillquit remarked that the president had looked preoccupied and tired. At first he had seemed inclined to give the Socialist delegation "a short and perfunctory hearing, but as we proceeded with our argument he became interested and animated and our interview developed into a serious and confidential conversation." The president had informed the delegation that he had considered a similar plan, but had failed to act upon it because "with the exception of the United States every neutral government was definitely committed in its sympathies to the one side or the other in the war. He hinted at the possibility of a direct offer of mediation by the ... United States and assured us that he would continue to study the question with deep and serious interest." Hillquit, 161–62; James H. Maurer, *It Can Be Done* (New York: Rand School of Social Science, 1938), 215–16; *New York Call*, January 26, 1916, 1.
54. *New York Call*, January 30, 1916, 1.
55. *American Socialist*, February 5, 1916, 1.
56. *New York Call*, February 6, 1916, 1.
57. *American Socialist*, February 19, 1916, 1.
58. *Ibid.*, *New York Call*, February 6, 1916, 8; *Appeal to Reason*, February 19, 1916, 3.
59. *American Socialist*, February 12, 1916, 1.
60. *Congressional Record*, 64th Congress, 1st Sess., 3111–3112; *American Socialist*, March 4, 1916, 2.
61. *New York Call*, February 14, 1916, 2.
62. *American Socialist*, February 19, 1916, 1.

63. Henri H. van Kol, the Socialist leader in the upper chamber of the Dutch Parliament, cabled London that the Dutch Socialist Party agreed with his proposal and would cooperate if his action met with success. The Norwegian Socialist leader, Magnus Nillissen, also cabled his party's approval as did the Social Democrats of Denmark. The Danish Socialists notified London that they had already begun to work for peace through the International Socialist Bureau. *New York Times*, February 11, 1916, 3; *New York Call*, February 13, 1916, 1; February 17, 1916, 1; *Milwaukee Leader*, February 16, 1916, 1.

64. U.S. House of Representatives Committee on Foreign Affairs, *Hearings on Congress of Neutral Nations, House Joint Resolution 38* (Washington, DC, 1916), 3. The committee met with Henry D. Flood of Virginia presiding. Due, however, to the armed ship controversy, the meeting lasted a short time.

65. *Ibid.*, 4. Among the speakers introduced by London on the first day of the abbreviated hearings were Morris Hillquit; Samuel B. Montgomery, representing the United Mine Workers; Edward Janney, chairman of the Friends General Conference; and Dr. Kasimir A. Zurizewski of the Polish National Defense Committee.

66. *Ibid.*, 4-9. One of the highlights of the morning was the statement of New York representative Isaac Siegel, the only congressman other than London to testify on behalf of the resolution. Siegel, an advocate of preparedness, called for its approval without the preamble, "as many of us undoubtedly differ with the preamble's contents and believe most wisely in a reasonably increased Army and Navy." *Ibid.*, 20-22.

67. *Ibid.*, 23 Among the other speakers were Charles Pegler, representing the Bohemian National Alliance and the Bohemian Federation of the Socialist Party; James H. Maurer; Socialist assemblyman Abraham Shiplacoff of New York, who represented the Jewish National Workmen's Committee, the United Hebrew Trades, the Amalgamated Clothing Workers and the Jewish Socialist Federation; Isaac Hourwich, spokesman for the Jewish National Worker's Alliance and the Poale Zion; Mrs. Jessie Hardie MacKaye, delegate from the Women's Peace Party; and Doctor John Szulpos, representing some seven hundred thousand Lithuanians in the United States.

68. *Ibid.*, 60. London read a cable from the secretary of the British Independent Labor Party which stated that a motion had been introduced in Parliament calling upon the government to accept the good offices of the neutrals and provide for the evacuation of invaded territory and respect for the principle of nationality. Parliament, London stated, had debated the motion on February 23. *Ibid.*, 59-60.

69. *New York Call*, March 4, 1916, 1.
70. *Ibid.*, March 6, 1916, 6.
71. *Ibid.*, March 8, 1916, 1.
72. *Ibid.*, March 9, 1916, 1.
73. *American Socialist*, March 25, 1916, 1, 3.
74. *New York Call*, March 26, 1916, 5.
75. *Ibid.*, March 27, 1916, 4.
76. Link, *Wilson: Confusion and Crises*, 4:195-216.
77. *New York Call*, March 11, 1916, 4.
78. *Ibid.*, March 12, 1916, 1.
79. *Congressional Record*, 64th Congress, 1st Sess., 4097-98; *New York Times*, March 15, 1916, 1; *New York Call*, March 15, 1916, 1.
80. *Ibid.*, March 1, 1916, 1.
81. *American Socialist*, March 25, 1916, 1. The *Appeal to Reason* commended London. He had remained true to his class and the ideals of international socialism. "Like Liebknecht's daring stand against the war in the German Reichstag, so will London's vote in the Mexican crisis make history." Local New York also endorsed his stand. *Appeal to Reason*, March 25, 1916, 4; *New York Call*, March 27, 1916, 4.
82. *Congressional Record*, 64th Congress, 1st Sess., 5020-23.
83. Link, *Wilson: Confusion and Crises*, 4:280-83.
84. *Congressional Record*, 64th Congress, 1st. Sess., 9888.
85. *Ibid.*, 9992-93. Huddleston stated that he regarded the proposed draft as conscription. *New York Times*, June 24, 1916, 1.
86. Link, *Wilson: Confusion and Crises*, 4:303-12.
87. Among the other speakers were Morris Hillquit; Allan L. Benson, the Socialist candidate for president; and Algernon Lee, director of the Rand School of Social Sciences. *New York Times*, June 25, 1916, 1:5; *New York Call*, June 25, 1916, 1.
88. Link, *Woodrow Wilson: Revolution, War and Peace*, 142-44.
89. *Ibid.*, 209-12.
90. *Ibid.*, 209-14.
91. *Congressional Record*, 64th Congress, 1st Sess., 3638.
92. *New York Call*, March 3, 1916.
93. Link, *Wilson: Confusion and Crises*, 4:192-93. The House ignored London's proposal.
94. *Congressional Record*, 64th Congress, 1st Sess., 3638-40.
95. *Ibid.*, 3720; Link, *Wilson: Confusion and Crises*, 4:192.
96. *New York Times*, March 9, 1916, 3; *New York Call*, March 9, 1916, 1-2.
97. Link, *Wilson and the Progressive Era*, 214-18.
98. *Ibid.*, 186-87; Link, *Wilson: Confusion and Crises*, 4:327-29. The Hay bill increased the Regular Army by forty thousand officers and men.
99. *Congressional Record*, 64th Congress, 1st Sess., 4353-55.
100. *Ibid.*, 4630, 4633-35.
101. *Ibid.*, 4729. A legislative deadlock developed between the two houses over the major features of the military bill. It was not until May 13 that the conference committee finally agreed upon a compromise measure. The House ap-

proved the conference report by 351 to 25. London was among those voting against the measure. Link, *Wilson: Confusion and Crises*, 4:329–32; *Congressional Record*, 64th Congress, 1st Sess., 8406.
102. *New York Call*, March 24, 1916, 1; *Appeal to Reason*, April 8, 1916, 2.
103. Link, *Wilson: Confusion and Crises*, 4:334–35.
104. *Congressional Record*, 64th Congress, 1st Sess., 8894–95.
105. *Ibid.*, 9187, 9189–90; Link, *Woodrow Wilson: Revolution, War and Peace*, 189.
106. *Ibid.*, 190. It provided for the completion of the administration's program in three years and for construction during the next year of four battleships, four battle cruisers, four cruisers, twenty destroyers, thirty submarines and a number of smaller craft.
107. *Congressional Record*, 64th Congress, 1st Sess., 12696.
108. Link, *Woodrow Wilson: Revolution, War and Peace*, 191–92.
109. *Congressional Record*, 64th Congress, 1st Sess., 8374. As a Socialist, London advocated nationalization of monopolies as well as mines, railroads, the telephone and telegraph systems. *New York Call*, January 17, 1916, 6.
110. Link, *Woodrow Wilson: Revolution, War and Peace*, 192–95. The bill increased the income tax from 1 to 2 percent, without reducing exemptions, raised the surtax to a maximum of 10 percent on incomes over $40,000, imposed a federal estate tax ranging from 1 to 5 percent on estates oven $50,000 and levied a tax of from 1 to 8 percent on the gross earnings of munitions manufacturers, making a net profit of 10 percent and over. Claude Kitchin, the chairman of the House Ways and Means Committee, estimated that the bill would raise an additional $250 million, sufficient to defray the costs of the preparedness program.
111. *Congressional Record*, 64th Congress, 1st Sess., 2030–31.
112. *Ibid.*, 10747–48.
113. *Ibid.*, 10768; *New York Call*, July 13, 1916, 5.
114. Link, *Woodrow Wilson*, 195.
115. *Ibid.*, 224–25.

Chapter 7

1. Samuel Gompers to Meyer London, April 6, 1916, vol. 217:1019 and September 1, 1916, vol. 224:385, the Papers of Samuel Gompers, the Library of Congress; hereafter cited as the Gompers Papers. Other congressmen included in the group were David J. Lewis, chairman of the House Labor Committee; John I. Nolan; Carl Van Dyke; John G. Cooper; and Edward Keating, all members of the Labor Committee, and William J. Cary, John R. Farr, Isaac R. Sherwood and John J. Carey.

2. *New York Call*, December 13, 1915, 1.
3. *Ibid.*, December 19, 1915, 3.
4. *Congressional Record*, 64th Congress, 1st sess., 2856. The resolution proposed that Congress create a Social Insurance Commission to prepare a detailed plan for the creation of a national insurance fund and to report plans and recommendations for the relief of unemployment by the employment of workers on public work projects and by creating industries maintained by the federal government. *New York Call*, February 20, 1916, 4. For a brief history of the health insurance movement, see Forrest A. Walker, "Compulsory Health Insurance, the Next Great Step in Social Legislation," *Journal of American History* 56 (September 1969): 290–304.
5. *New York Call*, February 21, 1916, 1.
6. *Ibid.*, March 10, 1916, 1.
7. *Ibid.*, March 26, 1916, 1; *American Socialist*, March 25, 1916, 5.
8. *New York Call*, March 16, 1916, 5; *Appeal to Reason*, April 1, 1916, 4.
9. Others who testified were Juliet Stuart Poyntz, director of labor research of the Rand School of Social Science; Charles S. Nesbit, commissioner of Insurance for the District of Columbia; Royal Meeker, United States commissioner of Labor Statistics; Rufus M. Potts, state insurance superintendent of Illinois; Dr. N.I. Stone, former statistician for the United States Tariff Board; and Professor Joseph P. Chamberlain of Columbia University. *New York Call*, April 7, 1916, 1; April 8, 1916, 2.
10. Samuel Gompers, "Voluntary Social Insurance vs. Compulsory," *American Federationist* 23 (May 1916): 337. The *American Federationist* published in the May, June and August issues Gompers' testimony on the resolution before the House Labor Committee under the aforementioned title. *Ibid.*, 350–51.
11. *Ibid.*, 338–43.
12. *Ibid.*, 347–48. Samuel Gompers was the principal architect of voluntarism, the belief that workers should develop strong unions to advance their economic interests rather than using political action and looking to government. Michael Rogin, "Voluntarism: The Political Functions of an Anti-Political Doctrine," in *The American Labor Movement*," ed. David Brody (New York: Harper and Row, 1971), 118.
13. *Ibid.*, 357. Gompers believed that government interference would be detrimental to the welfare of the workers. "Compulsory sickness insurance," he stated, "was based upon the theory that they [the workers] are unable to look after their own interests and the State must interpose its authority." Wage earners had to work out their own salvation and solve their problems. Samuel Gompers, "Intellectuals Please Take Note," *American Federationist* 23 (March 1916): 198–99. The socialist press extensively covered the hearings. The *New York Call* reported that London would probably win a favorable report from the House Labor Committee. Congress distributed

a thousand copies of the proceedings, but when London requested additional copies, the chairman of the House Printing Committee refused on grounds of economy. The *American Socialist* charged that Congress wanted to suppress the London hearing to keep the truth about labor legislation from the public. *New York Call*, April 12, 1916, 1; *American Socialist*, April 15, 1916, 1; June 17, 1916, 2; *Appeal to Reason*, May 20, 1916, 3.

14. *Congressional Record*, 64th Congress, 1st Sess., 6147–51. London informed John B. Andrews that Gompers' resolution "would secure almost the same result" as his resolution. Chances appeared excellent, London wrote, that Congress would approve a plan to investigate the social insurance issue. Meyer London to John B. Andrews, April 12, 1916, John B. Andrews Papers, M.P. Catherwood Library, Cornell University Library, Ithaca, New York.

15. *Ibid.*, 10248.

16. *Ibid.*, 10372; *New York Call*, July 2, 1916, 1.

17. For a copy of the resolution, see the *Congressional Record*, 64th Congress, 2nd Sess., 2650.

18. Link, *Wilson: Campaigns for Progressivism and Peace*, 5:56–57.

19. *Appeal to Reason*, January 29, 1916, 2.

20. *Congressional Record*, 64th Congress, 1st Sess., 1591–92.

21. *Ibid.*, 2035; Link, *Wilson: Campaigns for Progressivism and Peace*, 5:57.

22. *Congressional Record*, 64th Congress, 1st Sess., 10916.

23. *Ibid.*, 10913–14.

24. Link, *Wilson: Campaigns for Progressivism and Peace*, 5:57–58.

25. *Ibid.*, 58–59.

26. *New York Times*, September 15, 1916, 9. London came to the aid of thirty-four thousand federal employees in Washington when Representative William P. Borland of Missouri offered an amendment to an appropriations bill to increase their working day from seven to eight hours. London urged the House to defeat the Borland amendment. The House later rejected the amendment 176 to 44. *Congressional Record*, 64th Congress, 1st Sess., 4090–91, 4094.

27. Link, *Wilson: Campaigns for Progressivism and Peace*, 5:83–90.

28. *Congressional Record*, 64th Congress, 1st Sess., 13594. During his speech to Congress, Wilson had called for the amendment of existing legislation to require arbitration of railroad labor disputes. Link, *Wilson: Campaigns for Progressivism and Peace*, 5:89.

29. *Congressional Record*, 64th Congress, 1st Sess., 13608, 13655.

30. *Ibid.*, 13881.

31. Link, *Wilson: Campaigns for Progressivism and Peace*, 5:327. See Maldwyn Allen Jones, *American Immigration* (Chicago: University of Chicago Press, 1960), 268–70; John Higham, *Strangers in the Land, Patterns of American Nativism, 1860–1925* (New Brunswick, NJ: Rutgers University Press, 1955), 191–204.

32. Isaac A. Hourwich, "Congressman London on Immigration," *New Review* 4 (May 1916): 137–38. London's statement on Chinese and Japanese immigration represented a modified position on Oriental exclusion as expressed at the Socialist Party Convention in 1910. See chapter 3. Isaac Hourwich criticized London's statement to the Immigration Committee. The Socialist congressman, he asserted, had no authority to speak in favor of Asiatic exclusion. London had apparently hoped to appease the American Federation of Labor, but there could be no compromise, Hourwich insisted, between the position of the Stuttgart Socialist Congress and that of the AFL.

33. *New York Call*, January 22, 1916, 1.

34. *Congressional Record*, 64th Congress, 1st Sess., 4793–94.

35. *Ibid.*, 4866.

36. *Ibid.*, 64th Congress, 1st Sess., 5166–67.

37. *Ibid.*, 5193–94.

38. *New York Call*, March 31, 1916, 1.

39. Link, *Wilson: Campaigns for Progressivism and Peace*, 5:327.

40. Gompers, *American Federationist*, 3:354–55.

41. H. Rogoff, 177.

42. Raymond Jones to Meyer London, May 14, 1916, London Papers.

43. Link, *Wilson: Confusions and Crises*, 4:350–56.

44. *Congressional Record*, 64th Congress, 1st Sess., 7204, 7213–14.

45. *New York Call*, May 22, 1916, 3.

46. *Congressional Record*, 64th Congress, 1st Sess., 8894.

47. *Ibid.*, 7475.

48. *New York Times*, May 6, 1916, 9. These remarks do not appear in the *Congressional Record*. See also Louis B. Boudin, "A Disgraceful Episode," *New Review* 4 (June 1916): 174–75. Boudin criticized London for apologizing rather than insisting upon his rights. "And not only that, he actually went back on himself, denying that he even uttered the words in which he should have gloried. And all this in such a miserably abject way, that the reading of the record of this scene is sickening and disheartening beyond measure." What, Boudin asked, had happened to London? Those who had observed him in Congress knew he was not a coward. "What cowed him was undoubtedly the thought that he might be expressing doctrines which were irregular, heterodox, revolutionary from the official Socialist point of view." This, Boudin noted, may have made the situation less disgraceful for London, but had made it more so for the American Socialist Party.

49. *Congressional Record*, 64th Congress, 1st Sess., 7476–78.

50. *Ibid.*, 846.

51. *Ibid.*, 8465–66.

52. *Ibid.*, 8466–68.

53. The Puerto Rico bill was finally adopted in an amended form in early 1917. It extended

Notes—Chapter 7

American citizenship to citizens of Puerto Rico, established an elective two-house legislature and gave the legislature virtual autonomy. Julius W. Pratt, *America's Colonial Experiment* (New York: Prentice Hall, 1950), 188–90. *New York Times*, December 7, 1915, 13. In other domestic matters, London fulfilled his promise to introduce the Susan B. Anthony amendment in the House. *Congressional Record*, 64th Congress, 1st Sess., 2130. London introduced bills to amend the United States Bankruptcy Law of 1898 by providing for a uniform system of bankruptcy, but the House Judiciary Committee buried them. *Ibid.*, 8427, 9368.

54. London was nominated by East Side branches in the Second, Third, Fourth and Sixth assembly districts on the evening of July 18. *New York Call*, July 19, 1916, 2.

55. *American Socialist*, July 8, 1916, 2; *New York Call*, July 10, 1916, 6; August 6, 1916; *Appeal to Reason*, July 22, 1916, 2; *Socialist Party Minute Books, Executive Committee Local New York*, August 16, 1916, MB 48, 13.

56. *Ibid.*, May 10, 1916, 309.
57. *Ibid.*, May 24, 1916, 313.
58. *New York Call*, September 6, 1916, 1. For a biographical sketch of Sanders, see Jacob Magidoff, *Der Spiegel fun der East Side*, 1.
59. *New York Call*, September 28, 1916, 6.
60. *Ibid.*, October 2, 1916, 4; October 2, 1916, 1; October 6, 1916, 3; November 4, 1916, 2; *New York World*, October 1916, 5. The International Ladies' Garment Workers' Union endorsed London at its annual convention in Philadelphia and contributed five hundred dollars to the Labor Conference campaign fund. ILGWU, *Proceedings 1916*, 98, 115, 117.
61. *New York Call*, October 14, 1916, 1.
62. *Ibid.*, October 17, 1916, 4.
63. Among these were the Workmen's Circle, the Poale Zion (Labor Zionists), the Marxian Philosophical Society, the Meyer London Students' League, the Women's Campaign League, the B'rith Abraham Meyer London League, the Young People's Socialist League, and the Meyer London Non-Partisan League. *Ibid.*, October 1, 1916, 4; October 16, 1916, 4; October 17, 1916, 3; October 18, 1916, 2; October 19, 1916, 3–4; October 29, 1916, 3.
64. See the *New York Call* and the *Daily Forward* for September and October 1916.
65. *New Republic* 8 (September 30, 1916): 204.
66. *New York Call*, October 27, 1916, 1.
67. *Ibid.*, October 18, 1916, 2; October 31, 1916, 1.
68. *Ibid.*
69. *Ibid.*, November 6, 1916, 1.
70. *Ibid.*, September 27, 1916, 1.
71. *Ibid.*, October 15, 1916, 1.
72. *Ibid.*, November 6, 1916, 1.
73. *Ibid.*, August 26, 1916, 6; September 28, 1916, 6.
74. *Daily Forward*, October 29, 1916, 8. The *American Socialist* published a detailed account of London's record in Congress. *American Socialist*, October 21, 1916, 2.
75. Questions about London's religious beliefs had also been raised in the 1914 campaign. See chapter 3.
76. *New York Call*, October 21, 1916, 6.
77. *Ibid.*, October 22, 1916, 2. The Independent Order of B'rith Abraham was founded by Hungarians in 1887, but welcomed everyone. It became the largest of all Jewish fraternal organizations. Rischin, 150.
78. *Ibid.*, October 18, 1916, 1.
79. A. Sheibar to Meyer London, October 25, 1916; Meyer London to A. Sheibar October 25, 1916, London Papers.
80. William W. Feigenbaum, "The Last Refuge of a Scoundrel," *New York Call*, October 21, 1916, 6.
81. *Ibid.*, October 23, 1916, 2.
82. *Ibid.*, October 24, 1916, 2. London supporters also charged that Sanders had arranged a gift of three thousand dollars to the ex-grand master of B'rith Abraham in order to procure Sanders' election as grand master. *Ibid.*
83. *Daily Forward*, October 27, 1916, 1; October 29, 1916, 5; October 30, 1916, 8; *New York Call*, October 31, 1916, 1; November 1, 1916, 2; November 2, 1916, 2.
84. *New York Tribune*, November 8, 1916, 6.
85. *New York Call*, October 31, 1916, 2; November 1, 1916, 1–2; November 2, 1916, 1–2; November 3, 1916, 2; November 7, 1916, 1. The Labor Conference furnished watchers and guards for all polling places.
86. *Ibid.*, November 7, 1916, 1–2.
87. The glass shades on which the returns had been marked were placed in wire baskets that slid over strings stretched across the street from the Forward Building. *New York Tribune*, November 8, 1916, 6.
88. *New York Call*, November 8, 1916, 3.
89. *Ibid.*, November 8, 1916, 1.
90. Leon Sanders (Democrat) 5,759, 42.17 percent of the whole vote.
Meyer London (Socialist) 6,102, 44.69 percent of the whole vote.
Louis Block (Republican) 968, 7.08 percent of the whole vote.
See *Official Canvass of the Vote Cast in the County of New York*, December 31, 1916, 235–36. According to the *New York Call*, Louis Block did not wage an active campaign. He ran on a platform of "vote for your neighbor and friend." *New York Call*, November 4, 1916, 3.
91. *Daily Forward*, November 8, 1916, 1; *New York Call*, November 9, 1916, 3.
92. *New York World*, November 9, 1916, 4; *New York Call*, November 9, 1916, 2.
93. *Ibid.*, November 9, 1916, 3.
94. *Ibid.*
95. H. Rogoff, 297.
96. *New York Call*, November 9, 1916, 6; November 10, 1916, 6. London's victory, the *Ladies'*

Garment Worker declared, strengthened the workers' faith in political action. He had not only won nationwide recognition and esteem, but had enhanced the prestige of his district. *Ladies' Garment Worker* 8 (December 1916): 7–8.

97. *New York Call*, November 25, 1916, 1.
98. *Ibid.*, November 26, 1916, 3; November 28, 1916, 1; November 29, 1916, 2; December 6, 1916, 2.
99. *Ibid.*, December 1, 1916, 2.
100. *Ibid.*, December 8, 1916, 1.
101. Eleven bills and resolutions were introduced in Congress aimed at dealing with the situation created by rising food prices. Gompers and several labor leaders met with the president and urged him to appoint a committee to investigate the matter. *New York Times*, December 5, 1916, 1.
102. *Congressional Record*, 64th Congress, 2nd Sess., 666; *New York Call*, December 22, 1916, 1; December 23, 1916, 1.
103. *New York Call*, December 22, 1916, 1; *New York Times*, December 24, 1916, 10; December 30, 1916, 1.
104. *New York Call*, December 23, 1916, 1; *American Socialist*, January 16, 1917, 1.
105. *Ibid.*, January 27, 1917, 2; *New York Call*, January 14, 1917, 1.
106. *Appeal to Reason*, November 25, 1916, 1; December 2, 1916, 2; December 16, 1916, 1; December 30, 1916, 1; January 6, 1917, 1; *American Socialist*, December 2, 1916, 1.
107. Paul H. Douglas, 391; George Soule, *Prosperity Decade: From War to Depression, 1917–1929* (New York: Harper and Row, 1968), 21.
108. Howard Zinn, *La Guardia in Congress* (Ithaca, NY: Cornell University Press, 1959), 23.
109. *Congressional Record*, 64th Congress, 2nd Sess., 3813–14.
110. Dana Frank, "Housewives, Socialists and the Politics of Food: The 1917 New York Cost of Living Protests," *Feminist Studies* 11, no. 2 (Summer 1985): 256–59. *Congressional Record*, 64th Congress, 2nd Sess., 3959; *New York Times*, February 23, 1917, 3; *New York Call*, February 23, 1917, 1.
111. *Congressional Record*, 64th Congress, 2nd Sess., 4184–85.
112. *Ibid.*, 4191–92.
113. *Ibid.*, 4192–93.
114. *Ibid.*, 4527.
115. Link, *Wilson: Campaigns for Progressivism and Peace*, 5:327–28.
116. *Congressional Record*, 64th Congress, 2nd Sess., 2450.
117. *Ibid.*, 2650.
118. *Ibid.*, 2651–52.
119. *Ibid.*, 2651.
120. *Ibid.*
121. *Ibid.*, 2652–53.
122. *Ibid.*, 2654. The *New Republic* stated that the vote on London's proposal showed how little the House was influenced by argument and how persistently it could overlook a timely suggestion.

New Republic 10 (February 17, 1917): 58. A two-thirds majority was need to suspend the rules.
123. Link, *Wilson and the Progressive Era*, 252–61.
124. *New York Call*, January 1, 1917, 1. The American Neutral Peace Conference sponsored the rally.
125. Link, *Wilson and the Progressive Era*, 261–65.
126. *Congressional Record*, 64th Congress, 2nd Sess., 390–91.
127. Link, *Wilson and the Progressive Era*, 266–68.
128. *Congressional Record*, 64th Congress, 2nd Sess., 2332.
129. *Ibid.*, 2441–42. Opposition came from the Republicans who unsuccessfully attempted to recommit the bill so that tariff duties would be increased to help produce revenue.
130. *Ibid.*, 3028.
131. *Ibid.*, 3239–40.
132. *Ibid.*, 3527–28.
133. *Ibid.*, 3528.
134. Link, *Wilson and the Progressive Era*, 271.
135. Link, *Wilson: Campaigns for Progressivism and Peace*, 5:348.
136. *Ibid.*, 5:349–53.
137. *Congressional Record*, 64th Congress, 2nd Sess., 49.
138. *Ibid.*, 4691–92.
139. Link, *Wilson: Campaigns for Progressivism and Peace*, 5:359–61.
140. *Ibid.*, 376–77.

Chapter 8

1. *New York Call*, March 5, 1917, 1.
2. *New York Tribune*, March 9, 1917, 2; *Socialist Party Minute Book, Central Committee Local New York*, March 14, 1917, MB 48, Folder 1, 90; March 24, 1917, MB 49, 31; March 30, 1917, MB 48, Folder 2, 97.
3. *New York Call*, March 10, 1917, 1; *New York Times*, March 10, 1917, 4. Rabbi Judah Magnes, with whom London worked to resolve the Fur Worker's strike of 1912, was a leader of the anti-war Emergency Peace Federation. Daniel P. Kotzin, *Judah L Magnes: An American Jewish Nonconformist* (Syracuse, NY: Syracuse University Press), 146.
4. Link, *Wilson and the Progressive Era*, 274–75. London greeted the March Revolution with great enthusiasm. "I rejoice over this greatest event," London told a distinguished audience gathered at the Astor Hotel on May 10 to celebrate the revolution, "not only because it emancipates the Jews, the Poles, etc., but because it gives a new soul to a people occupying one-sixth of the globe, to a people 180,000,000 strong." Russia, London stated, would never return to the past for she had suffered too greatly and liberty was too precious a thing to ever be surrendered by an aroused Russia. Among the other speakers were former pres-

ident Taft and Jacob Schiff. "Jewish Emancipation Banquet," *American Hebrew* 8 (May 18, 1917): 41–42.

5. Link, *Wilson and the Progressive Era*, 276; *New York Call*, March 22, 1917, 1.

6. *New York Times*, November 10, 1916, 3; *New York Call*, November 11, 1916, 1; November 17, 1916, 3; *Appeal to Reason*, November 25, 1916, 2. The four other "independents" were Charles H. Randall, Prohibitionist of California; Whit P. Martin, Progressive Protectionist of Louisiana; Thomas D. Schall, Progressive of Minnesota; and Alvin T. Fuller, Independent of Massachusetts.

7. Thomas M. Bell to Meyer London, November 14, 1916, London Papers; Homer Larry Ingle, "Pilgrimage to Reform: A Life of Claude Kitchin" (PhD diss., University of Wisconsin, 1967), 4.

8. *New York Call*, November 10, 1916, 2; *American Socialist*, March 24, 1917, 1. The *Independent* wrote that since neither the Republicans nor the Democrats had a working majority in the House, it was a pity that London was the only Socialist in Congress. Had Berger, Gaylord, Debs and Hillquit also been elected, "the country would have enjoyed a somewhat novel experience of having a party with a program of fundamental reconstruction hold the balance of power in the legislative halls of the nation." Editorial reprinted from the *Independent* in the *Appeal to Reason*, December 16, 1916, 4.

9. *New York Call*, February 18, 1917, 1; February 19, 1917, 1.

10. U. Solomon to Meyer London, February 21, 1917; February 24, 1917, London Papers.

11. *New York Times*, March 5, 1917, 1.

12. *Congressional Record*, 65th Congress, Special Sess., 107. Four of the "independents," London, Schall, Randall and Martin, voted with 213 Democrats to give Clark his margin of victory. *Milwaukee Leader*, April 2, 1917, 1; *New York Call*, April 3, 1917, 3.

13. *Congressional Record*, 65th Congress, Special Sess., 109–11.

14. *Ibid.*, 114.

15. *Ibid.*, 129; see the *New York Call*, April 3, 1917, 1, for copy of the resolution.

16. The House had bided its time while the Senate debated and adopted the resolution on the previous day by a vote of 82 to 6. Link, *Wilson and the Progressive Era*, 281–82.

17. *Congressional Record*, 65th Congress, Special Sess., 329–30. *New York Times*, April 17, 1917, 12; Rappaport, "Jewish Immigrants and World War I," 277.

18. *Congressional Record*, 65th Congress, Special Sess., 412–13.

19. The National Executive Committee, with war imminent, had issued a call on March 12 for a special convention of the Socialist Party to meet on April 7 in St. Louis to determine party policy in the eventuality of war. Van der Slice, 149.

20. Weinstein, 126.

21. *New York Call*, April 15, 1917, 2.

22. Weinstein, 129–30.

23. Epstein, *Profiles*, 8.

24. *Congressional Record*, 65th Congress, 1st Sess., 10270.

25. H. Rogoff, 104–5.

26. *Congressional Record*, 65th Congress, 1st Sess., 10269–70.

27. *Ibid.*, 690; Arthur S. Link, *American Epoch, A History of the United States Since the 1890s* (New York: Knopf, 1967), 200.

28. *Congressional Record*, 65th Congress, 1st Sess., 11046; *New York Times*, June 27, 1925, 1.

29. *New York Call*, April 10, 1917, 1; April 12, 1917, 1.

30. *Congressional Record*, 65th Congress, 1st Sess., 2815–16; Zinn, 22–23.

31. *Ibid.*, 2818–19.

32. Seward W. Livermore, *Politics Is Adjourned, Woodrow Wilson and the War Congress 1916–1918* (Middletown, CT: Wesleyan University Press, 1966), 17–18; Frederic L. Paxson, *American Democracy and the World War: America at War, 1917–1918* (Boston: Houghton Mifflin, 1939), 2:5–9; David M. Kennedy, *Over Here: The First World War and American Society* (Oxford: Oxford University Press, 1982), 18, 146–47. For a detailed discussion of the draft bill controversy see Livermore, 13–31.

33. *Congressional Record*, 65th Congress, 1st Sess., 1157.

34. The Central Committee of Local New York approved a recommendation of the Executive Committee that a campaign be started for the repeal of the Conscription Act. The Central Committee requested London to introduce a bill repealing the law. *Socialist Party Minute Book, Central Committee Local New York*, June 2, 1917, MB 49, 48; *New York Call*, July 8, 1917, 2:10; H. Rogoff, 107.

35. Weinstein, 140–45.

36. Principal opposition came from the Republicans led by George S. Graham of Pennsylvania, a member of the judiciary committee, who received support from most of the Republican leaders. Livermore, 34.

37. *Congressional Record*, 65th Congress, 1st Sess., 1779–80.

38. *Ibid.*, 1816. Representative Graham, who introduced the motion, stated that the section represented an attempt to prevent communication. *Ibid.*, 1808.

39. *Ibid.*, 1819; Livermore, 34; Kennedy, 25–26.

40. *Congressional Record*, 65th Congress, 1st Sess., 1823.

41. *Ibid.*, 1824.

42. *New York Call*, May 5, 1917, 3; *Congressional Record*, 65th Congress, 1st Sess., 1841.

43. Livermore, 35–36; London was among those who voted to recommit the conference report. *Congressional Record*, 65th Congress, 1st Sess., 3144–45.

44. *New York Call*, July 10, 1917, 1; Weinstein, 90–91. Among the nearly dozen Socialist publi-

cations banned from the mails were the *Halletsville Rebel, American Socialist, Appeal to Reason, International Socialist Review, Social Revolution, The Masses,* and the *People's Press* in Philadelphia; the *Socialist News* in Cleveland; and the *Michigan Socialist* in Detroit.

45. *Congressional Record*, 65th Congress, 1st Sess., 4931; *New York Call*, July 10, 1917, 1; July 11, 1917, 1; July 14, 1917, 6; *New York Times*, July 11, 1917, 3; *American Socialist*, July 14, 1917, 1; *Appeal to Reason*, July 21, 1917, 1.

46. *New York Call*, July 11, 1917, 1.

47. *Ibid.*, July 8, 1917, 1.

48. *Ibid.*, July 16, 1917, 1.

49. *Ibid.*, July 23, 1917, 1; July 24, 1917, 1; July 25, 1917, 2; *New York Times*, July 24, 1917, 16. According to the report in the *Call*, only five of the twenty-one members of the committee attended the hearing.

50. *Congressional Record*, 65th Congress, 1st Sess., 5569, 5634; *New York Call*, July 31, 1917, 4.

51. Weinstein, 145.

52. If London's point of order was sustained, the conference report would have been rejected. *Congressional Record*, 65th Congress, 1st Sess., 7417.

53. Senate amendment 127 stated that it "should be unlawful for any person, firm, corporation, on association to print, publish, or circulate, or cause to be printed, published or circulated, in any foreign language, news items, editorials ... matter respecting the Government of the United States, or of any nation engaged in the present war, or their policies, international relations, state or conduct of the war or, any matter relating thereto. This section shall not apply when the publisher ... has filed with the postmaster ... a true and complete translation of the entire article." Any newspaper or publication failing to conform to the translation requirement was denied mailing privileges. Furthermore, it was not only unlawful to mail, but to transport or otherwise distribute such matter. *Congressional Record*, 65th Congress, 1st Sess., 7421.

54. The conferees had disregarded House rules in three important respects. Firstly, they had extended Section 19 of the Senate bill to foreign languages other than German as originally provided in the section. Secondly, the conferees had also extended the section by prohibiting the circulation or distribution of these publications. Thirdly, and most important, they had added a section to the Espionage Act which prohibited the circulation and distribution of printed matter after the postmaster general had banned it from the mail. *Congressional Record*, 65th Congress, 1st Sess., 7421.

55. *Congressional Record*, 65th Congress, 1st Sess., 7421–28; *New York Call*, September 26, 1917, 1. In a statement to the *New York Call* several days later, London urged the Socialist Party and socialist publishers to organize their own distribution agencies. Such a step, he said, would not be contrary to the law, for only the courts, not the postmaster general, had the authority to determine what could be excluded from the mails. *Ibid.*, September 29, 1917, 3.

56. The miners, engaged in a strike against Phelps-Dodge Co., were forcibly expelled from the town by a sheriff's posse urged on by a local loyalty league. They were transported across the state line in cattle cars and left in the desert without food or water for some thirty-nine hours. Federal authorities rescued the miners and placed them in a detention camp in Columbus, New Mexico. A mob took Little from his boarding house in Butte, Montana, on August 1, 1917, and hanged him from a railroad trestle. Melvyn Dubofsky, *We Shall Be All: A History of the IWW* (New York: Quadrangle, 1969), 385–91; 391–92.

57. *Congressional Record*, 65th Congress, 1st Sess., 7908–9; *New York Call*, October 7, 1917, 1.

58. Frank, "Housewives, Socialists and the Politics of Food," 255–88.

59. Livermore, 48–52; Link, *American Epoch*, 203–4; Paxson, *American Democracy*, 2:80–87. Gompers to London, Gompers Papers, June 9, 1917, 711.

60. *Congressional Record*, 65th Congress, 1st Sess., 666.

61. *Ibid.*, 3980–81. The *New York Times* reported that the galleries applauded when London "twitted" the House for refusing to support his food resolution. *New York Times*, June 21, 1917, 2.

62. *Congressional Record*, 65th Congress, 1st Sess., 4190.

63. *New York Call*, June 26, 1917, 6.

64. Editorial in *Advance* 1 (April 20, 1917), 4.

65. [Karl Dannenberg], "Meyer London's Miss," *Radical Review* 1 (July 1917): 64–69.

66. *American Socialist*, May 15, 1917, 4.

67. H. Rogoff, 107. In a similar vein, the Third Annual Convention of the Jewish Socialist Federation commended him for his work on behalf of the workers, but expressed regret for his vote on the War Loan Act. It would have been more tactful and in keeping with party policy, the convention declared, had London voted against the measure. Hertz, 165.

68. *New York Call*, April 20, 1917, 1; *New York Times*, April 20, 1917, 1.

69. H. Rogoff, 106.

70. *New York Call*, April 21, 1917, 1. Hillquit refers to a cable signed by eleven pro-war Socialists including John Spargo and William English Walling which stated that a separate peace between Germany and Russia would be "disastrous to the progress of the international Socialist movement." *New York Call*, May 10, 1917, 6. Spargo criticized Hillquit's position in a letter which appeared in the *Call*, characterizing it as "pro-Germanism rampant." In reply, Hillquit stated that he considered their cable a pro-war message and an attempt to convey the impression that it represented Socialist sentiment in the United States. As for London's cable, Hillquit stated that his principal objection was that it had been sent simultaneously with the other, thus

lending official sanction to the "free lance message" of the other. Letter to the editor from John Spargo, *Ibid.*; letter to the editor from Morris Hillquit, *Ibid.*

71. *Milwaukee Leader*, April 28, 1917, 4.

72. *New York Post*, April 21, 1917, 1; *New York Call*, April 22, 1917, 1; *New York Times*, April 22, 1917, 1:3.

73. *Congressional Record*, 65th Congress, 1st Sess., 4534–40.

74. Seymour Stedman to Meyer London, April 23, 1917; London to Seymour Stedman, April 27, 1917, London Papers. Jacob Liebstein to the editor of the forum, *New York Call*, July 8, 1917, 2:10.

75. *New York Times*, May 24, 1917, 7. See Arno J. Mayer, *Wilson vs. Lenin: Political Origins of the New Diplomacy, 1917–1918* (Cleveland: World Publishing Company, 1963), 191–214, for an excellent discussion of the Wilson administration's attitude toward the Stockholm Conference and other Socialist peace initiatives. Van der Slice, 151; Hillquit, 155–56; *Milwaukee Leader*, June 5, 1917, 1.

76. *New York Times*, May 24, 1917, 7.

77. *Ibid.*, May 31, 1917, 12; Meyer London, "Socialism and the Terms of Peace," *Academy of Political Science Proceedings* 7 (July 1917): 289–93.

78. *New York Call*, May 26, 1917, 1.

79. *Congressional Record*, 65th Congress, 1st Sess., 7909; ibid., 2nd Sess., 5908, 5912.

80. *Ibid.*, 1st Sess., 5814; *New York Call*, August 5, 1917, 1.

81. *Ibid.*, *American Socialist*, August 11, 1917, 1; *Appeal to Reason*, August 18, 1917, 1. The *Appeal* stated that the fate of the resolution was a foregone conclusion, but there were millions of people throughout the world who would like to know more about Allied war aims.

82. Weinstein, 149–54.

83. *New York Call*, September 8, 1917, 4; September 20, 1917, 3.

84. *Ibid.*, October 21, 1917, 2.

85. *New York Times*, October 22, 1917, 4; *New York Call*, October 22, 1917, 3. The *Call* report made no reference to London's comments on the war or the heckling. H. Rogoff, 107.

86. *New York Times*, October 23, 1917, 12.

87. *New York Call*, October 23, 1917, 3; October 25, 1917, 3; October 26, 1917, 3; October 27, 1917, 3; October 29, 1917, 5; October 30, 1917, 3.

88. *Ibid.*, November 6, 1917, 1.

89. Weinstein, 154.

90. *New York Times*, November 9, 1917, 2; November 10, 1917, 2.

91. [Ludwig Lore], "Our Obedient Congress," *The Class Struggle* 1 (November–December, 1917): 44–45. Lore expressed such views in *The Class Struggle*. London, he wrote, had violated the St. Louis Manifesto by neglecting every opportunity to assert opposition to the war. His congressional career had been a "complete fiasco." London was "completely dead," Lore declared, but other Londons might appear to discredit the party unless it abandoned the practice of seeking popular candidates rather than selecting men of recognized principles and integrity who would adequately represent the Socialist movement, particularly in perilous times. [Ludwig Lore], "Meyer London," *The Class Struggle* 1 (September–October, 1917): 100–101.

92. *Socialist Party Minute Book, Central Committee Local New York*, November 24, 1917, MB 49, 90.

93. *Ibid.*, December 1, 1917, 92–93; H. Rogoff, 108–9. The *New York Call* later reported that the National Executive Committee planned to meet with London at its next session. In the meantime, it designated Seymour Stedman to confer with London on proposed legislation for the second session of the Sixty-Fifth Congress. *New York Call*, December 25, 1917, 2.

94. *New York Times*, December 4, 1917, 5.

Chapter 9

1. Livermore, 62–65.

2. Ray S. Baker and William E. Dodd, eds., *War and Peace: Presidential Messages, Addresses, and Public Papers (1917-1924) by Woodrow Wilson* (New York: Harper and Brothers, 1927), 1:128–29.

3. *Congressional Record*, 65th Congress, 2nd Sess., 90–91.

4. *Ibid.*, 92.

5. *Ibid.*, 96.

6. *Ibid.*, 97–98. Other congressmen critical of London were Lenroot of Wisconsin and Campbell of Kansas. Lenroot doubted that London represented a very large portion of those who voted the Socialist Party ticket. *Ibid.*, 91–92, 97. Campbell declared that London spoke for himself and a few New York Socialists, but not "midcontinent" Socialists. *Ibid.*, 97–98.

7. *Ibid.*, 99–100. The *New York World* and the *New York Times* viewed his vote as another indication of Socialist support for Germany. Its greatest significance, the *World* stated, would be to further equate socialism with "Kaiserism" in the minds of the American people. *New York World*, December 8, 1917, 10; *New York Times*, December 9, 1917, 2:6.

8. Livermore, 68–90.

9. *Congressional Record*, 65th Congress, 2nd Sess., 53.

10. *New York Call*, December 8, 1917, 3; *Eye-Opener*, December 15, 1917, 2; December 22, 1917, 4.

11. In drafting his address, the president was influenced by diplomatic steps taken by the Bolshevik government. The Bolsheviks began to move toward a separate peace with Germany. They called for a general peace conference to provide "for a just and democratic peace" which would exclude forcible territorial annexations and indemnities. Leon Trotsky transmitted the proposed treaty to the Allies and the United

States. He invited them to join the negotiations, and requested that they state their war aims. The Allies failed to reply. In drafting his Fourteen Points address, President Wilson sought to answer the Bolshevik demand for an explanation of war aims and to persuade Russia to stand by the Allies in their defense of liberal and democratic principles. Mayer, *Wilson vs. Lenin*, 342. Also see John Milton Cooper Jr., *Pivotal Decades: The United States, 1900–1920* (New York: Norton, 1990): 344–46.

12. *Congressional Record*, 65th Congress, 2nd Sess., 853–57.
13. *Ibid.*, 860–62.
14. *Ibid.*, 271, 373.
15. *New York Call*, December 16, 1917, 3. A headline in the *Eye-Opener* read, "Meyer London Wins New Labor Victory in Congress." *Eye-Opener*, December 22, 1917, 1; *New York Call*, December 18, 1917, 4; *New Appeal*, December 29, 1917, 4.
16. *Congressional Record*, 65th Congress, 2nd Sess., 740–41; *New York Call*, January 11, 1918, 4; January 13, 1918, 5.
17. *Ibid.*, 903–4.
18. *Ibid.*, 905–6. The *New York Call* declared that Democratic and Republican "reactionaries" in the House had defeated the measure. *New York Call*, January 18, 1918, 1; January 20, 1918, 5.
19. London referred to an order issued by the fuel administrator, Harry A. Garfield, shutting down all factories, with the exception of a few munitions plants, east of the Mississippi River for a week beginning January 18. Non-essential industry would go on a five-day week until March 25. Kennedy, 124.
20. *Congressional Record*, 65th Congress, 2nd Sess., 1044–45.
21. *Ibid.*, 1192.
22. *New York Call*, January 27, 1918, 4.
23. *Congressional Record*, 65th Congress, 2nd Sess., 3454–56.
24. *Ibid.*, 7920–24. In addition to his fight for social insurance, London worked on behalf of government employees. He opposed an amendment to the Legislative, Executive and Judicial Expenses bill lengthening the working day for government employees in the District of Columbia from seven to eight hours. The House adopted the amendment, but President Wilson vetoed the bill. The House upheld the veto on July 1 by a substantial majority. *Ibid.*, 2936–37, 3561–62, 8577–88. London also supported bills providing higher wages for Postal Service employees and establishing a minimum wage for all government employees in the District of Columbia. *Ibid.*, 4027, 8880.
25. Soule, 8:34–35; Kennedy, 252–56.
26. *New York Call*, January 8, 1918, 5; Meyer London, "Why Federal Management of Railroads Is Not Socialism," *Fur Worker* 2, no. 26 (January 1918): 6.
27. *Congressional Record*, 65th Congress, 2nd Sess., 2544–45.

28. *Ibid.*, 2832.
29. Martin Dies should not be confused with his son who also served in the House from 1931 to 1945 and from 1953 to 1958. Martin Dies Jr. was chairman of the controversial House Un-American Activities Committee and like his father had a reputation as a labor-baiter and staunch anti-communist.
30. *Appeal to Reason*, March 23, 1918, 2.
31. *Congressional Record*, 65th Congress, 2nd Sess., 2576–77.
32. *New York Times*, February 24, 1918, 1:14.
33. Soule, 73; Paxson, *American Democracy*, 2:77.
34. *Congressional Record*, 65th Congress, 2nd Sess., 4416, 4446.
35. *Ibid.*, 4414. London later told the delegates to the annual ILGWU convention in Boston that Congress had limited the authority of the secretary of labor because it feared that construction of houses for the working people might become a permanent policy of the government. Nevertheless, government authority was extended, although temporarily, to another sector of the economy. ILGWU, *Proceedings of the Fourteenth Annual Convention*, May 20–June 1, 1918, 291.
36. In late April, the House considered a measure providing federal funds to encourage the production of rare metals essential to the war effort. London expressed opposition to subsidizing private ownership to develop natural resources. Nevertheless, he voted for the bill because he considered it necessary for the prosecution of the war. *Congressional Record*, 65th Congress, 2nd Sess., 5793–94, 7082–83; *New York Call*, April 27, 1918, 1.
37. *Congressional Record*, 65th Congress, 2nd Sess., 5295.
38. *Ibid.*, 8797.
39. Kennedy, 126–27. Also see Livermore, 170–72.
40. *Congressional Record*, 65th Congress, 2nd Sess., 1572–73.
41. *Ibid.*, 1872–73. Rainey also charged that London had during one week demanded roll calls consuming one-sixth of the hours occupied in legislative work. "Now if that is not legislative sabotage, if this is not the method of the I.W.W. and the Socialists injected into this body, I do not know what it is."
42. *Ibid.*, 1873–74.
43. Kennedy, 79–81.
44. *Congressional Record*, 65th Congress, 2nd Sess., 172.
45. *Ibid.*
46. Paxson, *American Democracy*, 2:291–94.
47. *Congressional Record*, 65th Congress, 2nd Sess., 172–73.
48. *Ibid.*, 6179–80.
49. Among the group were Gard of Ohio, Graham of Pennsylvania, Johnson of Washington, Norton of North Dakota, and Quin of Mississippi. *Ibid.*, 6180–83.
50. *Ibid.*, 6184–85.

51. *Ibid.*, 6186; *New York Times*, May 8, 1918, 5.
52. *Congressional Record*, 65th Congress, 2nd Sess., 7401–2.
53. *New York Call*, May 12, 1918, 8; "The Socialist Congressman," *The Public* 21 (May 18, 1918): 626.
54. *Ibid.*, 9125.
55. *New York Call*, March 5, 1918, 4. The *Call* reported that London's "attack" on the Lenin-Trotsky regime met with disapproval from the audience.
56. *Congressional Record*, 65th Congress, 2nd Sess., 3028; *New York Times*, March 5, 1918, 2. The *Times* printed the text of the resolution. See also *New York Call*, March 6, 1918, 1. The Executive Committee of Local New York sent a letter urging adoption of London's resolution to President Wilson. *Socialist New York Party Minute Book, Executive Committee Local*, March 6, 1918, MB 48, 207; *New York Times*, March 8, 1918, 1; *New York Call*, March 9, 1918, 1.
57. *New York Call*, March 5, 1918, 4.
58. Roy Watson Curry, *Woodrow Wilson and Far Eastern Policy, 1913–1921* (New York: Bookman Associates, 1957), 223. See pages 213–48 for an excellent discussion of the Siberian intervention.
59. *New York Times*, March 2, 1918, 1.
60. *New York Call*, March 14, 1918, 1.
61. Curry, 230–32.
62. *New York Tribune*, July 1, 1918, 1.
63. *New York Times*, July 2, 1918, 1; *New York World*, July 2, 1918, 1. The *World*'s report was similar to the *Times*.'
64. *New York Call*, July 3, 1918, 2. The *Call* headline read "London Bares *Tribune* Lie on Russian Stand." See also *New York World*, July 3, 1918, 3.
65. *New York World*, July 3, 1918, 3.
66. *New York Call*, July 3, 1918, 1.
67. *New York World*, July 3, 1918, 3. Wilson, however, had informed London that the assignments to the commission had already been made. Woodrow Wilson to Meyer London, May 1, 1918, Letterbook 40 of Series 3, 338, Wilson Papers, Library of Congress. For a complete discussion of the Root Mission, see Philip C. Jessup, *Elihu Root* (New York: Dodd, Mead, 1938), 2:353–71.
68. *New York World*, July 3, 1918, 3.
69. M.R., "Applied Londonism," *Radical Review* 1 (January 1918): 308–10.
70. *New York Call*, June 21, 1918, 2.
71. H. Rogoff, 159.
72. *New York World*, June 28, 1918, 13; *New York Times*, June 27, 1918, 4; *Daily Forward*, June 27, 1918, 1; "Congressman London Re-nominated in Twelfth Congressional District," *Fur Worker* 2, no. 31 (June 1918): 4.
73. *New York World*, July 2, 1918, 7.
74. *Socialist Party Minute Book, Central Committee Local New York*, July 13, 1918, MB 49, 137. Three members abstained, and seventy-six did not attend.
75. *Congressional Record*, 65th Congress, 2nd Sess., 9125–26.
76. *Socialist Party Minute Books, Central Committee Local New York*, July 15, 1918, MB 48, 241.
77. *Ibid.*, July 17, 1918, MB 49, 138. Six members failed to vote, and fifty-five were absent.
78. *New York Times*, July 18, 1918, 9.
79. *New York World*, July 19, 1918, 8.
80. *New York Times*, July 20, 1918, 8.
81. Between July 13 and August 19, the two houses adhered to the constitutional requirement not to adjourn for more than three days at a time. Twice a week several members would meet, discover that no quorum was present and adjourn for three days. Livermore, 136–37; Paxson, *American Democracy*, 2:354.
82. The Democratic leadership in the House broke with the president on the need for a larger draft army. See Livermore, 176–78, for a complete discussion of the fight to change the selective service law.
83. *Congressional Record*, 65th Congress, 2nd Sess., 9506–7.
84. Livermore, 134–36.
85. *Congressional Record*, 65th Congress, 2nd Sess., 10270–71.
86. *Ibid.*, 10548.
87. Livermore, 244.
88. *Congressional Record*, 65th Congress, 2nd Sess., 9603–4.
89. *Ibid.*, 10269–70.
90. Van der Slice, 186.
91. *New York Call*, October 22, 1918, 1.
92. *Congressional Record*, 65th Congress, 2nd Sess., 11; *New York Call*, October 6, 1918, 1; Benjamin Meimon, "Congress Considers Reconstruction," *Advance* 2 (October 11, 1918): 5.
93. *Congressional Record*, 65th Congress, 2nd Sess., 11376–77.

Chapter 10

1. *New York Times*, July 10, 1918, 12.
2. *New York Sun*, July 14, 1918, 4; *New York Times*, June 13, 1918, 11; July 10, 1918, 12.
3. *New York Times*, July 13, 1918; *New York Call*, July 16, 1918, 2; Naomi Cohen, "The Public Career of Oscar S. Straus" (PhD diss., Columbia University, 1955), 446–47.
4. *New York Call*, July 20, 1918, 2.
5. *Ibid.*, August 4, 1918, 2; *New York Times*, July 31, 1918, 3.
6. *Ibid.*, August 1, 1918, 1.
7. *Ibid.*, August 2, 1918, 6. See also *Ibid.*, August 4, 1918, 2.
8. *Ibid.*, August 22, 1918, 2.
9. *Congressional Record*, 65th Congress, 2nd Sess., 9604. Livermore, 164–67. See Kennedy, *Over Here*, for the origins and program of the National Security League.
10. Hertz, 190. A pro-Bolshevik group called the *Advante Garde* left the Jewish Socialist Federation and opposed London.

11. *Ibid.*, 169.
12. Meyer London to S. Sernatzky, September 6, 1918, London Papers.
13. Epstein, *Profiles*, 181.
14. Meyer London to S. Sernatzky, n.d., London Papers.
15. Epstein, *Profiles*, 181–82.
16. Among its sponsors were the International Ladies' Garment Workers' Union, the International Fur Workers' Union, the Amalgamated Clothing Workers of America, the United Hebrew Trades, the Cloakmakers' Union, the Ladies' Waist Makers' Union, the Boot and Shoe Workers, the White Goods Workers, the Cleaners and Dyers' Union, the Bed Spring Makers, the Embroiderers' Union and the Grocery Clerks' Union. *New York Call*, September 28, 1918, 3; September 20, 1918, 3; September 22, 1918, 3; September 24, 1918, 3; September 26, 1918, 5; September 29, 1918, 3; October 1, 1918, 3; October 2, 1918, 3; October 13, 1918, 3; October 19, 1918, 8; October 21, 1918, 4; "N.Y. Furriers to Help Reelect Meyer London for Congress," *Fur Worker* 2, no. 34 (September 1918): 1.
17. *New York Call*, September 28, 1918, 7; October 3, 1918, 3; October 5, 1918, 5; October 26, 1918, 2; "Meyer London Must Be Reelected," *Fur Worker* 2, no. 36 (October 1918): 1; "Our Members' Duty on Election Day," *Ibid.*, 6; *Daily Forward*, October 25, 1918, 2.
18. *New York Call*, September 28, 1918, 3; October 1, 1918, 3; October 20, 1918, 2; October 29, 1918, 3; October 31, 1918, 3.
19. *Ibid.*, September 30, 1918, 3; October 2, 1918, 3–4; October 5, 1918, 3; October 15, 1918, 3; October 16, 1918, 4; October 20, 1918.
20. *Ibid.*, October 21, 1918, 2; October 23, 1918, 4; October 25, 1918, 3.
21. *Ibid.*, October 3, 1918, 3; "Socialist Party Going Strong in This Year's Campaign," *Fur Worker* 2, no. 36 (October 1918): 7.
22. *Daily Forward*, October 24, 1918, 1; *New York Call*, November 2, 1918, 7.
23. *Ibid.*, September 4, 1918, 3; See also Meyer London Papers, September 2, 1918, for text of speech which was partly delivered in Yiddish.
24. Livermore, 185; *New York Times*, October 6, 1918, 1:17; *New York Call*, October 21, 1918, 4; October 22, 1918, 2. The *Ladies' Garment Worker* reported that London spoke with "heart and soul" for the Liberty Loan at a rally sponsored by the United Hebrew Trades on the evening of October 10. "Jewish Workers Active in Fourth Liberty Loan," *Ladies' Garment Worker* 8 (November 1, 1918): 25.
25. The disease had reached the United States that summer from Europe, and during September and October killed nearly half a million Americans and affected millions more before waning in late fall. New York City health officials took steps to discourage public gatherings. As a result, the Twelfth Congressional Campaign Committee and the Trade Union Conference announced that they would hold more outdoor meetings, use more advertising and distribute more campaign literature. Livermore, 185–86; *New York Call*, October 8, 1918, 1; October 21, 1918, 1; October 22, 1918, 1; October 31, 1918, 1; November 1, 1918, 3.
26. Socialist Alderman B. Charney Vladek and other Socialists protested the board's decision to enforce a law that was previously ignored. Two weeks before the campaign ended, the Board of Education reversed itself. *New York Call*, October 10, 1918, 1; October 23, 1918, 3; October 24, 1918, 5.
27. London restricted his campaign appearances to weekends while Congress was in session. Only during the last two weeks of the campaign did he feel free to fully devote himself to seeking reelection. *New York Call*, October 9, 1918, 3.
28. *New York American*, August 21, 1918, 1; *New York Call*, August 22, 1918, 2; "Congressman London Defines His Position," *Ladies' Garment Worker* 8 (September 1918): 28–29.
29. *New York Call*, August 22, 1918, 2; October 23, 1918, 3. The *Call* stated that Goldfogle's colleagues in the House referred to him as the "perpetual dodger" because of his high rate of absenteeism. The socialist daily charged, once again, that Goldfogle had failed to vote on measures vital to workers such as the so-called "phossy-jaw" bill, a bill to regulate injunctions, a child labor bill, the women's suffrage and direct election of senators amendments. *Ibid.*, September 16, 1918, 3; October 11, 1918, 3; October 21, 1918, 4.
30. *New York Call*, September 29, 1918, 2; October 10, 1918, 2; October 23, 1918, 3; October 24, 1918, 5; October 28, 1918, 4.
31. *Ibid.*, September 29, 1918, 2.
32. *Ibid.*, October 24, 1918, 5.
33. *New York American*, August 21, 1918, 1; *New York Call*, August 22, 1918, 2.
34. H. Rogoff, 160; *New York Tribune*, November 6, 1918, 1; *New York Times*, November 5, 1918, 8.
35. *Daily Forward*, November 4, 1918, 1.
36. In the synagogue service, an *aliyah* is the act of going up to pulpit to read a portion of the Torah. It is considered an honor to receive an *aliyah*.
37. *Daily Forward*, November 5, 1918, 1. When the Governor of Iowa declared that no one could worship in Hebrew, London alone had spoken against this in the House. London had also called attention to discriminatory hiring practices against Jews by businessmen with government contracts.
38. *New York Call*, October 24, 1918, 1; *New York Tribune*, November 6, 1918, 2. Marshall and Schiff had previously worked with London on the Protocol of Peace and had praised his leadership. Kotzin, *Judah L. Magnes*, 152.
39. *New York Call*, November 3, 1918, 1; *New York Tribune*, November 6, 1918, 1.
40. *New York Evening Mail*, November 5, 1918, 9; *New York World*, November 5, 1918, 8; *New York Times*, November 5, 1918, 8.
41. *New York Call*, October 25, 1918, 1.
42. *Daily Forward*, November 5, 1918, 1.

43. The New York Legislature passed a bill on February 19, 1918, giving women the right to vote. *New York Times*, February 20, 1918, 1.
44. *New York Call*, November 6, 1918, 1.
45. Henry Goldfogle (Democrat) 7,452, 48.61 percent of the whole vote
Meyer London (Socialist) 6,625, 42.45 percent of the whole vote
See *Official Canvass of the Vote Cast in the County of New York*, November 1918, 95–6. Election officials did not count 568 blank ballots and 650 void ballots. The number of void ballots was six times greater than in 1916.
46. *New York World*, November 7, 1918, 10.
47. *New York Times*, November 7, 1918, 14.
48. *New York Evening Mail*, November 6, 1918, 8.
49. Ludwig Lore, "The Election," *Class Struggle* 2 (December 1918): 621.
50. *New York World*, November 6, 1918, 5; November 7, 1918, 11.
51. Danish also claimed that in the Nineteenth Election District of the Fourth Assembly District, 102 votes for London had been marked void, and officials, therefore refused to count them. Election officials placed lead under a fingernail so they could mark up a ballot, thus invalidating it according to election law. He further charged that in the Twenty-Second Election District of the Fourth Assembly District, officials had crumpled and smeared sixty-seven ballots with ink. *New York Call*, November 6, 1918, 1–2; *Daily Forward*, November 6, 1918, 1, 4.
52. *Daily Forward*, November 7, 1918, 1; November 8, 1918, 4.
53. *New York Call*, November 6, 1918, 10; November 7, 1918, 8.
54. "Socialist Vote Increased," *Advance* 2 (November 8, 1918): 1.
55. *New York Call*, November 11, 1918, 1; Julius Gerber to Meyer London, November 7, 1918, London Papers.
56. *New York Call*, November 14, 1918, 2; November 15, 1918, 1; November 16, 1918, 1; November 22, 1918, 1.
57. *New York Times*, November 22, 1918, 12; *New York Call*, November 23, 2918, 1; November 26, 1918, 5. While Socialists and trade unionists anxiously awaited the decision of the court, they continued to perfect plans to secure a recount for London. They appealed to the unions for both moral support and financial assistance. In addition, a nationwide appeal was made to Socialist locals and Workmen Circle branches. *New York Call*, November 26, 1918, 5.
58. *New York Times*, December 7, 1918, 13.
59. *New York Call*, December 18, 1918, 1.
60. *Ibid.*, January 4, 1919, 1.
61. *Ibid.*, January 9, 1919, 1.
62. Ibid., January 16, 1919, 1.
63. *Socialist Party Minute Books, Executive Committee Local New York*, January 15, 1919, MB 48, 291–92.
64. H. Rogoff, 165; "How to Elect Socialist Candidates," *Fur Worker* 4, no. 60 (September 1920): 1.
65. Peace negotiations between the United States and Germany based on Wilson's Fourteen Points had begun in October 1918. On November 9, the kaiser abdicated and fled to Holland. The armistice was signed two days later. See Alexander De Conde, *A History of American Foreign Policy* (New York: Scribner, 1963), 468–69.
66. Link, *American Epoch*, 231–34.
67. *Congressional Record*, 65th Congress, 3rd Sess., 961. Efforts by London and several other representatives to amend the Sundry Civil Appropriations Bill to provide ten million dollars for the continuation of employment exchanges failed. Ibid., 4662–65.
68. For an excellent discussion of the conflict between pro-war and anti-war elements in the United States, see H.C. Peterson and Gilbert C. Fite, *Opponents of War, 1917–1918* (Madison: University of Wisconsin Press, 1957).
69. Robert K. Murray, *Red Scare: A Study in National Hysteria, 1919–1920* (Minneapolis: University of Minnesota Press, 1955), 33–56.
70. *Congressional Record*, 65th Congress, 3rd Sess., 179.
71. *Ibid.*, 3230–32.
72. *Ibid.*, 3232.
73. *Ibid.*, 3976–77.
74. *Ibid.*, 4067.
75. Link, *American Epoch*, 237–40. In other domestic matters, London opposed the Naval Appropriation bill and a bill providing for the leasing and sale by the government of valuable oil and gas lands. *Congressional Record*, 65th Congress, 3rd Sess., 2828. On February 18, London told the House that the bill to lease and sell oil and coal lands was "mischievous" and represented an attempt "at public plunder in the expiring days of the session." The bill passed 233 to 109. *Ibid.*, 3172, 3710.
76. *Ibid.*, 2828–29.
77. *New York Call*, March 4, 1921, 1.
78. Levine, 339–40; *New York Call*, January 4, 1920, 3; January 6, 1920, 1.
79. *New York Times*, January 10, 1920, 18; *New York Call*, January 10, 1920, 1, 3.
80. *New York Call*, January 12, 1920, 6; January 13, 1920, 1; January 15, 1920, 1; *New York Times*, January 15, 1920, 11.
81. *New York Call*, January 27, 1920, 1; Levine, 340.
82. *New York Call*, January 27, 1920, 3.
83. *Ibid.*, October 15, 1920, 5.
84. Foner, *The Fur and Leather Workers Union*, 96. See Foner for a detailed account of the strike. According to Foner, the Greek workers had been kept out of the union by its leaders.
85. *New York Call*, November 14, 1920, 3; November 16, 1920, 5.
86. *Ibid.*, November 6, 1920, 5.
87. *Ibid.*, November 17, 1920, 3.

88. Foner, *The Fur and Leather Workers Union*, 103.
89. Weinstein, 177–210; Shannon, 126–49; Draper, *The Roots of American Communism*, 148–75; Bell, "The Background and Development of Marxian Socialism in the United States," 1:318–24.
90. Weinstein, 209–21; Shannon, 150–53. The American Socialist Party applied for membership in the Third International in March 1920, but never received an official answer. The Third International later adopted twenty-one points as conditions for affiliation which the American Socialists refused to accept.
91. *New York Call*, October 1, 1919, 1.
92. *Ibid.*, October 28, 1919, 1; October 30, 1919, 2; October 31, 1919, 3. For complete coverage of the 1919 campaign, see the October and November issues of the *New York Call*.
93. James Berton Rhoads, "The Campaign of the Socialist Party in the Election of 1920" (PhD diss., American University, 1965), 55. The five elected Socialists were Louis Waldman and August Claessens, who represented districts on the Lower East Side; Samuel Orr and Samuel A. DeWitt of the Bronx; and Charles Solomon from Brooklyn.
94. *Ibid.*, 236; William E. Leuchtenburg, *The Perils of Prosperity, 1914–1932*, 2nd ed. (Chicago: University of Chicago Press, 1993), 66–83; Link, *American Epoch*, 237–40. The suspension was the outgrowth of an investigation conducted by the Lusk Committee of the New York Legislature which sought for some time to establish that the Socialist Party supported violent revolution. It also took place against the background of a new wave of anti-radical hysteria that had begun to sweep the country.
95. *New York Times*, January 12, 1919, 3.
96. See Rhoads, 55–81, for a full discussion of the proceedings against the expelled Socialists.
97. *New York Call*, April 2, 1920, 1.
98. *Ibid.*, April 14, 1920, 3.
99. See Rhoads, 140–243, for a complete discussion of the convention.
100. *Ibid.*, 172–77.
101. Socialist Party, *Minutes of the Eighth National Convention*, May 8–14, 1920, New York City, MB 51, Folder 6, 98. Copy in the Bobst Library, New York University. Hereafter cited as *Minutes*, 1920.
102. Rhoads, 186–90.
103. *Minutes*, 1920, MB 51, Folder 5, 25–27.
104. *Ibid.*, 30–33; *New York Call*, May 13, 1920, 2.
105. Rhoads, 193–97.
106. *Minutes*, 1920, MB 51, Folder 5, 95–98.
107. *Ibid.*, MB 51, Folder 6, 14–19.
108. Rhoads, 122.
109. *New York Call*, May 15, 1920, 5; May 16, 1920, 8; Rhoads, 178–79.
110. *New York Call*, July 3, 1920, 3; July 4, 1920, 1:2; July 5, 1920, 1; *New York Times*, July 5, 1920, 9.
111. *New York Call*, July 8, 1920, 6; July 9, 1920, 4.
112. *Ibid.*, July 10, 1920, 11.
113. *New York Times*, May 31, 1920, 4.
114. *New York Call*, June 2, 1920, 4.
115. *Ibid.*, August 13, 1920, 7; August 16, 1920, 7; *New York Times*, August 13, 1920, 3.
116. In mid-August, Governor Al Smith issued proclamations calling for special elections on September 16 to fill the five Assembly vacancies caused by the expulsion proceedings. *New York Times*, August 13, 1920, 1.
117. August 28, 1920, 5. See Rhoads, 81–85, for discussion of the special election.
118. *New York Times*, August 29, 1920, 2.
119. *Ibid.*, September 2, 1917, 1.
120. *New York Times*, September 17, 1920, 17; *New York Call*, September 17, 1920, 1.
121. *New York Call*, September 22, 1920, 1.
122. *Ibid.*, September 25, 1920, 1.
123. Rhoads, 330–31.
124. *New York Call*, September 15, 1920, 1–2. In a letter to Theodore Debs, Lucy Robbins, a labor and radical activist who attended the meeting, lauded London and Gompers. "I believe," she wrote, "both you and Gene would have been very happy to listen to the wonderful talks of both men." Constantine, 3:120–21.
125. *New York Call*, July 19, 1920, 7; August 13, 1920, 6; September 28, 1920, 2.
126. *Ibid.*, *New York Call*, September 28, 1920, 1–2; September 29, 1920, 1, 7.
127. *Ibid.*, August 26, 1920, 2.
128. *Ibid.*, October 1, 1920, 2; October 15, 1920, 5; October 16, 1920, 5; October 19, 1920, 5; "Cloakmakers' Socialist Committee Conducts Rousing Campaign," *Justice* 2 (October 15, 1920): 1; "Cloakmakers Determined to Elect London and Hillquit," *Justice* 2 (October 22, 1920): 1.
129. *Ibid.*, *New York Call*, October 1, 1920, 1; October 9, 1920, 2; October 10, 1920, 6.
130. "Cloakmakers' Socialist Committee Conducts Rousing Campaign," 1.
131. *Ibid.*, October 26, 1920, 5. Among the other unions which endorsed London's candidacy and worked actively for him were Bakers' Union Local 100, the Embroidery Workers' Union, Cap Makers' Union Local 1, Chandelier Workers' Union, the Fancy Leather Goods Workers' Union, the Seltzer Workers' Union, the Bed Spring Makers' Union and the Butchers' Union. *Ibid.*, September 30, 1920, 6; October 22, 1920, 5.
132. Open cooperation between the Socialist Party and the Farmer Labor Party or any other working-class political group was prohibited by the Socialist Party's constitution. Rhoads, 370–75; *Milwaukee Leader*, October 22, 1920, 10. Although this writer found no evidence regarding London's position on the issue, his willingness to accept non-socialist support in past elections no doubt led him to accept it on this occasion as well.
133. *New York Call*, October 4, 1920, 1.
134. *New York Times*, October 30, 1920, 10.

135. *New York World*, November 1, 1920, 4.
136. *New York Tribune*, November 1, 1920, 10.
137. *New York Call*, October 18, 1920, 1.
138. *Ibid.*
139. *Daily Forward*, October 28, 1920, 1.
140. *Ibid.*, November 2, 1920, 1.
141. *Ibid.*, October 29, 1920, 3; October 30, 1920, 1.
142. *New York Call*, October 28, 1920, 5.
143. *Ibid.*, November 4, 1920, 4.
144. *New York Tribune*, November 3, 1920, 2; *New York World*, November 3, 1920, 8.
145. *Ibid.*, November 3, 1920, 4.
146. *Ibid.*, November 4, 1920, 8; *New York Tribune*, November 4, 1920, 2:4. The *New York Times* called London's victory "the greatest" in the city. *New York Times*, November 4, 1920, 1.
147. Henry Goldfogle (Democrat) 8,646, 45.81 percent of the whole vote
Meyer London (Socialist) 10,212, 54.06 percent of the whole vote
See *Official Canvass of the Vote Cast in the County of New York*, December 31, 1920, 217.
148. London ran ahead of all other Socialist congressional candidates. Hillquit polled 9,441 votes in the Twentieth Congressional District, but was defeated by Isaac Siegel who received 12,602. *New York Call*, January 22, 1921, 7; Rhoads, 668–69.
149. *New York World*, November 4, 1920, 8.
150. *New York Call*, November 4, 1920, 2; November 8, 1920, 2.
151. "Cloakmakers' Campaign Committee Win Congress Seat for London," *Justice* 2 (November 5, 1920): 1. London appeared before the Joint Board of the Cloakmakers shortly after the election to thank them for their support. "Cloakmakers' Joint Board Rejoices Over Election of Meyer London," *Justice* 2 (November 12, 1920): 1.
152. A. Rosenburg, "Congressman Meyer London — Congratulations," *Fur Worker* 4, no. 61 (November 1920): 5.
153. *New York Call*, November 15, 1920, 7.
154. *Daily Forward*, November 3, 1920, 4.
155. *New York Call*, November 20, 1920, 2. London was undoubtedly amused when he received congratulations from Clarence B. Miller, secretary of the Republican National Committee. Clarence B. Miller to Meyer London, November 9, 1920, London Papers.
156. *New York Call*, November 14, 1920, 3.
157. *Ibid.*, December 22, 1920, 4.
158. *Ibid.*, December 1, 1920, 7; December 4, 1920, 11.
159. *New York Times*, November 30, 1920, 17. While in Chicago, London addressed a December 5 meeting attended by some two thousand Socialists. The changes sought by American Socialists, he told them, would vary from the methods used in Russia. "Russia had the right to work out her destiny without interference from outside powers, and American Socialists will fight for Russia's right to do so. But American Socialists ... , will also reserve the right to work out the problems in this country without outside dictation." London's comments brought boos and hisses from the communists in the audience. *New York Call*, December 6, 1920, 1. According to the initial *New York Times* report, several fights broke out, and the police were summoned. However, before they arrived, London restored order. The following day the *Times* stated that riot reports were erroneous. *New York Times*, December 6, 1920, 5; December 7, 1920, 6.
160. *New York Call*, January 17, 1921, 5. See also the *New York Call*, November 20, 1920, 2; December 10, 1920, 3; January 23, 1921, 7; March 4, 1921, 1.
161. *Ibid.*, December 10, 1920, 3.
162. *Ibid.*, January 31, 1921, 1, 3.
163. *Ibid.*, March 4, 1921, 6.
164. *Ibid.*, March 26, 1921, 2; March 29, 1921, 1.
165. Samuel Gompers to Meyer London, April 2, 1921, Gompers Papers, vol. 270:140.
166. *New York Call*, April 5, 1921, 1; *New York Times*, April 5, 1921, 21; "Labor Amnesty Committee Sees Pres. Harding," *Justice* 2 (April 8, 1921): 1.

Chapter 11

1. Link, *American Epoch*, 322–25; Leuchtenburg, 103.
2. President Harding had called a special session of Congress to deal with important fiscal matters left undone by the Sixty-Sixth Congress. Frederick L. Paxson, *American Democracy and the World War: Postwar Years; Normalcy, 1918–1923* (Berkeley: University of California Press, 1948), 3:201. London was assigned to the Committees on Labor, Mines and Mining, and Reform in the Civil Service. *Congressional Record*, 67th Congress, 1st Sess., 408.
3. The delegation included James Oneal, a leading socialist publicist; Swinburne Hall, a progressive lawyer; Fisher Kane, a former federal district attorney; Mrs. Winnie Branstetter, wife of the Socialist Party's National Executive Secretary; and Harry W. Laidler, a prominent socialist writer. *New York Call*, April 14, 1921, 1.
4. *Ibid.*
5. *Congressional Record*, 67th Congress, 1st Sess., 461.
6. *New York Call*, April 19, 1921, 1.
7. *Congressional Record*, 67th Congress, 1st Sess., 3323–25; *New York Call* July 2, 1921, 6; *New York Times*, July 2, 1921, 4. London also presented resolutions, petitions and memorials from Socialist, labor, veterans and other groups requesting the release of political prisoners. *Congressional Record*, 67th Congress, 1st Sess., 8143–44, 8151–53.
8. *New York Times*, December 24, 1921, 1.
9. *New York Call*, December 24, 1922, 1–2.
10. *Congressional Record*, 67th Congress, 2nd Sess., 1534; *New York Times*, January 22, 1922; *New York Call*, January 22, 1922, 1.

11. *Ibid.*, March 1, 1922, 1–2.
12. *Ibid.*, March 17, 1922, 1; April 19, 1922, 8.
13. *Ibid.*, May 12, 1922, 1–2.
14. *Congressional Record*, 67th Congress, 2nd Sess., 7078–79.
15. *Ibid.*, 8352–53.
16. *Ibid.*, 8354.
17. *Ibid.*, 13178–79; *New York Call*, September 23, 1922, 1.
18. Peterson and Fite, 283.
19. *Congressional Record*, 67th Congress, 2nd Sess., 1365–66. The *New York Call* praised London's speech as "masterly." *New York Call*, January 20, 1922, 8. See Weinstein, 63–47, for a discussion of the Socialist Party's position on African-Americans.
20. *Congressional Record*, 67th Congress, 2nd Sess., 1795. London's support for the measure brought a note of thanks from James Weldon Johnson, secretary of the National Association for the Advancement of Colored People. James W. Johnson to Meyer London, January 21, 1922, London Papers.
21. Paxson, *American Democracy*, 3:353–54. The issue lay dormant until 1935 when the Roosevelt administration made a new but unsuccessful attempt to pass an anti-lynching bill. See Arthur Schlesinger Jr., *The Politics of Upheaval* (Boston: Houghton Mifflin, 1960), 436–38, and John Hope Franklin, *From Slavery to Freedom* (New York: Knopf, 1967), 486–87.
22. Jones, 272–76; Higham, 310–11.
23. *Congressional Record*, 67th Congress, 1st Sess., 515–16.
24. *Ibid.*, 550–52.
25. *New York Call*, April 23, 1921, 1.
26. *Congressional Record*, 67th Congress, 1st Sess., 1442.
27. *New York Call*, May 20, 1921, 3; Jones, 276. London voted against extending the Immigration Act of 1921, which the House passed overwhelmingly on February 20, 1922, *Congressional Record*, 67th Congress, 2nd Sess., 2801, 5076, 5083.
28. Paxson, *American Democracy*, 3:219–24; John D. Hicks, *Republican Ascendency, 1921–1933* (New York: Harper and Row), 54. The Farm Bloc consisted of about twenty senators and a slightly larger number of representatives from the agricultural states of the Middle West and the South who sought relief for farmers from falling farm prices.
29. *Congressional Record*, 67th Congress, 1st Sess., 355.
30. *New York Call*, July 28, 1921, 2.
31. Hicks, 54–55.
32. Paxson, *American Democracy*, 3:292.
33. *Congressional Record*, 67th Congress, 1st Sess., 3728–30.
34. *Ibid.*, 3949; *New York Call*, July 17, 1921, 1–2. London considered the rule adopted for the consideration of the Fordney bill as "vicious" as the bill itself. *Congressional Record*, 67th Congress, 1st Sess., 4058.
35. *Ibid.*, 4058–59.

36. *Ibid.*, 4197–98.
37. The Senate failed to act upon the bill until August 19, 1922, because of lengthy deliberations by the Senate Finance Committee. Thus, Congress found it necessary to extend the Emergency Tariff. The House approved the extension on October 18, 1921, by a vote of 200 to 74, with London once again in opposition. *Ibid.*, 6468; Hicks, 56; Paxson, *American Democracy*, 3:297–300.
38. *Congressional Record*, 67th Congress, 2nd Sess., 11655.
39. *Ibid.*, 12521.
40. *New York Call*, September 14, 1922, 1; Paxson, *American Democracy*, 3:297–304.
41. *Congressional Record*, 67th Congress, 2nd Sess., 12718.
42. Hicks, 57.
43. Paxson, *American Democracy*, 3:259.
44. *Congressional Record*, 67th Congress, 1st Sess., 5145.
45. *Ibid.*, 5282.
46. *Ibid.*, 5359–60.
47. It provided for the repeal of the excess profits tax, the continuance of existing income tax rates for the remainder of 1921 with the maximum surtax to be 50 percent thereafter, a 2.5 percent increase in the tax on net corporate income taxes and no change in inheritance taxes. Hicks, 54. London voted against the conference report. *Congressional Record*, 67th Congress, 1st Sess., 8086–87.
48. Samuel Gompers to Meyer London, April 23, 1921, Gompers Papers, vol. 278:122.
49. *Congressional Record*, 67th Congress, 1st Sess., 1333–35.
50. *Ibid.*, 1891. A joint commission consisting of seven members of each house would investigate whether existing unemployment was due to a concerted effort by businessmen to reduce wages, as well as other causes of unemployment; the feasibility of a national system of employment exchanges; a national system of unemployment insurance; the advisability of a national minimum wage law; legislation for the elimination of child labor; the undertaking of public works; and legislation to reduce the recurrence of unemployment.
51. *New York Call*, May 28, 1921, 1; *New York Times*, May 29, 1921, 2:1.
52. *Congressional Record*, 67th Congress, 1st Sess., 5497; *New York Times*, August 24, 1921, 1.
53. *New York Call*, August 23, 1921, 1.
54. Samuel Gompers to Meyer London, September 22, 1921, Gompers Papers, vol. 283:357.
55. Paxson, *American Democracy*, 3:234–35; Bernard Mandel, *Samuel Gompers: A Biography* (Yellow Springs, OH: Antioch Press, 1963), 489.
56. *New York Call*, September 12, 1921, 2.
57. President Harding and Secretary of Commerce Herbert Hoover, the chairman of the conference, suggested to the delegates that they limit their recommendations to those things which could be achieved through voluntary private initiative rather than through government "paternalism" and spending. Mandel, 489.

58. *Ibid.*, 490.
59. *Congressional Record*, 67th Congress, 1st Sess., 6462–63.
60. *Congressional Record*, 67th Congress, 2nd Sess., 2415–56; *New York Call*, February 11, 1922, 1.
61. *New York Call*, February 25, 1922, 7; *New York Times*, February 24, 1922, 12.
62. *Congressional Record*, 67th Congress, 2nd Sess., 4421–22.
63. *New York Call*, March 24, 1922, 1.
64. Philip Taft, *Organized Labor in American History* (New York: Harper and Row, 1964), 353–54.
65. *Congressional Record*, 67th Congress, 2nd Sess., 1341.
66. *New York Call*, January 20, 1922, 1.
67. Hicks, 69.
68. *Congressional Record*, 67th Congress, 2nd Sess., 6219–20. For London's speech on May 5, see *Ibid.*, 6417–18.
69. Hicks, 70–71.
70. *New York Call*, August 20, 1922, 2.
71. *Congressional Record*, 67th Congress, 2nd Sess., 11719–21.
72. *Ibid.*, 12349.
73. *Ibid.*, 13027–28. The House also passed a bill, which London supported, extending the Interstate Commerce Commission's power and providing for the appointment of a Federal fuel distributor. *Ibid.*, 11935–36.
74. Hicks, 71.
75. The Bankruptcy Act provided that claims of wages to the extent of one hundred dollars earned within ninety days prior to the filing of bankruptcy proceedings enjoyed priority, if there were any remaining assets. Before, however, any money could be used for the payment of employees' wages, provision had to be made for the payment of administrative expenses. This practice, coupled with fraudulent concealment of property by employers, deprived thousands of workers of a large part of their earnings. *Congressional Record*, 67th Congress, 2nd Sess., 2357; *New York Call*, June 10, 1921, 1.
76. *Ibid.*
77. *New York Call*, November 1; *Congressional Record*, 67th Congress, 1st Sess., 7055–56.
78. *Congressional Record*, 67th Congress, 1st Sess., 807; *New York Times*, January 13, 1922, 4; *New York Call*, January 13, 1922, 1.
79. See Link, *Woodrow Wilson and the Progressive Era*, 189–90, for a description of the program. Senator William E. Borah had introduced a resolution requesting the president to invite representatives from Great Britain and Japan to a conference on naval disarmament. Hicks, 32–33.
80. *Congressional Record*, 67th Congress, 1st Sess., 620.
81. *Ibid.*, 809–10. See also *Ibid.*, 67th Congress, 2nd Sess., 5753.
82. *New York Call*, April 29, 1921, 1. On June 29, the proponents of disarmament scored an important victory when the House agreed to accept a Senate amendment to the navy bill authorizing the president to invite the British and Japanese governments to send representatives to a conference on naval limitation. President Harding, who opposed the amendment, nevertheless signed the bill on July 12, 1921. *Congressional Record*, 67th Congress, 1st Sess., 3223; Hicks, 34. For a detailed discussion of the Washington Arms Limitation Conference, see Paxson, *American Democracy*, 3:232–50, and Hicks, 34–39.
83. *Congressional Record*, 67th Congress, 2nd Sess., 4268–70.
84. Paxson, *American Democracy*, 3:207–8.
85. *Congressional Record*, 67th Congress, 1st Sess., 2444.
86. *Ibid.*, 2461–63.
87. *Ibid.*, 2546–47, 2549. London proposed that the conference consider the following: the creation of a permanent international parliament, the cancellation of Allied war debts, a revision of the Versailles Treaty based upon the recognition of the equal rights of all nations, international free trade and, finally, universal disarmament. *New York Call*, June 14, 1921, 1. The Senate accepted the House version of the resolution, and the House agreed to the conference report on June 30. President Harding signed it on July 2, 1921. Paxson, *American Democracy*, 3:209.
88. *Congressional Record*, 67th Congress, 1st Sess., 2430.
89. *New York Call*, June 11, 1921, 1; *New York Times*, June 11, 1921, 2.
90. *Congressional Record*, 67th Congress, 2nd Sess., 428–30.
91. *Ibid.*, 9626. *New York Times*, February 4, 1922, 2; *New York Call*, February 4, 1922, 4.
92. The *New York Tribune* and the *New York World* reported that the Republicans hoped to ensure the reelection of Congressman Nathan D. Penman in the Fourteenth Congressional District. Penman was the son-in-law of Samuel S. Koenig, Republican boss of New York County. *New York Tribune*, April 12, 1922, 10; *New York World*, April 15, 1922, 7.
93. *New York World*, March 23, 1922, 1; Louis London to Meyer London, March 22, 1922; Julius Gerber to Marx Lewis, May 31, 1922, London Papers. *Congressional Directory*, 68th Congress (Washington, DC, 1923), 72.
94. *New York Call*, March 22, 1922, 1. Julius Gerber, executive secretary of Local New York, told the *New York Call* that those responsible for the Tolbert-Ullman bill had not listed it in the alphabetical index under the heading "Redistricting of Congressional Districts." Only after checking bills introduced by Tolbert had he discovered that it had been presented on March 1, the last day for such action in the current legislative session.
95. *Ibid.*, March 23, 1922, 4.
96. *Ibid.*, March 28, 1922, 4.
97. *Ibid.*
98. *Ibid.*, April 6, 1922, 3; April 9, 1922, 1; April 10, 1922, 1; April 11, 1922, 1.

99. The delegation included Marx Lewis, London's congressional secretary; Benjamin Schlesinger, president of the ILGWU; William F. Kehoe, secretary of the Central Trades and Labor Council; Morris Kaufman, president of the International Furriers' Union; and Senators Edmund Seidel and August Claessens, Socialist members of the New York Legislature. *Ibid.*, April 12, 1922, 1, 3.

100. John Block, "Memorandum in Opposition to the Gerrymander Bill," April 11, 1922, London Papers; *New York Call*, April 12, 1922, 1, 3. Under the present bill, the Eleventh District would have 212,719 people, the Thirteenth 191,803, the Fourteenth 173,369 and the Twelfth only 147,476.

101. *Ibid.*

102. *Ibid.*, April 15, 1922, 1.

103. H. Rogoff, 301–2. London discussed this sense of futility and loneliness while discussing the unemployment issue in the House on February 10, 1922. He had raised the question of unemployment on six occasions, he said, and was tired of it. "I am weary of playing the part of the one disturber." *Congressional Record*, 67th Congress, 2nd Sess., 2145. For a description of the Socialist Party in the 1920s, see Shannon, 163–67; Irving Howe, *World of Our Fathers* (New York: Harcourt Brace Jovanovich, 1976), 312. Howe points out that in 1912 the proportion of registered voters on the Lower East Side was the lowest in New York.

104. *New York Call*, July 8, 1922, 1.

105. H. Rogoff, 303. Julius Gerber wrote Marx Lewis that it had been a "rather hard job to persuade London to accept the nomination, and he was not sure what made him change his mind. Julius Gerber to Marx Lewis, August 26, 1922, London Papers.

106. Shannon, 168–69.

107. *New York Call*, July 2, 1922, 1.

108. *Ibid.*, July 17, 1922, 1; November 7, 1922, 6.

109. *Ibid.*, October 16, 1922, 2.

110. *New York Times*, August 26, 1922, 20; *New York Call*, August 28, 1922, 10.

111. *New York Call*, September 21, 1922, 5–6.

112. *Ibid.*, August 30, 1922, 1.

113. *Ibid.*, October 5, 1922, 2.

114. *Ibid.*, October 18, 1922, 3.

115. *Ibid.*, October 16, 1922, 2.

116. *Ibid.*, October 5, 1922, 2. Dickstein served in the House until 1945. For a biographical sketch of Dickstein see U.S. Library of Congress, *Biographical Directory of the American Congress, 1774–1961* (Washington, DC, 1961), 811.

117. *New York Call*, October 22, 1922, 9.

118. *Ibid.*, November 6, 1922, 8.

119. *Ibid.*, October 1, 1922, 11; October 17, 1922, 7; October 18, 1922, 3; October 19, 1922, 7; October 23, 1922, 7; October 27, 1922, 1; November 1, 1922, 7.

120. *Ibid.*, September 30, 1922, 11; October 5, 1922, 9; October 8, 1922, 9; October 2, 1922, 9.

121. "Cloakmakers Active in Meyer London's Campaign," *Justice* 4 (October 27, 1922): 1; *New York Call*, October 30, 1922, 7.

122. *Ibid.*, November 4, 1922, 9; *Daily Forward*, November 3, 1922, 1.

123. *New York Call*, October 22, 1922, 9; October 23, 1922, 8; October 26, 1922, 9; October 28, 1922, 2; October 30, 1922, 7; November 1, 1922, 4; November 5, 1922, 2; October 6, 1922, 11.

124. Draper, *The Roots of American Communism*, 378–79, 383.

125. *Daily Forward*, October 29, 1922, 6; October 30, 1922, 2; October 31, 1922, 7; November 1, 1922, 6; November 2, 1922, 6; November 3, 1922, 4, 5, 8, 10.

126. *New York Call*, October 18, 1922, 3; October 23, 1922, 8.

127. *Daily Forward*, October 29, 1922, 1; *New York Call*, October 29, 1922, 1.

128. *Ibid.*, October 21, 1922, 1.

129. *Ibid.*, October 28, 1922, 1. In one tenement house occupied by Italian families, twenty-six men had registered, but Gilbert's investigation showed that none of them lived there and that no one in the building knew them.

130. *Ibid.*, October 29, 1922, 1. The *New York Call* questioned whether Banton refused to act because Tammany did not want to alarm the floaters and repeaters it had planted to steal votes. *Ibid.*, October 30, 1922, 8. The *New York Tribune* deplored the fact that differences existed between Banton and Gilbert over the indictment of election law violators. *New York Tribune*, November 7, 1922, 14.

131. *New York Call*, October 24, 1922, 7.

132. *Ibid.*, November 1, 1922, 4.

133. *Ibid.*, November 2, 1922, 7; November 5, 1922, 1; November 6, 1922, 1–2.

134. *Ibid.*

135. *Ibid.*, 8; *Daily Forward*, November 7, 1922, 1.

136. Samuel Dickstein (Democrat) 11,027, 60.08 percent of the whole vote

Meyer London (Socialist) 5,900, 32.55 percent of the whole vote

Louis Zeltner (Republican) 1,183, 6.51 percent of the whole vote

See *Official Canvass of the Vote in New York County*, November 7, 1922, 63.

137. *Ibid.*, London failed to carry the Fourth Assembly District in all of his bids for Congress in the Twelfth Congressional District. *New York World*, November 8, 1922, 2; *Congressional Directory*, 68th Congress (Washington, DC, 1923), 72.

138. *Daily Forward*, November 8, 1922, 1.

139. John D. Buenker, *Urban Liberalism and Progressive Reform* (New York: Norton, 1978), 10–11.

140. *New York World*, November 7, 1922, 2.

141. *New York Call*, November 9, 1922, 8.

142. Paxson, *American Democracy*, 3:351–53.

143. The Democrats reduced the Republican majority in the House from 168 to 18 and in the Senate from 22 to 8. *Ibid.*, 311.

144. *Congressional Record*, 67th Congress, 3rd Sess., 73.
145. *Ibid.*, 429.
146. Paxson, *American Democracy*, 3:354–56.
147. *Congressional Record*, 67th Congress, 4th Sess. 1603, 2207–8, 1603, 3370–72.
148. *Ibid.*, 2088; *New York Call*, January 21, 1923, 3.

Chapter 12

1. H. Rogoff, 304–6; Hertz, 274.
2. *New York Times*, October 6, 1924, 3; October 7, 1924, 22. See Kenneth MacKay, *The Progressive Movement of 1924* (New York: Octagon, 1966 [1947]), and Weinstein, *The Decline of Socialism in America*, for the Socialist role in the Progressive Party.
3. *New York Times*, November 5, 1925, 6.
4. Richard Hofstadter, *Age of Reform* (New York: Vintage, 1955), 98. Hofstadter writes, "The moral and intellectual leverage of the Socialist Party and Socialist ideas in the Progressive era have never been sufficiently recognized." See Gordon J. Goldberg "Meyer London and the National Social Insurance Movement 1914–1922," *American Jewish Historical Quarterly* 65 (September 1975): 59–73.
5. London left a small estate of four thousand dollars (valued at about fifty thousand dollars in 2010 dollars) to his wife Anna and his daughter Isabel. *New York Times*, June 25, 1926, 6.
6. H. Rogoff, 209, 305–6; *New York Call*, March 5, 1922, 1. Samuel Gompers stated that London had "stood with all his ability for the men who toil for the City of New York and the United States."
7. *New York Times*, June 7, 1926, 1.
8. *Ibid.*, June 10, 1926, 1.
9. *Ibid.*

Bibliography

Archival and Manuscript Sources

John B. Andrews Papers. M. P. Catherwood Library, Cornell University, Ithaca, New York.
August Claessens Papers. Bobst Library, New York University.
Constantine, Robert J., ed. *Letters of Eugene V. Debs.* 3 vols. Urbana: University of Illinois, 1990.
Samuel Gompers Papers. Library of Congress.
International Ladies' Garment Workers' Union. *Proceedings of Annual Conventions, 1902–1918.*
Meyer London Papers. Bobst Library, New York University
Minute Books of the New York Local of the Socialist Party. Bobst Library, New York University.
Minutes of the Executive Board of the International Ladies' Garment Workers' Union, 1913–1917. M.P. Catherwood Library, Cornell University.
Socialist Party. *Proceedings of National Conventions, 1904–1922.* Bobst Library, New York University.
Woodrow Wilson Papers. Library of Congress.

Federal and State Government Publications

The City Record, Official Canvass of the Votes Cast in the Counties of New York, Bronx, Kings, Queens, and Richmond, 1904, 1910, 1911, 1912, 1914, 1916, 1918, 1920, 1922, 1925.
New York Secretary of State. *Manual for the Use of the Legislature of the State of New York,* 1896, 1898, 1899, 1904.
U.S. *Congressional Record,* 64th, 65th, 67th Congresses.
U.S. House of Representatives. *Hearings on Congress of Neutral Nations, House Joint Resolution 38.* 64th Cong., 1st Sess. Washington, DC: Government Printing Office, 1916.
U.S. House of Representatives. *Hearings on Commission to Study Social Insurance and Unemployment,* 64th Congress, 1st Sess., Washington, Government Printing Office, 1915.
U.S. Library of Congress. *Biographical Directory of the American Congress, 1774–1961.* Washington, DC: Government Printing Office, 1961.
U.S. Library of Congress. *Official Congressional Directory for the Use of the United States Congress.* 64th Congress, 1st Sess. 3rd ed. Compiled by Edgar E. Mountjoy. Washington, DC, May 1916.
U.S. Library of Congress. *Official Congressional Directory for the Use of the United States Congress.* 65th Cong., 1st Sess. Compiled by Edgar E. Mountjoy. Washington, DC, April, 1917.

Books

Ameringer, Oscar. *If You Don't Weaken.* New York: Henry Holt, 1940.
Antonovsky, Aaron. *The Early Jewish Labor Movement in the United States.* New York: YIVO Institute for Jewish Research, 1961.
Baker, Ray S., and William E. Dodd, eds. *War and Peace: Presidential Messages, Addresses, and Public Papers (1917- 1924) by Woodrow Wilson.* Vol. 1. New York: Harper and Brothers, 1927.
Baron, Salo W. *The Russian Jew Under Tsars and Soviets.* New York: Macmillan, 1964.
Buenker, John D. *Urban Liberalism and Progressive Reform.* New York: Norton, 1978.
Burgin, Herz. *Di Geschichte fun der Idisher Arbeiter Bewegung in Amerika, Rusland, England.* New York: United Hebrew Trades, 1915.
Carpenter, Jesse Thomas. *Competiveness and Collective Bargaining in the Needle Trades 1910–1967.* Ithaca, NY: Cornell University Press, 1972.
Chafee, Zechariah. *Free Speech in the United*

States. Cambridge, MA: Harvard University Press, 1941.

Claessens, August. *Didn't We Have Fun*. New York: Rand School of Social Science, 1953.

Cohen, Julius Henry. *They Builded Better Than They Knew*. New York: Messner, 1946.

Cooper, John Milton, Jr. *Pivotal Decades: The United States, 1900–1920*. New York: Norton, 1990.

Curry, Roy Watson. *Woodrow Wilson and Far Eastern Policy, 1913–1921*. New York: Bookman Associates, 1957.

Danish, Max, and Leo Stein, eds. *ILGWU News-History, 1910–1911*. New York: International Ladies' Garment Workers' Union, 1950.

De Conde, Alexander. *A History of American Foreign Policy*. New York: Scribner, 1963.

Douglas, Paul H. *Real Wages in the United States, 1890–1926*. Boston: Houghton, 1930.

Douglas, Paul H., and Aaron Director. *The Problem of Unemployment*. New York: Macmillan, 1934.

Draper, Theodore. *The Roots of American Communism*. New York: Viking, 1957.

Dubofsky, Melvyn. *We Shall Be All: A History of the IWW*. New York: Quadrangle, 1969.

Epstein, Melech. *Jewish Labor in the U.S.A., 1914–1952*. Vol. 2. New York: Trade Union Sponsoring Committee, 1953.

———. *Profiles of Eleven*. Detroit: Wayne State University Press, 1965.

Faulkner, Harold U. *The Decline of Laissez Faire, 1897–1917*. Vol. 7 of *The Economic History of the United States*, ed. Henry David, Harold U. Faulkner, Louis M. Hacker, Curtis P. Nettels, and Fred A. Shannon. New York: Harper and Row, 1968.

Fine, Nathan. *Labor and Farmer Parties in the United States, 1828–1928*. New York: Rand School of Social Science, 1928.

Foner, Philip S. *The Fur and Leather Workers Union*. Newark, NJ: Nordan Press, 1950.

———. *History of the Labor Movement in the United States*. Vol. 2. New York: International Publishers, 1955.

Franklin, John Hope. *From Slavery to Freedom*. 3rd ed. New York: Knopf, 1967.

Fuchs, Lawrence H. *The Political Behavior of American Jews*. Glencoe, IL: Free Press, 1956.

Gaddis, John Lewis. *Russia, the Soviet Union and the United States: An Interpretive History*. 2nd ed. New York: McGraw-Hill, 1990.

Ginger, Raymond S. *The Bending Cross: A Biography of Eugene Victor Debs*. New Brunswick, NJ: Rutgers University Press, 1949.

Greenwald, Richard A. *The Triangle Fire, the Protocol of Peace, and Industrial Peace in Progressive Era*. Philadelphia: Temple University Press, 2005.

Henderson, Thomas M. *Tammany Hall and the New Immigrants*. New York: Arno Press, 1976.

Hertz, Jacob S. *Der Idisher Sotsialist Bewegung in Amerika*. New York: Der Wecker, 1954.

Hicks, John D. *Republican Ascendency, 1921–1933*. New York: Harper and Row, 1966.

Higham, John. *Strangers in the Land: Patterns of American Nativism, 1860–1925*. 2d Ed. New Brunswick, NJ: Rutgers University Press, 1988.

Hillquit, Morris. *Loose Leaves from a Busy Life*. New York: Macmillan, 1934.

Hoffman, B. *Fuftsig Yor mit di Clokemacher Union, 1886–1936*. New York: Local 17, 1936.

Hofstadter, Richard. *Age of Reform*. New York: Vintage, 1955.

Howe, Irving. *World of Our Fathers*. New York: Harcourt Brace Jovanovich, 1976.

Howe, Irving, and Lewis Coser. *The American Communist Party, 1919–1957*. Boston: Beacon, 1957.

Hurwitz, Maximillian. *The Workmen's Circle: Its History, Ideals, Organization, and Institutions*. New York: Workmen's Circle, 1936.

Jessup, Philip C. *Elihu Root*. Vol. 2. New York: Dodd, Mead, 1938.

Jones, Maldwyn Allen. *American Immigration*. Chicago: University of Chicago Press, 1960.

Keating, Edward. *The Gentleman from Colorado: A Memoir*. Denver, CO: Sage, 1964.

Kennedy, David. *Over Here: The First World War and American Society*. New York: Oxford University Press, 1982.

Kipnis, Ira. *The American Socialist Movement, 1897–1912*. New York: Columbia University Press, 1951.

Kotzin, Daniel P. *Judah L. Magnes: An American Jewish Nonconformist*. Syracuse, NY: Syracuse University Press 2010.

Leuchtenburg, William E. *The Perils of Prosperity, 1914–1932*. 2nd ed. Chicago: University of Chicago Press, 1993.

Levine, Louis. *The Women's Garment Workers: A History of the International Ladies' Garment Workers' Union*. New York: B.W. Huebsch, 1924.

Link, Arthur S., with the collaboration of William B. Catton. *American Epoch: A History of the United States since the 1890's*. 3rd ed. New York: Knopf, 1967.

_____. *Wilson: Campaigns for Progressivism and Peace, 1916–1917*. Vol. 5. Princeton, NJ: Princeton University Press, 1965.

_____. *Wilson: Confusions and Crises, 1915–1916*. Vol. 4. Princeton, NJ: Princeton University Press, 1964.

_____. *Wilson: The Struggle for Neutrality, 1914–1915*. Vol. 3. Princeton, NJ: Princeton University Press, 1960.

_____. *Woodrow Wilson: Revolution, War and Peace*. Arlington Heights, IL: Harland Davidson, 1979.

_____. *Woodrow Wilson and the Progressive Era, 1910–1917*. New York: Harper and Row, 1954.

Livermore, Seward W. *Politics Is Adjourned: Woodrow Wilson and the War Congress, 1916–1918*. Middletown, CT: Wesleyan University Press, 1966.

Livesay, Harold C. *Samuel Gompers and Organized Labor in America*. Boston: Little, Brown, 1978.

MacKay, Kenneth Campbell. *The Progressive Labor Movement of 1924*. New York: Octagon, 1966 [1947].

Magidoff, Jacob. *Der Spiegel fun der East Side*. New York: Author, 1923.

Mandel, Bernard. *Samuel Gompers: A Biography*. Yellow Springs, OH: Antioch Press, 1963.

Mann, Arthur. *LaGuardia: A Fighter Against His Times*. Philadelphia: Lippincott, 1959.

Mason, Alpheus Thomas. *Brandeis: A Free Man's Life*. New York: Viking, 1956.

Maurer, James H. *It Can Be Done*. New York: Rand School of Social Science, 1938.

Mayer, Arno J. *Wilson vs. Lenin: Political Origins of the New Diplomacy, 1917–1918*. Cleveland: World Publishing Company, 1963.

McCreesh, Carolyn Daniel. *Women in the Campaign to Organize Garment Workers 1880–1917*. New York: Garland Publishing, 1985.

Michels, Tony. *A Fire in Their Hearts: Yiddish Socialists in New York*. Cambridge, MA: Harvard University Press, 2005.

Miller, Sally M. *Victor L. Berger and the Promise of Constructive Socialism, 1910–1920*. Westport, CT: Greenwood, 1973.

Morgan, H. Wayne. *Eugene V. Debs: Socialist for President*. Syracuse: Syracuse University Press, 1962.

Murray, Robert K. *The Politics of Normalcy: Governmental Theory and Practice in the Harding-Coolidge Era*. New York: Norton, 1973.

_____. *Red Scare: A Study in National Hysteria, 1919–1920*. Minneapolis: University of Minnesota Press, 1955.

Parmet, Robert D. *The Master of Seventh Avenue: David Dubinsky and the American Labor Movement*. New York: New York University Press, 2005.

Paxson, Frederic L. *American Democracy and the World War: America at War, 1917-1918*. Vol. 2. Boston: Houghton Mifflin, 1939.

_____. *American Democracy and the World War: Postwar Years; Normalcy, 1918–1923*. Vol. 3. Berkeley: University of California Press, 1948.

Peterson, Horace C., and Gilbert C. Fite. *Opponents of War, 1917–1918*. Madison: University of Wisconsin Press, 1957.

Pratt, Julius W. *America's Colonial Experiment*. New York: Prentice Hall, 1950.

Preston, William, Jr. *Aliens and Dissenters: Federal Suppression of Radicals, 1903–1933*. New York: Harper and Row, 1963.

Quint, Howard H. *The Forging of American Socialism: Origins of the Modern Movement*. New York: Bobbs-Merrill, 1964.

Rischin, Moses. *The Promised City: New York's Jews, 1870–1914*. Rev. ed. Cambridge, MA: Harvard University Press, 1977.

Rogoff, Harry. *An East Side Epic: The Life and Work of Meyer London*. New York: Vanguard, 1930.

Russell, Charles E. *Bare Hands and Stone Walls*. New York: Scribner, 1933.

Salvatore, Nick. *Eugene V. Debs: Citizen and Socialist*. Urbana: University of Illinois Press, 1996.

Sanders, Ronald. *The Downtown Jews: Portraits of an Immigration Generation*. New York: Harper and Row, 1969.

Schlesinger, Arthur, Jr. *The Age of Roosevelt: The Politics of Upheaval*. Boston: Houghton Mifflin, 1960.

Seidman, Joel. *The Needle Trades*. New York: Farrar and Reinhart, 1942.

Shannon, David A. *The Socialist Party of America*. New York: Macmillan, 1955.

Sorin, Gerald. *The Prophetic Minority: American Jewish Radicals 1860–1920*. Bloomington: Indiana University Press, 1985.

Soule, George. *Prosperity Decade: From War to Depression, 1917–1929*. Vol. 8 of *The Economic History of the United States*, ed. Henry David, Harold U. Faulkner, Louis M. Hacker, Curtis P. Nettels, and Fred A. Shannon. New York: Harper and Row, 1968.

Swisher, Carl Brent. *American Constitutional Development*. Cambridge, MA: Houghton Mifflin, 1954.

Taft, Philip. *The A F of L in the Time of Gompers*. New York: Harper, 1957.
——. *Organized Labor in American History*. New York: Harper and Row, 1964.
Trachtenberg, Alexander. *American Socialists and the War*. New York: Rand School of Social Science, 1917.
Tyler Gus. *Look for the Union Label: A History of the International Ladies Garment Workers' Union*. New York: M.E. Sharp, 1995.
Urofsky, Melvyn I. *American Zionism from Herzl to the Holocaust*. New York: Anchor Press/Doubleday, 1976.
——. *Louis D. Brandeis: A Life*. New York: Random House, 2009.
Van der Slice, Austin. *International Labor, Diplomacy and Peace, 1914–1919*. Philadelphia: University of Pennsylvania Press, 1941.
Von Drehle, David. *Triangle: The Fire That Changed America*. New York: Atlantic Monthly Press, 2003.
Waldman, Louis. *Labor Lawyer*. New York: Dutton, 1945.
Walling, William English, ed. *Socialists and the War*. New York: Rand School of Social Science, 1915.
Weinstein, James. *The Decline of Socialism in America, 1912–1925*. New York: Monthly Review Press, 1967.
Zinn, Howard. *La Guardia in Congress*. Ithaca, NY: Cornell University Press, 1959.

Articles

Bell, Daniel. "The Background and Development of Marxian Socialism in the United States." In *Socialism and American Life*, vol. 1, ed. Donald Drew Egbert and Stow Persons. Princeton, NJ: Princeton University Press, 1942.
Boudin, Louis. "A Disgraceful Episode." *New Review* 4 (June 1916): 174–175.
——. "Milwaukee and New York." *New York Call*, November 24, 1910, 6.
——. "Socialist Congressional Responsibility." *New Review* 4 (January 1916): 26–27.
"Cloakmakers Active in Meyer London Campaign." *Justice* 4 (October 1922): 1.
"Cloakmakers' Campaign Committee Win Congress Seat for London." *Justice* 2 (November 1920): 1.
"Cloakmakers Determined to Elect London and Hillquit." *Justice* 2 (October 1920): 1.
"Cloakmakers' Joint Board Rejoices Over Election of Meyer London." *Justice* 2 (November 1920): 1.
"Cloakmakers' Socialist Committee Conducts Rousing Campaign." *Justice* 2 (October 1920): 1.
"Cloakmakers' Socialist Committee in Whirlwind Campaign Finish." *Justice* 2 (October 1920): 1.
"Congratulations to Our Elected Congressman." *Ladies' Garment Worker* 7 (December 1916): 7–8.
"Congressman London Defines His Position." *Ladies' Garment Worker* 7 (September 1918): 28–29.
"Congressman London Does Not Fear Results." *Fur Worker* 2, no. 33 (August 1918): 3.
"Congressman London Renominated in Twelfth Congressional District." *Fur Worker* 2, no. 31 (June 1918): 4.
Danish, Max. H. "The Campaign in the Ninth." *New York Call*, November 29, 1910, 6.
——. "Monthly News and Events." *Ladies' Garment Worker* 6 (July 1915): 11.
[Dannenberg, Karl]. "Londonism and Party Discipline." *Radical Review* 2 (October–December 1918): 213–214.
——. "Meyer London's Miss." *Radical Review* 1 (July 1917): 64–69.
Dubofsky, Melvyn. "Success and Failure of Socialism in New York City, 1900–1918: A Case-Study." *Labor History* 9, no. 3 (Fall 1968): 361–375.
Editorial in *Advance*, April 1917, 4.
Editorial in *Ladies' Garment Worker* 3 (November 1912): 1–2.
Feigenbaum, William F. "Child of the Workers." *New Leader*, June 12, 1926, 1.
Frank, Dana. "Housewives, Socialists and the Politics of Food: The 1917 New York Cost of Living Protests." *Feminist Studies* 11, no. 2 (Summer 1985): 255–285.
Goldberg, Gordon J. "Meyer London and the National Social Insurance Movement 1914–1922." *American Jewish Historical Quarterly* 65 (September 1975): 59–73.
Gompers, Samuel. "Intellectuals Please Take Note." *American Federationist* (March 1916): 198–199.
——. "Voluntary Social Insurance vs. Compulsory." *American Federationist* 23 (May 1916): 333–357.
——. "Voluntary Social Insurance vs. Compulsory." *American Federationist* 23 (June 1916): 453–466.
——. "Voluntary Social Insurance vs. Com-

pulsory," *American Federationist* 23 (August 1916): 669–681.
Gorenstein, Arthur. "A Portrait of Ethnic Politics: The Socialists and the 1908–1910 Congressional Elections on the East Side." *Publication of the American Jewish Historical Society* 50, no. 3 (March 1961): 202–238.
Hourwich, Isaac A. "Congressman London on Immigration." *New Review* 4 (May 1916): 137–138.
"How to Elect Socialist Candidates." *Fur Worker* 4, no. 60 (September 1920): 1.
"International Members Active in Labor Party Campaign." *Justice* 4 (October 1922): 1.
"Jewish Emancipation Banquet." *American Hebrew* 108 (May 1917): 41–42.
"Jewish Workers Active in Fourth Liberty Loan." *Ladies' Garment Worker* 7 (November 1918): 24–25.
"Labor Amnesty Committee Sees Pres. Harding." *Justice* 3 (April 1921): 1.
Lang, Harry. "Every Bit a Man." *American Federationist* 33 (August 1926): 982–984.
Lee, Algernon. "Meyer London." In *Dictionary of American Biography*, ed. Dumas Malone, 11 (New York: Scribner, 1933).
Lewis, Marx. "Meyer London in Congress." In *American Labor Year Book*, vol. 3, ed. Alexander Trachtenberg, 421–427 (New York: Rand School of Social Science, 1919).
———. "Meyer London in Congress." In *American Labor Year Book*, vol. 4, ed. Alexander Trachtenberg, 410–413 (New York: Rand School of Social Science, 1921).
Liesin, A. "Der kongressional campayn oifn New Yorker east side." *Zukunft* 19 (November 1914): 1082–1088.
London, Isabel M. *Meyer London: An Appreciation*. London Papers, Bobst Library, New York University.
London, Meyer. "Democrats Join Republicans in Betrayal of Nation to Militarism." *American Socialist*, December 1915, 1.
———. "Di vahl resultaten un di brenendste frage oif den tagsordenung." *Zukunft* 20 (December 1915): 1067–1073.
———. "The Government as Grocer." *Independent* 89 (March 1917): 451–459.
———. "Meyer London's Address." *Ladies' Garment Worker*, July 1914, 8–9.
———. "The Nation and the Problem of Unemployment." *American Labor Legislative Review* 5 (June 1915): 446–449.
———. "The Promise of Great Russia." *Independent*, November 1917, 367–368.
———. "Socialism and the Terms of Peace." *Academy of Political Science Proceedings* 7 (July 1917): 289–293.
———. "There Must Be an End." *The Masses*, May 1915, 18.
———. "The Unemployed." *The Masses*, April 1915, 20–21.
———. "The Veto Power of the Supreme Court." *American Federationist* 30 (March 1923): 224–231.
———. "Why Federal Management of the Railroads Is Not Socialism." *Fur Worker* 2, no. 26 (January 1918): 6.
Lore, Ludwig. "The Elections." *The Class Struggle* 2 (December 1918): 621.
———. "Meyer London." *The Class Struggle* 1 (September–October 1917): 100–101.
———. "Our Obedient Congress." *The Class Struggle* 1 (November–December 1917): 44–45.
Meimon, Benjamin. "Congress Considers Reconstruction." *Advance* 2 (October 1918): 5.
"Meyer London." *Fur Worker* 10, no. 115 (June 1926): 4.
"Meyer London Must Be Reelected." *Fur Worker* 2, no. 36 (October 1918): 1.
M.R. "Applied Londonism." *Radical Review* 1 (January 1918): 308–310.
"N.Y. Furriers to Help Reelect Meyer London for Congress." *Fur Worker* 2, no. 34 (September 1918): 1.
"Our Candidates." *Justice* 2 (October 1920): 4.
"Our Members Duty on Election Day." *Fur Worker* 2, no. 36 (October 1918): 6.
"The Representative with a Million Constituents." *Independent* 80 (November 1914): 280–281.
"Results of the Election." *Justice* 2 (November 1920): 4.
Rogin, Michael. "Voluntarism: The Political Functions of an Anti-Political Doctrine." In *The American Labor Movement*," ed. David Brody. New York: Harper and Row, 1971.
Rosebury, A. "Congressman Meyer London-Congratulations." *Fur Worker* 4, no. 61 (November 1920), 6.
Schapiro, J. Salwyn. "Henry Moskowitz: A Social Reformer in Politics." *Outlook* 102 (October 1912): 446–449.
"The Socialist Congressman." *The Public* 21 (May 1918): 626.
"A Socialist Digest." *New Review* 3 (December 1915): 368–369.
"Socialist Party Going Strong in This Year's

Campaign." *Fur Worker* 2, no. 36 (October 1918): 7.
"Socialist Terms of Peace." *New Review* 4 (January 1916): 1–2.
"Socialist Vote Increased." *Advance* 2 (November 1918): 1.
Tattler. "The Solitary Socialist." *Nation* 102 (May 1916): 478.
Todd, Laurence. "The Lone Congressman," *Advance* 10–11 (June 1926): 2.
_____. "Report of the Work in Congress of Meyer London, Representative of the Twelfth New York District." *American Labor Year Book*, vol. 1, ed. Alexander Trachtenberg (New York: Rand School of Social Science, 1916): 102–104.
"A Victory for Socialism and the Worker." *Ladies' Garment Worker* 5 (December 1914): 12–13.
Walker, Forrest A. "Compulsory Health Insurance: The Next Great Step in Social Legislation." *Journal of American History* 16 (September 1969): 290–304.
Weinzweig, Irving. "The Life of a Fighter." *Advance* 10–11 (June 1926): 8.
Yellowitz, Irwin. "The Origins of Unemployment Reform in the United States." *Labor History* 9, no. 3 (Fall 1981): 338–360.

Newspapers

The American Socialist, (Chicago), 1914–1917.
Appeal to Reason (*New Appeal*) (Girard, Kansas), 1910–1922.
Eye Opener (Chicago), 1917–1920.
Milwaukee Leader, 1914–1916, 1918, 1920, 1922 (October–December).
New York American, 1914, 1916, 1918 (November), 1920 (August, November), 1922 (November).
New York Call (New Leader), 1908–1926.
New York Daily Forward (Yiddish), 1910, 1912, 1914, 1916, 1918, 1920, 1922 (October–November).
New York Evening Journal, 1914 (November).
New York Evening Mail, 1918 (November).
New York Evening World, 1915 (December).
New York Post, 1914–1922, passim.
New York Press, 1914 (November).
New York Sun, 1914, 1918 (November).
New York Times, 1910–1926.
New York Tribune, 1914, 1916 (November), 1917 (March–April), 1918 (July, November), 1920 (November), 1922 (April, November).
New York World, 1914, 1916 (October–November), 1917 (December), 1918, 1920 (October–November), 1922 (October–November, April).
New Yorker Volkszeitung (German) 1896, 1897–1898 (November).
People (Anti–De Leon) (New York), 1900.
Social Democrat (Milwaukee), 1897–1898.
Social Democratic Herald (Milwaukee), 1897–1900.
Der Tag (Yiddish) (New York), 1914, 1918 (November).

Unpublished Works

Anderson, Paul H. "The Attitude of the American Leftist Leaders Toward the Russian Revolution, 1917–1923." PhD diss., Notre Dame University, 1942.
Berman, Hyman. "The Era of the Protocol: A Chapter in the History of the International Ladies' Garment Workers' Union, 1910–1916. PhD diss., Columbia University, 1956.
Cohen, Naomi Wiener. "The Public Career of Oscar S. Straus." PhD diss., Columbia University, 1955.
Dubofsky, Melvyn. "New York City Labor in the Progressive Era, 1910–1918: A Study of Organized Labor in an Era of Reform." PhD diss., University of Rochester, 1960.
Ewald, Peter Kenneth. "Congressional Apportionment and New York State." PhD diss., New York University, 1955.
Ingle, Homer Larry. "Pilgrimage to Reform: A Life of Claude Kitchin." PhD diss., University of Wisconsin, 1967.
Iversen, Robert W. "Morris Hillquit, American Social Democrat: A Study of the American Left from Haymarket to the New Deal." PhD diss., University of Iowa, 1951.
Muzik, Edward John. "Victor L. Berger: A Biography." PhD diss., Northwestern University, 1960.
Rappaport, Joseph. "Jewish Immigrants and World War I: A Study of American Yiddish Press Reactions." PhD diss., Columbia University, 1951.
Rhoads, James Berton. "The Campaign of the Socialist Party in the Election of 1920." PhD diss., American University, 1965.
Rogoff, Abraham M. "Formative Years of the Jewish Labor Movement in the United States, 1890–1900." PhD diss., Columbia University, 1945.

Index

Numbers in **bold italics** indicate pages with photographs.

Abendblatt 8
Adamson Act 129
Advance 166, 212
Agricultural Tariff Bill 245
Amalgamated Clothing Workers 136, 205, 221, 228, 232, 261
American Association for Labor Legislation 90
American Civil Liberties Union 241
American Federation of Labor 8, 19, 39, 122–23, 129, 137, 205, 237, 240, 248–49, 292n32; *see also* Gompers
American Labor Party 276
American Neutral Peace Conference 294n124
American Railway Union 8–9
American Socialist 88, 100, 105, 109, 111, 163, 166–67, 281n30, 283n124, 288n27, 288n30, 292n13, 293n74
Ameringer, Oscar 266, 284n17
Andrews, John B. 122, 292n14
Appeal to Reason 290n81, 295n44, 297n81
Arbeiter-Zeitung 8
Army Bill 116–17; *see also* preparedness
Asquith, Herbert H. 107
Austin, Richard W. 111-35

Bailey, Warren Worth 107
Balfour Declaration 205
Bankruptcy Bill 253–54, 268, 305n75
Barondess, Joseph 8–9, 44, 46
Bell, Thomas M. 155
Bennett, William 169, 171
Benson, Allan L. 158, 290n87
Berg, Michael 46
Bethmann-Hollweg, Theobald von 107
Bisbee, Arizona 164
Black, Eugene 21
Block, John S. 258, 261
Block, John W. 51, 53
Block, Louis M. 135, 141
Bloomfield, Meyer 21, 25
Bolshevik Revolution 153, 171, 202, 221–22, 270
Borowsky, Benjamin 72, 285n64
Boudin, Louis B. 106, 282n64, 288n21, 289n45, 292n48
Boyle, Edward M. 220
Brandeis, Louis 40, 73; mediator New York

Garment strike 21–23, 27, 29, 30, 279n34, 279n35, 279n70; Protocol of Peace 29, 32, 34, 36
Branstetter, Otto 235
Branting, Halemar 109
Britten, Frederick 117
Brooklyn Trolley Strike 11, **137**
Brotherhood of Painters and Paper Hangers 49
Bryan, William Jennings 11–12, 83–84, 87
Buchanan, Frank 84
Bund 46, 281n22
Burleson, Albert S. 162–63
Burnett immigration bills 129–132, 139, 145
Businessmen's League 58
Byrns, Joseph W. 182

Cahan, Abraham: cloak makers' strike 48; *Daily Forward* editor 8; early connection to socialism 7–8, 10; election (1914) 71, 76; (1918) 210, 232–33; (1920) 261; at London's funeral 271; Shirt Waist strike 18–19; supports Franklin D. Roosevelt and New Deal 275–76; tenth anniversary service 271–72, 275
Cannon Joseph 53
Cannon, Joseph D. 84
Carey, James F. 13
Carranza, Victoriano 111, 113–14; *see also* Mexican Revolution
Carrizal, Mexico 113
Central Federated Union 18, 82, 84, 136
Chamberlain, Joseph P. 291n8
Claessens, August 170, 234, 257, 263, 306n99, 320n93
Clark, Champ 99, 155, 159, 166–67, 268, 288n7
Class Struggle 171, 212, 297n91
Cloak Makers' Strike (1912) 19–27, **33**
Cohen, Isadore 36
Cohen, Julius Henry: attorney for Manufacturers' Association 2–25; Protocol of Peace 27–31, 33–36, 40, 279n63
Cohen, Samuel 281n19
Communist Labor Party 222
Communist Party (American) 262, 275
Conscription bill 159–60, 198, 242, 295n32, 299n82

315

Index

Coolidge, Calvin 240, 242
Crosser, Robert 161–62
Cutters' Union Local 10

Daily Forward (Forverts) 4, 8, 13; elections: (1898) 44; (1908) 47; (1910) 52, 54, 282n80, 282n92; (1912) 60, 283n121; (1914) 67–70, 73, 284n25, 284n29; (1916) 138–39; (1918) 210, 212; (1920) 232, 235; (1922) 262–263; Garment Workers' strike (1910) 19, 279n47; praises London on civil liberties 300n37; supports defensive war 289n34
Danish, Max H. 56, 212, 270n40, 282n94, 287n51
Darrow, Clarence 163
Dawson, Miles M. 122
Debs, Eugene V. 1, 95, 267, 287n72, 302n124; "Amnesty Day" 228, 237; candidate for president (1900) 12–13; (1904) 45; (1908) 47; (1912) 97–98, 275; (1920) 225; Congressional candidate (1914) 142; (1916) 295n8; in Federal prison 206, 215; Harding's pardon 241; on London's request for amnesty 223, 228, 233; on London's victory (1914) 142, 285n85; opposes war 154; organizes Social Democracy of America 8–10; organizes Social Democratic Party 10, 12, 13; Peace Resolution meeting 107–108, 295n85; supports London's candidacy (1910 and 1916) 59–60, 295n8; supports Susan B. Anthony amendment 287n73
Deis, Martin 145, 183–85
Deis, Martin, Jr. 298n9
De Leon, Daniel 8, 11–12, 44, 277n18, 277n19
De Silva, Albert 241
De Witt, Samuel 234
Dickstein, Samuel 260, 263, 306n136
Donnelly, James 213
Dreier, Mary 18
Dysche, John 21, 31

East Side Citizen's League 58
East Side Peddlers' Association 51, 58
East Side Voters' League 58
Eastern European Jews 44, 108, 280n1
Eastman, Max 206
Educational Alliance 6, 8
elections *see* Meyer, London
Elkus, Abram I. 210
Emergency Peace Agency 294n3
Engdahl, John Louis 163–164
Espionage Act 1, 160–64, 212, 215, 217–218, 228, 240, 242
Eye-Opener 298n15

Factory Inspection Commission 36
Farmer-Labor Party 229, **230**, 259–61
Faygnboym, Benyomen *see* Feigenbaum, Benjamin
Feigenbaum, Benjamin 18, 76, 277n1

Feigenbaum, William M. 193, 293n80
Filene, A. Lincoln 21, 25–27
Fisher, Irving 122
Flood, Henry D. 290n64
Focht, Benjamin K. 200
Foley, James A. 213
food boycotts 144–45, 165
Ford Peace Expedition 110
Fordney–McCumber Tariff 239, 247
Fourteen Points 89, 178, 219, 298n11, 301n65
Fourth Liberty Loan 207, 300n24
France, Joseph I. 188, 240
Fuller, Alvin 295n6
Fur Workers' strike (1912) 36–39; *see also* Fur Workers' Union
Fur Workers' Union 2, 16, 62, 206, 224, 229, 238, 280n4, 300n16

Gard, Warren 180, 298n49
Garrison, Lindley M. 100–1
Gaylord, Winnfield 158, 295n8
Gaynor, William J. 51, 282n64
Gerber, Julius 58, 66, 68, 135, 197, 301n55, 305n93, 306n105
German Socialists (New York) 7, 85, 207, 211, 277n18
Ghent, William 158
Gillis, Meyer 284n20
Gitlaw, Benjamin 222
Gladden, Washington 147
Goff, John W. 24–25
Goldfogle, Henry M.: background 47; Congressional elections of: (1908) 47; (1910) 51–55, 282n73, 282n90; (1912) 60–61, 283n123; (1914) 67–72, 285n64, 285n67; (1916) 135, 141; (1918) 204, 206, 208–11, 213–14, 300n29, 301n45; (1920) 227–28, 231–34, 303n147; Tammany Hall connections 51–52
Gompers, Samuel **253**; amnesty 228, 237, 302n124; endorses London (1910) 50, (1912) 58, 283n104 (1922) 261; on food control program 165, 294n101; Fur Workers' strike (1912) 38; Garment Workers' strike (1912) 19, 22; and House labor group 121, 248, 291n1; on immigration 75, 132, 281n46; on London 40; London criticizes Gompers' war support 84; on London's death 307n6; and National Social Insurance 122–23, 125–26, 268, 291n1, 291n10, 291n12, 291n13, 292n14; on postwar unemployment 248–49; Shirt Waist Workers' strike (1910) 18–19
Gordon, William 177, 198
Gore-McLemore Resolution 114–16, 150
Gorgas, W.C. 122
Greene, Frank L. 161–62
Grossman, Charles 228, 271

Hampton, Richard J. 110
Hardie, Kier 88

Harding, W.L. 189
Harding, Warren G. 239; amnesty 237, 240–42; coal strikes 251–53; election (1920) 235; London opposes Harding domestic policies 3, 223, 231, 244, 247, 303*n*2; naval expansion 254, 305*n*82; peace treaty 255–56, 305*n*86, 305*n*87; signs London's Bankruptcy bill 254; unemployment 249–254, 304*n*57
Harriman, Job 12–13
Hay, James 101, 112, 116–17, 290*n*98
Hayes, Max 13
Hearst, William Randolph 51, 68, 282*n*65
Heath, Fred 13
Hersey, Ira G. 242
Hickey, Thomas A. 163
Highland, John F. 171
Hillquit, Morris 29, 66, 80, 89, 168, 221, 224, 238, 261, 267; anti-war activist 84; appointed ILGWU counsel 64–65, 283*n*9; attraction to socialism 7; as candidate: Ninth Congressional District (1904) 282*n*73; (1906) 46, (1908) 47; Twentieth Congressional District (1916) 135–37, 142, 175, 295*n*8; (1918) 211; (1920) 226, 229, 232, 234, 303*n*148; civil liberties issues 163; criticizes Goldfogle (1901) 14; drafts St. Louis Manifesto 157; endorses London (1910) 50–51; eulogizes London 266, 271, 274; immigration restriction 48, 281*n*46; intervention in Russia 192; leads anti–De Leon revolt 11–12; meeting with President Wilson 107–10, 289*n*53; opposes London resolution on international parliament 225; peace resolution testimony 110; preparedness 104, 290*n*65; replaced by London in new Twelfth Congressional District (1910) 41, 46–48, 281*n*58; separate peace with Russia 167, 296*n*70; Socialist candidate for mayor of New York City (1917) 169–71; Socialist unity 12; supports London (1914) 68–69, 73, 76 (1916) 137; Third International 224–26
Holt, Hamilton 29
Honest Ballot Association 69, 73
Hoover, Herbert 165, 304*n*57
Hourwich, Isaac M. 8–10, 31–36, 64–65, 222, 280*n*82, 283*n*1
Huddleston, George 113, 178, 290*n*85

Independent Labor Party 11–13
Independent Order of B'rith Abraham 293*n*77, 293*n*82
Independent Voters' League 58, 282*n*7
Indianapolis Convention 1901 14–16
International Ladies Garment Workers' Union (ILGWU) 89, 205, 220, 266, 268, 275, 280*n*102, 298*n*35, 306*n*99; amnesty meeting with Harding 237; appoints London counsel 28–30; conflict with Hourwich 34–36; creates American Labor Party 275–76; founding and early years 17–21; growth of 36; Hillquit appointed counsel 64; Hillquit/London relationship 281*n*58, 283*n*5, 283*n*9; supports London's congressional campaigns (1910) 49; (1912) 58; (1914) 66–67, 70, 284*n*20, 284*n*23; (1916) 136, 293*n*60; (1918) 206, 300*n*16; (1920) 228–29, 234; (1922) 261
International Socialist Congresses (1914, 1917) 64, 66, 168
Irwin, Charles 266

Jaeger, Henry 234
Jerome, Tavers 51, 282*n*65
Jewish Agitation Board 48
Jewish Daily Worker 53, 71
Jewish Relief Commission of America 89
Johnson, Albert 129, 164
Jones, William A. 132

Kahan, Abraham *see Daily Forward*
Kahan, Alexander 69, 212
"Kangaroos" 11
Kaufman, Morris 220, 229, 306*n*99
Keating, Edward 117, 126–27, 135, 137, 146, 164, 179–80, 208, 291*n*1, 300*n*29
Kelley, M. Clyde 150
Kerensky Government 196
Kern-Mc Gillicuddy Act 127
Kishinev Pogrom 5
Kitchin, Claude 98, 100 155, 159, 291*n*110, 259*n*7
Knights of Labor 8
Koenig, Samuel B. 61, 203, 305*n*92
Kremer, Arcady 46
Kruse, William F. 224
Ku Klux Klan 161

Labor Committee on Amnesty for Political Prisoners 237–38
Ladies' Garment Worker 58, 74, 293*n*96, 300*n*24
Ladies Tailors' and Dress Makers' Union Local 38–39
Ladies' Waist Makers Union Local 25, 18
La Follette, Robert 52, 151, 266
La Guardia, Fiorello H. 159
Lane, Henry 105
Lanferseik, Walter 73, 80, 107, 111
Lansing, Robert 113–14, 168–69
Lassalle, Ferdinand 65
Lehman, Irving 24
Lemlich, Clara 18
Lennon, John B. 19, 23
Lenroot, Irvine 159, 297*n*6
Lever Act 165–66
Lewis, John L. 252, **253**
Lewis, Marx 306*n*99
Liebnecht, Karl 50

Little, Frank 164
Little Germany ("Kleine Deutchland") 7
Loeb, Mitchell 122, 212
Logan Act 168
London, Anna Rosenson 17, 20, 33
London, Ephraim 5–6
London, Horace 142, 213–214, 217
London, Isabel 20, 278n5
London, Louis 5–6
London, Meyer: Bankruptcy Bill 253–54, 268, 305n75, Bund, support for 46, 281n22; Congressional elections: Ninth Congressional District (1910) 46–57, 282n58, 282n73, 282n84, 282n90; Twelfth Congressional District (1912) 57–64, 282n100, 283n106 283n109, 283n111, 283n112, 283n123; (1914) 65–67, 284n19, 284n20, 284n23, 284n24, 284n46, 285n60; (1916) 135–43, 293n60, 293n63, 293n75, 293n90; (1918) 194, 196–98, 203–14, 300n25, 300n26, 300n27, 300n28, 301n45, 301n51, 301n57; (1920) 226–35; 302n128, 302n131, 301n132, 310n47, 301n148; (1922) 259–64, 305n72, 305n94, 305n99, 305n100, 305n103, 305n116, 305n129, 305n130, 305n138 305n147; Counsel for Workmen's Circle 50; early years in Russia 5–7; Educational Alliance 6, 8; embraces socialism 7–8; emigration to America 6; family 5–6, 17, 20, 33, 142, 213–14, 217, 278n5; House of Representatives: (64th Congress) 99–107, 109–18, 121–26, 130–35, 143–51, 290n81, 291n109, 291n4, 291n13; (65th Congress) 79–83, 85–89, 151, 154, 156–57, 159, 160–69, 171–73, 175–76, 179–83, 185–93, 195–96, 198–201, 215–16, 219, 296n70; (67th Congress) 239–57, **253**, 264–65, 304n19, 304n34, 305n75, 305n87; Jewish community relations 21–22, 25, 27, 40; joins Social Democracy of America 8–10; labor lawyer 16–17, 19–36; 50, 36–39, 64–65, 89, 287n49; New York University Law School 7; post–Congressional years 266–71, **269**, **272**, **273**, **274**; pre–Congressional elections 8, 46, 57, 62, 281n29; Social Democrats 10–11, Socialist Party of America 14; Triangle fire 36; on unemployment 90–93; on women's suffrage 93–96
London, Rebecca Berson 5
London Star 107
Lore, Ludwig see *Class Struggle*
Lunn, George R. 66
Lusitania 81, 83, 114

Magnes, Judah L. 294n3, 300n38
Mahler, James P. 181
Mailly, William 13
Malone, Dudley Field 147
Manchester Labor Leader 107
Mann, James R. 97–98, 146, 288n13

Marshall, Louis 25, 27, 40, 210, 213, 300n38
Martin, Whit P. 291n9
Marx, Karl 7, 170, 267
Maurer, Charles A. 289n51
Maurer, James Henry 107–109, 111, 137, 289n53, 190n67
Maxim, Gregory 46
McAdoo, William G. 182–83
McCormick, Medill 180, 268
Mensheviks 11
Merchants' Society of the Ladies Tailors and Dress Makers of New York 30
Mexico 97, 111–14, 119, 137, 290n81, 296n56
Meyer London Memorial Committee 273–274
Meyer London Professional League 51, 58, 206
Meyer London Trade Union Conference 206
Michels, Tony 276, 277n15, 280n9, 281n24, 282n60
Miller, Clarence B. 303n5
Miller, Louis 7–8, 44
Miller, Nathan 258
Milwaukee Leader 108, 285n73, 289n46, 289n51; see also Berger, Victor
Mitchel, John P. 169, 171
Moon, John L. 163
Moore, J. Hampton 146, 180
Morning Journal 209
Morningstar, David M. 69
Moskowitz, Henry W. 32, 40, 57, 59, 70–72, 141, 279n69, 282n101, 283n101
Most, Johan 7
"Moths of Division Street" 20
Murphy, Charles F. 203, 213, 285n67

National Civic Federation 21
National Security League 83, 117, 160, 203–5, 226–27, 231, 286n30, 299n9
National Social Insurance bill 1, 37, 268, 276, 307n4; bill's provisions 291n4; House Labor Committee hearing 122–24; House rejects 146, 151; Labor Committee approves 125–26; London argues for bill in House 124; London introduces National Social Insurance bill 121; London optimistic 292n14; London presents modified version 125; resumes fight for National Social Insurance program 179–183, 215
National Women's Trade Union Convention 94
National Workingman's Committee on Jewish Rights in the Belligerent Countries 89, 109
Navy Bill 117–18, 305n82
Nesbit, Charles S. 291n9
New Post 19, 32, 34
New York American 72, 207, 209, 285n59, 285n75, 285n77, 285n79, 285n80, 300n28, 300n33

New York Call 183, 286*n*47, 287*n*1, 287*n*61; on Cloak Makers' strike (1910) 16, 19–20, 279*n*34, 279*n*47, 279*n*55, 277*n*58; Congressional elections (1908) 46–70; (1910) 48–50, 53, 55; (1912) 58, 60–61; (1914) 67, 69, 73; (1916) 135–36, 138–39, 141–42, 293*n*54, 293*n*63, 293*n*85, 293*n*90; (1918) 203–4, 212–14, 300*n*16, 300*n*23, 300*n*25, 300*n*26, 300*n*27, 300*n*29, 301*n*51, 301*n*57; (1920) 226, 235, 302*n*131, 303*n*148; (1922) 257–59, 261–64, 305*n*94, 306*n*; endorsed London's opposition to Sedition bill 189; on Fur Workers' strike (1912) 280*n*14; interview with London 171; letters criticize London 105; London booed by Communists 303*n*159; on London committee assignments 97, 287*n*2, 287*n*5; London urges unemployment conference 249; on London's death 307*n*6; on London's fight for food control 166; on London's importance in Sixty-Fifth Congress 155; London's position on intervention in Russia 192; peace conference 88; plans to meet with constituents 102, 288*n*27; preparedness 86, 99; sinking of *Lusitania* 83; supports general strike to end war 82, 286*n*24; supports London's peace resolution 106, 108, 110; on suppression of Socialist publications 296*n*5; Susan B. Anthony amendment 95; unemployment legislation 90; war 78; Woodrow Wilson meets with London, Hillquit and Maurer 109, **109**
New York Evening Journal 68, 282*n*73
New York Evening Mail 211
New York Evening World 101
New York Joint Board of the Cloak and Suit Makers' Union 17, 19, 27, 30–36, 38, 64–65, 67, 89, 261, 280*n*114, 303*n*151
New York Peace Society 81
New York Post 74, 284*n*57
New York Socialist Party State Executive Committee 165, 167, 192
New York Sun 72, 285*n*75
New York Times 4, 292*n*26, 292*n*48, 293*n*43, 296*n*61, 297*n*7, 299*n*56, 302*n*116, 303*n*159; comments on Congressional elections (1914) 74; (1918) 197, 211; (1920) 231 260, 303*n*146; defends London's war position 170; Dutch support London's peace proposal 290*n*63; food bills 294*n*41; Hillquit on London's death 266; London heckled at meeting 287*n*61, 303*n*154; London on expulsion of New York Socialist Assemblymen 223; London on position of interventionists 83–84; London on unemployment (1915) 287*n*52; London's Congressional goals 64; London's estate 307*n*5; London's Russian position 191–92; London's speech at Union Square meeting 92; trial of cloakmakers 287*n*50, 287*n*51

New York Tribune 69, 74, 154, 191, 231, 233, 262, 285*n*67; 293*n*87; 305*n*92; 306*n*130
New York Women's Trade Union League 18
New York World 72, 74, 76, 141, 192–93, 197, 211–12, 231, 233, 264, 285*n*67, 285*n*86, 288*n*27, 299*n*63, 305*n*92, 306*n*137
New Yorker Volkszeitung 7, 288*n*21
New York's Lower East Side 41, **42**, 43
Nonpartisan Businessmen's League 206
Norton Patrick Daniel 200, 298*n*49

Order of Lions 266
Orr, Samuel 227, 234, 392*n*93
Orth, Charles D. 203–4, 226

Pacifists 87–88, 198
Pale of Settlement 2, 5, 45, 277*n*1, 281*n*22
Palmer, A. Mitchell 228, 230
Panken, Jacob 76, 89, 194, 204, 225, 233, 261, 271
Pauly, Albert 105
People 277*n*18
Pershing, John J. 113, 119
Philbin, Eugene A. 213
Philippine Islands Independence bill 132–133, 264
Phillips, Isadore 12
Pinchot, Amos 206
Pine, Max 13, 19, 48, 67, 237, 284*n*20
Poale Zionists (Workers of Zion) 50, 205–6, 293*n*60; *see also* Zionists
Porter Peace Resolution 256
Potts, Rufus M. 291*n*9
Poynitz, Juliet 291*n*9
Preparedness movement 1, 3, 78, 80–89, 96–97, 99–104, 106–7, 109, 111, 117–19, 148–49, 152, 158, 269
Protocol of Peace 27–31, 33–36; *see also* Garment Workers Strike 1910
Puerto Rico 99, 133–35, 292*n*53

Quin, Percy 176, 189, 298*n*49

Radical Review 166, 193
Railroad strike (1916) 128–29
Rainey, Henry 178, 180, 186–87, 298*n*41
Randall, Charles 295*n*6
Reconstruction 182, 201, 208, 214–15
Reed, John 222
Reefer Makers' Association 17
Reefer Makers' strike of 1907 17–19, 278*n*9, 283*n*106, 284*n*24
Regan, Michael J. 21
Revenue bills 148, 199
Roosevelt, Franklin D. 275–276, 304*n*21
Roosevelt, Theodore 3, 52, 59–61, 81, 127, 136, 203, 209–210
Root Commission 193, 299*n*67
Rosenberg, Abraham 17, 21, 35, 49, 64–65
Rubinow I.M. 122

Russell, Charles Edward 170–71; campaigns for London (1914) 69–71, 73; (1916) 137–38, 141; criticized for war stance 198; New York City mayor (1912) 62; refused to support St. Louis Manifesto 158; Socialist candidate for New York governor (1910) 49–50, 52, 55–56; Socialist delegate to International Socialist Congress 66, 284n17; supports preparedness 104; telegram to Kerensky 167; United States Senate New York (1914) 65

Sabbath, Adolph 152, 175, 243
St. Louis Manifesto 157–58, 160, 166–67, 169, 172–73, 187, 194, 205, 295n19, 297n91
Schaffer, Louis 66, 68–69, 135
Schewitsch, Sergius 7
Schiff, Jacob E. 25, 40, 210, 294n4; 300n38
Schlesinger, Benjamin 17, 64, 237, 284n20, 306n99
Sedition Act 188–89, 217
Seidel, Emil 66
Sherley, J. Swagger 133, 145, 180, 182
Siberian Intervention 190–91
Simons, Algie M. 158
Sinclair, Upton 158
Slabodin, Henry L. 68
Smith, Alfred E. 25, 36, 214, 220, 235, 263–264, 267, 280n103, 302n116
Smitkin, Leonard A. 61
Social Democracy of America 8–10
Social Democrat 5, 7
Social Democratic Herald 44
Social Democratic Party 10–13
Socialist Labor and Trade Alliance 8
Socialist Labor Party 7–9, 11–12, 15, 44, 277n88, 280n10, 282n90
Socialist Party of America 48, 51, 73–74, 80, 84, 106, 167, 178, 205, 236, 307n4; amnesty 228, 237–40; anti-war position 84, 288n30; approves Russian Revolution 3; decline of 203, 275; Eighth National Convention 224; endorses London's food bill 143; and Farmer-Labor Party 302n132; founding 14–15; growth 45; on immigration 281n40, 281n41; internal dissent 221–22; International Socialist Congress 168; London's peace plan 89, 107–8, 110–11; on *Lusitania* 83; national social insurance program 122, 124; opposition to Espionage Act 163; on outbreak of war 78; peace program 80, 256; on Root Commission 193; St. Louis Manifesto 157, 160, 295n19; supports suffrage 93; and Third International 222, 302n90
Socialist Party of Local New York 40, 46, 76, 213, 284n19, 286n37, 295n34
Socialist Party of New York County 109, 226
Socialist Party of New York State 92, 94, 96, 111, 153

Socialist Press Club 86
Solomon, Charles 98, 227, 234, 302n93
Spanish Influenza epidemic 203, 207
Spargo, John 158, 198, 296n70
Stafford, William H. 164, 180, 189
Stedman, Seymour 13, 163, 168, 225, 297n3
Stockholm Conference 168–69, 297n75
Straus, Nathan 212
Straus, Oscar S. 61, 204
Stuttgart Congress (1907) 48, 281n49
Suffrin, Solomon 136
Sulzberger, Cyrus 73, 206
Sundry Civil Appropriations bill 182, 301n67
Susan B. Anthony Amendment 78, 95–96, 292n53
Sussex sinking and pledge 116, 147

Taft, William Howard 177, 209, 294n4
Tageblatt 47, 53, 68, 70–71, 232, 284n49
Third International 221–24, 302n90
Todd, Laurence 98
Trading with the Enemy Act 164
Treaty of Brest-Litovsk 190, 196, 200, 270
Triangle Shirtwaist Factory Fire 18, 36, 279n24
Trotsky, Leon 100, 177, 190–92, 196, 198, 270, 297n11, 299n5
Tscheidse, N.C. 167

United Hebrew Trades: amnesty 228, 237; appeal to London to assist Solomon Metz 89–90; creation of 7; sponsors Liberty Bond rally 300n24; supports Cloak Makers', Ladies Waist Makers' and Fur Workers' strikes 18–19, 36; supports London's Congressional campaigns (1910) 48–49; (1912) 283n71; (1914) 284n20; (1916) 136; (1918) 300n16; (1922) 261, 283n106, 300n16; unemployment Day sponsor 90
United States Railroad Administration 133
University Settlement House 59
Untermeyer, Samuel 210
"Uprising of Twenty Thousand" 18

Vail, William N. 236
Van Kohl, Henri M. 290n63
Vann, David M. 49
Villa, Francisco 111–13
Volk, Herman 213

Wagner, Robert, 4, 36
Waldman, Louis, 227, 234, 261, 302n93
Walling, William E. 158, 296n70
Walsh, Franklin P. 163, 181, 218, 286n49
Weinstein, H.B. 19
Weiser, Nathan, 58
Whitman, Charles S. 62
Wilson, William B. 181–82, 185
Wilson, Woodrow 298n24, 305n79; abandons Continental Army proposal 116;

against Gore-McLemore resolutions 114–15; armed merchant ship authorization 150–51; endorses Henry M. Goldfogle (1918) 204; McAdoo appointed Railroad Administrator 118, 182–83; meeting with Socialist delegation 108; Mexican intervention and withdrawal 113–14; opposes immigration restriction 129–32, 145; opposes Japanese intervention in Siberia 190–91; peace initiatives 146–48, 298n11; Philippine Islands autonomy 132–33; preparedness 3, 86, 97, 99–102, 107; Puerto Rico autonomy 133–35; railroad crisis 127–29, **128**, 183–84, 292n28; refuses to release political prisoners 218–19; reluctant decision for war 154–56; response to anti-war sentiment 160, 162, 164; response to *Sussex* sinking 116; Root Commission 193, 299n67; split with Secretary of War Garrison 101; Stockholm Peace Conference 297n75; supports reform measures 127–28; vetoes Fordney tariff bill 245; vetoes joint resolution to end war unilaterally 255; war measures 118, 159, 165–66, 198, 290n98, 290n101 291n110
Winchevsky, Morris 8, 76
Wise, Stephen A. 210
Wolf, Alexander 61, 283n123
Women's Meyer London League 58
Women's Peace Party 83, 109–110, 290n67
Woods, Arthur H. 69, 73, 146
Workmen's Circle: London as counsel and advisor 1, 47, 50, 220, 266, 275; origins and growth 281n39; supports London's congressional campaigns (1910) 50; (1912) 53–54, 283n106; (1914) 66, 68, 284n20; (1916) 293n63; (1918) 206, 301n57; (1920) 228, 232; (1922) 261

Zametkin, Mikhail 7
Zhitlowsky, Chalm 50
Zimmerman Telegram 150–51
Zionism 203
Zukunft 47, 67, 86

www.ingramcontent.com/pod-product-compliance
Lightning Source LLC
Chambersburg PA
CBHW051209300426
44116CB00006B/485